Gus J. Solomon

Liberal Politics, Jews, and the Federal Courts

To Diana B. Kerman

Gus J. Solomon

Liberal Politics, Jews, and the Federal Courts

by HARRY H. STEIN

Oregon Historical Society Press
Portland

This book is made possible with the generous support of the U.S. District Court Historical Society, Portland, Oregon

Oregon Historical Society Press
1200 SW Park Avenue, Portland, OR 97205, USA
www.ohs.org

The paper used in this publication is acid-free. It meets the minimum requirements of American National Standard for Information Sciences— Permanence of Paper for Printed Library Materials, ANSI Z39.48—1984. ∞

Distributed by the University of Washington Press

COVER DESIGN: Dean Shapiro
PRINTER: Friesens

COVER PHOTO: Courtesy of Richard B. Solomon

Library of Congress Cataloging-in-Publication Data
Stein, Harry H.
Gus J. Solomon : liberal politics, Jews, and the federal courts / by Harry H. Stein.
p. cm.
Includes bibliographical references and index.
ISBN-13: 978-0-87595-298-7 (alk. paper)
ISBN-10: 0-87595-298-4 (alk. paper)
1. Solomon, Gus J. (Gus Jerome), 1906-1987. 2. Jewish judges--Biography. I. Solomon, Gus J. (Gus Jerome), 1906-1987. II. Title.
KF373.S63S74 2006
347.73'14092--dc22
2006005350

Contents

Acknowledgments

This book is the product of many years and many helping hands. It could never have been done without the interest and assistance of Richard B. Solomon. I wish his mother, Elisabeth W. Solomon, had survived to read this biography. Dick and Libby made Gus J. Solomon's papers available to me (and then presented them to the Oregon Historical Society) and furnished other essential aid. I am thankful that the U.S. District Court of Oregon Historical Society established the Solomon Biography Project and a special contributions committee and provided manuscript reviewers. The Hon. Owen M. Panner of the U.S. District Court for Oregon enthusiastically supported this project since its inception and furnished all manner of kind assistance. Not least of all, Diana B. Kerman has been an unfailing and loving supporter and adviser during my labors.

Many individuals generously helped me. Robert D. Johnston, Steven L. Wasby, and Tim Garrison provided influential critiques of my first manuscript draft. I also benefited from later manuscript reviews by George H. Fraser, Christian B. Fritz, Stephen Gillers, Gersham Goldstein, Cheryl Greenberg, Michael Janeway, Diana B. Kerman, William F. Long, the Hon. Owen M. Panner, and editor Dennis Stovall.

Additional valuable aid came from Clerk of Court of the U.S. District Court for Oregon Don Cinnamond, E. Kimbark MacColl, Sr., Michael Munk, Sandy Polishuk, and commentators on my papers on Solomon at sessions of the Northwest Independent Scholars Association, Oregon Historical Society, and Western History Association. For generous hospitality on research trips, I thank Warren McKay, Dr. Michel D. Stein, Dr. Ruth P. Stein (of blessed memory), Junko Toll, and William Toll.

It has been a pleasure working with Oregon Historical Society Press Director Marianne Keddington-Lang and Production Editor Eliza Jones. I also thank the talented and dedicated staffs of the Oregon Historical Society Library, especially Steve Hallberg and James Strassmaier, Multnomah County Library, especially its Interlibrary Loan Department,

Multnomah County Law Library, especially Jacquelyn Jurkins, Portland State University Library, Lewis and Clark Law Library, U.S. District Court for Oregon Law Library, especially Scott McCurdy, and, as also listed in my bibliography, the staffs at many other libraries, archives, and record centers as well as those individuals who allowed me to use privately-held material.

I am indebted to a hard-working special contributions committee of the U.S. District Court of Oregon Historical Society. Headed by Richard B. Solomon and Henry Richmond II, it included Jonathan Ater, Leonard J. Bergstein, Henry S. Blauer, Ernest Bonyhadi, Keith Burns, E. Kimbark MacColl, Sr., and Thomas B. Stoel.

Major financial support for the Solomon Biography Project came from the Kohlberg Foundation, Inc. and Jerome Kohlberg, Jr. Additional support came from the Oregon Community Foundation (Tom and Caroline Stoel Fund), the Oregon Jewish Community Foundation (the John and Janet Sherman Family Fund and the Mrs. Moe Tonkon Fund), the Milton and Moselle Pollack Foundation, the Harold and Arlene Schnitzer Care Foundation, the Herbert A. Templeton Foundation, the Rose E. Tucker Charitable Trust, the Weisman Foundation, the Oregon Chapter of the Federal Bar Association, the Schnitzer Investment Corp, and the law firms of Kell, Alterman & Runstein, LLP, Gevurtz, Menashe, Larson & Howe, PC, Newcomb, Sabin, Schwartz & Landsverk, LLP, Stoel Rives, LLP, and Sussman, Shank, LLP.

I also thank the many individual contributors to the Solomon Biography Project: Richard Adelman, Jonathan Ater, Henry and Gerel Blauer, Ernest Bonyhadi, Keith Burns, Milt Carl, the Hon. Irving Cypen, Joyce C. Dahl, Stuart Durkheimer, Carol Edelman, Barnes Ellis, Paul Gamson, Maurice O. Georges, Stephen Gillers, Ivan L. Gold, Gersham Goldstein, Mr. and Mrs. Dan Goldy, Leonard Gumport, Allan Hart, Harold C. Hart, Lee L. Holzman, Bernard Jolles, Garry and Judith Kahn, J. Kenneth Kaseberg, Mr. and Mrs. Myron B. Katz, Jerome S. Katzin, Drs. Louis and Annette Kaufman, Jack L. Kennedy, Diana B. Kerman, John J. Kerr, Jr., Randall Kester, Dennis Lindsay, Charles F. Luce, Dan and Pat O'Leary, Sidney I. Lezak, Mr. and Mrs. Monford Orloff, the Hon. Owen M. Panner, Michael Pertschuk, T.W. Phillips, C. Delos Putz, the Hon. James A. Redden, Milton A. Rudin, Harold and Arlene Schnitzer, Norman Sepenuk, Mrs. Freda Silberman, Mark Silverstein, Elisabeth W. Solomon, Phillip W. Solomon, Richard B. Solomon, Leigh Stephenson, Robert L. Weiss, and Wendell Wyatt.

Introduction

District judges are the federal judiciary's acknowledged workhorses and, with few exceptions, the first — and often the final — interpreters of federal laws. While their courts by and large make federal law and while district judges are the federal judiciary's largest segment, they remarkably are its least studied. Rarely are they biographical subjects. Instead, scholars have emphasized the appellate courts, especially the United States Supreme Court, assuming perhaps that only their denizens had epic or near-epic careers of influence. Inspired district judges such as Gus J. Solomon, whose impact on the law and on other important aspects of life — most often felt regionally rather than nationally — have been woefully ignored. During his long career, Solomon participated in significant decisions at the district and appellate levels, improved the administration of justice, and affected many lives. He was a vital, vivid individual and the source of endless stories. In some ways, Solomon was a typical long-serving and appreciated district court judge. In others, he was unique.

In this biography, Gus Solomon appears within his social, cultural, political, economic, and legal environments, especially the parallel and convergent histories that informed his life and that he, in turn, affected or tried to affect. We can know the boy Solomon, growing up before the Great Depression, in relation to his family, changing communities, and national and local trends. During the 1930s and 1940s, Solomon is best seen in relation to American legal practice, the struggles of Jews in society and as minority lawyers, and the accomplishments and failures of liberal political and legal activists devoted to constitutional liberties and democratic change. Judge Solomon appears in this book in relation to the inner workings of the federal courts and their politics, issues, personalities, and interests, as the courts passed from the comparative quiet of the 1950s into a seeming crisis in the 1960s and 1970s.

Solomon was a representative grassroots liberal leader in the decades of liberalism's great success in the United States, from the

1930s into the 1970s. He pushed against conservatism in government, politics, and the law and for liberal policies, standards, and precedents, particularly New Deal and Fair Deal ideas and programs. A bright figure on the canvas of twentieth-century Jewish activism, he was also a characteristic one in urban Jewish communities and national Jewish affairs. And on the twentieth-century federal court, Solomon was a district judge who immediately, if not always enduringly, influenced the course of the law and his own district's structures and processes.

Solomon's life illuminates major aspects and shifts in American law, politics, and group life throughout most of the twentieth century. In politics from 1929 to 1949, Solomon's life as an attorney shows how practical-minded citizen-activists engaged in partisan politics, fighting for liberalism, civil libertarianism, and popular democracy. As a judge after 1949, his life reveals the sometimes torturous passage of American liberals and liberalism through the Cold War and the rapid changes that followed. Finally, in law and politics from 1949 until his death in 1987, Solomon's life lets us learn how district judges were chosen and how they behaved and were expected to behave on and off the bench.

The sort of individual Solomon was — and the past he bore — figured significantly in the brawl set off by his bid for a federal judgeship in 1949 and 1950. Conservatives vigorously contested the bid, as did prominent Republicans and Democrats. Leaders of private utilities and the wood products industry as well as newspaper editors and publishers choked when contemplating Solomon as a judge. He was a liberal Democrat and New Dealer-Fair Dealer, a grassroots political activist, an arch civil libertarian, and a Jew to boot in a traditionally Republican, white Protestant state. The portly, bespectacled lawyer was opposed for his years of toil on behalf of civil liberties and the public-power movement and other allegedly radical causes. Republicans did not want a pro-union New Dealer–Fair Dealer or Democrat in the judgeship. And neither the people of Oregon nor the bar were prepared to accept a Jewish federal judge, some opponents said.

Within a few years, however, Gus Solomon was the dominant figure in the U.S. District Court for Oregon. Two years after death ended his storied thirty-seven-year career in 1987 — the longest service of any federal judge in the state's history — what many people considered his true home was renamed the Gus J. Solomon United States Courthouse. In many minds, Solomon *was* the district court in

Oregon. By then, all antipathies had disappeared.

Nobody ever questioned Solomon's devotion to justice or his rage against injustice. Groups ranging from civil liberties advocates to trial lawyers praised his intellectual and legal abilities, his dedication, hard work, and keenness for justice, and his volunteer service. He accumulated honorary degrees, awards, and other commendations. In 1975, he received an honorary Doctor of Laws degree from Reed College for a career "distinguished by its deep concern for the dignity of the individual and the protection of the rights of the less fortunate members of society." Solomon would have said that he tried to hold himself to the best dreams of his youth, dreams that carried him from a modest Jewish neighborhood in Southeast Portland to a distinguished and memorable career on the U.S. District Court.

Chapter 1

Early Years

*Residence in a Jewish neighborhood and associational ties with
other Jews brought one into the orbit of the community, in "a
world of Jewish unconsciousness."*
      — Deborah D. Moore, *At Home in America*

BEGINNINGS

Gus Jerome Solomon was born in Portland, Oregon, into a still-im-migrant urban America. Gould, as he was named on August 29, 1906, was the youngest of three sons and two daughters of Jacob and Rose Solomon. Their fourteen-block-long South Portland neighborhood ran from the busy Willamette River westward six to ten blocks to end in a giant garbage dump. Many South Portlanders barely eked out a living. It was a classic first-settlement neighborhood for its mostly immigrant east European Jewish and Italian Catholic residents. Jacob Solomon, a prospering small merchant, wanted to move his family to a better one soon.[1]

Jacob and Rose Solomon had fled lands where Jews were despised as alien outsiders and where the weight of their collective heritage was being chipped away by new economic, social, and political forces. Jacob had been born in 1872 in the village of Hoosh, in what became Romania. His mother died in childbirth, and his father died young. Poor relatives raised their children. Barred by law from school, Jacob likely received only a Hebrew school education, which prepared males at age thirteen — the beginning of adult reasoning and responsibility, according to Orthodox Judaism — for a Bar Mitzvah. If he had meant to follow a favored poor boy's route, it closed when he was twelve, when Jews were barred from town and city peddling. It was Romania's "era of legal persecution," called a "cold pogrom," by another historian, when the government "defined Jews as enemies of the nation, removed them from the state school system, and encouraged occasional violence." Jews were almost entirely disqualified from citizenship, periodically expelled from villages, deported, and worn down by poverty. Western Jewry worried about their very survival.[2]

Fourteen-year-old Jacob Solomon was one among only 518 Romanian Jews thought to have arrived in the United States in 1886. Bearing decidedly one-way tickets, they constituted a mere four percent of the east European Jewish tide arriving between 1880 and 1920. Jacob lost contact with an older sister who immigrated before he did and had only occasional contact with an older brother who settled in Matanzas, Cuba, and opened a store. For two years, Jacob attended a night school, where he learned to write a crude English, perform mathematical calculations, and read newspapers. He then moved to Key West, Florida, home to a big Romanian community, and for four or five years lived in Tampa. Selling trinkets and notions, he followed the fairs and may have peddled shoelaces during the 1893 World's Fair in Chicago. Around 1895, he gravitated to Portland, where he knew Romanian Jews.[3]

Jacob always hated Romania, and both Solomons hated Rose's Russian homeland. They painfully associated Europe with privation, ferocious anti-Semitism, life-threatening events, and migration. Rose was born Rifka Rochel Rosencrantz in 1872 near Kiev in Czarist Ukraine. For Russian Jews, there were "no civil rights, ruinous restrictions on trading, and periodic expulsions from towns and villages," and pogroms savaged them early in the 1880s. Evictions from cities, new discriminatory laws, and heightened violence worsened conditions in the 1890s. "A Yiddish thesaurus needs nineteen columns of fine print for all the synonyms for 'misfortune,'" Gerald Sorin, a historian of American Jewry, reminds us; "'good fortune' needs only five."[4]

Between 1880 and 1920, millions of people from Europe, the Ottoman Empire, and Asia created the greatest immigration era in United States history. In these years, a third of east European Jewry left for a fabled United States, which in 1880 had only a quarter-million Jews, about a sixth from eastern Europe. By 1900, some 600,000 more east European Jews had arrived, 45 percent of them women and girls. Rose's brothers, Abraham and Jacob Rosencrantz, brought the twenty-two-year-old to Portland in 1894; other siblings followed later. Similar networks of relatives and friends encouraged Atlantic crossings and helped newcomers. The Rosencrantz brothers became leading figures in Jewish South Portland, respected for their learning in Talmud. Abraham became a well-known cantor in small congregations — Shaarie Torah and Neveh Zedek Talmud

Torah — and an interim rabbi. Jacob, called John, became a synagogue sexton.

Rose and Jacob were married not long after she arrived in Portland. Until 1919, they lived among or near foreign-born Jews and their native-born children in one of Portland's language and cultural enclaves. The city contained the urban Far West's second highest percentage of foreign-born people in 1890 and 1900, most of them clustered in the same neighborhoods. Portland was not highly segregated, however, and no "single nationality group, including Jews, ever constituted a majority in any area as large as a half-mile square." In 1910, in a city of 207,000, some 5,000 Jews, almost half from eastern Europe, belonged to Portland synagogues. There is no estimate of those who were not affiliated. In 1920, at least 11,000 religiously affiliated Jews lived in the city of 258,288 people, some 6,000 of them in or near South Portland. But they lacked the visibility of their multitudinous brethren in New York, Chicago, Philadelphia, Baltimore, and Boston. Most Portlanders knew little about them, their aspirations and achievements, their fretting and divisions. It was not an unwelcome situation. Jews were historically sensitive to slights and bad treatment and prone to feelings of collective pride and disgrace. Nervous about differences among themselves and about embarrassing themselves before non-Jews, they customarily preferred inattention to keen notice.[5]

Jacob and Rose Solomon arrived in Portland during the severe depression of 1893-1897. In time-honored fashion, the peddler opened a small second-hand store, first with Max Barrell, also from Hoosh, and later with Morris Augustin. Portland Jews seldom sought mill or factory employment, which were not numerous in any event. The city had prospered as the Pacific Northwest's leading financial, commercial, port, and rail center; and by 1910, it ranked twentieth-eighth in urban population and fifty-fifth in manufacturing value. Portland Jewry largely came from that sizable minority of Jewish immigrants who entered the economy through trade and commerce. "In Portland, Oregon, Columbus, Milwaukee, and Minneapolis, too," Sorin writes, "innovative East Europeans followed the paths of the German Jews who preceded them and borrowed capital from friends, relatives, and cooperative loan societies to pursue the often risky process of building small businesses." South Portland's tailors, shoemakers, and storekeepers largely served workers' families. William Toll estimates that 60 percent of its Jewish heads of households in 1910 "were either proprietors or clerks, while another eighteen percent were on the fringe of proprietorship as expressmen or peddlers." Many barely eked out a living.[6]

With the depression's end, Portland began rebuilding its services and small industries and re-establishing its trade with the northwestern interior, California, Europe, and Asia. Employment rose, boosting Jacob Solomon's sales of work clothing and sundries. He acquired his first small properties. Population, house- and bridge-building, and businesses exploded between 1905 and 1911. The city absorbed nearby towns. The population crested, not to do so again until after the Second World War. Residency on the east side of the Willamette River, which bisected the city, rose from 32,000 to 178,000 between 1900 and 1916; west-side residency increased from 58,000 to 96,000 — all to the Solomons' benefit.[7]

Tradition contested Americanizing trends in urban immigrant enclaves. Immigrants' categories of identity, ideas of national loyalty, and relation to power displayed real flexibility in the America that emerged between 1880 and 1920. In Portland, many "individuals and groups straddled the fluid line between working class and middle class," Robert D. Johnston writes. As the Solomons rose into the middle class, they retainded certain cultural attitudes and forms but borrowed and invented others to partially remake themselves. Before Gus Solomon was born, the family members symbolically entered the mainstream by Americanizing their names. Rifka became Rose; the eldest child, born in 1896 when his parents acquired citizenship, took the name Eugene. The other children became Sam, born in 1898, Claire born in 1900, and Delphine born in 1902. Before he was four, boys began calling Gould "Gus" for the comic strip character Gasoline Gus, who he later joked, "like me had no front teeth, large ears, and a big smile." Gus he became, and in adulthood officially Gus Jerome Solomon.[8]

South Portlanders felt pressured to be model citizens and rapidly assimilate. Everywhere, as Eric L. Goldstein writes, American Jews between 1900 and 1940 manifested both "the desire to accommodate to the demands of white America and the desire to mark themselves off as different from other whites." For decades, E. Kimbark MacColl tells us, a "restrained civic style — moderation bordering on dullness — had characterized Portland city life as a whole." Respecting decorous behavior, the Solomons identified with a dominant staid and respectable white Portland. In the early 1900s, Portland was a wide-open town, still notorious for shanghaiing sailors, but respectable folk averted their gaze from the city's raucous underbelly. Civic corruption long endured despite bouts of reform. Gambling, bootlegging, opium dens, and a lively sex trade operated more or less openly. Jacob Solomon knew about this other Portland, at least through his hardscrabble clientele of mill hands, loggers, sailors, ranch hands, and farm workers, and he apparently sheltered his children from it.[9]

Jacob Solomon's generation "worked very hard," his youngest son said. "That's all they knew." Fathers devoted themselves to making "money and taking care of their families." Life, their children were taught, was work, and hard work promised good income and respectability. Long store hours seven days a week and attendance at Odd Fellows and Woodsmen of the World events often kept Jacob away from dinner at home. He and his wife exercised fairly strict discipline and insisted on promptness, integrity, and honesty. They also expected their children to work in the family's stores, a task performed grudgingly by a teenage Gus Solomon. Jacob and some other small Jewish merchants and dealers in old and junked material raised their families into the comfortable middle class before the First World War. Better neighborhoods became available; few restricted renting or selling properties to Jews. When Gus was two years old, the Solomons moved to a larger home in adjacent, slightly tonier Goose Hollow, and Jacob built the large Caruthers Apartments in South Portland. But Rose's customs and her poor English frustrated relations with the family's new non-Jewish neighbors. She loved fraternizing and pined for the old neighborhood. In 1911, they returned to South Portland to occupy a fairly opulent four-bedroom house, denoting their move upward in the world.[10]

His family and Jewish South Portland cultivated Gus Solomon's basic sense of himself as an American, a Jew, and a white middle-class male. They engendered basic values and attitudes, including near-tribal feelings of obligation to Jews and to the weak, oppressed, and suffering. Part of his consciousness included the religious commandment that Jews were responsible for one another and other *mitzvoth* (commandments to do virtuous, kind, considerate, ethical deeds), which stressed Jewish obligations to society at large. Judaism's prophetic tradition emphasized *zedakeh* (righteousness), which taught that the poor deserved support from the better off as a matter of right. It was not something to be earned or limited.

Patriotism was burned into his consciousness at home and in school. "My father and mother, particularly my father," Solomon later remembered, "were very patriotic." Gus repeatedly heard how the United States furnished a haven of acceptance, opportunity, and recognition. His parents apparently had a quasi-messianic sense of America as a promised land of equality and liberation, where east European Jews, in David Biale's words, "might escape their historic destiny" as a vulnerable, ill-treated minority "and become part of the majority." Jacob and Rose Solomon angrily refused to speak of their past and never understood why their adult children visited Europe. Being Americans gave them pride and hope. Whatever its injustices, they insisted, be loyal to this land.[11]

Jacob Solomon proudly, or perhaps warily, carried his naturalization document at all times. Like many of the foreign-born during the First World War, he heavily purchased Victory Bonds, as if to prove his loyalty. And he criticized neighbors whose sons did not volunteer to fight. The Solomon family liked to think that twenty-one-year-old Eugene was Oregon's first U.S. Army volunteer. At Oregon State College, Sam enrolled in officer training and entered the service. The war occasioned their youngest brother's first shuddering experiences with chauvinistic flag-wavers: a yellow stripe painted on a house where a son would not join the army and young women dragging men into enlistment offices.[12]

Gus Solomon recalled growing up in a "close" family that was conscious of its recognizably Jewish name. "We had a good life," he said — largely a contented, tranquil, comfortable, and uneventful one. They endured little economic anguish or conflict with non-Jews, two themes in writings about the urban American Jewish experience. Living in a city with few cosmopolitan pretensions helped ease their way. Each summer, Gus, his mother, and two sisters vacationed for several weeks on the Pacific coast, joined some weekends by Jacob. The Solomons enjoyed Portland's parks, silent movies, and the Baker Theater. Gus was allowed to quit piano lessons to play baseball. "Above all," William Toll writes, "people reared in South Portland remembered . . . family as the center of social life." Fifty to seventy-five Rosencrantzes and Solomons often gathered for backyard and park picnics, where the children played while the adults drank tea, talked, and played baseball or cards. In Solomon's fond memory, the families frowned on judging others by their income or house size. They valued hard work, getting ahead, respectability, promptness, charitableness, family loyalty, and perpetuating Jewish customs and a Jewish identity — that is, the perception of oneself as Jewish and different from the majority.[13]

From 1912 to 1919, Gus attended the immigrant-filled Shattuck School on Park Street near Jackson. Some 35 percent of its students were Jewish, and many others were Italians. Gus could write well, which helped him earn "pretty good grades." He felt smarter than most students but not as smart or motivated as several of his Jewish friends. Neither of his parents encouraged hard study, but he still assumed — along with other newly middle-class students — that high school and college lay ahead.[14]

Community "had been a powerful and defining force for Jews in Eastern Europe, notwithstanding their many intractable internal disagreements," writes Jonathan D. Sarna. This was also the case in Portland. There were at least a thousand Jewish organizations in the city between 1893 and 1940, creating a context that helped immigrants remember and act out their Jewishness and find their way through new experiences. These organizations preserved customs, structured mutual aid, and helped newcomers and their native-born children adapt and feel safe. The nation's South Portlands nourished Jewish identity for decades before intimate private spheres and references to a sovereign self primarily came to fashion it, Steven M. Cohen and Arnold M. Eisen conclude. "Residence in a Jewish neighborhood and associational ties with other Jews," Deborah D. Moore tells us, "brought one into the orbit of the community, in 'a world of Jewish *unconsciousness.*'" No American Jew had "to take out membership, nor was one forced into the community primarily by anti-Semitism."[15]

Religious institutions counted heavily in these neighborhoods. The Solomons, like Rose's brothers, adhered to Conservative Judaism. Founded in the United States, this branch of Judaism existed between the nominal orthodoxy of many east European Jews and a Reform Judaism that, to them, meant snobbish, patronizing German Jews who betrayed classical Judaism. Conservatism accepted elements of modernity while preserving aspects of Mosaic Law. Its synagogues emphasized the social, cultural, and ethnic — not just the religious — dimensions of Judaism. Conservative Judaism supported, and Gus Solomon always accepted, the ideas of a Jewish people and a Jewish national homeland in Palestine. For the Solomons, Judaism possessed more of a communal or ethnic meaning than a spiritual one. If not particularly observant of rites and rituals, they knew how to comport themselves in their community. Services were dutifully attended at a Neveh Zedek Talmud Torah, which nurtured the children's Jewish identity and provided the family prestige and social support. The Solomons sustained Jewish traditions of mutual assistance, followed European Jewish holiday customs, and adored European Jewish cuisine. While Gus's formal Jewish education was minimal, he was not, as he claimed, "from a generation of Jewish illiterates who grew up in an atmosphere of spiritual darkness." Four afternoons a week for two years, Gus attended the Hebrew Language School to prepare for his Bar Mitzvah. Located in Neighborhood House at 3030 Southwest Second Street, the school was "a major vehicle of the expression of South Portland's passionate support for both a Jewish homeland" and for its own spiritual and cultural regeneration.[16]

Attendance at the school required occasional flights from gauntlets of children who called Gus a "Christ-killer," a taunt familiar to generations of urban Jewish youth. "As much as American Jews believed that they had fully embraced American civic ideals and saw themselves as distinct from nonwhite minorities," Victoria Saker Woeste writes, "the dominant culture" after the 1918 Armistice "regarded them as 'the white other,' neither clearly marked by color as a subordinate class nor fully welcomed as citizens." Institutionalized and unconscious anti-Semitism of indiscriminate depth and breadth were accepted features of American life, making Jews acutely sensitive to its manifestations and disguises. Condescension toward and stigmatization of Jews were common and, like overt discrimination, deeply resented. Vaudeville bills caricatured Abies, Ikies, and Abie Kibbibles. Christian-only advertisements filled employment columns. Jews were routinely barred from many jobs and places and only partially incorporated into the local and national economies.[17]

Anti-Semitism sharply cut Solomon, edging his personality and his plans. Childhood incidents taught him "that I was different. I was a Christ-killer," and discrimination against him as an adult "in education, job opportunities and social activities" reinforced the message and recalled past humiliations. Even when he was an elderly judge, he still felt "the hurt that I experienced as a young man being discriminated against because I was a Jew." Years earlier, his resentment translated into action. "Largely as a result of these experiences, and the emphasis on social justice in the Jewish tradition, I became active as a young lawyer in the problems of the poor" and in the struggle for civil rights and liberties, "not for the Jews alone — but for everyone."[18]

During his life, Solomon assailed popular notions of America as a melting pot. White ethnic groups were supposed to peacefully assimilate, and ethnic consciousness was to gradually disappear. Becoming American "meant you went through a blender or grinder and came out looking and talking and acting like everybody else." Though Jews were not made to repudiate or condemn their religion, he said, they were made to feel ashamed and wanted to abandon their former language, culture, and national loyalties. To Solomon, melting-pot sentiments victimized those lacking a strong Jewish education and many foreign-born Jews.[19]

The Solomon children "always knew that we were Jews" and different from German and Sephardic Jews, and nowhere in urban America was a Jewish community truly homogenous, despite expectations of solidarity and lives organized around similarities. The variety of Jewish associations in Portland, as elsewhere, and their dizzying array of political and cultural expressions revealed economic, gendered, political, cultural, and religious differences. Jews held a myriad of political beliefs, at least in large cities. Some Jews disdained other Jews' religious practices and ways. Still, in Portland, east European and German Jews skirted the often racking conflicts that occurred in larger Jewish communities. German Jews congregated in the Reform temple and, having prospered, usually lived in better homes in Portland Heights or on South Portland's periphery. A few were among the city's wealthiest citizens. Since the nineteenth century, some dozen Jewish merchants and lawyers had held public office and exercised conspicuous authority in the Republican Party. Prominent German Jews sympathized with the Portland newcomers' difficulties and generously supported their needy, but other German Jews saw in the immigrants distasteful Jewish or foreign attributes that might heighten anti-Semitism.[20]

Cultural and class condescensions created resentment. Throughout his life, Gus Solomon retained South Portland's bias that German Jews were overly jealous of their own reputation for respectability and, considering themselves "better than we were," were loftily condescending toward South Portlanders. In his later years, he reeled off the names of boyhood friends to illustrate the superior talent and intellectuality of east European Jews: economic historian Joseph Dorfman, musician Louis Kaufman, attorney Moe Tonkon, composer David Tamkin, scientist Milton Harris, pharmacologist Louis Goodman, and artist Marcus Rothkovitz, who became world famous as Mark Rothko. That attitude, however, never prevented his forming strong friendships with German Jews.[21]

HIGH SCHOOL

The Solomons flourished in the wartime economy of 1914–1919, which stimulated regional agriculture, manufacturing, and commerce. Wartime growth profited their store and a temporary branch near one of the several busy shipyards. With their properties rising in value, family worth neared $250,000. After the 1918 Armistice, Jacob Solomon opened a store to outfit loggers in Klamath Falls, in southern Oregon, where he also bought timberland. In 1919, the family settled across town in the upscale, tree-lined Irvington neighborhood in Northeast Portland. Jacob opened a second Portland store. A new wholesaling operation also gave him "quite a corner on working clothes" by 1921. By then, his youngest son was accustomed to substantial comfort, wealth, and security. His parents' circle, part of a sober generation of new comfort, judged that their gamble had paid off: America had ended exile, expulsions, ruin, and annihilation, if not grief or separation. Having installed themselves in the middle class, they owned cars, homes, and properties. In heavy accents, they boasted of their naturalization, new wealth, and country. Well-behaved, well-dressed, well-fed offspring gave them pride. Their anxieties about succeeding were muted, but they still worried over whether they were ignoring what they owed others who had *not* succeeded. Sensitivity over loyalty issues lingered as well. How could they be both American and Jewish — and in more than their own minds? Restrictive social and economic boundaries between Jews and non-Jews still existed; their difficulties as Jews and aliens had hardly vanished.[22]

Lincoln High School, where about 10 percent of the students were Jewish, took Gus Solomon a step outside his insular community. Before 1919, he had known a few non-Jews and German Jews from wealthy homes in Oswego, Dunthorpe, and Portland Heights. Financially, he fit in. Solomon was "never pinched for funds," Morton Goodman remembered, due to a bountiful ten-dollar weekly allowance, most of which he saved at a brother's insistence. Solomon's friends were talkative Jewish boys much like himself, Americanized children of immigrants or immigrants, plus a few from an earlier generation of German Jews. They enjoyed swimming, basketball, and card games; and they disdained riches, social privilege, personal complacency, and boorishness. While boys such as Sam Wilderman and Mark Rothkovitz worked part-time to help support their families, most of his Jewish friends had only to study and play. They sprang from the new middle class of clerks, managers, teachers, shopkeepers, and salespeople who were emerging as Portland's Jewish community leaders. "Young people, particularly, wanted to talk English only, even in their homes," Solomon recalled. Talking "with a Yiddish accent was something to be avoided. It marked one as a greenhorn." Their speech, education, and claims to worldliness made them feel more culturally advanced than their parents. "We lived in a blissful era," Solomon's friend Ted Swett remembered. "Everybody was supposed to be successful" after securing a good job or entering a profession. "It was a world of confidence." Morton Goodman saw something else, too. Gus had "very strong feelings about a lot of things, and sometimes he was very sensitive [and] easily hurt" by perceived rejections based on his weight or east European Jewishness.[23]

Charles E. Wright, a non-Jewish high school classmate, remembered Solomon as a bright student who had "sort of a tough time being Jewish." Tensions rooted in "ethnic and class differences were clear" at Lincoln, according to Rothko's biographer, where Jews were excluded from its social clubs and teams. Things were no different at Washington High School, where Leo Levenson, Solomon's future office mate, felt left out when he "wasn't asked to join" its all-Christian clubs and teams. Facing exclusion at Lincoln, Solomon, Gilbert Sussman, Max Naimark, and Aaron Director organized their own debating team at Neighborhood House in South Portland. They frequented the gym at the B'nai B'rith building; and Solomon, Ted Swett, Sam Suwell, Phil Silver, and Phil and David Weinstein attended the Junior Menorah Society meetings in the South Portland building on Saturday nights. Meanwhile, Rose Solomon was the president of a charity and was working as a Zionist aiding Jewish settlement in Palestine. Jacob Solomon was a heavy contributor to the synagogue and served as its treasurer, but he avoided religious services, as did his youngest son Gus and Louis Goodman. When possible, the two boys slipped out to play baseball.[24]

Gus's low grades at Lincoln High School upset Rose, who demanded that he transfer to Jefferson High School nearer home in Northeast Portland. There, Hyman Samuels introduced him to overnight camping, and they became lifelong friends. But Solomon missed his Lincoln friends and had a meager social life. In January 1922, he persuaded his mother to let him return for a final year at Lincoln, where his grades improved. He joined the debate team and was assistant manager of the yearbook and business manager of the class play. Graduating at sixteen in January 1923, he entered the University of Washington in Seattle.[25]

American ways and Old World Jewish habits had been fusing in the adolescent. As a "second generation" Jew, Gus had developed his American identity while retaining an ethnically Jewish one. One need not exist at the expense of the other, he had decided. Solomon had acquired a middle-class gestalt of hard work, personal proficiency, patriotism, self-confidence, community responsibility, and an unquestioned regard for education, propriety, individual merit, and upward social mobility. He liked having forums in which others acknowledged him and in which he recognized and respected himself. He wanted neither a humdrum adulthood nor an unnoticed existence.

For Solomon, identity and purpose were inextricably interwoven. Obligation to Jews and non-Jews and a sense of the centrality of community had become imbedded in his sense of himself as well as an awareness of himself as a Jew of distinctive east European background and sensibilities. To German Jews, he identified himself as an east European Jew; to non-Jews, as a Jew. Being Jewish, as he would refine it in college, distinguished him from most of the world; and, because of memories and fresh persecutions of many groups, it obliged him to aid minorities and the weak. To be Jewish, above all, meant fulfilling a moral identity connected to the love of justice. Jewish communal ways had prepared Solomon to act through the group rather than out of personal preference. Having adopted universalistic claims to treat the people of the world as his brothers, he further struggled to integrate liberal universalism and Jewish particularism.

COLLEGE

Because his friends expected to attend college, Solomon did, too. Living alone in a small room, he endured six months at the University of Washington, where he reportedly made above-average grades. "I was awfully young," he remembered; the university seemed too big, and many students seemed anti-Semitic. The experience was "a disaster for me because I was absolutely unqualified and in despair." That summer, he took a public-speaking course at the University of Oregon in Eugene; and in September 1923, he transferred to Portland's small, tree-shaded Reed College. He was to spend two blissful years among its 240 students, bridged in 1924 by summer school at the University of California in Berkeley.[27]

"I loved Reed," he often declared, and "sort of found myself" there. The college nourished serious intellectuality, spacious liberalism, and easy sociability. It was open to Jews, hiring them for the faculty and rejecting the so-called quota system, a ceiling on Jewish student applicants then being imposed through much of American higher education. Since opening in 1911, Reed had tried to attain the excellence of the best eastern colleges. It required a core curriculum in the history of Western civilization, theses, seminars, and comprehensive examinations and dispensed with competitive intercollegiate sports, fraternities, and sororities. Excited by its offerings, Solomon abandoned vague thoughts of a medical career for a major in political science. Reed attracted serious-minded students, most of them Portlanders who commuted to the college by streetcar. Solomon took the helm of Reed's chapter of the Menorah Society, in a period when interest in Jewish affairs was low among Jewish students. Anticipating the work of the Hillel Foundation, some eighty campus chapters of the society took their direction from the influential *Menorah Journal*, which promoted Jewish ideals and a positive and secular Jewish identity, satirized the staid respectability of Jewish elders, celebrated ethnic differences, and tried to neutralize the effects of anti-Semitism and assimilationism on Jews. The journal called for a Jewish humanism, the formation of a Jewish vanguard, and the creation of an American Jewish cultural renaissance. In 1925, Solomon had the Menorah Society bring speakers to Reed, a campus where some twenty-five Jewish students appeared "reluctant to identify as Jews." The chapter, he explained, was trying "to create an interest in Jewish affairs where such an interest does not exist."[28]

The college was one of Oregon's small liberal engines. Faculty families, students, and alumni figured noticeably in events and organizations devoted to bettering labor and race relations, advancing social welfare, civil liberties, religious understanding, and world peace. They perpetuated the democratic ideal, visions of social solidarity, and the condemnation of rampant individualism that ran through much of pre-war progressivism. Solomon began college as a mild union sympathizer, embarrassed by union picketing of Sunday openings of his family's store. Reed brought him closer to Judaism's protest traditions and the tradition of *tikkun olam*, the obligation to repair or improve the world. "At Reed, I became quite a liberal," he remembered, more sympathetic to the less fortunate (of whom he knew little) and more interested in "issues like the right to vote and equality of opportunity. Being a Jew, naturally I was influenced in that direction because of the discrimination some people suffered."[29]

Reed stimulated Solomon socially and intellectually. "For the first time," at Reed, "I had a real social life. I began to go to dances and parties" and to spend time with women. Before long evenings of study, he enjoyed dancing in The Commons after dinner, and he played on the freshman football team. Friends opened new vistas to him. Fellow Portlander Max Gordon, for instance, introduced Solomon to the theater, which he loved, and had him read Thomas Hardy, Henrik Ibsen, Gerhart Hauptmann, Knut Hamsum, and August Strindberg. Reed also strengthened his interest in world affairs, broadened his terms of reference, fueled his outrage at injustice, and polished his political consciousness. At Reed, "I learned to appreciate the opinions of others and to question my own opinions and goals," he said. "I quickly learned that many of the things that I had taken for granted were not true." Reed friends and faculty taught him "about the good life and one's obligations to one's community." He joined the campus chapter of the recently formed League of Nations Non-Partisan Association (LNA). Abandoning his family's nominal Republicanism, he called himself a Democrat by 1926.[30]

His liberalism was more a set of high-minded meanings, symbols, and connotations than a systematic philosophy. Reed's young intellectuals were largely interested in world politics, Solomon remembered. But the Ku Klux Klan could not have escaped their concern. It was Oregon's first significant organized anti-Semitic group, and it claimed between 14,000 and 35,000 white Protestant members by the end of 1923. Fifty-eight Klaverns were formed, mainly in southern Oregon and Portland, home to around 2,500 African Americans, the lowest number among West Coast cities in 1920. The Klan burned crosses on Portland's hillsides and initiated members at its annual Rose Festival in 1923. By then, "most observers felt that the Ku Klux Klan was substantially in charge of the legislature, and — with good reason — perhaps even the Portland mayoralty and the governor's office," Robert D. Johnston writes. In 1922, mainly to restrict Oregon's roughly 8 percent Catholic minority, the Klan and Scottish Rite Masons sponsored an initiative outlawing private and parochial schools. By 1925, the Klaverns had split and politically exhausted themselves, and the Supreme Court, in *Pierce v. Society of Sisters*, had struck down the school initiative.[31]

Solomon would have entered his senior year at Reed, where his grades were average, except that faculty deaths and sabbaticals left nobody to teach history or political science. In 1925, he transferred to the University of Chicago on the advice of Harry Kenin, a Reed graduate who had just earned a doctorate at the university. Concentrating on historical studies, Solomon thrived intellectually, but the year was emotionally difficult. Living in an off-campus room, he made few friends. He disliked mandatory weekly chapel services and, despite weekend visits to his brother Eugene and other Chicago relatives, felt lonely. At nineteen, he graduated in June 1926 with a B-minus average.[32]

He wanted an academic career, but anti-Semitism kept him and large numbers of intellectually oriented Jewish students from pursuing it. Historians at the University of Chicago made it "clear that a Jew wasn't going to get into a History" graduate program and that only the most brilliant Jews succeeded in academic careers. Solomon returned to Portland and was looking for work when a small fellowship offer arrived. He had to reject the opportunity when his father refused to supplement it. Jacob's retail profits had fallen to a modest level, his wholesale business had badly deteriorated, and a decline in the real-estate market had cut the value of his holdings. Fires had destroyed his southern Oregon timber, and a downtown store fire had cost him between $75,000 and $100,000. Jacob clung to the Caruthers Apartment, but, as Solomon later remembered, "I think my father lost practically all of his money before the great depression of 1929."[33]

The slowing regional economy contributed to Jacob's losses. Lumbering, in which Oregon was the nation's second largest producer, ranked with agriculture and the coal, rail, and textile industries as distressed national activities during the 1920s. Soft spots had appeared in Portland's important commercial, trade, and banking sectors by 1926. Local construction declined, and some banks failed. The Solomons moved to a smaller house, and in the summer of 1926 their cash-starved son and Max Gordon entertained themselves by haunting the public library and taking brisk walks. The business world projected a diminishing future. Not that Solomon was interested. Law seemed "a pretty good profession," he thought, though he was woefully ignorant of it. He had never been inside a law school or a courthouse, did not know what happened in them, knew no attorney other than his brother Eugene in Chicago, and knew nothing about how lawyers behaved.[34]

LAW SCHOOL

Harvard Law School accepted Solomon in 1926, but he chose Columbia, which was then on the frontier of American legal scholarship. Unprepossessing grades from prestigious colleges won him entrance at the two elite law schools at a time when few required applicants to have finished more than two years of college. Bearing the $1,500 fee and further guarantees from his father, who apparently favored a law rather than an academic career, he and Max Gordon entered Columbia under its 25 percent Jewish quota. They shared a dormitory room for six weeks until Gordon abandoned law classes for a Bohemian existence of artists and musicians. A Portland friend, Gilbert Sussman, moved in, and Gordon used an unreported cot. Rather than studying law, Solomon attended history, anthropology, and political science classes. Gordon introduced him to Brooklyn relatives and young people he knew, including one who became a girlfriend, and they frequented the theater with other Portlanders. Near the final month of the school year, Solomon finally "began to study law. I studied quite hard, and I passed all my classes."[35]

Columbia's law school was in a golden era. In 1926, it bulged with 725 students, and entrants were told that high standards would drive away a third of them by June. In 1927, new faculty member William O. Douglas concluded that the "students were the lion and the teacher was the tamer. Utter precision was demanded and sarcasm plus occasional humor was the technique." During the 1920s and 1930s, Columbia, Yale, and Harvard were centers of a revolt "against the sterile formalism and conceptualism of nineteenth-century jurisprudence and the case study" teaching method, Peter Irons writes.[36]

Beginning in 1922, several Columbia professors, later termed legal realists or Realists, reconceived their approach. Law was supposed to be studied empirically, they argued, and understood in its cultural context and as it related to other disciplines. Look closely at the actual landscape surrounding the law, Realists taught, and at the politics and other factors influencing judicial decision-making. Do not absorb the law as a set of abstract or static legal rules or doctrines. Realists, Laura Kalman writes, stressed "the role of [human] idiosyncrasy in the formation of private and public law, the importance of focusing on the particular context of a factual situation, and the utility of social sciences such as economics in illuminating legal issues." Legal rules reflected social and historical forces and so were inherently discretionary and malleable. Allegedly neutral judicial decision-making masked the judges' subjective choices, which were rooted in their individual personalities, conscience, environment, policy preferences, and general outlook. During the approaching depression, the Realists' "skepticism toward law as a 'symmetrical structure of logical propositions'" would prove "sufficient to redirect energy from law as a pillar of the status quo to law as an instrument of social reform," Jerold S. Auerbach adds. Their implicit political view that judges had been making and implementing bad social policy and that the law should better meet the challenges of the bureaucratic and welfare state would come to the fore. Solomon happily recalled Columbia's "upheaval in [my] thinking" and his Realist teachers Karl Llewellyn, Hessel Yntema, and Herman Oliphant. He adopted their view that enduring principles did not determine the law's course. He learned other lessons as well, including that lawyers should know something about any industry in question. His later practical and fact-based approach to adjudication owed much to this legal realism.[37]

But anti-Semitism diminished the educational virtues. "At Columbia University you really knew you were a Jew," he remembered. "You were discriminated against, not only in the classes, but also in social life and by the law clubs and fraternities." Moot Court barred Jews, for example, and anti-Semitism shrank career possibilities and made Jewish students, including the young Oregonian, feel inferior or unworthy.[38]

In May 1927, speeches on the Columbia campus sponsored by the American Civil Liberties Union (ACLU) left an indelible mark on him. After ranging over America's grim record on civil liberties, the ACLU's Roger Baldwin and Arthur Garfield Hayes, Professor Karl Llewellyn, and City College philosopher Morris R. Cohen protested the impending executions of anarchists Nicola Sacco and Bartolomeo Vanzetti for a Massachusetts murder-robbery. Liberals and radicals had angrily charged that their 1921 trial had been conducted by a prejudicial judge and that the two men had been tried for their radical views rather than any crime. To them, it was the decade's most famous case involving injustice to American radicals and immigrants. The plight of Sacco and Vanzetti also became a Jewish cause. Solomon remembered: "This ACLU meeting opened up new horizons for me and had a great impact on my life." He acutely felt the wrongs visited on the two men and legions of Americans.[39]

Solomon was ready to believe that wholesale violations of individual liberty had violated the promise of America. He was primed to agree with demands by unions, immigrants, and racial, political, and religious minorities for full constitutional protection. Constitutional remedies, he believed, must be deployed to right the wrongs Sacco and Vanzetti and other outcasts suffered. Within a few years, he decided that American society could not depend on judges to grant rights. Citizens had to peacefully challenge illegitimate authority and strengthen the institutions through which individuals and groups might undo injustices — that is, rights were realized by collective efforts and a civil support structure, as embodied, he was beginning to think, in the ACLU and other rights organizations. The executions of Sacco and Vanzetti on August 23, 1927, staggered him. Sleepless, he roamed the beach all night in Seaside, Oregon, where he was recuperating from an appendix operation. He shared the conviction of the western left and liberal worlds that two innocent men had been unjustly executed.[40]

At home during that summer of 1927, Solomon volunteered in the law firm of Arthur Goldsmith and David Robinson, whose representation of farm cooperatives and fledgling public power interests he supported. Wanting "to learn how the law actually works," he received a little business law tutoring, learned how to draft and handle legal papers and debt collection letters, assisted Robinson in *pro bono* representation of indigents, attended two trials, and glimpsed through both men the prosperous and more acculturated world of German Jews. He decided to find a legal internship after graduation.[41]

Ill health — the removal of his appendix and a possible gall bladder problem — made his return to Columbia questionable. Also, his father was losing money and worried about revenue. Solomon transferred to Stanford Law School, which charged only $285 a year, started two weeks later than Columbia, and was only a day's train ride away. Life there would have to be simpler, he thought. Stanford was a "very easy place to go." Palo Alto was a "wonderful place to live" and was near San Francisco's rich cultural offerings. But the school lacked Columbia's cutting-edge approach. Students analyzed portions of appellate decisions to derive the narrow, technical principles that judges supposedly used in resolving disputes, and lectures prevailed. Legal realism was a distant noise. Gratefully, there "was very little discrimination at Stanford" against the few Jewish law students there.[42]

Stanford "was a good traditional law school," Solomon remembered, "dedicated to turning out good, competent business-oriented lawyers." Many hoped to succeed as corporate presidents or partners in large law firms. Few "were restless or . . . wanted to dedicate themselves to the public good." While "I didn't study law as much as I should have, I did read a great deal," he remembered, particularly *The Nation, The New Republic, Atlantic Monthly, Harper's, Current History*, and novels. He was attracted to the national liberal sensibility and new politics featured in these periodicals: freedom of speech, the producing classes, the rights of minorities and women, academic freedom, economic justice, natural resource conservation, and world peace were championed; the Ku Klux Klan, religious fundamentalism, censorship, and restrictive immigration policies were opposed. From New York, Joseph Dorfman directed Solomon to read Thorstein Veblen's biting social criticism. Classmates apparently sought him out as a skeptical, nonconforming spirit. For nonlegal and political subjects, he said, "I became a sort of an arbiter" among them. As at Columbia, he considered himself a person first and a law student second.[43]

Plagued by an undefined health problem, he spent the first two quarters at Stanford feeling poorly, making few friends, and dating nobody. Three difficult weeks spent painting the Caruthers Apartments in the summer of 1928 prompted his enrollment in Stanford's summer session. By then, his father was rapidly losing money; only accumulated savings from allowances and limited parental assistance permitted a final year in Palo Alto. It was a happy one. Solomon felt better and could swim regularly, and roommate Ted Swett helped him meet bright students and find new friends. Male friendships were cemented over bridge and poker tables, where he won a reputation for prowess. In 1928, Solomon registered as a Democrat and, like the greater majority of Jews, voted for Al Smith.[44]

Returning to Oregon with his law degree in June 1929, Solomon was more purposeful than ever. He meant to pass the state bar examination and secure a business-law apprenticeship. Professionally, he felt unfinished. He knew himself ignorant of swaths of statutory and case law, and he was untutored in Oregon law. He had no real training in litigation or negotiation, and he had only glimmerings of how to be an advocate or counselor or how to build a practice. He did know how to critically analyze statutes and cases and to test for their limits and exceptions. While he had no real interest in legal abstractions or doctrines, in legal realism he had a guide to understanding and treating the law and the judicial process.

Personally, he felt himself part of a wider world than that of the law or of his Jewish or white male identities. With horizons broadened by education and experience and with principles yet untested, Solomon returned to an essentially uncharted territory, meaning to find his way to a life larger than law might afford. There would be no "living in a mental ghetto," which he later said contributed "to the perpetuation of a system that would ghettoize all Jews and all members of minority groups." With his moral and political references largely set, he planned to commit himself to liberal causes rather than just pursuing a career or merely voicing conventional and grand sentiments. And he meant to be heard. So, as the world plunged into instability and depression, he returned confidently to his overwhelmingly Republican and white Protestant state.[46]

Chapter 2

Young Lawyer

I look upon the practice of law as an opportunity to participate in great social movements.

— *Gus J. Solomon, c. 1951*

NOVICE

Gus Solomon "never considered going any place but Portland. This was my home," he said. "I liked it here." Still, Americans were only dimly aware of Oregon. It was distant from the centers of money and influence, rural and small town in its economy and habits, and provincial in its outlook. In 1930, Oregon had about one percent of the nation's population — 953,786 people — and produced about one percent of the nation's income. Portland, its single urban place, contained some 302,000 mostly native-born residents, 98 percent of them white, plus sizable numbers of unrecorded transient workers seeking employment throughout the West.[1]

Following his licensing as a lawyer in September 1929, Solomon meant to do what the legal profession largely did: service business. What "lawyers do is no mystery," Lawrence M. Friedman writes. "Big-firm lawyers work for big business, small-firm lawyers for small business."[2]

Solomon expected Portland to brim with possibilities, but then he stunningly encountered the strong prejudices that faced Jews and liberals in legal circles. In Oregon, the profession was dominated by a Protestant social hierarchy and business values that distrusted or detested outsiders, active government, minorities, unions, radicals, and dissent. Its leading law firms, as elsewhere, hired no Jews, nor did their powerful lumber, utility, rail, and shipping firm clients. The Republicans' two-to-one electoral majority kept Oregon a GOP citadel. Every county had voted for Harding, Coolidge, and Hoover; and Democrats had lacked an electoral majority since 1876. No Democrat had reached the U.S. Senate since 1914. They had remained in the minority throughout the Boom Decade, primarily because of divisions over prohibition, nativism, religious fundamentalism, and publicly owned electrical power. Because only its primaries counted and his young Republican friend Harry Kenin planned a legislative bid, Solomon registered as a Republican in 1930. Kenin's bids for a congressional nomination in 1934 and 1936 kept Solomon a titular Republican even as his politics became fully crystallized.[3]

Although Oregon was generally considered the Far West's most politically conservative state, insurgencies before the First World War — demanding greater democracy and egalitarianism — had swept its politics and government. Ordinary Portlanders had fought the great economic and political power of the city's elite, and grand insurgencies "shook Progressive Era Portland, from the single tax to antivaccinationism," writes Robert D. Johnston. Pre-war Oregon pioneered in protective labor laws and created the nationally renowned Oregon System, a bundle of electoral initiatives that included the direct primary, the recall, the direct election of United States senators, and direct legislation. The initiatives found ready use.[4]

The untried twenty-three-year-old made the rounds of uninterested law firms as the Boom Decade deflated. Given the prevailing material conditions, social structure, and cultural values, Solomon's hometown was not suffused with infinite opportunities. The Pacific Northwest's natural resource economy hovered on disaster even as his own family's fortunes plunged. Jacob Solomon, already in difficulty, watched his monthly store receipts drop from about $5,800 to $900 during the last nine months of 1929. A brother had to lend Gus $200 for the bar examination fee and new clothes meant to impress interviewers.[5]

Solomon expected to compete for legal success; but if he could help it, he did not want a legal practice to compromise his high principles or the lofty ones the bar and law schools expounded. An elevated sense of professional and community obligations regulated his ambition. Neither law nor politics should be rooted in raw power or self-interest, he believed. A legal career should embody civic virtues, not just be another kind of business. Attorneys ought not to be amoral professionals, mouthpieces for wealth, special-favor seekers, uncritical plan executors, or mere problem-solvers. He was appalled by the Oregon bar's undisguised commercialism and indifference to laws that addressed social wrongs and furthered justice. Representing Oregon's leading business and financial interests, the major law firms, he charged, employed those intent on "making money as rapidly as possible with the least possible effort" while avoiding unpopular causes. Attorneys occupied two camps, he oversimplified — social blinders and avarice defined one, while the other recognized the legal enterprise's larger responsibilities and promoted the collective good.[6]

Other job-seekers, he remembered, "were horrified at my lack of respect for corporation lawyers and my belief that the practice of law is a privilege which carries with it responsibilities to society as a whole." During interviews, Solomon probably conveyed these sentiments to business attorneys, a group that in Robert W. Gordon's estimation tended "to see themselves as extensions and technical instruments of their clients' projects, agents who 'grease the wheels' of American capitalism, rather than as an independent estate with independent functions."[7]

Trudging from one law office to another dampened Solomon's hopes. New law graduates held little appeal in that economy. Interviewing proved uncomfortable, and anti-Semitism hurt his pride and confidence. "For the Jew," religious philosopher Mordecai M. Kaplan wrote in 1934, "the primary need of earning a livelihood is beset with humiliating obstacles." In employment, housing, accommodations, recreation, and college admissions, obstacles were the rule rather than the exception. Private-club bans helped make Jews outsiders in business and law, Solomon came to think. Oregon's vast wood-products industry employed no Jewish lawyers partly because they could not negotiate deals in private clubs.[8]

Hurtfully, Portland Jews discriminated, too. Some hired non-Jewish lawyers, believing that courts favored them over Jewish ones. Some Jewish attorneys used non-Jewish co-counsel as window dressing. Leading local German Jewish businessmen were so enamored of respectability, Solomon later fumed, that they only hired non-Jewish legal help. Further, prominent Jewish families feared "'rock[ing] the boat.' They wanted to identify with the wealthy and the well-born and with the people 'who counted.'" It incensed him that a Jewish delegation tried to persuade Harry Kenin to withdraw from the Republican congressional primary contention because Jews, especially controversial ones such as Kenin, should not become too conspicuous. Solomon never forgave parvenu Jews for spurning him professionally and opposing worthy people and causes.[9]

Job discrimination proved to be a raw and defining experience, bringing out Solomon's constructive, prolonged anger but also sustaining activities to advance equitable employment opportunities for everybody. Solomon never forgave the unnamed authors of his anti-Semitic "rejections." In 1929, he remembered, he felt "offended more by the way I was treated by prospective employers than by my failure to get a job." No leading firm, including those with Jewish clients, would hire a Jew, and Jewish attorneys could not afford apprentices. "Other young men — who were not Jews and who had less qualifications — got jobs, but I didn't." After two weeks, he only approached firms recommended by family friends. Able to live at home, he asked for fifty dollars a month, then twenty-five dollars, and then for an empty law office desk.[10]

Confidence in his own talent and credentials apparently made him feel that discrimination could soon be overcome. He somehow ignored the common knowledge in law schools and legal circles that major law firms employed Jews only under exceptional circumstances. Jews had long coped with this exclusion by establishing solo practices, relying mainly on a Jewish clientele, developing the least lucrative legal areas, and finding supplementary income. Clustering in urban areas, they largely focused on tort, real estate, bankruptcy, and criminal matters. Leo Levenson counted ninety Jews practicing in Portland and two elsewhere in Oregon in 1925. Recent Jewish law graduates normally had to take other jobs. On lunch hours, Portland journalist Sam Wilderman, Solomon's friend, reportedly "would hustle down to the municipal court and hang around hoping to be appointed a lawyer for some poor crook."[11]

Solomon entered practice alone, "not because I wanted to, but because I couldn't get a job." If he lacked the now-declining patronage enjoyed by Protestant law graduates, he gained a slippery footing through his own kinship and ethnic networks. A brother-in-law, Bernard Cantor, engaged him part-time to represent the Retail Credit Association in collection suits. He received fifty dollars a month, an office, and time to find his own clients. He mainly attracted Jews: business people, relatives, and family friends who needed scant experience or shrewdness. But drafting contracts, wills, and other documents bored him. When collection work grew distasteful and threatened his standing among Jews, he abandoned the arrangement. At the same time, Solomon did not troll for clients in every club, association, or committee. He never joined the business-heavy B'nai B'rith chapter or other service organizations. And no Jew was wanted in the prospect-filled private clubs or on prestigious committees or boards.[12]

In a seedy downtown building just after the stock market crash,

Solomon opened a solo practice on October 29, 1929, one of the 60 percent of America's attorneys who worked alone in 1930. "As late as 1947, the average firm contained only 1.64 lawyers," one study reported. Portland, with 32 percent of the state's population in 1930, was home to some 860 attorneys, 54 percent of the lawyers in the state. By 1940, there were only 650. In the nation's stratified bar, sole urban practitioners bulked the largest in numbers and the lowest in income, prestige, and influence. Below what his former professor Karl Llewellyn called the era's "blue-stocking . . . respectable bar" came the "catch-as-catch can bar" of the sole practitioners. They appeared almost exclusively in state and local matters. They might share cramped space, a few books, common expenses, and cases. A narrow range of real-estate transactions, property transfers between generations, personal injury claims, and business litigation paid them meagerly. These lawyers largely performed highly repetitive work in sectors where the law changed slowly: "wills, estates, divorces, incorporations, bank loans, home sales and purchases, and personal injuries," Sol Linowitz recalled. "There were limits on making decisions, and on how fast they could move things along."[13]

The elite Portland bar desired corporate and other institutional clients but necessarily sought clients in every nook and cranny, except where unions, public power, or other supposedly radical elements lurked. Each of the three largest firms employed as many as seven partners and associates and operated much like the catch-as-catch-can bar. Five-and-a-half days a week, a lawyer prepared his (rarely her) own evidence discovery, research, drafting, and arguments. The two bar sectors were generally unacquainted. After five years of practice, Solomon said that he knew few prominent attorneys.[14]

Beginning lawyers struggled to retain their knowledge, stay current with the law, gain experience, find attorneys who would share their knowledge, and survive during the nation's greatest crisis since the Civil War. The Great Depression rapidly dislocated lives, consumed ambitions, and subjected more than attorneys to a dread that only hard necessity laid ahead. Just to learn, Robert A. Leedy begged Portland firms in 1933 "for the privilege of sitting in their library and reading and serving their papers" without compensation. Almost no such opportunity existed. Starting out grew no easier as the Depression wore on. Only the top 10 percent of Harvard Law School graduates secured paid positions in 1936, Raymond M. Kell noted, and they merely secured "a desk in a firm that was keeping its head above water and that would pay the new associate on a piece basis for the work and errands he performed plus any fees that he could generate." In 1937, attorney Charles E. Wright gave up a four-year struggle in Portland "because the remuneration was so little, you couldn't live."[15]

"It was a terrible time. I saw people selling apples and fruit on the street, and begging and living in these Hoovervilles," Solomon remembered. By 1933, some 13 million Americans, almost a quarter of the workforce, were unemployed; millions more worked drastically shortened hours. Countless Americans were being stripped of their worldly goods and place in society and vaunted ideas of progress and the virtues of marketplace economics and democracy appeared in doubt. Americans desperately searched for answers. Confidence reeled, along with farms, industries, and businesses. Total income in Oregon declined by 29 percent between 1929 and 1932. Almost 20 percent of Portland was on relief in 1932; two-thirds of its small businesses were tax delinquent in 1933. The state's farm cash income of around $136 million in 1929 plummeted to $49 million by 1933. Rural areas pursued a grim semi-subsistence existence, worsened by the Great Dust Bowl drought east of the Cascade Mountains. During this frightening four-year period, Oregon's employment rolls dropped by some 60 percent and wages by 77 percent. Strings of sawmill towns and logging camps disappeared, and almost 90 percent of Oregon's lumber firms verged on bankruptcy. The historically important workforce in the lumber industry was cut in half.[16]

Insecurity dogged the American bar, especially for lawyers like Solomon. Surveys revealed the particular "vulnerability of young lawyers, solo lawyers, and lawyers from ethnic minority groups," Jerold S. Auerbach writes. In California, 51 percent of those admitted to the bar between 1929 and 1931 could not support their families on their first year's income; 33 percent could not by their third year. A wretched legal income in a worsening economy might have dampened Solomon's spirit if he had not thrown himself into grassroots causes.[17]

LEVENSON, SOLOMON, AND GOODMAN

In those troubled times, attorneys often pooled their resources to survive and fashioned crude clientele and support networks, ethnic and otherwise. Longtime friends Maurice E. Tarshis, Sam Wilderman, and Gus J. Solomon gathered with Leo Levenson and other young Jewish lawyers over cheap lunches at a restaurant "stag table," at free public events, in parks and homes, and on the Oregon coast. They discussed the world and their hopes and enjoyed themselves. Solomon's academic credentials and intellect impressed Levenson, who had worked his way through the downtown, privately owned Northwestern Law School. Each recognized the other's strong appetites for life, hard work, and legal experience. Solomon's "ideas about life and mine seemed to coincide," Levenson recalled. Both were strong liberals and civil libertarians. Both jabbed at individual pretensions to superiority and "stuffed shirts," scorned falsity, and liked unpretentiousness and "the little people." Levenson asked: "Why don't you move over to the Yeon Building and associate with some first-class lawyers?" Levenson could contribute a skimpy personal injury practice and brief-preparation skills — a hearing loss barred courtroom appearances — and Solomon could bring family contacts. In September 1930, the two lawyers associated without a formal partnership. A newly licensed Erling J. Hangerud rented some of their space at Fifth and Alder.[18]

In the Yeon Building, attorney Philip Chipman and Solomon struck up a companionship. The two bachelors regularly dined inexpensively before attending some free lecture — "from antivivisection to Christian Science to politics and all things in between," Kell recalled — and then dissected it. Levenson and Solomon had ample time to mull over world events and the law and to give time to civil liberty and political projects. Undemanding cases in 1930 and 1931 provided a bare living, with assignments increasing only slightly in 1932. Solomon's brief helped win an Oregon Supreme Court order for a new trial for Levenson's bootlegger client; they won a small creditor's suit and its appeal, but the debt was uncollectible. Solomon represented family friends and his father, for whom he lost in circuit court but won a favorable Oregon Supreme Court judgment on store rent. But they had little chance to captivate judges and juries with oral arguments and graceful, powerful writing. A bustling business law practice — depicted in New York as one that has "deals to complete and nail down contracts to negotiate, loans to arrange, securities to issue, bills to collect" — escaped them.[19]

Starved for clients, Solomon and Levenson seized on Irvin Goodman's invitation to collaborate. But they meant to share an office and larger clientele, not his radicalism. In October 1932, Goodman "wanted to get someone who believed in civil [liberties]," Solomon remembered, "although he was much more to the left than either Leo or me." Ten years Solomon's senior, Goodman was a cousin of the two lawyers' friends Morton and Louis Goodman and, as a major International Labor Defense (ILD) attorney in the Pacific Northwest, Oregon's leading radical lawyer. Widely considered the legal arm of the Communist Party, USA (CPUSA), the ILD had mobilized mass protests and furnished legal aid to thousands of Communists, labor organizers, and African Americans since its founding in 1925. After the political left's rebirth in the early Depression years, left-wingers seized during demonstrations, raids, and strikes and aliens under threat of deportation turned to Goodman. At his request, in 1931 Solomon had located an expert witness to testify for Ben Boloff, who faced state criminal syndicalism charges. It was Solomon's first modest venture into legally aiding protest movements.[20]

Goodman "didn't have the patience and maybe not the skill to work on briefs, and Leo Levenson was a good briefer," Solomon recalled. Sharing many convictions, an east European Jewish background, and occupational needs, they combined without a formal partnership. The younger attorneys anticipated more and better cases; Goodman foresaw enough relief from civil actions to focus more on criminal, divorce, and civil liberties matters. His "criminal law work attracted civil cases for us," Levenson recalled. "We built up a helluva practice representing both plaintiffs and defendants in civil suits." Representing unpopular groups alienated some potential clients, but "we gained more than we lost."[21]

Irvin Goodman soon drew Solomon into ILD cases, one of which always disturbed him. In 1933–1934, he worked on its appeal brief for Theodore Jordan Jr., an African American sentenced to death for murder. To Solomon, the trial transcript reeked of a plaintiff who likely had been terrorized into a confession and defended by an incompetent, court-appointed counsel. The ILD intended to face the state's highest court for "the first time [with] the question of discrimination against blacks, and the fact that the blacks were often deprived of opportunity to get a fair trial" in Oregon. Goodman must have substantially reworked the twenty-seven-year-old attorney's draft. (Solomon's later briefs were measured, concise, and without belletristic streaks.) The final brief overflowed with hyperbole, literary quotations, and unnecessary legal citations. Its authors claimed never to have "read a colder transcript of evidence where a more reckless disregard of the fundamental rules of evidence were so completely forsaken." The trial had been "a star chamber session of the defendant's entire life. Fair play, common decency and justice were overlooked." Jordan lost in the high court. Governor Julius Meier, responding to a public furor inspired by radicals, appointed a review committee, which reported that racial prejudice had tended "to prevent a fair and impartial prosecution and consideration of his case." Meier commuted Jordan's sentence to life in prison. The ILD did not appeal to the U.S. Supreme Court, even though it had begun sympathetically to take up issues of coerced confessions and ineffective counsel in race-related criminal procedure cases.[22]

Through Irvin Goodman and his own affiliations, Solomon fitfully joined the long-running debate between liberals and radicals. He knew that Goodman represented the Communist Party but always doubted that he belonged to it. Later, he pretended to know little about Goodman's radicalism. Yet, Goodman had stumped California for convict Tom Mooney, a "class war" prisoner adopted by the CPUSA, before they combined offices. Goodman's defense of United Front groups, in which Communists cooperated with Socialists, liberals, and other non-radicals in the early 1930s, had been widely reported. Associating with Goodman and groups within the United Front and its Popular Front successor — in which Communists in 1935–1939 partnered with liberals and Socialists to oppose fascism abroad and support the New Deal at home — damned Solomon in many conservative quarters. As conservative Portland lawyer Chester E. McCarty later remarked, he "had the guts to take on cases some other lawyers didn't want to touch." But being seen as an anti-Establishment figure did not faze the young Solomon. Neither did it prohibit his participation in staid bar association committees, a conservative-minded legal aid society, and an internationalist organization that attracted elite lawyers.[23]

A revolving cast passed through their law office: struggling merchants and homeowners; the injured and unemployed; union, public power, and civil liberties figures; radical agitators; and individuals with too much time on their hands. Early in the Depression, Solomon helped represent Communist-organized unemployment councils pressing for more generous relief payments. He wrote ACLU supporting briefs for ILD-defended firebrands and minorities. In about 1938, he persuaded the Works Progress Administration to allow its local employees to join the Communist-influenced Workers Alliance of America. He shared public platforms with radical speakers and argued with public authorities about violations of radicals' civil liberties. In a time of fluidity across the left-liberal political spectrum, Solomon behaved like any self-respecting liberal activist and civil liberties counsel in making common, though selective, cause with radicals. Conviction tempered by deepening skepticism dictated his relations with the ILD. Outside the office, he saw little of Goodman and much of Levenson, Hangerud, and other liberals. As time passed, he and Goodman, both possessed of hard streaks of determination, engaged in increasingly heated political arguments. A politically ambiguous relationship had its drawbacks.[24]

LAW PRACTICE

"I came to have a very active practice," Solomon later remembered. "For the most part I represented local business." Small civil actions, many paying only if Solomon won and the losers paid, provided little income but enough to quit the family home in 1934. Seeing less of his extended family and more of friends and political allies, Solomon occupied a series of seedy houseboats and apartments for the remainder of the decade. Disputes that were significant only to the contending parties usually filled his time — such as, merchants staving off creditors or wanting bills paid. "He was for the small man," charged very little, and gave lots of free advice, service station owner James Caputo Sr. remembered. Solomon and another lawyer, for example, lost a bulb-grower's suit at trial and on appeal but secured only a modest judgment. Solomon negotiated and litigated for injured people and widows faced with loss of property or denied insurance benefits. In the process, he and other plaintiff attorneys developed considerable antipathy toward insurance companies.[25]

The legal results were mixed. In an era when Oregon tort law severely limited compensation in wrongful death and negligent injury cases and in any recovery if the plaintiff bore any contributory fault, Solomon and two others secured a $7,500 award for an injured client for whom they had asked $52,000. After losing two similar suits, Solomon won them on appeal. He also lost a foreclosure appeal on a widow's home and land. When he and another lawyer teamed against powerful insurers in a wrongful death claim, they overturned a state commission's decision. But the verdict was set aside and a new trial ordered, after which the Oregon Supreme Court sustained the commission. In his sole federal appearance, he successfully argued an insurance appeal for Cohn Brothers, his cousins' furniture store, in the Ninth Circuit Court of Appeals.

Campaigning for causes that, for him, occupied the moral high ground kept Solomon from becoming absorbed in earning a living. Public power became one of his particular enthusiasms. Looking back, he said: "I don't know of anything of which I'm more proud than my [work] for the establishment of PUDS and Co-op[s], except for my civil [liberties] fights, and I think that what success we've had in the region, developing industries [has] largely been due to the PUD's." As an occupational niche, public power opened when Oregon attorneys overwhelmingly rejected the nascent People's Utility Districts (Public Utility Districts, or PUDs) and Rural Electrification Authority cooperatives (REAs) as disreputable or evil entities. That urban liberals, the Oregon State Grange, the Oregon-Washington Farmers' Union, and the State Federation of Labor all supported the public power effort, making public power appear even more illegitimate to conservatives.[26]

The controversy over public-versus-private power convulsed the Pacific Northwest and other regions for years. In Oregon, the issue divided the minority Democrats and most Republicans. (Outside the well-served urban districts, public power won support among rural and small-town Republicans.) In favoring public ownership of electric systems (some added water and bus systems), Solomon shared a growing opinion that the public — through governments, consumer-users, or both — should rightfully own, develop, and deliver electric power to everyone at low cost. To help create and support a healthy economy, he and other liberals expected the federal government to take the lead in turning western rivers into inexpensive power sources.

Principle and self-interest ran through a dispute that was ultimately related to conflicting visions of what would contribute the most to a healthy society. Utilities unhesitatingly fought their dismantling and replacement by public-power entities, especially the threat of PUD condemnation proceedings. Public ownership and rural electrification interests assailed private utilities, especially the dominant utility holding companies (outlawed in 1935), as plundering speculators that abused free enterprise, contaminated public opinion, exploited ratepayers, and ignored unserved areas. Opponents countered that public power brought an unwanted planned economy, Socialism or Communism, and a needless bureaucracy and that investor-owned utilities could ill afford to serve many areas. Heated rhetoric, bitter feelings, threats, and reprisals marked the public-power fight.

As a sentiment and an institution, public power surged during the Depression, dramatically so in the Pacific Northwest. Oregon and Washington possessed nearly a third of the nation's potential hydroelectric power in 1930, the year Oregon elected the pro-public power independent Julius Meier as governor and amended its constitution to allow PUDs to exist. In 1932, a State Power Authority was voted into Oregon's constitution. The legislature enacted a PUD law covering waterpower and hydroelectric delivery but no State Power Authority. Initiatives and referenda rendered state public-power laws "a hopeless botch" by 1938, journalist Richard L. Neuberger reported. Twelve Oregon PUDs managed to form between 1932 and 1950; but despite the availability of federal aid, only four acquired or built facilities. Fierce utility and business resistance, a difficult legal process, and a wartime hiatus frustrated them.[27]

Solomon became a member of the Oregon Public Power Association in 1931 or 1932, and public power quickly became a cause that channeled his legal and political energies. He became the "unpaid legal information bank for the public power movement, including the Oregon State Grange," its former counsel wrote. Because of Solomon's almost unbroken string of PUD victories in the Oregon Supreme Court between 1939 and 1948 and other achievements, the Master of the Oregon Grange called him the state's "outstanding authority" on municipal utility law. For years, liberal circles viewed Solomon as an idealistic, accomplished, and canny public-power adviser, litigator, negotiator, and coalition-builder — a reputation that frightened away potential clients. Like civil liberties and union representation, public-power work was not for the posturer or the faint of heart. Adversaries and skimpy fees would have ground down either. Until the post-war period, PUDs and REA representation paid Solomon little, and payment sometimes came years afterward when private systems were purchased. The Northern Wasco County PUD and the new Clatskanie and Central Lincoln PUDs hired him, as did the Northwest Public Power Association. After passage of the 1935 Rural Electrification Act, several rural electrical and telephone and agricultural cooperatives also employed him. "There again, I worked for nothing, practically," he remembered. Three years' labor for one REA yielded $840, less than a dollar an hour at a time when office expenses exceeded three dollars an hour. Rewarding loyalty, the REA rehired him for more profitable tasks.[28]

For public power and numerous other causes, Solomon was no morally neutral legal technician but, rather, a fervent agent of change. He believed in the law's redeeming promise of justice and, as a legal realist, presumed that the law was not separate from power or policy. He was, at heart, a "cause lawyer," sharing with clients a vision of a higher good and responsibility for the ends promoted. He participated, for instance, in unsuccessful efforts led by Harry Kenin to win Portland voters' approval of a PUD in 1940 and a municipally owned utility in 1941 — the same year the Oregon Committee of the Public Ownership League honored Solomon and others at a banquet.[29]

Oregon's growing unions created a narrower occupational niche for Solomon. With few Oregon lawyers willing to represent organized labor, Goodman, Solomon, and Levenson gladly handled tasks for affiliates of the fledgling Congress of Industrial Organizations (CIO). In 1938, CIO unions within Solomon's anti-Communist faction in the Oregon Commonwealth Federation secured his services. Primarily "through friends in Seattle," he remembered, "I was hired by trade unions, particularly the International Woodworkers of America to handle some cases." The IWA-CIO had him defend (unsuccessfully at trial and on appeal) its takeover of one Oregon Carpenters Union-AFL local, and IWA's Columbia River District Council asked him to negotiate with government agencies during a ferocious AFL-CIO jurisdictional dispute in 1938. IWA representation ended once radical Harold Pritchett headed the parent union and purged his predecessor's lawyers. In 1938, the state CIO employed Solomon and others to prepare its portion of a joint AFL-CIO constitutional challenge to the Oregon's anti-picketing statute, and CIO unions sent him members with potentially lucrative wage, hour, and injury claims. He handled the first Oregon cases under the federal minimum wage law for women and the first wage and hour claims under the Fair Labor Standards Act of 1937. Had more CIO affiliates been interested in his services — by 1941, he admitted being friendlier to them than to American Federation of Labor (AFL) affiliates — he would have jumped at the chance.[30]

Solomon's only significant labor case was *CIO v. Bain* (the companion to *AFL v. Bain*). In 1938, Oregon had banned secondary boycotts and all picketing in or near an employer's premises unless a majority of employees had a bona fide dispute with that employer over wages, hours, or working conditions. The statute was one of the nation's most stringent regulations of union activities, "objectionable on so many grounds," Solomon predicted, "that I cannot see how even the lower court will sustain its constitutionality." The case set off a joint AFL-CIO challenge. In February 1939, Solomon traveled east to confer with CIO General Counsel Lee Pressman and his staff about the statute and with the ACLU legal staff about the IWA-CIO's separate case, *Harris v. Backman*. He appeared in May alongside union lawyers before a circuit court panel considering the consolidated anti-picketing challenge. The case was dismissed.[31]

The AFL headed the appeal to the Oregon Supreme Court in February 1940. At Solomon's urging, the ACLU filed an *amicus curiae* brief. Together, the unions and ACLU argued that the U.S. Supreme Court's developing doctrine, that union picketing was a form of speech protected by the First Amendment, applied to states through the Fourteenth Amendment. In April, in *Thornhill v. Alabama* and *Carlson v. California*, the Supreme Court raised peaceful picketing as constitutionally protected communication to a legal pinnacle. Oregon's statute was automatically invalidated, Solomon claimed: "You can't enact a catch-all and attack the right to picket because it's one of the manifestations of free speech in order to get at a different end." The Oregon justices speedily applied *Thornhill* and *Carlson* to render unconstitutional all but one section of the anti-picketing law. Contrary to Solomon's hopes, *Bain* failed to become an American constitutional landmark.[32]

CIVIL LIBERTIES COUNSEL

The ACLU became the most important vehicle for Solomon's unrelenting constitutionalism from 1934, when he became an ACLU activist and cooperating volunteer attorney. In 1933, Goodman and national Communist Party leader Elizabeth Gurley Flynn, who lived in Portland, had recommended him to ACLU Director Roger N. Baldwin as a dedicated civil libertarian and "a real Liberal" capable of branching out from a mundane legal practice. He could inspire Portland's lackluster Oregon Civil Liberties Committee, they suggested. Formed in 1932, the Committee had done little more than persuade the mayor not to unleash war veterans on an unemployment march. Earlier, Solomon had approached Millie R. Trumbull, a member of the Oregon Industrial Welfare Commission, about forming an ACLU affiliate; but she had not been interested, and the famous pre-war progressive William S. U'Ren had opposed the idea. Now, Baldwin welcomed him into the rank of ACLU volunteer lawyers. In his first assignment for the ACLU in 1934, Solomon silently observed a state criminal syndicalism sentencing. Three years later, he prepared the ground for the statute's replacement.[33]

Criminal syndicalism laws in thirty-four states had wreaked havoc among real and alleged Socialists, anarchists, Communists, and trade unionists since the First World War and the Russian Revolution. Following the deportation of aliens in the early 1920s and renewed fears of revolution, and in settings of unconstrained law enforcement, states in the early 1930s revised the statutes and enforced them anew. Oregon did both in 1933. Its original law prohibited the advocacy of force, violence, or sabotage as a means of instituting political change or labor organization. The amended version banned assemblies or organization that taught violence or sabotage at meetings or attempted to advocate syndicalism with oral or written communications. To obtain evidence and suppress Communism, the Portland police Red Squad increased its spying and raids, disbanded meetings and marches, blacklisted union activists, and made arrests.[34]

American law had not yet developed a "constitutional culture," a core set of substantive ideals held and implemented by the nation's judiciary. No consensus had developed, according to Cass R. Sunstein,

> that the Constitution protects broad rights to engage in political dissent; to be free from discrimination or mistreatment because of one's religious convictions; to be protected against torture or physical abuse by the police; to be ruled by laws that have a degree of clarity, and to have access to court to ensure that the laws have been accurately applied; [and] to be free from subordination on the basis of race and sex.[35]

"Each generation has its own civil [liberties] problems," Solomon recalled, "and during the 1930's our problems grew out of the great depression and out of the struggle between capital and labor." As Jerold S. Auerbach specified, "Radicals, especially Communists, were the primary victims of suppression for their unionizing efforts, hunger marches, public demonstrations, picket lines, and advocacy of social change." Dissident organizations were infiltrated and harassed, and people were jailed and brutalized for speech-making, publications, or their presence in banned places, such as Portland's skid road area after a police-imposed 6 PM curfew. Racial minorities widely suffered from eruptions of violence, police third-degree tactics, and forced confessions.[36]

Portland's ACLU "became sort of a spokesman, the litigat[or] for those who were being pushed around," Leo Levenson recalled. It remained a magnet for the hurt and the disaffected. Hobbled by disagreements and poor financial, legal, and membership resources, the organization relied more on negotiation, persuasion, and alliances than on independently battling the crippling courtroom and legislative odds. Yet, it did try twice, on Solomon's recommendation, to overturn the state's criminal syndicalism law. In southern Oregon, after Kyle Pugh had received a five-year sentence for unlawfully selling radical literature, the ILD asked the ACLU to join its appeal to the Oregon Supreme Court. With national ACLU approval, Solomon previously had rejected comparable ILD requests. In this period, however, ACLU-ILD cooperation was cautiously re-emerging in the country, but not at the trial level and only if the ACLU considered an appeal as not directed primarily to Communist Party organizing and propaganda. National ACLU officials, who normally trusted Solomon's judgment, left the decision about the Pugh appeal to its Oregon Committee. Solomon read the draft ILD brief and chose an independent ACLU role. In 1935, he and others asked Oregon's highest court to grant the ACLU friend-of-the-court status. Chances of success "are very poor," he wrote an ACLU official, "and I believe that our only possible chance is to get an imposing list of legal scholars on our amicus curiae brief." Recruit them, he advised, from among ACLU notables on the law faculties at Harvard and the University of Chicago, where two of the Oregon justices had graduated.[37]

When the petition was rejected, Solomon unusually conferred with a sympathetic justice, J.O. Bailey, on a revised approach. His colleagues might reverse themselves, he heard, "if they felt that a great number of 'respectable' people" — such as Harvard's Felix Frankfurter — "were opposed to the decision." ACLU headquarters agreed. The resubmission stressed the applicants' national ACLU connections, listed its board members' prestigious affiliations, and indicated an interest in Pugh's case from philosopher-author Corliss Lamont and Senator Burton K. Wheeler from Montana. This time, friend-of-the court status was approved.[38]

Solomon sighed that Pugh was "a very difficult case in view of the record, but the records in all of these cases are usually very bad." The brief by Solomon, Levenson, and three New York attorneys discounted the language in the publications Pugh sold. While citing *Gitlow v. New York* (1925), *Stromberg v. California* (1931), and other rulings, they focused on the words in the pamphlet that had been used to convict him. In conceding, to ILD disgust, "that Communism considers armed insurrection necessary and inevitable, and, indeed the only way of attaining a new social order," the ACLU team claimed that the offending item "merely expounds this viewpoint as an abstract doctrine" and in no way advocated or urged action to accomplish it. That is, they took the traditional liberal path of rigorously distinguishing violent action from speech or thought. The team also argued that Pugh had been arrested before he sold the pamphlet and that no evidence showed him sympathetic to any radical group or doctrine or belonging to the Communist Party. The intercessors had combined orthodox first principles — citations, facts, and argument — with hard-nosed calculations about judicial personalities. As legal realists, they had focused on the context of Pugh's situation and assumed that the law was fluid and that judicial neutralism masked subjective choices. The Oregon justices were simply expected to be subject to prestige claims and other extrajudicial considerations. Solomon's ten-minute oral argument focused on the notable Americans who endorsed the ACLU brief. While the justices refused to declare the criminal syndicalism statute unconstitutional, they did reverse Pugh's conviction.[39]

As an advocate, Solomon believed that he was acting in a terrain of struggle in which the legal culture and his training, not just his causes, demanded victory. Uncertainties that could be found in virtually every statute, administrative mandate, and court ruling permitted a skilled counsel to make a plausible argument for almost any claim. Persuasively leading judges through the gray areas was an attorney's responsibility. "I never thought when I was a lawyer I was searching for the truth; I was searching for a verdict," Solomon said. "I wanted to put my best foot forward without engaging in any bad tactics." That is, trial lawyers should truthfully present rules of law and selected facts that help clients and otherwise try to persuade all-too-human judges to adopt their version of the facts and the law.[40]

THE DEJONGE CASE

Gus Solomon's most important case, decided when he was only thirty years old, led to an American constitutional landmark. It began in Portland on July 27, 1934, when the police arrested Dirk DeJonge and others at an orderly rally called by the Communist Party. Referring to events during a bloody West Coast waterfront strike, DeJonge and other speakers protested county jail conditions, the police shooting of strikers, and police raids on homes and the local CPUSA's headquarters and bookstore. They urged listeners to recruit people into the Communist Party, buy Communist Party literature, and attend another meeting. DeJonge and other Communists were indicted under Oregon's revised criminal syndicalism statute for participating in a meeting conducted by a political party that taught and advocated the violent and unlawful overthrow of the government.

At trial, the prosecution produced evidence that the CPUSA had called for the violent overthrow of the government and that it had organized the event. Multnomah County's Circuit Court decided that DeJonge and Edward R. Denny had violated the law, even though no one at the rally had actually advocated the overthrow of the government or any other unlawful action. The two men were tried and convicted and in 1936 began seven-year sentences for participating in a meeting of persons who in other places and times advocated outlawed acts. At trial, an ILD team led by Irvin Goodman had argued that under both the statute and the indictment the state had to prove the meeting was under Communist Party auspices *and* that it vocally championed unlawful actions.[41]

Based on Solomon's report on the bitter three-week trial, the local ACLU concluded that "the Court permitted a great number of things in evidence that were clearly erroneous and which constitute reversible error." The judge, "a big American Legion man . . . very amenable to pressure from the so-called respectable groups," rejected the ILD's claim that the prosecutor had engaged in serious misconduct. Before the sentencing, Solomon asked ACLU members on the Columbia law faculty to appeal for leniency to the judge, an alumnus. "Nothing should be left to the Judge's imagination because he has none," he wrote. The letters did not succeed. Years later, a still angry Judge Solomon declared that the long sentences awarded were "outrageous."[42]

The ACLU Committee, advised by national ACLU officials, refused the ILD's request to join its appeal to the Oregon Supreme Court. The Oregon majority, with two justices dissenting, upheld the convictions. Following common state court practice in applying anarchism and syndicalism statutes, the court ruled that mere membership in an organization advocating the proscribed doctrine constituted grounds for conviction, without any need to prove a defendant's adherence to the doctrine or that he had said or done anything at a meeting. The decision meant that, in Oregon, anybody who helped publicize, presided over, or took an active role in any peaceful Communist Party-sponsored meeting could be imprisoned.[43]

Solomon had initially recommended that either the ILD or the ACLU appeal DeJonge's conviction to the U.S. Supreme Court. The ILD's planned request for an Oregon Supreme Court rehearing gave the ACLU an opportunity. When asked by Solomon if the ILD would take the case to the U.S. Supreme Court, Irvin Goodman supposedly quipped "that the Communist Party didn't want the appeal because some people do their best work for them in jail" as class-war prisoners useful for organizing and propaganda. To many in the ACLU, the remark showed once again that the ILD was only interested in winning a Communist following and exploiting revolutionary situations. Still, Solomon's interest persisted, and he and others overcame the strong hesitancy within the Portland ACLU to collaborate with the ILD. ACLU-ILD collaboration had been stormy and tenuous, but it now was cautiously re-emerging in Oregon, in the Scottsboro Defense Committee, and in the lead-up to the Supreme Court's ruling in *Herndon v. Georgia* in May 1935.[44]

Solomon was now a driving force in DeJonge's appeal. Late in 1935, Allan Hart, a younger lawyer who became one of Solomon's best friends and allies, persuaded him that the ACLU should make its own rehearing request to the Oregon Supreme Court. He ought to argue that the First Amendment applied to the states, Hart urged, and cite *Herndon v. Georgia* that a constitutional question must be "seasonably raised in the court below or passed upon by that court" for the Supreme Court to consider an appeal. When the ILD asked the Oregon Supreme Court for a rehearing, Solomon persuaded the reluctant Oregon Civil Liberties Committee to submit a friend-of-the-court brief. The brief, written by Levenson and Solomon, contended that DeJonge's conviction violated the Oregon constitution and that the First Amendment applied to the states. Solomon remembered: "We in the ACLU were not interested in any of the attacks made by DeJonge's counsel in either the trial or appellate court other than the one charging" violation of a federal right. As expected, a rehearing was denied, and DeJonge entered prison on January 25, 1936. But the federal question had been raised. If the national ACLU agreed to play its part, as Solomon recommended, an appeal could be filed with the U.S. Supreme Court.[45]

Solomon believed that DeJonge would fare well in that venue. Still, fearing ILD abandonment of DeJonge, he proposed to ILD attorneys, the Communist Party's district organizer, and the national ACLU that the ACLU take over the appeal. On reflection, all agreed. Solomon, Levenson, and Goodman, none of whom had "experience appealing a case from the State Supreme Court to the United States Supreme Court," would appear as "of counsel," Solomon reported. "We can write the brief in Portland," he said, but help was needed from lawyers who had argued before the Supreme Court. Somebody in the East would have to make the oral argument. A young Osmond K. Fraenkel, a national board member and the New York Civil Liberties Committee co-counsel, was made the principal *DeJonge* counsel.[46]

For several months, Solomon and Fraenkel traded ideas. The Portlander conveyed suggestions from the CPUSA district organizer. He had Goodman review a proposed filing to the Court, apparently Goodman's only work on the appeal, and Fraenkel discussed the brief with ILD attorneys. He already had taught Solomon how to use a new Supreme Court rule that an appellate team could file a brief in support of jurisdiction. After jurisdiction was noted, Solomon learned that all along "the Supreme Court was looking for a case of that kind, or some of the law clerks were, and they grabbed onto this case."[47]

Solomon and a friend who was assigned to argue the state's case, Portland's Deputy City Attorney Maurice E. Tarshis, began negotiating a stipulation of facts for the Supreme Court in lieu of a two-thousand-page trial transcript, which they could not afford. Assuming that Tarshis would use CPUSA literature to demonstrate that the party advocated violence, Solomon repeated the tactic the ACLU had used in *Oregon v. Pugh*. He tentatively agreed with Tarshis that the Communist Party taught and advocated the violent overthrow of governments. "I cannot see how we can be prejudiced" by admitting that some literature introduced at trial offended the statute, he wrote, "for the whole theory of our appeal is that DeJonge was not charged with distributing literature, but only with assisting in presiding at an assemblage of persons which taught and advocated prohibited doctrine." Communist Party officials reacted angrily, and Irvin Goodman reportedly vetoed the admission. Then, Solomon later recalled, DeJonge and ILD Acting National Secretary Anna Damon "came to me and said that he had been told by the Communist Party to fire me," at least "theoretically," he laughed, because Fraenkel was the principal counsel. Joseph Brodsky, ILD national counsel, would represent DeJonge, and he was informed that Brodsky must clear any ACLU *amicus curiae* brief prior to submission. The ACLU advised Solomon against making the admission but permitted a substitution of excerpts from official Communist literature, which made the same point. Now claiming that they were too busy and wanted to retain Fraenkel as principal counsel, the ILD lawyers allowed the submission. The ACLU kept the appeal authority, and the stipulation was filed on June 2, 1936.[48]

Fraenkel said that, on appeal, he would define the issue as simply as possible so as not to "challenge the state court's finding with regard to the character" of the Communist Party and its position on the forcible overthrow of the government. He concentrated "on the fact that he [DeJonge] had not been charged with membership in the Party." Constitutionally, the ACLU brief emphasized that the statute, as applied, violated a person's right to petition for redress of grievance and the right to peaceable assembly. Fraenkel questioned a law that "punishes a person for participation in a lawful meeting, called for lawful purpose, merely because the meeting was called by an organization which, it is charged, advocated prohibited doctrines." Because the CPUSA had been on the 1932 Oregon ballot, it called the punishment disturbing. Oregon asked the justices to apply the "bad tendency" test, contending that advocating for the Communist Party might spur into action the "morons, especially those who are class conscious, and who believe that men in high places got there through imposition upon the toilers."[49]

On December 9, 1936, Fraenkel presented the case to the U.S. Supreme Court in eight uninterrupted minutes. He asked: "Does a man, whether he is a Communist or not, become liable, criminally liable, if he speaks at a meeting called under the auspices of the Communist Party, no matter how lawful the subject matter of that meeting may be?" Tarshis spoke next, defending the constitutionality of the Oregon statute. As four of the justices sat silently, the most conservative ones barraged him with questions, leaving him ten minutes for argument. Was DeJonge a criminal under the Oregon law if he discussed the tariff? Yes, Tarshis replied. If he presided over a meeting where only resolutions were passed or deceased Communists were memorialized? Yes again. Fraenkel sensed victory.[50]

In a swift ruling on January 4, 1937, a unanimous Court invalidated the statute as it applied to DeJonge and reversed the conviction. Writing for the Court, Chief Justice Charles Evans Hughes referred to its 1931 ruling that freedom of speech and the press were protected in the states by the due process clause. Hughes held that for the states the "right of peaceful assembly is a right cognate to those of free speech and free press and is equally fundamental." He declared: ". . . peaceable assembly for lawful discussion cannot be made a crime. The holding of meetings for peaceable political action cannot be proscribed." A Communist was "entitled to discuss the public issues of the day and in a lawful manner, without incitement to violence or crime, to seek redress of alleged grievances. That was of the essence of his guaranteed personal liberty." States could prohibit incitement to violent overthrow of the government, he added, but they must "preserve inviolate the constitutional rights of free speech, free press and free assembly in order to maintain the opportunity for free political discussion" so government might respond "to the will of the people" and changes could occur peacefully. The Court did not declare the statute unconstitutional. It did not decide whether Communist Party doctrines were inherently seditious or whether CPUSA membership could be prohibited, and it refrained from establishing a general test or rule for evaluating sedition and syndicalism laws. The case was decided on the narrow grounds that the statute had been erroneously applied to DeJonge and was "repugnant to the due process clause of the Fourteenth Amendment."[51]

The victory was a heady one for Solomon. "The ACLU is batting 1,000 percent in Oregon!" he wrote the ACLU's national office. "Both the Kyle Pugh case and the Dirk DeJonge case, the only ones in which we have participated, have been reversed on appeal." Except "for our activities both men would now be in the penitentiary." In 1971, an elderly DeJonge gratefully acknowledged Solomon's central role in securing his freedom. Without his shrewd and persistent legal and organizational contributions, the case would have ended with the ILD's failed appeal to the Oregon Supreme Court. Solomon had helped develop the basic legal strategy and arguments that led to a majestic expansion of First Amendment rights.[52]

The Supreme Court used *DeJonge v. Oregon* to incorporate the First Amendment's freedom of assembly provision — and by implication the right to petition the government for a redress of grievances — into the due process clause of the Fourteenth Amendment. *DeJonge* continued the process of applying the Bill of Rights to the states, initiated for freedom of speech in *Gitlow v. New York* (1925) and *Stromberg v. California* (1931) and for freedom of the press in *Near v. Minnesota* (1931) and *Grosjean v. American Press Company* (1936). Nationalizing the Bill of Rights protected individual rights that had been left exposed to the variations of local authorities. *DeJonge* also foreshadowed Supreme Court attempts, Martin Shapiro writes, "to distinguish between those Communist party members and activities devoted to constitutionally protected advocacy and those implicated in incitement to revolutionary violence."[53]

DeJonge v. Oregon became a staple of constitutional history and law texts and a reference point for Solomon when he became a judge. But within two years of *DeJonge*, local press references to his connection faded away. Thereafter, aging Oregon practitioners were the only ones who associated him with the constitutional landmark, a common fate of supporting counsel in such cases. Even on the heels of the decision, Solomon's aid surprisingly was not solicited by a group of Oregonians who launched an effort to discard the offending statute. The 1937 legislature repealed it and substituted a simple conspiracy law.[54]

One group displayed too much interest. Because "I represented DeJonge and because I belonged to the Communist organization, the ACLU," Solomon said, Portland's Red Squad initiated a lengthy boycott of him. "Portland has always been a conservative community, but its businessmen have been a frightened lot. — Let's not be hasty. And, above all, let's not get in any controversy — keep away from controversial people," Solomon recalled. "In the middle and late 30's, the people in our community were even more frightened than they were 10 or 15 years later during the McCarthy period." The boycott "had some success with some of my clients, and other clients didn't need that push." The recession of 1937-1938 likely reduced calls upon his services as well. His income plunged from around $3,000 in 1936 — already about $1,400 below the national average for nonsalaried attorneys — to $800 in 1937. Thanks to Levenson's loans, he survived. The boycott failed to separate him from liberal grassroots activism or drive him from Portland.[55]

Chapter 3

Grassroots Activist

I believed in more concern by the government for the poor, and at the time I also believed in strong labor unions. I also was beginning to get interested in public power.

— *Gus J. Solomon,* 1984

CROSSING BOUNDARIES

"I look upon the practice of law," Gus Solomon told young lawyers in 1951, "as an opportunity to participate in great social movements." Since the 1930s, he had preached that lawyers had a duty to contribute to needed social change. They and other change-makers had to make courageous commitments, act collectively and practically (especially at the grass roots), and employ power. Eleanor Roosevelt, biographer Blanche W. Cook tells us, was "a team player, surrounded by allies and hard-fighting friends." Like Eleanor Roosevelt, Solomon "understood that politics was not an isolated, individualist adventure." Work as a cause lawyer, he had known from the outset, meant entering a terrain of struggle where popularity, prestige, and income might be sacrificed. He did not fear alarming or angering people. Solomon was confident of his values, intelligence, enterprise, and force of will; disdainful of merely talking about the nation's ills and promises; and thought about himself as a scrappy man of action. He "was a hot-tempered, fiery little guy," Wendell Gray observed, "a little man in a big hurry."[1]

Strong cultural, political, and professional traditions urged attorneys such as Gray and Solomon into many arenas. Attorneys had long understood that law was a major entry point to public life; it was a profession that exercised huge influence on the nation's codes, rules, and institutions. "Historically," Robert W. Gordon writes, "American lawyers imagined great roles for themselves as state-builders, as protectors of the Constitution and the common-law framework of rights against both populist and plutocratic excess, and as reformers whose task was to keep the law up to date with social change and fulfill the promise of equal justice." [2]

Solomon wanted to make a difference, not just a career, and early on believed that he might best do so as a liberal leader. Beginning in 1929, he threw himself into the then-vibrant world of membership organizations that were devoted to change. Offering high purposes and small-group communities, these value-driven organizations helped adherents such as Solomon find or maintain a sense of a larger community. Some were single-purpose in nature; others boldly encompassed divergent class, ethnic, racial, or political interests. They were small in scale but big in aspiration. But they were hobbled by rudimentary structures, slim material and political resources, small leadership bases, and atmospheres of amateurism, uncertainty, and grim resistance. Finding enough people with the inclination and skills to build and sustain these sometimes-fragmented organizations was difficult. Solomon's membership in these organizations (but not their parents) seldom lasted five years, if that. [3]

Between 1929 and 1950, Solomon became a driving force in several liberal organizations and, thus, in battles over the meaning and implementation of federal policies in Oregon and the Pacific Northwest. He became one of the state's best-known liberals and part of the nation's loosely connected liberal community. Causes associated with the New Deal, civil liberties, and public power particularly roused his hopes. Along with the Democratic Party, the causes opened worlds of possibility for him in the form of contacts, influence, and personal breadth, understanding, and satisfaction. Still, as someone who always intermingled the political, professional, and personal, he was tested by the hurts, setbacks, and frustrations triggered by these affiliations. As he had already learned, dissenting views could easily be brushed aside — and not just in Oregon. [4]

Solomon was at heart a centrist liberal. The nation's enormous disparities in income, possessions, and privilege appalled him. Unbridled materialism, unrestrained individualism, and unfettered capitalism, he believed, lessened the promise of American life. So, too, did class, racial, and ethnic barriers to individual and group opportunity. The promise of the America in which he believed was bound up with political democracy, civil liberties, equal opportunity, a regulated capitalist order, and a vibrant civil society and government open to the exercise of peaceful action.

Three values pulsated at the core of his liberalism. First, he believed in social justice, which meant society must ensure fair and compassionate treatment of its weaker and poorer members. Second, there is a positive role for government, one intervening widely and strongly in society to create good in its own right, to counterbalance "special interests," and to restrain profit-seekers from trampling human needs. Third, there should be social-political inclusiveness so that marginal and excluded groups could realize their legitimate needs and enjoy the opportunities inherent in a democratic order.

Government ought to embrace great causes and do great things, Solomon believed. It should solve domestic problems, better lives, alleviate inequality, promote justice, protect vulnerable minorities, and support international cooperation. He later remembered: "I believed in strong labor unions" before the Depression started. "I believed in social security," in "more concern by the government for the poor" than the Republicans wanted, and in a better "deal" for unions. He shared the New Deal conviction that government was duty-bound to aid distressed Americans and foster growth; that is, it should help people obtain jobs, care, and other resources so they might win a secure place in society and better their lives. "These are the things that the liberal Democrats stood for" in the 1930s, he said.[5]

In the dams, irrigation and electrical systems, and other infrastructures being constructed in the Pacific Northwest, Solomon celebrated a New Deal that was publicly investing for everyone. For him, governmental initiatives and regulations took precedence over private property rights. He rejected the conservatives' opposition to income redistribution from the more to the less privileged and their claim that the greatest danger to liberty lay in the abuse and extension of government power. Government should not simply protect citizens and their property and remove barriers to a person's material advancement, he believed. A vigorous government and civil society, guided by an alert citizenry and democratically minded lawyers, best ensured liberty, equality, and opportunity.

Civil liberties undergirded a healthy and secure American democracy, Solomon argued. The Constitution and Bill of Rights spelled out basic protections and, he came to believe, helped farmers, workers, minorities, urbanites, and people of small means defend themselves during the Depression against state and private exploitation. The struggles to win equal opportunity illuminated the centrality of constitutional rights, for people had to fight against great odds to win the rights to speak and associate freely, work securely, and live safely. Individual rights, for Solomon, rested not only on the Constitution and Bill of Rights but also on Americans forging a civil society that fostered virtues beyond self-interest. Attorneys bore a special responsibility; unless they advanced constitutional freedoms, cherished rights were merely phrases.

Solomon's liberalism acquired a deepening anti-Communist hue as the 1930s wore on and as he came to believe that the Communist Party only searched for exploitable revolutionary situations. He quietly and then publicly opposed Communists, except in their enjoyment of constitutional freedoms. By the mid-1930s, he considered Communism to be an anti-democratic force and was convinced that it preached the limitless predominance of the class struggle in human activity and the ultimate necessity of violent proletarian revolution. Even though the CPUSA cooperated with non-Communists during the Popular Front of 1935-1939, Solomon thought that it had not abandoned its revolutionary views. "I never believed you can achieve anything by force and violence," he later said. In his Jewish historical memory, violence was a dreaded happening.[6]

Solomon's anti-Communism was first apparent around the time that Irvin Goodman and Elizabeth Gurley Flynn recommended him to the ACLU as a good liberal. During the West Coast waterfront strike in the spring of 1934, he quietly advised union counsel B.A. Green on tamping down Communist influence in Portland's longshoremen's union. Four years later, Solomon conferred with two Oregon IWA–CIO leaders on ousting the allegedly Communist president of their international union. While negotiating with the state of Oregon over the stipulated facts in the DeJonge case — at a time when the CPUSA disavowed armed revolution and identified Communism with American reform traditions — he had agreed that the CPUSA meant to violently overthrow the government. As Maurice E. Tarshis later swore, "Mr. Solomon's antagonism toward the Communist Party and its program was apparent" in 1936.[7]

Involvement in Depression-era liberal causes and mass politics gave the warily optimistic Solomon a heady sense of participating in the nation's great social movements. Events and agents channeled Americans into strikes, new groups, and mass movements. He sympathized deeply with demands by groups and individuals for more say in their workplaces, government, and society. Further, he acted, rallying small farmers, union members, Jews, African Americans, and others into Democratic Party and New Deal formations.[8]

Solomon opened a law office and took his first political steps in September 1929. Seeking enlightened policies abroad to accompany progressive policies at home, he helped launch a chapter of the League of Nations Non-Partisan Association (LNA) and became its treasurer. Mainly a popular education organ, the LNA endorsed international cooperation, America's association with League agencies, an end to isolationist policies, and ultimate League membership. The national organization wanted "the principles of political and economic liberalism" to undergird a peaceful, prospering, interdependent international system. For the LNA, "reason, comity, justice, and impartial expertise would ultimately prevail over power politics and unbridled nationalism." The *Oregonian*, the *Oregon Journal*, and old Wilsonian Democrats delighted in the LNA. Solomon's chapter immediately deployed Youth Crusaders door-to-door in silk-stocking neighborhoods to win support for its positions. The LNA's local membership of professionals and businesspeople associated with Reed College and the First Unitarian Church broadened Solomon's non-Jewish associations. Many were the "nice people" who his mother and her friends wished him to represent, including the chapter's president, Bert Haney, appointed to the Ninth Circuit Court of Appeals in 1935, and its secretary, A.L. Wirin, who would serve as counsel for the southern California ACLU and Solomon's collaborator in some civil liberties pursuits.[9]

CIVIL LIBERTIES AND UNIONS

During the early 1930s, civil liberties and domestic politics occupied Solomon far more in attention and effort than international concerns. Opponents in the Oregon Civil Liberties Committee initially frustrated his doing "my best to make the Portland branch a very active one." Attorney and chair Henry M. Esterly, child labor opponent Sadie Orr Dunbar, William S. U'Ren, and others did not believe Solomon and Irvin Goodman when they denied spearheading a Communist takeover attempt of the committee. They also seemed unwelcoming to young activists in the group. "Both Irvin and I feel that we can get within a very short time at least twenty-five interested Liberals" into the ACLU, Solomon declared, and, expand its work. Criticism of the Committee's inaction during the 1934 West Coast waterfront strike weakened its leadership. Without intervention from the Committee, the police, sometimes with strong-arm volunteers, had attacked, wounded, and jailed strikers, broken up meetings, and raided the Portland ILD and the Communist Party headquarters and bookstore.

And criminal syndicalism charges had been lodged against DeJonge and Denny. Esterly was forced to resign and was replaced that autumn by the Rev. Ross W. Anderson.[10]

The Committee, essentially a Portland group, groped with how best to find its voice, unify its members, grow, and set its course. Internal divisions persisted over its positions, its independence, and its choices about organization building, litigation, negotiation, and lobbying. Suspicion about Communist influence in the Committee dogged it. The group had few successes — decisive interventions such as *DeJonge* and *Pugh* were rare. It issued a few reports. It failed to persuade the legislature to repeal Oregon's criminal syndicalism law and fitfully interested itself in a few deportation cases. Internal disagreements and inadequate recruiting contributed to its tiny size, with no more than sixty people belonging statewide during the 1930s. Ordered by the national office to disband or reorganize in 1936, it reorganized and made Solomon treasurer. But the group still rejected his ideas. "The only ones that give me any support at all are three or four old ladies past sixty," he said. The rest "are afraid of their own shadows."[11]

Other Committee members frustrated Solomon's tendency to confront and resist adversaries and taught him the virtue, or at least the necessity, of tactical compromise. He glumly acceded to the Civil Liberties Committee's refusal to sponsor an appearance by the Rev. Harry F. Ward, the perennially controversial chair of the ACLU and national secretary of the American League Against War and Fascism, the nation's leading Popular Front organization. The Committee, Solomon said, was "fearful of becoming contaminated by associating its name with that of the League." Overcoming opposition from veteran and patriotic organizations, the Committee did rent a school auditorium for a different sponsor of Ward and, after reportedly promising no "offensive or shocking" behavior or words, another one for a Portland Scottsboro Defense Committee speaker. "My position as a buffer between the Portland committee of the ACLU and other organizations such as the ILD and League Against War and Fascism, is not a very pleasant one," Solomon complained. "I am blamed by the ACLU here because I am too radical, and by the ILD and the League because I am not radical enough, or because the ACLU isn't willing to cooperate with them."[12]

Increasing worker activism and union organizing triggered appeals for aid that almost swamped Portland's small band of civil libertarians. Oregon had suddenly become a big labor battleground. After only 30 strikes from 1928 to 1933, Oregon experienced 122 industrial disputes between 1934 and 1939, directly involving between 9,273 and 17,941 people each year. Compared to the rest of the nation — at its Depression height, 2 percent of the workforce struck in 1936 — the total was small, yet it was no less polarizing or traumatic in Oregon than in large industrial states.[13]

With employers clashing with unions, AFL and CIO unionists locked in conflict, and the police, non-strikers, and strong-arm squads confronting strikers, labor disputes spurred Oregon's greatest popular mobilization between 1933 and 1939. Affecting broad swaths of life (including constitutional understanding), the disputes activated both pro-union and anti-union sentiment, groups, and structures and previously uninvolved people. The four strikes that took place in Oregon in 1932 involved only 590 employees. The next year, there were ten strikes with 10,067 workers. Brief walkouts in 1933 and 1934 failed to unionize hopfields and hopyards. And then the bloody eighty-two-day West Coast waterfront strike idled over 3,000 waterfront workers in Oregon in 1934. Maritime trade all but ceased, laying off at least another 50,000 Oregon workers. The International Longshoremen's and Warehousemen's Union (ILWU) subsequently won Pacific Coast bargaining rights and collaborated closely with other new CIO unions in the western lumber, fishing, salmon canning, and inland boating industries. Unions secured footholds in Oregon's pulp and paper mills and in Salem's woolen mill and expanded in Portland's food, beverage, and pinball industries. In 1937, the CIO tried to organize Oregon food processors; Portland hotel clerks and Safeway grocery employees walked out a year later. Printers' strikes the next year temporarily closed Portland's three daily newspapers.[14]

Lumber unionism thrived in the early 1930s before splitting in 1937 into antagonistic AFL and CIO affiliates. A traumatic strike ran through the woods and mills of the Pacific Northwest's immense Douglas-fir belt. The IWA–CIO, representing some 50,000 employees, held on to about 80 percent of the region's lumber mills and logging operations against fierce attacks by the Carpenters Union–AFL, which claimed 35,000 lumber workers. "No jurisdictional battle between the AFL and the CIO during the 1930s was more bitter," Ronald L. Filippelli writes. According to Robert A. Christie, it triggered "mobs, vigilante, and goon-squad actions, mass picketing and counter-picketing, boycotting and counter boycotting" that battered communities from mid-1937, when 90 percent of the region's lumber mills were paralyzed, to late 1941. Neither union "emerged completely victorious." Portland was a major battleground in the struggle. Largely because of AFL boycotts and blockades, many of its IWA sawmills closed in 1938. Violence among unionists and police attacks on the CIO rippled through Portland; and officials, labor and employer groups, the clergy, and others voluntarily or unwittingly were drawn into the fray.[15]

Portland's Red Squad thrust itself into the disputes. Liberals such as Solomon hated the Squad's marauding through the region's labor and political arenas. Aligned with war veterans groups, the Teamsters, and fiercely anti-union employers, the shadowy Red Squad conducted extensive surveillance, provocation, and disinformation campaigns. By 1937, it boasted that it had a 10,000-file cache on Communists and their sympathizers, and it blacklisted union members who were forced out of work. Portland's anti-New Deal Democratic mayor and Red Squad patron Joseph K. Carson Jr., "with the help of the newspapers and various employers' associations, whipped up a mob hysteria against labor unions," leading to mass arrests, Solomon reported. No doubt "most of [the strikers] are guilty of acts of force and violence, varying from throwing bricks through windows, to burning of buildings" in 1938. Nearly all the CIO men "were severely beaten at the time of arrest and subsequently." By November, Solomon said, AFL "strong arm tactics" had injured many CIO members and caused substantial property damage. At a protest meeting organized by the Civil Liberties Committee, Solomon, Goodman, and others called on Senator LaFollette's Subcommittee on Violations of Civil Liberties to investigate Oregon's "'goon violence,' police 'labor spy activities,' state police 'lawlessness and third-degree methods,' and labor racketeering generally." The protests, Solomon thought, at least slowed police depredations.[16]

As he likely suspected, Solomon's name began appearing in secret reports. Informants for the Red Squad, state police, Oregon National Guard, and Immigration and Naturalization Service routinely identified him among alleged or admitted Communists. One of Governor Charles H. Martin's imaginative operatives placed him at the Twelfth District Communist Party Plenum in Seattle in 1937, even though Solomon's anti-Communist views were becoming well known by then. A different operative did not mention his presence.[17]

The Civil Liberties Committee failed, in Solomon's subsequent estimation, to effectively confront the Red Squad. Whenever someone proposed ways during the Depression and war years "to protect the rights of the unpopular minority through an independent action, through parallel action or by intervention in a pending act, there were those who prophesied disaster for our organization," he later remonstrated. Few pre-war complaints to the local ACLU inspired court dates; they only happened when the parent organization furnished aid. Committee leaders did issue statements, write telegrams and letters, address meetings, speak on the radio, and cajole public officials; but Solomon wanted more action and often volunteered to effect it. In litigation, he served as the ACLU's principal Oregon counsel, sometimes with Leo Levenson. He conferred regularly with ACLU headquarters, signed the National Lawyers Guild's study of Portland's Red Squad, and advocated free speech to "Labor Hour" radio listeners. In 1938, he wrote the Portland city commissioners and talked to Mayor Carson about a police assault on a Socialist–Labor Party (SLP) street speaker. He negotiated revocable speaking permits for the SLP at certain police-supervised corners, which it was forced to accept. By now, Solomon displayed proficiency in legal and political strategizing and negotiation, legal argumentation, opinion influencing, and organization building. He was becoming an accomplished grassroots leader, counselor, and scold.[18]

LEGAL ACTIVIST

"The whole character of the practice of law was changing" during the Depression, Solomon remembered. "Lawyers were becoming activists. They wanted to use the law not only for the protection of property rights but for the advancement of human rights." Solomon belonged to a segment of the bar that wished to make the country "more democratic by making the law more responsive." Through the ACLU, a legal aid society, and the National Lawyers Guild, he joined a national drive to realize constitutional freedoms and other far-reaching goals. Through the National Lawyers Guild and Portland's Blackstone Club, he fought for broad-based juries.[19]

"They were a conservative group," Solomon said of the Oregon Legal Aid Society he helped create. In the 1920s, judges and attorneys from elite eastern firms had initiated a movement to furnish competent paid counsel to the poor. They countered the prevailing American bar view that no one had a basic right to an attorney, even in criminal cases. State bars grudgingly supported legal aid societies for their practical advantages, according to Earl Johnson Jr. The hope was that they would siphon off undesirable nonpaying clients, keep people off relief rolls by securing them back wages and alimony, educate the public on the usefulness of legal counsel, provide good bar public relations, and employ some younger lawyers. The societies assisted a narrow range of poor applicants and generally ignored the conditions that caused poverty. Solomon, who had been representing indigents *pro bono* at the request of David Robinson and state and federal judges, saw how well three out-of-state legal aid societies took depositions to support a divorce petition he handled. Oregonians should try again to establish a similar organization, he decided.[20]

In July 1935, Robinson, Solomon, and others sent for a national legal-aid leader, Duke University law professor John S. Bradway, to advise lawyers and county judges on getting started. A new Works Progress Administration (WPA), eager to employ attorneys and secretaries, promised most of the initial financing, and Judge James W. Crawford and Solomon raised additional sums from a reluctant bar. At a Multnomah County Bar Association meeting in September, Solomon was accused of taking bread from lawyers' mouths and was denounced as a Communist, anarchist, and Socialist. Nevertheless, in October, he won sponsorship for a Legal Aid Committee by the newly formed Oregon State Bar, to which by statute all lawyers belonged.[21]

From the outset, a tiny staff and skimpy resources were stretched over as many clients as possible. Between mid-February and September 1936, more than 1,700 requests for advice and assistance swamped the Legal Aid office. After 250 were refused, some 3,000 court appearances resulted. They overwhelmingly related to nonsupport of women and children, evictions, wage garnishments, and juvenile court hearings. Like its counterparts elsewhere, the Oregon Legal Aid Society gave no divorce or bankruptcy assistance. Instead, bar volunteers such as Solomon handled a few divorces "involving some social problem of grave concern to the public" and some bankruptcy requests. Its Portland office expanded from two to six attorneys plus supporting staff. But withdrawal of WPA funds proved to be near fatal in August 1937, when a single lawyer and secretary were left to act on growing requests. Everywhere, Legal Aid Societies entered a long period of stagnation.[22]

To accomplish a limited good through Legal Aid, Solomon reined in his strong inclination to face inequality and injustice head-on. Writing annual committee reports, he disguised his view that Legal Aid met too few needs. His dispassionate, fact-laden reports did not preach equal justice or the bar's moral responsibility but stressed Legal Aid's careful, responsible methods. Most applicants "are socially maladjusted," he reassured his readers. Still, they conveyed his worries about hard-pressed women and children. A casual remark in his 1938–1939 report unexpectedly ended his connection. He wrote that Legal Aid "looks forward to extending an ever-widening service in the years to come." Conservative supporters said that they looked forward to closing or shrinking the office. "I thought that was ridiculous because I was sure that there would always be a time when there would be poor people" requiring free legal assistance. "You no longer need me," Solomon angrily responded. He quit report writing and, in time, overseeing Legal Aid but kept a *pro bono* role in state and federal courts.[23]

Solomon felt deeper affinities for the locally organized Blackstone Club and the National Lawyers Guild. Compared to Legal Aid, they were more militant and clearer about the influence of social class on legal affairs. Portland's most liberal bar segments — union, personal injury, and small business lawyers — established the Blackstone Club in about 1936 mainly to counter the practices of well-organized insurance company attorneys. It linked democratic rights to its members' occupational interests. In 1937, for instance, the Club challenged the jury list prepared by the Multnomah County Clerk solely from tax rolls and not, as previously, from both voter and tax rolls. The change reportedly had shrunk the jury pool from about 182,000 to 52,000 adults and created a situation where injury lawyers had to face "persons who came from the higher purchasing power districts" and all-male juries, rather than more potentially sympathetic working-class and female jurors. The list, the Club complained, "is undemocratic, results in class distinctions not sanctioned by law," and violates "the fundamental concepts of our free popular institutions." Solomon remembered the county clerk also discarding from jury rolls "the names of people whom he didn't like because of their age, occupation or residence, or just because he didn't like their names" — including his own. Through *mandamus* suits that challenged two juries, the Club won court orders for regular panels composed of the same numbers of prospective jurors from each precinct, selected by lot from the voting lists. "In other words, we anticipated the Federal Jury Selection Act of 1968 by at least 30 years," he later boasted. The Blackstone Club also helped defeat a bill requiring certain property ownership qualifications for Oregon jurors.[24]

Club members gravitated to the National Lawyers Guild. Learning of its creation on February 19, 1937, Solomon and five others formed a Portland chapter and enrolled some fifty lawyers and judges, who chose him as secretary. To Allan Hart, the chapter's president, the group was "New Dealish in its liberalism" and contained both liberal and "fairly non-political lawyers and judges." Unlike the American Bar Association (ABA), which disqualified applicants because of race, gender, or political belief, the Guild accepted without these limits three thousand attorneys nationwide in 1937 but fewer than one thousand in 1938. The Guild challenged the ABA's professional hegemony and its opposition to the New Deal. It supported the National Labor Relations Act, the Social Security law, a child labor amendment to the Constitution, public defenders, neighborhood legal bureaus, and Franklin Roosevelt's 1937 proposal to reorganize the Supreme Court. During a stormy Multnomah County Bar Association meeting, Solomon and fellow Guild members B.A. Green, and Clifford O'Brien gamely defended the presidential proposal. Solomon mischievously complimented his fellow Republicans for their sudden interest in civil liberties, which was supposedly violated by the proposal. To applause, William S. U'Ren and others harshly responded, with U'Ren declaring that he had quit the ACLU because of its "communistic" tendencies. By a lopsided vote, the bar association opposed Roosevelt's plan.[25]

To Jerold S. Auerbach, the Guild "spoke to lawyers committed to the liberal issues of the day: the right of workers to organize; civil liberties; and minority rights. It appealed to lawyers who were prepared to discard precedent in novel circumstances, who viewed law," according to the Guild's preamble, "as a living and flexible instrument which must be adapted to the needs of the people." The Guild rallied "liberal lawyers with strong ties to the professional establishment, radical attorneys with equally strong commitments to the political Left, law teachers who were dismayed by the commercial tone of the organized bar," and, in another unintended characterization of Solomon, "low-status urban practitioners from ethnic minority groups who were frustrated in their quest for professional success."[26]

Chapters of the National Lawyers Guild largely functioned autonomously. Differences between liberals and radicals wracked many of them, but not the Portland group. The chapter apparently had formed to confront Red Squad marauding, and its sole activity was its investigation. Allan Hart and Thomas S. Wilson, in a May 1938 report signed by Solomon and others, exposed Red Squad depredations in Oregon, its links to the American Legion, and its recent private disguise. They failed to uncover its infiltration of the Oregon Commonwealth Federation. After Hart and Wilson left the state, however, Guild membership rapidly dwindled. Solomon and others decided that Communists and their sympathizers overly influenced the parent organization. Early in 1939, a year before nationally known liberals such as Robert Jackson, Adolf Berle Jr., and Jerome Frank abandoned the Guild, Solomon and most local members quit in mass and returned their charter. Fearing renewed Communist infiltration, he refused to help reactivate the chapter after the war.[27]

PUBLIC POWER

"I was attacked on the radio and in the press for being a Communist because only Communists believed" in public power, Solomon sarcastically recalled. In well-financed campaigns, private utility executives and squads of publicists and agents monitored and fought the emerging PUDs and REAs. Living in the stronghold of investor-owned utilities, Solomon felt vilified for his stance on public power by the *Oregon Journal*, "the worst Red-baiting sheet in the city." His law business suffered. The president of the Pacific Power and Light Company warned an executive that a friendship with Solomon endangered his future in the company, and a printing firm refused Solomon's order for fear of offending a big utility account. Opposition from "many people in the Establishment," Solomon concluded, would "have been much less vigorous had I not been a Jew."[28]

Nothing ever shook Solomon's faith in public power. Solomon's exposure to its human features in 1934 and 1935, when only 31 percent of Oregon's farms were electrified, charged the struggle with nearly as much emotion as civil liberties. In those years, Morton Tompkins, Ray Gill, Vern Libsy, and other Oregon State Grange and Oregon–Washington Farmers' Union leaders sent Solomon to confer with PUDs and REAs struggling into existence on the Oregon coast, in the Willamette Valley, and along the Columbia River. Witnessing shocking poverty and unemployment, he absorbed stories of uncaring utilities denying electricity to those who sorely needed it. These companies, he decided, were partially responsible for the state's poor, socially marginalized, and over-worked people.[29]

Solomon's engagement in public power gave him a heady sense of belonging to a mass movement, one with large followings, popular programs, skilled leaders, and regional and national endorsement and momentum. Through public power, he identified in a concrete way with ordinary (rather than politicized or radical) citizens. Associating with rural and small-town modernizers galvanized him and provoked in him something of the nation's exaltation of the common people. He told and retold stories of individuals who celebrated or wept in gratitude for their new electrical service. One very poor area went online after "three heart-breaking" years, he believed, only because he had REA members employed as line builders to pay their home wiring and utility bills. Frankly, "nothing I have done in the practice of law gives me more satisfaction than the work which I did for the people of that area." He felt pride "every time I go there and see how electricity has lightened the burden for all of them, increased the value of their property, and made living easier and more meaningful." He later remembered: "It didn't give me very much money but the psychic compensation which I received far exceeds" the payments received.[30]

Solomon apparently expected public power to revolutionize the Pacific Northwest once it became a keystone of Roosevelt's New Deal and PUDs and REAs spread. Central to public-power hopes were the federally built Columbia River dams; a new Bonneville Power Administration, which transmitted and marketed the electricity produced at the dams, and the Bureau of Reclamation projects that added power infrastructures for economic development. Only inexpensive public power, he thought, could attract industry, enrich the Columbia Basin's resource-based economy, and better the lives of the rural and urban poor who lived in an area that stretched from Oregon and Washington into Idaho, Montana, and Wyoming.[31]

Solomon became "one of the pioneers of the rural electrification movement in this state," Oregon Grange Grand Master Tompkins glowingly wrote in 1949. "His counsel has played a large part in the success of the movement in this state." By the late 1940s, the much-traveled attorney was known in many Oregon and Washington locales, where year after year he acted as public power's goad and tactician, a liaison to liberal groups, a cheerleading intermediary between public-power agencies and their constituencies, and a lobbyist at the Portland headquarters of the Bonneville Power Administration (BPA) and in REA and Agricultural Department agencies. By June 1941, he felt closer to the public-power "problem than anyone else in the Northwest aside from the men" in the BPA. In September, the Public Ownership League of Washington honored him and others. When their cause appeared divided and disheartened that December, he urged its leaders "to keep the public-power forces in good spirits and not let them lose faith in the president and in the Department of Interior."[32]

To fellow public-power lawyer Raymond M. Kell, Solomon was "Mr. Public Power." Handling most of Oregon's important PUD cases, he influenced state utility law. He advised PUD and REA negotiators and organizers, represented PUDs and REAs in state utility-rate cases, and lobbied for them in the legislature. Most of his work in setting up Oregon and Washington PUDs and arranging for their purchase and erection of distribution facilities came after the Second World War. Long before that, however, BPA and other federal agencies recognized him as a public-power advocate and Democratic Party fundraiser. He supported the BPA and its placement in Harold L. Ickes's Interior Department, the appointment of James D. Ross as its first administrator, and the agency's commitment to long-range regional development. For Solomon, connections, patronage, and personalities — not just law — influenced important matters.[33]

Public power and civil liberties causes increasingly linked Solomon to liberals in the federal government, the Democratic Party, and the media. Jack R. Cluck and Paul Coughlin — Seattle lawyers, civil libertarians, and labor and public-power advocates — became valuable allies, vouching for him to Washington farm and union leaders. He began forging links to future liberal Senators Warren G. Magnuson, Hugh B. Mitchell, Henry M. Jackson, Mon Walgren, and other rising political figures in Washington state. Columnist Robert S. Allen, Drew Pearson's partner, corresponded on Oregon politics. Solomon developed useful relations with Arthur Goldschmidt, Abe Fortas, Oscar L. Chapman, and other liberal Interior Department executives. Chief Counsel C. Girard Davidson and others at BPA's Portland headquarters and liberals in western REA and Agriculture Department offices came to trust him. BPA Assistant Administrator Ulrich J. Gendron and BPA lawyers J. Kenneth Kaseberg and Allan Hart were his regular poker partners. BPA attorney Kell remembered how Solomon's office was "my second office and his clients and public power activities were fruitful grounds for my covert activities" for the agency between mid-1941 and mid-1943.[34]

Through this network, Solomon gave and received advice and favors, won aid for Oregon New Dealers, raised funds for Democratic candidates, found jobs for people, advanced client interests with governmental agencies, and recharged his crusading spirit. His network became an "unofficial, non-paid employment agency" for recent law graduates and unemployed attorneys and young lawyers from around the country who had heard that he would help find them a position in Oregon. Solomon placed people when possible in Portland's law firms and courts and at the BPA, the Farm Security Administration, and other federal agencies. Remembering his own ill treatment as a jobseeker, his goal was to further equal opportunity, not to build influence among grateful recipients, but he did not spurn it when it happened.[35]

THE OREGON COMMONWEALTH FEDERATION

Solomon was drawn to the Oregon Commonwealth Federation (OCF) because of its endorsement of public power, its provision of a coherent program of mass politics, and its potential as a statewide grassroots coalition. In December 1937 or January 1938, Monroe M. Sweetland, the young director of the OCF, came to Solomon's office, enrolled him, obtained a contribution, and, apparently broke and hungry, was invited to lunch. The tall, gangly Sweetland returned "almost every day if he didn't have anybody else to take him to lunch," Solomon remembered. "We became quite good friends."[36]

By July 1938, Solomon was OCF treasurer. That year, he finally registered as a Democrat after he and Sweetland persuaded legislator Henry L. Hess to launch a last-minute Democratic primary challenge to Governor Charles H. Martin. They belabored conservative Democrats such as Martin, who had repudiated the New Deal, for preventing Oregon party unification behind Roosevelt. The vitriolic governor had also resisted federal aid to Oregon's poor and forcefully opposed the growth of unions and public power. With Federation support, Hess defeated Martin but lost to moderate Republican Salem newspaper publisher Charles A. Sprague in November.[37]

Strife between reform (New Deal) Democrats such as Solomon and regular or machine (Old Guard) Democrats such as Martin erupted in dozens of states in the aftershock of the New Deal's realignment of voting behavior, from a majority Republican to a majority Democratic vote in the nation. Oregon's Democrats feuded over policies, personalities, and control of party apparatuses, candidate lists, and patronage. In that era, Democrats were not part of any serious political calculations in nearly all Oregon locales. Their party resembled the "hodgepodge of small formal organizations, informal networks linked to these organizations and masses of unorganized Democratic voters" that David Plotke identified as the Democratic Party in many Depression-era states. Despite the number of registered Democrats, which rose to 48 percent of the Oregon electorate during the 1930s, the Oregon GOP largely dominated its fractious rival in nonpresidential races. No Oregon Democrat reached the U.S. Senate during that decade and only one the House of Representatives. The biennial legislature stood as a Republican redoubt, little shaken by Democratic control of its lower house in 1935 and 1937. Republicans in 1938 captured the statehouse, the legislature, and two of the state's three congressional seats.[38]

In 1937, Democrats, Republicans, and Socialists established the Oregon Commonwealth Federation "to unite the progressive forces of our state, irrespective of race, religion or political affiliation." That April, the OCF rallied to a New Deal that was slowing down after the defeat of Roosevelt's Court-reorganization plan and as major administration programs were being cut back. The OCF wanted to bridge Oregon's rural-urban, ethnic, racial, political, and class divisions; change Oregon's conservative and Republican direction; strengthen member groups; and create a mass, statewide following and an all-county electoral network. Refusing to become a Farmer–Labor Party or to merge with the Democrats, the OCF affiliated with the CIO's new Labor's Non–Partisan League that October. While the Federation made nonpartisan endorsements, it largely came to support the national Democratic Party's objectives and purposes.[39]

Issue-oriented and, in time, outward-looking, the Federation quickly grew into the largest and most influential grassroots political grouping in pre-war Oregon. Solomon called it "a political holding company for practically every CIO union in the state, also the Workers Alliance [successor to the Unemployed Councils], pension groups, religious organizations, farm organizations, and various others who are interested in the New Deal." Youth organizations belonged along with individuals like himself. The Communist Party was denied membership but not the unions it influenced or party members. The heavy CIO presence kept antagonistic AFL unions away. In 1938, Solomon blamed the defeat of Oregon's New Deal ticket partly on reactionary AFL unions failing to cooperate with CIO unions and the Federation.[40]

Solomon believed that public-power and Federation activities brought him in close touch with the real needs of Americans for improved jobs, better wages, higher living standards, economic security, community betterment, social equality, and democracy. The OCF, in his eyes, provided a coherent plan and ideology for harnessing support for a new relationship between the people and their government.

Public power headed its platform, seeking — more sweepingly than Solomon preferred — "public ownership of all natural resources, utilities, banks, and monopolies." The Federation called for support of PUDs and publicly built transmission of the future Bonneville Dam's power to everyone in the state and a blanket rate to its distributing agencies. It endorsed worker and union rights, greater civil liberties protections, improved social-welfare benefits, and, in time, popular mobilization against fascism at home and aggression abroad.

The OCF also participated in the broad movement led by liberals and leftists to create greater racial democracy in the nation. Together with Portland's tiny chapter of the National Association for the Advancement of Colored People (NAACP) — an OCF member — it held a meeting in June 1937, supposedly Portland's first inter-racial dinner in a first-class restaurant. In 1938, the NAACP endorsed the Federation's call to establish public housing, which both the Portland city commissioners and a citywide advisory referendum rejected. In 1938–1939, a joint OCF-NAACP drive failed to win legislative passage of a law that would guarantee equal access to apartments and hotel rooms. Because of these and other actions, private utility spokesperson and former Democratic Governor Oswald West labeled Federationists as drunks, punks, bums, and Communists. To Governor Martin, who with Portland's Mayor Carson damned the OCF, democratic government was under siege by "Jew Communists" and "shanty Irishmen." Martin's informants had no difficulty portraying the Federation to him as a thoroughly Communist group.[41]

Its size and reach made the 25,000- to 30,000-member Federation more than a minor liberal irritant. Many voters had remained members after joining the OCF in order to defeat Governor Martin in 1938. (Some 80 percent of the Federationists were registered Democrats by 1941.) In 1940, Monroe Sweetland reported that between 700 and 1,000 Democratic Party precinct committee members were under OCF influence, compared to fewer than 100 identified with farm and labor organizations four years earlier. That year, the Roosevelt administration gave the OCF control of employment for the census in Oregon, its first serious patronage gain; and the 1940 legislature reportedly had its heaviest representation of union-backers to date, mostly from Federation affiliates.[42]

But tempers, jealousies, and squabbles sometimes got in the way. The Federation was Solomon's most challenging organizational challenge to date. At the same time, it gave him chances to control his truculence, hone effective leadership skills, and build influence in the state and among New Dealers. In the Federation, Sweetland believed, his friend bridged "the gap between the social and professional level at which he operated and the rank-and-file of people." He "took special pains to know every member of our scattered, far-flung board of directors." These "were working people, the unemployed, . . . old timers, pensioners, the rural public power advocates," individuals who lacked Solomon's "urban and urbane background." Solomon gladly collaborated with local NAACP leaders, attended their functions, and was one of the few white Federationists ready to host inter-racial gatherings in his home. Visiting New Dealers visited Solomon's home to meet OCF leaders. Solomon was committed to building a viable and lasting political movement, Sweetland thought. While he could be "very short with people in controversy" within the Federation's board, "that wasn't the essence of his personal tactic, which was to be considerate and to listen and reserve judgment until he was pretty sure of his ground."[43]

Solomon was a forceful, resourceful, and militant presence in OCF councils and meetings. A strong, fluid talker, he regularly expressed himself — if sarcastically about seeming opportunistic acts and rhetoric — on almost every topic under consideration. Volunteering for task after task, he called for less talk and more action. He drummed up members and allies, lobbied officials, negotiated and raised money for the OCF, gave it free legal advice, and found its members government employment. To Sweetland, he was "a tireless enthusiast for the things that we were doing," somebody who brought "new contacts and new elements into" the organization. Come to weekly lunches and "chew over current political questions," Solomon invited potential adherents.[44]

Some were already his friends. Every active Oregon liberal, he remarked in 1938, had many enemies but also many good friends. His friends mainly came from the old neighborhood, from new causes, and from work. Bound together by liberal politics and sometimes by their Jewishness, they were young, jaunty, bright, companionable, educated, civil liberties-minded, and politically engaged people who cherished "doing." They felt a responsibility for the character of their society and a deep sympathy for the underdog, and they looked optimistically at the nation's potential and the promises that government might fulfill. Trying to prevent their own slide to the bottom, they also were marrying and starting families. Solomon and his friends vacationed inexpensively together on the Oregon coast. Several of them, like Solomon, had a lifelong love of physical activity. At five foot, ten inches on a slim frame, he had not yet acquired the portliness of his later years. In Portland, the men rode horses and played baseball. As often as three times a week, Solomon, Gilbert Sussman, Nathalie Panek, and the Harts, Sweetlands, Morton Goodmans, and others gathered to eat, talk, and strategize. Opinions flew, and arguments broke out. Goodman once watched Solomon misinterpret a longtime friend's remark and fly into a rage, ending their friendship. More and more, people were noticing his fits of pique.[45]

Sweetland, Panek, Solomon, journalist Richard L. Neuberger, BPA publicist Stephen Kahn, and Wendell Barnett of the Farmers' Union forged an effective anti-Communist majority on the OCF board. Communists had captured the better-known Washington Commonwealth Federation, they warned, and meant to control the OCF and Oregon labor, farm, professional, and liberal organizations. In a forerunner of Cold War tactics, they monitored Communist Party support for the Soviet Union and used its startling policy shifts in 1939–1941 to identify, isolate, and defeat apparent Communists in their organization. So, after the CPUSA announced the death of the Popular Front, denounced Roosevelt, and opposed military preparedness, Solomon and other OCF members examined an individual's stances toward the Russo–Finnish war, the Nazi–Soviet Pact, the outbreak of war in Europe, Russian entry into Poland, and Roosevelt's renomination. On October 15, 1939, Solomon excoriated fellow board members who "had favored intervention in European affairs" three weeks earlier "but were ardent isolationists now." He charged them with being disciplined Communists. By prior arrangement, they were then defeated in board and OCF convention votes.[46]

Solomon's bloc persuaded the 1939 OCF convention to reject a pro-Soviet rationale for the Soviet intervention in Poland. Instead, the delegates regretted "the partition of Poland by Germany and the Soviet Union, and . . . the invasion of Finland by the Soviet Union, and the Oregon Commonwealth Federation condemns the governments of Germany and the Soviet Union for these acts." Solomon reportedly argued that the OCF "had condemned fascist and nazi aggression, so why not soviet Russian aggression?" He also helped persuade the OCF to break its ties to the Washington Commonwealth Federation and to oust the last Communists from its own board in 1940. By 1941,

Communists had been ostracized in the OCF, Sweetland claimed. But the Federation still had much to do, Solomon insisted, in areas that concerned him as a Jewish activist.[47]

JEWISH ACTIVIST

Gus Jerome Solomon was Jewish in the way a journalist said Charles de Gaulle was French — "by birth, instinct, tradition, and resolve." His Jewishness took on new forms and expressions during his early thirties. Nazi expansion of power in Europe and the volatile growth of anti-Semitism at home transformed his resolve. He determined to be more than a liberal democrat, a humanistic internationalist, or a civil libertarian — more than a lawyer-activist who happened to be Jewish. In deciding to seriously participate in Jewish organizations, he entered the orbit of the American Jewish Congress (AJCongress) in 1938–1939, drawn by its mission of acting on behalf of Jews as a group with distinct political interests. This affiliation represented a major turning point: the politicizing of Solomon's Jewish identity or, in different terms, his full public embrace of both his American and Jewish identities. Commitment to a string of Jewish causes and interests followed, as he made himself a leader in Oregon's small Jewish community and in a major national Jewish group.[48]

Neither his Jewish background, appearance, or name nor his support of a Jewish homeland in Palestine had led to any formal Jewish affiliation until the late 1930s, Solomon later reminisced. He had begun to tithe 10 percent of his personal income to causes, but not yet to any Jewish one. It worried him that "some people did things solely because they were Jews," so he had opposed Hitler and the Nazis "because they were against human rights for all persons." Worsening insecurity for European Jewry and the Roosevelt administration's apathetic response to the persecution of German Jews, however, changed his thinking. He began rallying support for recognition and respect for the rights of Jews as an oppressed group in the U.S. as well as protection of Jewish communities abroad. In other words, Solomon became a proponent of personal identity politics, one based on the belief that he belonged to a meaningful group that shared a distinct history and that his group had a mission of acting on or acting out its unique identity. At the time, he remembered, "I began to realize that everyone should know who he is, and that it was important that a person born a Jew should know who he is, and it's only by knowing one can lead a satisfied life." Jews, he believed, benefited themselves by adopting a more assertive and prideful Jewish posture and claiming a more visible place in society. Exemplifying American Jewry's repeated redefinition of Jewishness in American terms, he reconciled personal identity politics and universalistic doctrines. Being a Jew, liberal, and American democrat was not contradictory. He meant to act as a Jew while advocating the fundamental unity of all humanity.[49]

Nazi Germany galvanized American Jews without imposing a single meaning of Jewishness or a single anti-Nazi strategy. Synagogues rang with protest. About one hundred Jewish Community Relations Committees emerged after 1933 and infiltrated and exposed pro-Nazi groups. Membership in B'nai B'rith and other Jewish organizations rose dramatically in the 1930s, as did support for Zionism and a Palestinian homeland for Jews. Efforts got underway to get Jews out of Germany and alert the world to Nazi dangers. Nonsectarian and Jewish groups, including B'nai B'rith and the American Jewish Congress, launched disorganized boycotts of German goods in 1933. Aid to refugees and boycott exertions leaped after Germany's devastating Kristallanacht pogrom in 1938, rousing further the millions of Americans opposed to increased German aggression.[50]

In 1933, the year Hitler came to power, American Jews were experiencing sharply rising anti-Semitism. Fed by economic discontent and social calamities, 119 new rabidly anti-Semitic organizations formed between 1933 and 1940, up from the five that had existed earlier. The new, openly fascist Silver Legion of America (Silver Shirts) found much of its support for its blustering, quasi-military force in rural West Coast communities. In 1936, several hundred Oregonians filled its posts in Portland, Eugene, Vernonia, and elsewhere. An ally, the German–American People's League (Bund), which favored Nazi-like Brown Shirt attire, enrolled fewer than fifty Portlanders. But in 1938, in steep decline among German speakers everywhere, the German–American Bund (as it was also called) reached out to English-speakers. In Oregon, it distributed stridently anti-Semitic publications, ran meetings, and propagandized on the radio.[51]

Such groups found fertile ground. In 1938, one-fifth of all respondents in a national poll wanted to "drive Jews out of the United States." That year, Fr. Charles E. Coughlin's wildly popularly weekly newspaper and broadcasts turned openly anti-Semitic. Synagogues and Jewish cemeteries were defaced, and gangs of Coughlin's Christian Fronters broke windows of Jewish-owned stores and beat and brawled with Jews in northeastern cities. After war broke out in Europe, a Committee to Defend America First rally cheered Charles A. Lindbergh's widely believed charge that Jews wanted intervention for selfish reasons. An anti-Semitic candidate roamed Oregon's First Congressional District in 1940. The American Jewish Committee anxiously reported that "Nazi-inspired anti-Semitism had become a potent factor in the American political scene" by mid-1941.[52]

Anti-Semitic speakers attracted Portland crowds — 250 for Silver Shirt orators in the spring of 1938, 500 (700 by another count) early in 1939 — before halls were denied the Silver Shirts and Bund. In Portland, where most Jews were immigrants or children of immigrants, the crowds and the spread of Jew-baiting handbills intensified Jewish worries. Bundists left the flyers on streetcars and doorsteps and nailed them on Jewish-owned shops. One night, hastily assembled B'nai B'rith members scattered through two sprawling eastside neighborhoods to rip down fresh Bundist posters.[53]

Major assaults on racist, anti-Semitic, and anti-foreign traditions had been underway in the country for several years before Anti–Defamation League (ADL) regional director David Robinson recruited Solomon. Across the country, the ADL engineered interfaith meetings and educational programs and infiltrated and reported on Bundists, Silver Shirts, and similar groups to the FBI, the Justice Department, and police Red Squads. In about 1938, Robinson asked Solomon to write and distribute pamphlets aimed at labor — "Hitler Smashes Trade Unions" — and at churches — "Hitler Destroys Churches." In churches and union halls, Solomon delivered anti-Nazi addresses and assailed racial and religious discrimination. He kept the Oregon Commonwealth Federation and CIO unions abreast of local anti-fascist activity and urged Federation endorsement of the emerging Jewish political agenda. For him, the OCF in 1938 was "the strongest force in Oregon fighting fascism." He prod it to endorse a speedy American military buildup, the institution of a draft, and a congressional proposal to admit refugee children. He was certain that Jews, as part of the political culture and Roosevelt's coalition, ought boldly to assert their prerogatives and interests.[54]

With lasting consequences, he joined the American Jewish Congress. Early in 1938, Horace M. Kallen visited Portland and enthused Solomon, Richard L. Neuberger, and Harry Kenin about its reorganization and plans. The renowned thinker, educator, and activist impressed Solomon with his description of the small AJCongress, which "tended to attract more self-consciously progressive Jews who were dedicated to achieving social change through collective action and political protest." By comparison, the ADL and the American Jewish Committee attracted more affluent Jews and were more politically moderate. They defined Jews not as an ethnic, politically minded group — the AJCongress's position — but as a religion with few or no political interests.[55]

The AJCongress was known mainly as an instrument of working-class and lower-middle-class Jews of east European origin. Earlier in the century, its concerns about Jews domestically were secondary to protecting Jews abroad. Over the objections of many American Jews who were left feeling exposed and vulnerable, the AJCongress was a pioneer during the 1930s in "the use of law and social action as tools in combating prejudice and discrimination." In the history of what became known as the Rights Revolution, the "ACLU, the NAACP, and the American Jewish Congress formed the foundation of civil liberties and civil rights organizing for the first half (and more)" of the twentieth century. Of special interest to Solomon, the AJCongress in 1938–1940 launched studies into Jews' domestic problems, particularly economic discrimination.[56]

Appealing to his militance, the AJCongress in April 1938 collaborated in a renewed national boycott of German goods. Solomon and a few others launched a local drive: "We wanted to picket Jewish Department stores because they were doing business with Hitler," he said. The boycott peaked in most cities early in 1939, before declining under stiffening resistance from merchants of German Jewish background. Solomon fumed about the timidity and cowardice of unnamed Portland Jewish storeowners. In October, he, Kenin, and Neuberger established a local AJCongress chapter. "I realized through" Solomon, OCF's Monroe Sweetland said, "that there were as many differences among Jews on policy as there were in Oregon Democratic politics." He also was not surprised about how differences had perilously sharpened in Solomon's office. The three lawyers had reached a breaking point.[57]

Chapter 4

War and Peace

I am sorry to say that I was not involved in the beginning, when the Japanese-Americans were moved into concentration camps. I knew about it; I didn't like it; but I didn't protest. I don't know of any non-Japanese protests at the time.

—Gus J. Solomon, 1976

NEW BEGINNINGS

After heated arguments with Irvin Goodman, Solomon broke his lease and opened his own office in September 1939. Political differences had finally boiled over. Goodman and Solomon had "some real down-to-earth arguments on whatever was happening in legislation." After seven years, "we decided we must separate because the arguments were getting pretty tense sometimes in the office," Leo Levenson recalled. Gilbert Sussman later testified about "both Mr. Solomon's extreme anger over the Russian-German pact of 1939 and the Russian-Finnish war [1939–1940] and the conflict of views between him" and Goodman. As a member of the Oregon Commonwealth Federation, Solomon denounced the Soviet invasion of Finland and the Communist Party's sudden anti-war and anti-Allied stance. Their different work patterns had also created problems. Goodman and Levenson labored every day at all hours of the day and night, "very prodigiously on matters, not considering the consequences sometimes," Levenson admitted. After his own long work bouts, Solomon stayed away, which interfered with the odd office style. Further, his meetings "became just like a religion, the same group of people, same time, same speeches," Levenson remembered. "I got bored with" this devotion.[1]

During the official neutrality period before the U.S. entered the war, Solomon belonged to Citizens for Victory, the successor to the League of Nations Association, and pressed the OCF to endorse interventionist policies. When an advocate of aid to Great Britain and France, the Committee to Defend America by Aiding the Allies (CDA), formed in 1941, it recruited him for its local labor committee despite the national group's general view that Jews were warmongers. He reluctantly accepted, saying privately that the unions and the OCF had avoided Portland's CDA because it "was filled with a bunch of 'stuffed shirts' who are traditionally known to be antagonistic to labor."[2]

Still, money was on Solomon's mind. Three months into his new practice, he approached the Bonneville Power Administration about a legal position that paid around $3,800 a year. Seriously considered, he underwent a mandatory FBI screening. It was generally reported that he was smart and professionally qualified; but based on his political loyalties and affiliations, the FBI labeled him a Communist or fellow traveler. Diplomatically told that there was an inadequate congressional appropriation, he was not hired.[3]

A contemplated marriage and his mother's financial needs likely prompted the job-seeking. "I had a hell of a time making a living in Portland," he remembered, "but I did take care of my mother" from around 1938 until her death in 1947. Her difficulties had been mounting. The family's loss of its last properties had been followed by Jacob Solomon's deep depression. The couple lived apart from about 1935 to 1937, reunited briefly, and separated permanently in 1938. Jacob left town that year to peddle goods, the family heard, on Los Angeles streets. He returned in 1941 to open a surplus military goods store with his son Sam. Family appeals for reconciliation failed. An apparently embarrassed Rose Solomon sometimes listed herself as a widow in city directories.[4]

Gus Solomon preferred instead to talk about his beloved Elisabeth Willer, a medical technologist and Democratic Party precinct worker who, he had met at an Oregon Commonwealth Federation meeting in May 1938. Libby was liberal, Jewish, self-supporting, proudly independent, and "bitterly anti-Communist," he said. Born on March 9, 1909, in Czarist Boruisk (now in Belarus), she had arrived in Portland in 1914 with her parents and had briefly attended Reed College. The Solomon and Willer families lived near one another, the mothers were friendly, and Mr. Willer had sold plumbing supplies to Jacob Solomon.[5]

At an OCF meeting, Libby had accompanied her friend Helen Bradley, Solomon's young secretary, to verify the organization's liberal status and learn more about politics. She "thought Gus did the best job" as a speaker. "Helen told that to her boss, Gus," she later remembered, "and at that point he decided that I was smart." They saw one another at Federation events and spent time together. By August, they were informally engaged, but they delayed marriage until Gus was certain he could earn at least $1,800 a year, enough to support his mother and family. He was nearly thirty-three; she was almost thirty. Both wanted children immediately. While passing through Salem to attend a basketball game at the University of Oregon in Eugene in March 1939, they and another couple — Morton Goodman and Edith Schnitzer — decided on the spur of the moment to get married. Morton and Edith were married in Salem on March 18; the next day, March 19, 1939, Gus married Libby in Eugene. To satisfy their parents, both couples remarried in Portland synagogues.[6]

MAINTAINING LIBERALISM

The war's approach to America and wartime conditions shook the hopes and plans of visionaries like Solomon. "The war crisis, the influence of big business in defense industries," and other developments, he warned just before the attack on Pearl Harbor, meant "we may not accomplish very much in the near future." The public-power cause was in retreat despite efforts by the Public Ownership League of America and similar groups. In 1940, private utilities defeated ballot measures to establish PUDs and purchase electrical operations in nearly every Oregon county and in Tacoma, Washington. That year marked both public ownership's high watermark and the ebbing of its tide in the Pacific Northwest. By December 1941, only four of the 32 PUDs in Washington and none of the 12 authorized by Oregon voters were operating. Creating a public power dominion in the region appeared a more distant dream.[7]

Liberals felt dispirited. A surging popular conservatism was likening state interventionism to totalitarianism. In 1938, Portland officials and voters sharply rejected pleas to establish public housing. Realtors looked on in disbelief as Libby Solomon and others presented harrowing evidence of slum conditions to the city commissioners. After 1938, the national administration only passed domestic legislation that satisfied the new, ruling southern Democratic-Republican bloc in Congress. In 1942, conservatives tightened their congressional hold, blocked liberal policy advances, dismantled virtually every federal relief and public-works program, reduced planning and regulatory functions, limited strikes and union campaign contributions, overturned a cap on wartime salaries, and refused to consider civil rights legislation.[8]

"The political atmosphere of the war years discouraged American liberalism" and forced liberals "to reassess their positions," Alan Brinkley writes. Oregon's liberal organizations shrank, functioned poorly, or disappeared, and no significant replacements appeared until a group was formed to aid returning Japanese Americans late in 1944. War weakened and liquidated the liberals' largest vehicle, the "shabby, gay, starving, vital OCF," Nathalie Panek remembered. Public power seemed a spent force in 1942, when voters in Astoria rejected bond-selling by a barely approved PUD. REA and PUD development all but ceased, leaving almost a quarter of Oregon's farms without electricity. Portland's chapter of the AJCongress folded in around 1943, and the new Union for a Democratic America barely found a place in Oregon.[9]

By 1940, the Oregon Civil Liberties Committee lacked a structure, volunteers, and money and faced a short-lived rival on the left — the Emergency Council for Democratic Rights. A protest against the denial of Portland's public auditorium to the anti-interventionist Committee to Defend America First had to come from the national ACLU. In the 1941 Oregon legislature, ACLU and OCF lobbyists amazed themselves when they secured a ban on religious and racial attacks in the state's voters' pamphlet and defeated or watered down several unwanted bills. By 1942, the local ACLU was virtually extinct, partly because it had lost leaders and supporters to military service and out-of-state jobs. The national ACLU appointed a Northwest field representative and, as Bill of Rights caretakers, state correspondents. Solomon succeeded B.A. Green in that role between 1942 and 1949. He answered inquiries, kept the national office informed, occasionally acted for it, and conferred with its officials about reviving the branch.[10]

Apparent constitutional violations went unchallenged, if not unnoticed, by Solomon's ACLU remnant. A few violations were referred to the Northern California ACLU and the national office, which filed a brief supporting a 1943 complaint to the Fair Employment Practices Committee against Portland's Boilermaker's Union for forcing the discharge of African American workers (which was only won in 1945). Both the Northern California branch and the national ACLU ineffectually protested the persecution of Jehovah's Witnesses in small-town Oregon and elsewhere. Nationwide between May 1940 and December 1943, the Witnesses suffered as many as two thousand incidents of job firings, physical attacks, and bans on the education of their children. Federal courts jailed thousands of drafted Witnesses after denying them ministerial exemptions. In May 1942, Solomon overlooked these instances when reporting little change in the state's civil liberties scene since Pearl Harbor. "There has been no wholesale infringement of civil rights [civil liberties] but the feeling is still strong against the Japanese," he wrote. People of color in Portland faced added restrictions and "anti-Semitism is still quite prevalent but not very vocal," he noted. As John Morton Blum concluded, "Wartime public-opinion studies disclosed that Americans distrusted Jews more than any other European people except Italians."[11]

Oregon liberals lamented these trends and their own weakness. "There appears to be only slight interest in politics, Grange, Public Power, or anything else except the War," one complained in 1942. A year later, Portland liberals appeared to be "highly divided, discouraged, or inactive." Bemoaning their paltry legislative influence, they learned too late about an Oregon Senate bill that worsened the state's alien land law, but they did bottle up House Joint Memorials in 1945 calling for the deportation of Japanese aliens and the removal of all Japanese Americans from the Pacific Coast once they left internment. Communication among Portland liberals was so poor that neither Solomon nor a group of prominent liberal Christians knew in December 1944 that the other wanted to smooth the internees' return. Politics had not ceased, of course. His friends pondered "a quiet write-in campaign for Solomon for the Democratic nomination for district attorney" in 1942 and hoped to win him a place on the Ninth Circuit Court of Appeals. Both ideas went nowhere. Personally, Solomon was delighted by marriage and fatherhood. "Gus quite ebullient. Tractoring and fathering very nicely," Steven Kahn observed.[12]

Occasionally, however, Portland liberals were heartened, as when the Union for Democratic Action struggled to develop an agenda and policy proposals for a revised New Deal. On a larger scale, public hysteria about internal threats began waning early in 1942. There was no repetition of the First World War's extensive suppression of dissent, and the U.S. government assailed racist doctrines and spoke brightly about human freedom and social justice. The war also was making it official policy that the nation was no longer exclusively Protestant or white, a change that reduced the strain many Jews felt being both American and Jewish. It did not reduce their unspeakable grief on learning of the Holocaust.[13]

Importantly, prosperity was returning. Countless Americans were earning a good living, some for the first time. The rush of government capital, heavy and light industry, job-seekers, and military bases into the Pacific Northwest gladdened Solomon's pro-growth, patriotic soul. A great westward migration packed newcomers into the region's industrial places. Portland's populace grew by 20 percent, to 373,628, during the 1940s. Manufacturing — its Oregon workforce swelling 85 percent between 1939 and 1945 — and related sectors attracted some 72,000 migrants to Portland alone. Steel casting, scrap-iron, shipbuilding, and other industries crowded into Portland and Vancouver, Washington, just across the Columbia River. From 1940 to 1944, their combined populations grew by about a third to create one of the country's eight worst congested metropolitan areas, a subject of worried federal reports and special allocations.[14]

Portland gleefully rode the wartime wave, but it was not ready to house newcomers. Nor did many whites welcome a larger permanent African American community, which bounded from 2,000 to 15,000 residents during the war. Once rare, White-Only signs multiplied in the city as racial segregation and discrimination worsened. Local AFL unions kept people of color from better-paying jobs or assigned them to futureless segregated units. At the same time, new and restored industries, the virtual end to unemployment, and the barely restrained consumer buying aided Solomon's business clientele and, thus, his law practice. (Public-power representation had virtually disappeared by 1942.) The nation was poised on the point of an unparalleled affluence.[15]

Solomon carried on in familiar ways. There were elections to win, newly arrived Democrats to register and guide, New Deal programs to restart, and equal opportunity to support for African Americans in local war plants. He used his national liberal network so others could obtain patronage appointments, better jobs, and military commissions. He bought war bonds, performed favors for encamped soldiers, and wrote morale-boosting letters to distant compatriots. For Raymond M. Kell, whose young family the Solomons aided, the periodic letters on public power's tribulations brought welcome relief from his boredom in the South Pacific. Awaiting the birth of the Solomons' baby in 1943, one friend commented: "Gus is contemplating his flat feet which are weakened from week-end gardening." Solomon had a brush with the military early in 1944. Drafted at age thirty-eight, he was discharged after two weeks because of poor coordination and an allergy to khaki dye.[16]

The war neither discouraged Solomon's liberalism nor forced its reassessment. The thriving economy, the outlet that war gave his patriotism, and the optimistic rhetoric of wartime liberalism combined with a resilient, confident personality, a happy marriage, and the welcome birth of Gerald in 1941 and Philip in 1943 to strengthen his attachment to pre-war doctrines. He spoke and wrote in favor of the draft and of his faith in the Roosevelt administration and called on the disappearing OCF to shift in 1942 to educational work for "socialized medicine, disseminating information on question of the peace, etc." Like the Union for a Democratic America, his post-war agenda envisaged a society and politics predicated on social justice, economic security, and individual freedom.[17]

In May 1941, liberal and Socialist intellectuals had created the bipartisan, intervention-minded Union for a Democratic America (UDA). The organization opposed racism, Soviet and German foreign policies, and domestic Communists and Fascists and supported unions and civil rights. It tolerated the wartime Popular Front but remained "very edgy about extending any advantages [to the USSR] beyond the requirements of mutual military operations," member Monroe Sweetland recalled. Unique among national liberal groups, the UDA expressly banned Communists. Nonetheless, the House Committee on Un-American Activities charged that most UDA members belonged to an interlocking Communist directorate. And in 1944, an FBI informant falsely identified Solomon as someone active in the local Russian–American Club, which fostered good will and entertained Soviet crews picking up Liberty ships.[18]

Sweetland, Neuberger, Kahn, Hart, Panek, Solomon, Douglas Anderson, and other former OCF stalwarts were unable to persuade labor, farm, and liberal interests to form UDA chapters. In March 1944, a Portland group emerged from the Oregon Progressive Council, a ghost of the OCF, proclaiming itself a provisional UDA chapter, but it made bare inroads among federal employees and intellectuals. In Frank A. Warren's view, the national organization, which never reached much above ten thousand members, was little more than a public policy association that had influential liberals write letters and lobby. In a nation respectful of Soviet arms and tolerant of Communist enlistment in war ranks, it became, former UDA director James Loeb Jr. would admit, "the pariah of the liberal movement." Among its unremarked missteps was an unknown staff action that aroused Solomon's ire and for which, according to Panek, Loeb unsuccessfully apologized. "Gus should not have such a sensitive ego," she added.[19]

Efforts for the Democratic Party took Solomon further into the political mainstream. The year 1940 was partly given over to Oregon's Draft Roosevelt Committee, securing Republican voters for FDR, and obtaining campaign donations from unions and federal employees. Gus and Libby Solomon distributed material, ran campaign classes for Democratic women, and tried to persuade newspapers to print Libby's pro-FDR letters. In 1942, Gus was placed on the Democratic State Committee finance committee; in 1944, he was an alternate delegate to the Democratic National Convention. Too busy to attend, the attorney sent his wife to Chicago. They supported the visionary New Dealism of Vice President Henry Wallace and rued Senator Harry S. Truman replacing him on the ticket. Through the Norris–LaGuardia Committee in 1944, Solomon again urged Oregon Republicans to vote for the president.[20]

In the 1944 senatorial race, Solomon bolstered liberal and moderate Republicans against conservative Democrats. He favored Charles A. Sprague in the Republican primary and Republican victor Guy Cordon in the general election. Solomon persuaded several unions not to endorse Cordon's Democratic opponent, Willis Mahoney, and he enthusiastically backed Republican Wayne L. Morse's first-time senatorial effort. In 1936, Solomon had failed to persuade Morse, then dean of the University of Oregon law school, to become an ACLU sponsor. In the acrimonious 1944 Republican primary, liberal Democrats helped Morse challenge Senator Rufus Holman. Solomon obtained donations for Morse from public-power interests and Jews, and he and Libby invited reporters to their home to meet and play cards with the voluble dean. Almost any anti-Holman candidate would have won their aid. Holman, once a public-power advocate, was a pre-war isolationist, labor-baiter, and opponent of Lend Lease and liberalized refugee proposals. Morse accused Holman of prejudice and bigotry and was attacked in turn as someone financed by wealthy Jews. Democrats crossed over in large numbers to narrowly award Morse the victory, virtually ensuring his choice in November. Solomon belonged to a small group of friends "willing to stand up and support me," Morse later said, when most of his acquaintances believed that he had no chance of winning. The political correspondence between the two men quickened.[21]

JAPANESE AMERICANS

The nation's treatment of Japanese Americans after the attack on Pearl Harbor and his own passivity at the time lay forever on Solomon's conscience. More than 4,000 Japanese Americans, 60 percent of them born in America, lived in Oregon in 1940, some 1,680 of them in Portland. Solomon knew few of them, but he hated their forced removal. In 1942, he confessed: "I didn't protest. I don't know of any non-Japanese protests at the time." Even though the post-war ACLU of Oregon and the Japanese American Citizens League praised his principled support of Japanese Americans, Solomon guiltily recalled his own near-paralysis. Americans, including liberals, he believed, had not practiced their democratic pronouncements, when faced with racial stigmatization, hysteria, evacuation, and relocation. "I am sorry to say that I was not involved in the beginning," Solomon said, "when the Japanese Americans were moved into concentration camps."[22]

He did protest the internment at one unreported event. He remembered: "I was outraged by [Executive Order 9066], and I did speak before a meeting of the American Jewish Congress and told them how I felt about the thing." He told them "they have got to speak up against the treatment of the Japanese because today it's the Japanese and tomorrow it's the Jews." Those who viewed Japanese Americans as the Jews of the West were behind their expulsion, he apparently explained; interning citizens smacked of Nazi Germany. Putting somebody in a "concentration camp because of his color or place of origin" meant "you can do it because of his religion. . . . But I was the only Jew in Portland who was willing to stand up." He said nothing — then or later — about interning aliens of Japanese ancestry.[23]

Rumors sweeping the West Coast — such as one warning of an invasion abetted by an internal Fifth Column — made fair-minded intercession difficult. "War fever was raging," Solomon said, "and we were all fed propaganda that the Japanese might blow up our homes, our military installations and commit similar sabotage." A climate of racism and fear and a craving for Japanese Americans' properties enveloped communities on the West Coast. On January 2, 1942, Portland became the only city that prohibited business licenses to Japanese nationals. City commissioners called for interning all Japanese Americans. On February 12, Executive Order 9066 designated military zones from which anyone could be excluded, and the uprooting of Japanese Americans began. From Oregon, hundreds fled east to avoid evacuation and detention. Some 120,000 Japanese immigrants (Issei) and native-born Japanese (Nisei) from California, Washington, Oregon, and Arizona were forced into eighteen guarded camps, ten inland isolation areas, and, for agricultural labor purposes, Western Free Zones.[24]

Ironically, Solomon's inaction put him in the American mainstream. Almost no citizen, association, or organization publicly opposed the internment. His public-power ally, the Oregon Grange, had for decades venomously opposed Japanese aliens gaining citizenship and owning land. Once war began, Solomon's liberal Washington friends Mon Walgren and Warren Magnuson wanted everybody of Japanese ancestry removed from their state. Oregon's bar averted its gaze, too. Sudden news of Executive Order 9066, according to John F. Kilkenny, dismayed an Oregon State Bar Governing Board meeting, but bar leaders did nothing beyond privately agreeing that it constitutionally betrayed their fellow citizens. If "the order had been to hang all Japanese," Kilkenny volunteered, "I'd say that 50 per cent of the population might have gone for it."[25]

"Groups publicly committed to fighting discrimination," Eric Foner writes about the national scene, "either defended the internment or remained silent." While sporadic protest appeared in a few liberal and religious publications, liberals proved slow to awaken to the injustices and tragedies. The Union for Democratic America and American Jewish Congress were quiescent. The ACLU was divided on exclusion, then vacillated and eventually approved the internment order in principle even as some chapters and members challenged it in court. When early in 1942 the House of Representatives' Tolan Committee heard testimony on the West Coast regarding evacuation, small organized groups of former missionaries, pacifists, and others stepped forward to defend Japanese Americans and question mass internment — in San Francisco and Seattle but not in Portland. "In Oregon no public protest [of expulsion] was entered by any of the groups one might have expected to speak — churches, civil libertarians, the Red Cross, the YMCA and YWCA, international peace organizations — none stepped forward," Floyd J. McKay has found.[26]

Portland Jewry willfully looked the other way during the expulsion. The local Jewish newspaper continued its pleas for minority rights and tolerance but remained silent about the plight of Japanese Americans. Later explanations — that, like mainstream Jewish organizations, Jews in the Far West focused rightly on the destruction of European Jewry, had a well-founded fear of being labeled unpatriotic, or were eager to prove their allegiance to the white majority — did not fit Solomon. In any event, he always numbered himself among the unduly cautious who refused to act democratically when faced with the forced removal and relocation.[27]

On March 28, 1942, Minoru Yasui, Oregon's only Japanese American attorney, put the Constitution — and Solomon's commitments — to the test. Arrested in Portland for ignoring the 6 PM West Coast curfew for Japanese Americans, he challenged the curfew order, not the legality of the executive order or its enforcement statute. Before Yasui's April 22 indictment, Solomon urged the national ACLU "to come in with me" to defend him. Nervous about Yasui's previous employment by a Japanese consulate, disinclined to embarrass the Roosevelt administration, and seeking an appropriate test case of the evacuation order, the ACLU's board refused to help. A few months later, it reversed the decision, but by then Yasui had private counsel. As the Portland trial approached, California Attorney General Earl Warren obtained *amicus curiae* status to support the prosecution, and Judge James A. Fee appointed nine Oregonians to serve as nonparty friends of the federal court. Solomon claimed that he alone among them called the curfew unconstitutional; the others "made short shrift of me." Randall B. Kester, one of the nine, remembered differently: they all agreed that citizens did not fall under the curfew order and assumed the native-born Yasui was a citizen.[28]

Solomon recalled saying little, if anything, and objecting to much after the trial started on June 12. Nothing could be laid before the court, however, because Fee unexpectedly did not request any *amicus* brief. He ruled the curfew order unconstitutional as it applied to American citizens and surprisingly held that Yasui, because of his consulate employment, had renounced his citizenship and suffered the ban. Appeals by both sides were certified directly to the Supreme Court. On June 21, 1943, in *Hirabayshi v. U.S.*, *Korematsu v. U.S.*, and *Yasui v. U.S.*, the Court upheld the executive order and evacuation procedures as a military necessity. *Hirabayshi* upheld the curfew, making the citizenship issue irrelevant. The Court sustained Yasui's conviction. On remand, Fee recognized Yasui's citizenship and sentenced him to fifteen days of imprisonment. He had been in solitary confinement for almost a year. Seven years later, the former prisoner-of-conscience assured Judge Solomon "that your liberal views did reenforce my contentions" and that "your views were in accord with the highest ideals of American democracy."[29]

Solomon never believed that Americans knew what was happening in the western internment camps. Liberals in the War Relocation Authority (WRA) and clients in its Idaho camps gave him an inkling into their hard conditions. Once campaigns began to free internees to return home and groups formed to welcome them, Solomon publicly associated himself with their plight. It started in 1944, when the ACLU asked him to find a lawyer to constitutionally test the residence ban on Japanese Americans in Oregon. Any counsel "who could handle it would want a large fee," he responded, "and those who would be willing to handle it are fearful that they would lose their business if they did." A.L. Wirin, preparing a parallel California test case (another was in Washington), called him "probably the best man in Portland" to fight an Oregon action. After several lawyers declined, Solomon agreed to defend the claims of a disabled veteran recruited by the loyalist Japanese American Citizens League. In *Ex Parte Endo*, the Supreme Court acted first, unanimously ruling that the government could neither detain loyal Japanese American citizens nor bar them from the West Coast. The War Department rescinded the exclusion and detention order on December 17, 1944. The WRA announced that it was closing all of its camps within a year, and the agency would terminate in 1946.[30]

Solomon learned that Executive Order 9066 had been lifted when the *Oregonian* asked him for a reaction. Knowing his views were unpopular, he hesitated before declaring himself "glad to see the exclusion order rescinded." He hoped that "the Japanese are brought back gradually and established in communities where they will be well received." The mayor, sheriff, and president of the Portland Council of Churches issued cautious statements but no welcome. The next day, a man stopped Solomon to ask how he would like to have his home bombed and his children killed. People yelled at him over the phone that he was a Communist, anarchist, and traitor and threatened him. "I was accused of being a Communist because I didn't believe that American citizens of Japanese ancestry should be put in concentration camps without having charges filed against them."[31]

Opposition to the return of Japanese Americans had gathered force before the WRA announced it was shutting down. In Oregon, vigilantism and the deportation of ethnic Japanese were discussed in Hood River, Sherwood, Forest Grove, and Gresham. In the spring of 1945, the Oregon legislature tightened the old alien land law, which banned aliens from owning, operating, or controlling agricultural land or farm equipment and from deeding land to relatives. An older generation could no longer live on farms owned by American-born relatives. Solomon warned that the amended law served "the hate mongers around Hood River, Gresham, and the Snake River area" who had passed resolutions, held mass meetings, and urged Japanese not to return there. Now, "they can harass not only Nisei and Issei, but all persons who deal with them." How "can we expect people to leave the Relocation Centers and return to Oregon under such circumstances, particularly when the prohibitions of this law are magnified at the centers?" He wanted to challenge the law's constitutionality, but he was advised by the ACLU to secure Wirin's assistance first. Returnees promised to raise the needed money. Meanwhile, Solomon and others issued a Multnomah Bar Association report on the "Japanese Problem in Oregon," which concluded that threats to constitutional rights, fundamental justice, and human dignity were grave but not yet alarming.[32]

After Solomon's front-page *Oregonian* statement, Betty B. Sale of the local National Conference of Christians and Jews hurriedly invited him to join the meetings it was holding with the Portland Council of Churches on aid to returnees. Neither she, the Rev. Dr. I. George Nace, head of the Council of Churches, Isabel Gates of the Baptist Mission Board, nor the others knew him or his views. Amazingly to Solomon, "there were literally thousands of people who felt as I did. Among them were some of the outstanding leaders in the community," including social justice priest Fr. Thomas Tobin, socially liberal bank head E.B. MacNaughton, and several county bar leaders. Among state newspapers, only the *Oregonian* and Salem's *Oregon Statesman* spoke out for the returnees.[33]

From these meetings, the Portland Committee to Aid Relocation emerged, with Solomon as secretary and head of its employment committee. Counterparts formed in Gresham and Hood River and in communities in Washington and California. By mid-February 1945, about seventy-five professional and business people, their spouses, and a few others were members of the Portland group. These informal groups sent materials to WRA camps assuring internees a safe welcome and assistance. Many in the camps held their properties uncertainly and had few possessions left; and many would return, if at all, jobless, homeless, and afraid. Portland's Committee promised that Solomon, Gilbert Sussman, Herbert M. Schwab, and other ACLU co-operating attorneys would defend their rights and interests. It pressed legislators and officials from the Federal Housing Authority and other agencies to equitably and smoothly reintegrate the 859 internees who warily returned. The local group found them jobs, temporary shelter, and agricultural produce outlets and urged unions to enroll returnees. After lawyers in Hood River County refused to represent returnees, except those who were willing to sell their farms, Solomon was sent for. Fearing unsympathetic juries, he negotiated settlements that got "their property back, but many times I wasn't able to get very much by way of rental or profits for the use of their property" during the war.[34]

Solomon gave money to two Japanese American acquaintances he had known before the war to help reopen their businesses or return to school. Personally or through the Portland Committee, he helped others regain their homes, find jobs, and acquire business properties. Seattle returnees visited his home, where they — along with Wirin and liberal federal public-housing director Jesse Epstein in Seattle — kept him abreast of comparable efforts in Washington and California. In Oregon, Solomon had legislative friends introduce a bill to repeal the alien land law. When repeal failed, Allan Hart and Verne Dusenberry were hired to fight the law's constitutionality. "I guess I was miffed because [the challengers] did not come to me" instead of recruiting his two friends, he recalled. Hart remembered him "not only privy to it but contributing to" the legislative plans. The Oregon Supreme Court declared the law unconstitutional in 1947, while a year later the U.S. Supreme Court dealt alien land laws a deathblow in *Oyama v. California*.[35]

The Portland Relocation Committee worked to offset economic discrimination that the Solomons, as Jews, felt personally. After major Northwest fruit growers, florists, and produce merchants and the Seattle Teamsters union boycotted returnees' produce and flowers, he and Libby Solomon, in a nationally reported incident, gathered about fifteen committee members and federal officials one early March morning at Portland's Farmers' Wholesale Market. Three days earlier, a Japanese American farmer's unsold goods had to be dumped. Solomon observed his produce again languishing and offered to pay for two crateloads. Told that workers would not handle the goods, the lawyer futilely explained that as CIO members they would be ordered to do so after he called union officials. As police watched, the boycott held. Solomon yelled questions, but nobody responded, and the frustrated observers left. Twice more without results, the Committee sent the farmer to the market.[36]

Solomon's employment subcommittee acted. Episcopal pastor

Lansing Kempton, railroad lawyer Omar C. Spencer, lumber magnate Herbert Templeton, Ed Benedict from the IWA-CIO, merchant Harry Gervurtz from B'nai B'rith, and Solomon knew how to influence political and governmental figures, big purchasers, and the commercial food industry. Like its counterparts in other West Coast states, the Portland Committee obtained federal assistance, mobilized publicity, and arranged direct chain store, college, and hospital produce buying. It appealed to Senator Wayne Morse to press the War Food Administration to stop the boycott. By August 1945, after wholesalers rejected another of their pleas, the region's strongest boycott of Japanese American farmers ended. Marvin G. Pursinger traced its cessation to the Catholic Church's intervention among Italian Americans in the Portland wholesale market, but Solomon learned that the boycotted farmer had arranged purchases by Chinese American restaurant owners who were worried about the boycott's implication for themselves. Protests by the western aid groups brought an Agriculture Department cease-and-desist order to the Northwest Produce Dealers Association.

"The Portland Citizen's Committee," the WRA's Portland headquarters declared in its final report, "has been a courageous one and has never failed to take a stand." Just before the WRA suspended operations in 1946, three hundred Japanese Americans attended a Portland testimonial dinner honoring its personnel, the National Conference of Christians and Jews, the Portland Committee to Aid Relocation, and others. These small bands had mobilized racial liberals' knowledge, prestige, and influence and had reduced the considerable odds against a peaceful re-integration of Japanese Americans into metropolitan Portland. In the short run, the most crucial element in evacuees' successful re-entrance to the West Coast, according to Roger Daniels, "was the existence of a well-organized and active minority of whites who for one reason or another wanted what they considered justice for the Japanese Americans."[37]

LAW PRACTICE

The lean years were ending. Portland's bar lived "high on the hog because of war-time created work," Raymond M. Kell recalled. Solomon's business-law earnings swelled, and by the summer of 1944 he was very busy. As legal income generally corresponded to business conditions between 1929 and 1948, the improving wartime economy boosted the legal profession everywhere. Attorneys with small or moderate incomes did relatively better than those with large ones, according to one national study. Partners in old-line Portland Republican law firms, having lost personnel to the armed services, also resorted to hiring New Deal Democrats from federal agencies and to sharing work with liberals such as Gus Solomon.[38]

Importantly, numerous Jewish clients vaulted into middle or upper middle-class status. Owners of thriving sales, manufacturing, and distribution businesses requested more legal services. Small- and medium-sized firms worth between $50,000 and, in the immediate post-war run-up in values, $1,000,000 provided the bulk of Solomon's rising income. He represented buyers and sellers of properties and of a few small companies. He handled gifts, trusts, estates, and income tax matters and represented employers and employees before federal wage stabilization boards. He litigated liens and building contracts and handled mortgage foreclosures, bill collections, and negligence and insurance suits. Compared to public-power work, these were altogether more routine, emotionally detached, and lucrative tasks.[39]

Public-power interests grew more active after the war and renewed his services. Solomon's judicial victories for the People's Utility Districts placed them on a sound legal footing, established important precedents in municipal utility law, and burnished his liberal and professional reputation. In the Oregon Supreme Court in 1939, he established the constitutionality of the statute that enabled PUDs to form. *In Re Tillamook* arose when bankers had to be satisfied that the PUDs were constitutional before they purchased their bonds. Solomon won this approval in the circuit court and on appeal, persuading judges that PUDs should be treated as municipal corporations that possessed broad bond-issuing powers, not local improvement or special assessment districts.[40]

He countered almost yearly legal attacks on PUDs. Industry tactics and wartime interruptions prolonged the litigation. The Northern Wasco PUD was forced into three separate trials and three appeals, all handled by Solomon, during and after the war. In *Ravlin v. Hood River PUD*, Oregon's Supreme Court in 1940 agreed with him and Frank Kennan, a new associate formerly with the BPA, that the state had the authority to form a district that excluded those portions of the district where voters had rejected a PUD. The opinion permitted a new PUD election to determine the reformed boundaries. Two years later, in the trial and appeal of *Ollilo v. Clatskanie PUD*, Solomon established the validity and legality of the ballot authorizing a PUD board to issue revenue bonds to acquire a private system. A year later, the Oregon Supreme Court, in *Northern Wasco County PUD v. Kelly*, accepted his argument that other procedures used to form the PUD were legally valid. When the war ended and public power was reenergized, PUDs and REAs offered more legal work.[41]

In 1945, Americans celebrated the end of the war with relief, pride, and triumph. They braced for the demobilization and a depression that never came. Some 20,000 lawyers shed their uniforms and an unusually large number of new graduates entered practice, making competition difficult in Portland and elsewhere. Conditions rapidly improved as post-war projects multiplied. The nation — enormously richer, more self-confident, and now a vast worldwide presence — entered one of the longest and steadiest periods of growth and prosperity in its history. The legal profession shared in the prosperity. Law suits that had piled up due to wartime disruptions had to be settled or tried. Business and consumer prosperity and growing legislation and regulations created new legal commerce. The agricultural and forest industries reasserted their occupational dominance in Oregon. The legal corps swelled, Portland's from around 650 in 1940 to 1,181 in 1949, with another 728 practicing elsewhere in the state. Nationwide, lawyers and law firms exploded in numbers and specialization; some attorneys made fortunes.[42]

Solomon rebuilt his office after John McCourt was elected Multnomah County district attorney in 1946. Kell, given part-time employment by the Oregon State Grange, joined him. On all but paper the two cagey liberals became partners that April. Resurgent PUDs and REAs that wanted to build or acquire facilities employed them to deal with banks, utilities, public agencies, PUD elections, and court challenges. With Kell and others, Solomon continued winning in court. In 1946, the Oregon Supreme Court in *Seufert and Northern Wasco County PUD v. Stadelman* sustained the writ he had obtained forcing town officials to call an initiative election for the Northern Wasco PUD. Two years later, he was again upheld after winning at trial in *Gurdane v. Northern Wasco County PUD*, which validated its bond-issue ordinance. In three related suits in the circuit and high courts, he protected bond issuance by the Union County PUD but not the operating agreement that had secured its REA loan. In the appeal in *Fullerton v. Central Lincoln PUD*, the Oregon Supreme Court agreed with his contention that a PUD board could issue and sell revenue bonds without a prior vote of the district.[43]

Business law paid better than PUD representation, but his lingering "Communistically inclined" reputation, Solomon feared, hurt him with several important business prospects. He did labor lucratively for five years with Gunther F. Krause on a successful, stockholders' suit and, on behalf of Portland jewelers, persuaded the Oregon Supreme Court in 1948 that a personal property tax on pawned items was unconstitutional. (Solomon won nine of his ten final cases before that court.) Kell and he also defended gambling enterprises controlled in several states by Al Winter, the purported head of Portland's major criminal syndicate. "Gus, Al and I would [regularly] spend the better part of a Saturday afternoon with our limited library trying to develop a theory or theories that would either delay or strike down the offensive regulatory action," Kell recalled. Solomon represented unions before wage stabilization boards and workers denied union seniority, unemployment claims, and injury compensation. He counseled Herman D. Kenin (Harry's brother) of the Oregon local of the American Federation of Musicians. Business clients and local Jewish leaders had Solomon smooth their way with his friend Senator Morse and federal officials in the Pacific Northwest and Washington. His income shot up. By 1949, he could say: "Although my [law] business is not lucrative, I have a fairly large one." After twenty years at the bar, he earned $18,000 that year against a national net average of just over $8,000 for nonsalaried attorneys. "In those days," Kell recalled, "an income of $500 a month was adequate to keep a household of five operational." Solomon could finally consider himself a financial success.[44]

POLITICS

Politics challenged Solomon more than business law. In a nation experiencing considerable fluidity and rancor over its post-war political, economic, and foreign affairs options, new openings seemed possible. Against great odds, liberal Democrats strove to make inroads in the most Republican state west of the Mississippi River. "Oregon was a safe and solid republican [sic] state from city hall or courthouse to the national level," Kell recalled. Two Democrats served in its sixty-member House of Representatives in 1946. Howard Morgan and Richard L. Neuberger agreed that the Democratic Party in the state "had been in limbo for so long that the general public had gotten used to regarding it, if at all, as irrelevant." National party committees assumed nothing would change. Every four years, the Republicans sent $250,000 and the Democrats sent $15,000 to support their Oregon tickets.[45]

Morgan, Neuberger, Sweetland, Solomon, and others made their "primary objectives immediately after the war [the] rebuilding [of] the party at the grass roots and seizing control of positions of leadership in the party," according to Robert Burton. The contest "raged unabated from 1946 to 1952, destroyed unity and temporarily rendered the party powerless in state politics." New developments complicated their efforts. The emerging Cold War intensified liberal-leftist splits in many states after President Harry S. Truman fired Secretary of Interior Henry Wallace in 1946 and groups rallied to Wallace's call to preserve the wartime Russian alliance and Roosevelt's progressive policies. That the two Democratic camps had only recently shared the same New Deal convictions and appealed to many of the same constituencies blurred distinctions. Relations among Democrats were poisoned when many liberals dissociated themselves from former Popular Front connections and refashioned themselves into anti-Communists. Support for large-scale social changes became more difficult.[46]

The pro-Wallace Independent Citizens Committee of Arts, Sciences and Professions (ICC) formed just before Solomon's Union for a Democratic America transformed itself into the Americans for Democratic Action. "Many of the people whom we expected to join with us," he reported, instead joined the ICC Oregon chapter. "Some of them were willing to come into our organization as soon as it was started, but others were reluctant to leave the I.C.C. and were disturbed that we were setting up a competing liberal organization." After Solomon addressed the local ICC on legislative issues, UDA staff organizer Panek, considering it a Communist front, commented: "It would be ironical if, after all these years of militant fighting of the CP Gus were to be sucked in by the artists." She allowed that Oregon was considered "pretty hopeless by a good many people but it has at least one advantage — the absence of any material strength on the part of our comrades to the left."[47]

In December 1946, the Progressive Citizens of America, forerunner of the Progressive Party of May 1948, replaced the ICC as Wallace's primary instrument. The ADA, seeking to maintain New Deal influence and purge Communists from progressive ranks, opposed it as a Popular Front reincarnation. Wallace supporters in Oregon Democratic councils frightened Truman loyalists in 1948 when they discussed running Wallace as a Democrat in the state's preferential primary. "At one time, the Oregon state Democratic committee is believed to have been divided, 31 to 29, on the Wallace candidacy," Curtis D. MacDougal reports. When Wallace's name was not listed,

Solomon and others rushed to insert Truman's. They barely obtained enough signatures to place him on the ballot and just enough nominees to fill the party ticket. Listing Truman's name made the president vaguely aware of Solomon, Sweetland thought. "If it hadn't been for the help of Gus Solomon, and a few others like him, the Wallace crowd would have taken over the Democratic Party in Oregon," National Committeewoman Nancy H. Robinson informed the White House after the election.[48]

Antagonism by Sweetland, Neuberger, and Solomon toward the Progressive Party and Wallace's presidential bid almost destroyed their fledgling ADA chapter. Solomon had excitedly attended the national ADA's founding convention in March 1947, where he had met several rising young liberal politicians. Seattle Congressman Henry M. Jackson and Minneapolis Mayor Hubert H. Humphrey, as zestfully combative as Solomon, particularly impressed him. While the convention endorsed the administration's foreign policy, it conspicuously did not endorse Truman's re-election. Back home, Solomon represented Portland's chapter on the ADA board, his first national position, and in the Oregon Special Committee for the Defense of Public Power.[49]

The officially bipartisan ADA operated on the fringes of the Democratic Party. In Oregon, it tried but largely failed to establish chapters in several counties before retreating to Portland. In Astoria, a chapter captured the local Democratic Party before disbanding. The almost exclusively middle-class Portland organization, set up in May 1947, attracted anti-Wallacites from the Young Democrats and the new American Veterans Committee and one-time partisans of the Oregon Commonwealth Federation and Union for a Democratic America. By November, it had grown from twenty to nearly one hundred members. Portland still remained "glued to conservatism," Richard L. Neuberger told his readers; liberalism was "pretty much restricted to the intellectual level" and did not appeal to the AFL unions. "Portland has always been a lonesome place for liberals," a local ADA leader sighed. Few industrial unionists joined the chapter despite national CIO prodding. By August 1948, it had only "a spark of life left" and a determined board nucleus "trying to give it a little fuel." The chapter must "move into a new, young organization of people who have not been crying on each other's shoulders for the past twenty years," a staff organizer warned. An executive committee that included Solomon struggled to keep the chapter alive.[50]

Solomon closely fit the ADA member profile, except that he lived in the Pacific Northwest and had three children (Richard was born in 1946). In June 1948, 80 percent of its approximately 3,700 members clustered in five eastern states and the District of Columbia. According to ADA studies, the ADA's typical dues-payer was Jewish, male, nearing forty, college-educated, a professional, an owner or purchaser of a single-family dwelling, and married with almost two children. Solomon shared the ADA's faith in an active federal government and the welfare state and its respect for the power of interest groups in the Democratic Party. The ADA downplayed the New Deal's emphasis on redistributing wealth and power and on structural economic reforms. It called for less governmental control over major industrial operations and for more economic growth through high consumption levels, which dovetailed with Solomon's pro-growth and public-power doctrines. And he shared the ADA's commitment to civil liberties and civil rights and its resistance to monopoly power by the "interests."[51]

Solomon backed the officially bipartisan ADA in opposing both conservatives in the two major parties and Communists wherever they were. Like its predecessor, it defined Communists as criminal conspirators, equated them with fascists, and banned their belonging. The ADA endorsed Truman's Loyalty–Security Order of March 23, 1947, which tightened the loyalty reviews of federal employees and applicants and was later extended to all defense-industry workers. But as leftist and liberal New Dealers were purged from government jobs, the ADA warned against the use of closed loyalty hearings, the denial of the right of individuals to face their accusers, and forced testimony. Where the ADA stood on the loyalty-security matters confused liberals and kept many federal employees from joining. To believe in free speech and freedom of association and to support strong national-security restraints on domestic Communists at the same time created a host of conflicts.[52]

Experience representing friends and ADA members employed by the BPA convinced Solomon that Truman's loyalty program was careening out of control because it allowed political purges that were rarely susceptible to reversal by the courts or administrative appeals. No foundation existed for the BPA's attacks on his clients other than their having ACLU or Popular Front connections, he always maintained. Often accused vaguely and anonymously, his clients were fired or forced to retire early. What he could do for them was frustratingly little. Solomon helped Abraham A. Osipovich receive BPA loyalty clearance, for instance, but could not prevent his forced early retirement. The FBI meant, Solomon complained, "to drive non-Communist liberals out of the Government service" in the Pacific Northwest. In October 1947, he had his chapter ask the ADA to alter its position. It ought to object to the executive branch, he said, "in so far as [the Loyalty Order] does not safeguard the rights of individual employees" and job applicants. It must protest "the loose and careless statements which form the basis of some of the trials that are being held." He also opposed congressional investigation committee tactics and the new repressive loyalty legislation being enacted.[53]

The ADA, in turn, pressed chapters to do exactly what its Oregon, Minnesota, Wisconsin, and Michigan sections were trying to do: rebuild state Democratic parties on liberal programmatic lines from the bottom up rather than confront civic issues such as corruption, gambling, prostitution, and gambling. Portland's ADA guided its members into Democratic precinct committees and noisy internal party battles. The chapter attacked Republican legislators' voting records, joined farmers and unions in an electoral defeat of a statewide sales tax, endorsed an Oregon Fair Employment bill, and chastised segregated Portland neighborhoods and schools.[54]

Then there was the 1948 election. "The entire campaign [in Oregon] was rather spiritless and unenthusiastic, probably because the major party felt the election was in the bag and the minor party thought that its efforts were futile," one political scientist concluded afterward. Solomon's efforts stood out when conservative Democrats largely backed Thomas E. Dewey; and many liberals, anticipating Truman's defeat, never left the sidelines. Truman loyalists had to recruit a sacrificial gubernatorial candidate and Democratic conservatives to contest state offices. Exceptionally, Democratic voters — in the only state balloting on committee people — elected Solomon's allies Sweetland and Nan Wood Honeyman to the Democratic National Committee. The liberals secured a bare majority on the Democratic State Committee a year later.[55]

In Oregon, Solomon was an important contributor, fund-raiser, speaker, and pinch-hitting organizer for Truman. If someone else's name had not been needed to add luster to the party ticket, he would have been a Democratic presidential elector. A story circulated that Truman's cash-strapped whistle-stop campaign train could leave Portland in June 1948 only when Solomon, state treasurer of the Re-Elect Truman Committee, brought money aboard. Other versions named Solomon's client Abe Gilbert or Gilbert's brother as the cash-bearer.[56]

Oregonians chose Dewey and an all-Republican congressional delegation, filled all but one state office with Republicans, and awarded them seventy of the ninety legislative seats. The Progressive Party secured a minuscule 2.86 percent of the vote, one of Wallace's five best state results. According to that party's unofficial historian, "there was less local Red-baiting, more practical efficiency in party operations, and comparatively better newspaper treatment in Oregon than in most states." Nationally, Truman, promising merely to defend and renovate the New Deal, had barely held together union members, women, and racial and religious minorities from the old Roosevelt coalition. Liberals emphasized the positive — Truman's re-election. Everywhere they "mistakenly interpreted the election as a mandate to extend the New Deal," Steven M. Gillon writes — and, it should be added, as a mandate to keep anti-Communism and the Cold War in the forefront of Democratic liberalism. ADA's hopes soared, and its Portland enrollment climbed to 184 in March 1949. By then, Solomon was pursuing a federal judgeship, and the ADA could help.[57]

Chapter 5

Securing a Judgeship

The new Oregon judgeship is the first real test of strength between the new and the old factions [in the Democratic Party]. The new leadership is unanimous in its support for Gus J. Solomon for the post.

—Ben Buisman, editor, *Oregon Grange Bulletin*, 1949

PLANNING

Solomon almost failed to reach the federal bench, so great was the enmity and competition he faced. "The majority opinion seemed to be that Gus wasn't going to get it," recalled Oregon Democratic Party leader Howard Morgan. He

> would not survive in the confirmation process partly because Gus was Jewish, partly because he was accused falsely of being a crazy left-winger, partly because he had been an attorney for the various public power cooperatives, and for other reasons, and because there were both Republican and Democratic politicians who wanted that seat on the bench.

Attempts to defeat him persisted even as the Senate prepared to vote on his nomination. Solomon could not stop worrying about the wild cards his opponents might hold.[1]

Once on the bench, his life transformed, he did not forget who had done things either to or for him during the ordeal that had stretched from early 1949 into June 1950. He remembered supporters and seldom forgave those who had distorted or dismissed his legal competence or the worth and meaning of his Jewishness, his values, or his commitments or those who had personally attacked him and his wife.

The contest over the judicial post was largely rooted in persistent conflicts in Oregon. Virtually all the people and interests involved in the state had long opposed one another. The prejudices and concerns of their national allies, the growing Cold War fears, and the intricacies of the judicial recruitment, appointment, and approval processes within the Truman administration and a Democratic-controlled Senate projected the controversy — and Solomon's fate — into the national arena. Altogether, the contest restaged state, regional, and national disputes over public power, civil liberties, liberalism, Communism, the standing of Jews, and police and national-security authority. Some of those disputes cast lingering shadows on Solomon's judicial career.

It all began just after the 1948 Democratic primary. Raymond M. Kell, after clearing the idea with Oregon Grange chief Morton Tompkins, proposed that his officemate seek the seat allotted to the U.S. District for Oregon once Congress approved twenty-seven expected new judicial posts. Solomon called him crazy. "I just don't want to go through what I know I would have to go through" to reach the bench, he said: unrelenting scrutiny, inevitable attacks, personal expense, non-stop hard work, and detraction from making a living. U.S. Attorney Henry L. Hess already was soliciting his own labor and farm endorsements, Kell warned. Solomon told him to find them more clients because their public-power business was slackening.[2]

Kell nudged Solomon for days, stressing how his securing the post would strengthen Oregon's Democratic Party. They rightly assumed that the administration would handle the new judgeship as a patronage matter. President Truman's choice of a liberal, they agreed, would admirably stun their conservative Democratic rivals. Liberals could do better than Hess, they agreed. They also agreed that newly elected Democratic National Committeeman Monroe M. Sweetland would do anything for Solomon and that new state party rules gave him and the new committeewoman, Nancy H. Robinson, key authority. Because no Democrat held an important state office or congressional seat, only those two individuals could recommend appointments to the White House and the Democratic National Committee.[3]

Once Solomon decided to make a bid for the judgeship, a three-way race pitted him against Hess and Oregon circuit judge Earl C. Latourette, who Solomon had opposed for a federal judgeship in 1936. The conservative Howard Latourette, who Wayne Morse had defeated in the 1944 Senate race, again promoted his brother. A dozen other names surfaced in party discussions, but no Republican seriously sought the post. As Morse informed complaining Republicans, Truman had no reason to reward Dewey's champions. In fact, "92.5 percent of all 3,082 appointments to the lower federal courts (through 2004) . . . [went] to candidates affiliating with the president's party."[4]

Solomon initially told Sweetland that his bid was designed merely to attract new clients and that he held no illusions about winning. A "'good' law business comes from those people who are traditionally opposed to the things for which the OCF stood," he said. The "publicity should help me land some of the larger Jewish businessmen who are so sensitive to respectability." In fact, it was not uncommon for would-be judges to merely seek the advancement of their names before clients or the public. But within six months of entering his name, Solomon was hooked by the lures of a long judicial career and the influence he might have on human affairs.[5]

The potential opponents and the inexact selection standards of the Senate and White House made him cautious. He also was well aware that relatively few Jews had been placed on the federal bench. Lined up against him in Oregon were the private utilities, the wood products industry, veteran and patriotic groups, many Republicans, the largely Republican bar, and conservative Democrats and their *Oregon Journal* mouthpiece. He could not predict that U.S. District Judge Claude McColloch, the American Bar Association, conservative Democrats in Truman's administration, and the FBI would try to block him or that some national party figures, Cabinet members, and senators would weigh in so unfavorably. Solomon's only similarity to most of the other lawyers who obtained federal judgeships in this period was that he was a white male born and raised in the district over which he might preside. He came neither from an influential corporate law firm nor the office of a politically connected prosecutor or judge. Promoting young, energetic liberal Democrats was not the norm in the post-war federal judiciary.[6]

Politics — that is, partisanship and ideology — has been at the center of judicial selection since President John Adams commissioned "midnight judges" to afflict the incoming Jeffersonians. In Oregon, politics perennially affected the choices, Solomon's later colleague James A. Redden commented. It has "always been buffered by a sort of an openness about it so that nobody would get away with appointing their incompetent brother-in-law, but there's politics in it, no doubt." Solomon later explained that he was under consideration because of "my long and active support of the Democratic Party, I think my training and my experience, and the fact that both the Democratic National Committeewoman and the Democratic National Committeeman, a majority of the County chairmen in the state, have all urged my appointment." Contenders understood that they must engage in the political process even while pretending to do otherwise. A candidate ultimately had to satisfy the president and the Senate that he or she had made important marks, had an acceptable public philosophy and political background, and could be trusted to administer justice. "Though each appointment may be discrete," J. Woodward Howard Jr. writes, "the recipe usually boils down to three related ingredients — professional competence, political participation, and personal ambition — plus a pinch of luck."[7]

Just before Truman's inauguration in 1949, Solomon received support from Libby and from the *Oregonian*, partly to shield him from expected attacks by the private utilities and the pro-Latourette *Oregon Journal*. His candidacy also needed National Committeewoman Robinson's endorsement and help in mobilizing the fading New Deal elements within Truman's administration. And Solomon knew that he could depend on Monroe Sweetland.[8]

The "campaign," as Kell aptly termed it, began immediately. First, Solomon had to win the recruitment race. No contender, as Joel Grossman writes, publicly admits "that he is doing something as unseemly as 'running' for a judgeship. But running he is." On the evening of January 15, Multnomah County District Attorney John McCourt, a former officemate, visited Solomon's longtime friend Phillip Parrish, chief of the *Oregonian's* editorial page. While distancing itself from Solomon's liberalism, the Republican paper endorsed him and refused to print some unfavorable letters to the editor. By winter, Solomon would feel that the statewide daily had been wonderful to him. Additionally, publisher E.B. MacNaughton, a secret ADA member, recommended him to the White House and to Oregon's Guy Cordon and other senators and testified for him.[9]

Sweetland worried whether their campaign could win enough support in the state, whether Truman would approve somebody with "a liberal and left record," and whether the powerful Senate Judiciary Committee chairperson, Pat McCarran, a flogger of liberal subversion and a covert anti-Semite, might block his approval. At once, private utility lobbyist Willis Mahoney and a conservative Democratic friend, Secretary of Defense Louis A. Johnson, an acerbic former American Legion national commander, pressed Sweetland not to recommend

Solomon or, if he did, to make Latourette his second choice. Strengthened by Kell's visits, he resisted them. It was to be a difficult period
"of anxiety and of risky political operations" for Sweetland, who Kell
mainly credited for the appointment.[10]

Accustomed to rough politics, Solomon was not easily daunted.
He had no fear of what an open season on his private life might
expose. Given the social barriers, he likely anticipated a tolerable
amount of anti-Semitism. What he gravely underestimated was the
challenge to his legal stature by some Oregon lawyers and the potent
American Bar Association and the effectiveness of Red-baiting by individuals who equated Communism with the New Deal, the public
power movement, or civil libertarianism. There were also those who
simply wanted no critic like Solomon on the bench. The controversy
proved to be longer, nastier, and more wearing than he imagined.

Several post-war trends bedeviled people like Solomon. Masses of
Americans had come to deeply suspect the state interventionism and
federal authority expanded by the New Deal and war needs. Anti-
Communism was maturing into grim political abuse, punishing nerve
and principle. Proliferating public and private actions repressed civil
liberties and civil rights under the guise of repressing Communism.
Republicans scoured the Truman administration and liberals for ignoring, if not assisting, Soviet agents and their American accomplices.
Fears of the new People's Republic of China and a Soviet Union in
fresh possession of an atomic bomb further darkened moods. Wartime confidence, hope, and direction had been all but lost by 1949.
As a result, the political mainstream had gravely narrowed.[11]

In 1949, "anti-communism planted itself squarely in the nation's
political consciousness," Richard Fried specifies. Communists were
widely demonized and associated with infiltration, disloyalty, subversion, espionage, and sabotage. Anti-Communist crusades swept several states and locales before Senator Joseph R. McCarthy made his
first explosive charges in February 1950. Floyd J. McKay dated the
launch of Oregon's post-war Red Scare to just after the 1948 election, when the legislature barred anybody linked to Communism
from state employment. Congress fixed on the Red Menace by 1949.
The House Committee on Un-American Activities conducted stormy
hearings, the executive branch acceded to tough security measures,
and the FBI and Justice Department stretched Truman's loyalty restrictions. Major prosecutions of alleged subversives began. To Solomon,
a "widespread anti-Communist hysteria" lasted from the trial of top

Communist Party leaders in 1949 to the Supreme Court's approval of their conviction in 1951 for membership in a group that unlawfully advocated and taught the overthrow or destruction of the United States government by force and violence.[12]

CAMPAIGNING

In the spring of 1949, Monroe Sweetland named a tame advisory group to lend an aura of reasoned consideration to his coming endorsement. Kell, AFL and CIO lawyers, a former Bonneville Power Administration chief counsel, and others considered thirty names and duly chose Solomon. Conservative Democrats tried and failed to re-establish the state Central Committee's recommendation authority. "It's a question of who's speaking for the Democratic party," chairperson William L. Josselin plaintively said. He unexpectedly offered himself for the judgeship. Others, too, sought the office as a capstone to their legal careers.[13]

Hess and Latourette now "almost entirely concentrated on a stop-Solomon effort," Kell recalled. Hess supporters, mainly in the unions, argued that Solomon was too radical and too unsure of approval to merit support while privately promising to make no objection if he became the White House's choice. Invective, insinuations, and accusations came from Latourette's adherents. Conservative Democrats damned Solomon for having faithlessly supported Republicans. Opponents, aware of the potency of associating a person with public dangers or a chief executive's problems, called him a left-winger, a secret Communist, a Henry Wallace supporter. That he had been prominent in the anti-Communist UDA and the anti-Wallace ADA merely exposed Solomon's Red colors. So did his ACLU, public power, and National Lawyers Guild affiliations. Committeewoman Robinson reported "the same old lobby" of private power companies trying to block him.[14]

Sweetland, Robinson, and the Multnomah County Democratic chairperson sent Solomon's name to the White House and the Democratic National Committee in June 1949. They reported him coming in first, with Hess second, in a state party straw poll. Choosing Solomon, they argued, was vital for buttressing Oregon liberals, elevating Robinson and Sweetland in the state party, and revitalizing the Democrats. An Oregon Grange official framed the fight as "the first real test of strength between the new and old" Democratic factions. Robinson rated Solomon a "must" White House appointment.[15]

Solomon's law office orchestrated a shrewd campaign. In Portland, it was headed by Solomon and Kell and in Washington by Assistant Secretary of Interior C. Girard Davidson, the BPA's chief counsel from 1940 to 1946. Kell functioned as co-strategist, expert on bar politics, and general morale-builder. The officemates, sometimes joined by Sweetland, planned, inspired, and coordinated day-to-day tactics. Publicly, Solomon respected custom by projecting a grave, disinterested appearance. Having learned a measure of patience and indirection, he tried to use delicacy and tact to avoid the appearance of politicking on his own behalf.

Davidson was well versed in congressional and administration niceties. He belonged to the Wardham Park group, which had helped fashion Truman's winning re-election strategy in 1948. This small remnant of the New Deal had persuaded the candidate to pursue a more liberal course and rally a new coalition that included unions, centrist liberals, African Americans, and the new post-war middle class. Like Davidson, several in the Wardham Park group were well situated to promote Solomon, including Democratic National Committee chair J. Howard McGrath, White House aide Charles Murphy, Federal Security Agency head Oscar Ewing, Assistant Labor Secretary David Morse, and White House Counsel Clark M. Clifford. Clifford and Ewing were among the seven men who Truman took on a post-election celebration cruise, along with Mon Walgren, a longtime Solomon ally from Washington state. Less happily, Attorney General Tom C. Clark, a Latourette supporter, was another of the smiling celebrants.[16]

From the outset, Solomon's offensive crossed institutional, state, and party boundaries. His adroit campaign simultaneously sought a recommendation to the White House and Democratic National Committee, presidential selection, and senatorial confirmation. In Oregon, the strategy was meant to beat Hess and Latourette, demonstrate significant political and legal support for Solomon, and neutralize opponents. In the capital, it was designed to win Justice Department, Democratic National Committee, and White House approval, rally senatorial liberals, and win over enough conservative senators to secure a victory.

Senator Morse was invaluable. He gladly sponsored Solomon, aided by powerful Democratic Senator Warren G. Magnuson of Washington. After Sweetland discovered that Clark's Justice Department was "really digging deep" for information to disqualify Solomon, Morse warned the attorney general and his successor McGrath against attempts to "smear" Solomon's loyalty. The candidate had reason to worry about Oregon's Guy Cordon, however. The junior Republican senator opposed public power when, as Kell reported, "the public versus private power fight is still a hot one in Oregon." Yet, in 1944, Cordon had benefited when Solomon turned liberals against his Democratic senatorial opponent, Willis Mahoney. Insiders wondered about Cordon returning the "blue slip" that senatorial courtesy and reciprocity required from both home-state solons (signifying both approved of the nominee) before the Judiciary Committee would schedule hearings.[17]

Solomon gathered support from the Oregon Democrats' liberal wing, farm groups, public-power forces, and civil libertarians. State Senator Richard L. Neuberger, a rising party figure, warned the White House that nominating Latourette would demoralize Truman's supporters in Oregon. Speaking for a largely Republican constituency, the Master of Oregon's Grange extolled Solomon's contributions to the state's rural electrification movement. The ACLU and the American Jewish Committee warmly recommended him; and he drew endorsements from several judges, a reputable number of mainstream lawyers, and several bankers and businesspeople identified with public power.[18]

"The road to the federal bench is paved with good connections," wags say. Aided by the loose ADA network, the campaign reached into other states. Senator Magnuson, Representatives Hugh Mitchell and Henry Jackson, and recently defeated Representative Mon Walgren gave him strong support. In Colorado, Solomon won endorsements from National Farmers Union president James Patton and *Denver Post* publisher Palmer Hoyt, formerly of the *Oregonian*. (Hoyt later saw the attorney general on his behalf.) Judiciary Committee member Estes Kefauver and other senators from the public-power and liberal wings of the Democratic Party pledged votes. Liberal Senators Paul Douglas and James E. Murray lobbied the attorney general, and Senators Morse and Hubert H. Humphrey coaxed conservative Judiciary subcommittee members to support Solomon.[20]

Within the administration, the campaign mobilized Agriculture Secretary Charles Brannan and a fellow liberal, Interior Undersecretary (soon Secretary) Oscar L. Chapman. Chapman, who had known Solomon since the 1930s, visited an unfriendly Louis A. Johnson but failed to persuade the defense secretary that it had been Sweetland, not Solomon, who had opposed his 1940 vice-presidential ambitions. Willis Mahoney relayed that his friend Secretary Johnson planned in August 1949 to "go to the President if necessary to block Solomon."

But if new Democratic National Committee chair William Boyle Jr. "goes against us we wont [*sic*] fight it out in" the Justice Department. On October 4, either Johnson or former Portland Mayor Carson called J. Edgar Hoover's office at the FBI to complain about the purely political appointment of this "Communistic 'son-of-a-gun'" to the judgeship. Fortunately for Solomon, Truman was rapidly losing confidence in Johnson, who he forced to resign soon after the outbreak of the Korean War.[20]

Proponents and opponents jolted along public and concealed lanes. Solomon, the veteran of bruising battles, considered benchseeking to be another struggle where one doggedly rallied supporters and confounded adversaries. Facing tough, sometimes ruthless, opponents, he meant to get results. He and his camp animated, cajoled, and mollified individuals and groups. They meant to offend no one unless somebody gave serious offense. Sweetland was instructed not to praise socialized medicine when lobbying a mildly liberal federal appellate judge. Solomon did not mean to be all things to all people, but he and supporters were shrewd. They tailored appeals and evidence to the recipients' attitudes and interests so they would hear what they wished to hear. To partisan Democrats, he was a devoted Democrat. To moderate and liberal Republicans, he was a supporter of Wayne Morse. New Dealers and Fair Dealers were assured that he was in their camp. Anti-Communists were reminded of his strong anti-Communist record. Those sensitive to the opinions of veteran groups, the FBI, or prosecutors heard him favored by an individual or two from each background. They were invited to form inferences that ignored or downplayed criticisms of Solomon. Of course, the officeholders and political operatives among them were not naive about such evaluations.[21]

Cumulatively, the campaign cratered Solomon's existence. Three energetic sons, ranging from ages three to eight years old, bombarded their parents with questions about what was happening. The Solomons were not sure how to answer. Something bitterly partisan, ideological, and personal, adults might have been told. Solomon usually was cautiously optimistic, but now advisers sometimes had to calm him. Accumulating uncertainties and the tension from assaults on him and Libby might have brought on his prolonged "nervous stomach" in the fall of 1949 and his over-eating by spring. In March 1950, he said, "It seems to me that irresponsible attacks against me or members of my family will continue until I am confirmed."[22]

The opposition had to be continually dampened. Davidson asked: "Is there any way of getting Tom Mahoney, Les Josselin, etceteras to keep quiet?" Solomon futilely asked Democratic state chair Josselin to cease hounding him for past membership in the National Lawyers Guild and to stop insinuating that he was a Communist. He apparently used mutual friends to stop Josselin's Democratic partner, the influential state senator Tom Mahoney, from Red-baiting him. (John McCourt had defeated him for district attorney a year earlier.) Mahoney now complimented the candidate on separating himself from "former pink activities" and conforming to American traditions.[23]

Judge Latourette did not withdraw after Solomon's name reached the White House. Early in June 1949, he traveled to Washington to lobby the president, vice president, Attorney General Clark, the chief justice, high Democratic Party officials, and the state's Republican delegation. Weighing against him were his sixty-two years, since unwritten Justice Department policy established sixty as a nominee's age limit.[24]

For a year and a half, conservative Democrats and the Oregon business and Republican establishments "had a mild case of apoplexy" about Solomon's quest, Kell recalled. His "race and liberal affiliations were street corner and table conversations." Some opponents assumed that he could never divorce his strong personal views from his judicial role. Galling rumors circulated that he would favor Jewish over non-Jewish parties and lawyers. "I was called a Jew-Communist" despite an anti-Communist record, Solomon angrily recalled. His old antagonist, former Mayor Carson, "went to Washington to protest my nomination on the ground that the people of Portland didn't want a Jew for a federal judge" and to lobby for Latourette.[25]

Anti-Semitism, even McCarran's, never proved conclusive. The recent war, fought by an officially democratic and anti-fascist America, had brought dramatic changes in ethnic and racial attitudes and practices. The social and economic situation for Jews greatly improved after the war. In higher education, housing, recreation, and jobs, the opportunities for Jews improved while anti-Semitism, a historic element in fervent anti-Communist circles, grew less respectable, less articulated, and more evasive. In Oregon, organized anti-Semitic groups virtually disappeared, and anti-Jewish violence became rare. Genteel anti-Semitism and harsher club and employment barriers against Jews, however, remained intact.[26]

Such changes helped Jews to join the movement of other white ethnic groups into the American mainstream. By 1949, Protestantism, Catholicism, and Judaism were symbolic coequals in the public sphere. Jews increasingly were part of the business, legal, academic, and intellectual elite. Jewish families climbed into the middle class, abandoning immigrant neighborhoods for the expanding suburbs. The immigrant Jewish world virtually disappeared. As Beth Wegner writes, Jewish "life became solidly dominated by a generation of Jews whose ethnic identities and communal institutions reflected their American roots" — that is, by individuals such as Gus Solomon.[27]

The would-be judge affirmed his Jewishness while avoiding any appearance of being Jewry's stealth candidate. He did not solicit Jewish organizational support; but after the American Jewish Committee's Washington lobbyist volunteered to talk to senators, Solomon asked for an intercession with administration patronage-handlers. Once nominated, Solomon successfully cited anti-Semitism as one reason why a Nevada Jewish lawyer should urge McCarran to vote for him. Sweetland feared that McCarran and Republican Senator William Langer, from the reviewing three-member Judiciary subcommittee, meant to stop Solomon.[28]

Contrary to what Kell and Solomon thought, no coordinated opposition formed. Kell named Judge Claude McColloch of the U.S. District Court for Oregon as the anti-Solomon ringleader. The candidate gave the title to former Portland FBI Agent-in-Charge Howard I. Bobbitt. Solomon did know that McColloch, a Democrat whose judicial appointment the Oregon Commonwealth Federation had resisted in 1937, "was very much opposed to me" and was strongly for Latourette. An *Oregonian* columnist asked: "Does McColloch think his visit to Atty. Gen. McGrath to block Gus's appointment is secret?"[29]

Louis E. Starr, a past commander-in-chief of the Veterans of Foreign Wars — who had been embarrassed by Solomon when he was a 1930s Portland School Board member — also erected roadblocks. Starr sent senators old Red Squad reports that mentioned Solomon and intervened against him at top Washington levels. *Oregon Journal* editor Donald J. Sterling Sr., a Democrat, spearheaded another anti-Solomon cohort. He counseled Latourette and arranged letters, emissaries to Washington, and sympathetic coverage of him. Sterling closeted with Willis Mahoney, who was mailing old Red Squad reports to the White House, the Democratic National Committee, and Secretary Johnson. The *Journal* treated Solomon caustically in news and editorial columns, but its backing of Dewey in 1948 reduced Sterling's influence at the White House.[30]

Solomon later acknowledged that, due to his record on unpopular causes, he was not "the kind of man the leaders of the bar would go for." Nevertheless, he reported in July 1949, "The support I am getting from lawyers exceeds my fondest expectations." Everybody assumed that most members of the Oregon bar wanted a Republican or at least a conservative Democrat in the post. Before the Oregon State Bar polled attorney preferences, Kell lobbied every Democratic and liberal attorney he knew, especially the younger ones. While Latourette led the poll, Solomon won a solid minority of votes, keeping him the front-runner, Kell thought. Sweetland partly offset Latourette's showing by surveying party registrations of all bar members except in three counties. Newspapers reported that four and a half Republican lawyers practiced for every one who was a Democrat.[31]

Judges endorsed Solomon as well. Oregon Supreme Court Justices George Rossman and Arthur D. Hay and circuit judge James R. Bain provided letters or affidavits. From Tacoma, U.S. District Judge Charles H. Leavy, a former public-power attorney who had experienced his own confirmation difficulties, lauded Solomon to his friends Senators Magnuson and Kefauver and White House Assistant John R. Steelman. Like McColloch's behind-the-scenes intervention, these actions violated the popular notion that judges ought not to engage in political controversies.[32]

The American Bar Association, which Justice Douglas characterized as mainly representing "the big corporate and financial interests of the country," claimed to be the pre-eminent evaluator of would-be jurists. The Judiciary Committee wanted ABA review of nominees, but so far the committee had not accepted its recommendations. Senator McCarran declared that he was "firmly resolved the bar association shall not choose the judiciary of the country." Then, in the summer of 1949, a member of the ABA's Standing Committee on the Federal Judiciary slipped into Oregon and reportedly talked only to the state's outgoing delegate to the ABA Board of Governors, not its incoming pro-Solomon delegate or anyone else. On August 5, the ABA committee recommended Latourette and three others — not Solomon — to the Justice Department.[33]

FBI opposition was as least as potent as ABA disapproval, and the Bureau performed a mandated and basically unfriendly investigation. Agents relied heavily on former Red Squad informers and old Red

Squad reports. After summarizing largely derogatory, unsubstantiated, and rancorous information, accusations, and innuendoes, the Bureau concluded in September 1949 that the nominee "has been associated with several organizations which have either been cited by the House Committee on Un-American Activities as being Communist infiltrated or dominated or declared within the purview of Executive Order No. 9835 by the Attorney General." The House committee had reckoned the ACLU a Communist group, and the attorney general's list of subversive organizations included the National Lawyers Guild. J. Edgar Hoover called Solomon a "questionable applicant." Attorney General McGrath, Solomon said, now seemed "hesitant about recommending my appointment to the President because of the opposition of the private power companies and certain self-avowed patriots who are raising the 'Red' issue on me."[34]

NOMINATING AND CONFIRMING

The Justice Department had no clear-cut criteria for evaluating FBI reports and considered each on an *ad hoc* basis. Solomon passed McGrath's review, and the Democratic National Committee approved him. On October 13, 1949, the attorney general recommended him to the White House. President Truman, who typically ignored district court vacancies until he received the names, insisted on making all the final selections. Sweetland hurried to the White House to lobby staff members. Ushered unexpectedly into the Oval Office, he was asked at once if Solomon was or had ever been a Communist. "No, Mr. President, and I have here . . ." — Sweetland began, reaching for materials in his briefcase. Truman waved them away. "Oh, that's enough, that's enough. That's all I want to know," Sweetland remembered Truman saying. "Now let's talk politics." Sweetland always believed that the Oregon liberals' loyalty to Truman in 1948 was a major reason why the chief executive approved Solomon. "Truman put a lot of store in loyalty," Sweetland concluded. Political scientists agree on Truman's strong loyalty to those who backed him in 1948. He also sent more Jews (eleven) to district courts than any previous president had. The president sent Solomon's name to the Senate on October 15. For several days, "Solomon literally walked on air up and down the streets of downtown Portland to hear and feel the responses" to Truman's endorsement, Kell recalled.[35]

On October 15, Democratic senators fighting Truman over patronage issues blocked all judicial nominations. After Congress recessed, the president gave Solomon and his other nominees temporary commissions (recess appointments) on October 21. Solomon was sworn in on November 14, but he was careful to retain his law office furniture. Incumbency was an advantage. But, Sweetland figured, "We still weren't over the hump." Truman resubmitted all of the names of his recess appointees on January 5, 1950. Both Oregon senators returned Solomon's "blue slips," ending the threat of Cordon's informal veto. Cordon now wanted the subcommittee to hear the nominee respond to the filed accusations.[36]

In Solomon's favor was the strong presumption of senatorial confirmation, particularly of a sitting judge, if both home-state senators agreed — despite controversy in their state or in the executive branch. But these were not usual times. "These are days of hysteria here in Washington augmented by such attacks as those being made by McCarthy on the State Department," Morse reported in 1950. The "communist issue" was saturating several gubernatorial campaigns and many House and Senate contests. Democratic primaries and general elections would return a number of prominent liberals to private life.[37]

The ABA continued trying to keep Solomon a private citizen. In December 1949, it announced that neither his record nor other lawyers' opinions about his career justified making him a judge. The nomination, the ABA charged, had been made "for political reasons and not on the basis of merit." The statement set off an Oregon firestorm. Numerous lawyers — not just Solomon's supporters — called the ABA inquiry inadequate or the finding wrong and demanded specific evidence. Fifteen Oregon attorneys petitioned for an ABA reversal. An angry Senator Morse now offered to testify to the Judiciary Committee. Solomon wryly commented: "I did not know how many friends I had among the lawyers and judges in Oregon until I was being considered for the position." The *Oregonian* reendorsed him, and the *Oregon Journal* freshened its attack. A hard-pressed ABA reevaluated the nominee and on January 27, 1950, stated that it neither opposed nor recommended him.[38]

But there was still opposition. Top Portland General Electric Company officers assured the judge that company resistance had ended with his recess appointment, but Pacific Power and Light Company officers remained antagonistic. So did Portland General Electric's Washington lobbyist, Willis Mahoney, and his son Daniel, who was Judge McColloch's law clerk. The Mahoneys appealed to Senators Langer and McCarran, and Daniel Mahoney darkly warned McCarran against having "a man of Mr. Solomon's record to be not only Federal Judge but in charge of the Calendar" in a district near the Atomic Energy Agency plant at Hanford, Washington. The successful candidate, too, might rule on the Columbia Valley Authority (similar to the Tennessee Valley Authority), should Congress approve it.[39]

Through all these maneuvers, Solomon conveyed the immense deference that senators expected of nominees. Any hint of Judiciary Committee interest or disquiet produced appeasing details and affidavits that subtly burnished the senators' image of themselves as, in the words of Michael J. Gerhardt, "independent judges of the characters of the nominees and guardians of judicial independence, rather than just party hacks." Guided by Washington advisers Abe Fortas and former BPA Counsel Herbert S. Marks, Solomon warily and methodically prepared to face the subcommittee.[40]

Before the May 4 hearing in Salt Lake City, McCarran's assistant J.G. Sourwine told Solomon that it was improper for a nominee to be present unless asked, so the nominee only sent witnesses. Sweetland suspected the anti-Communist zealot Sourwine and wondered if he and McCarran had already disqualified Solomon. Solomon sent an establishment witness lineup, which included banker E.B. Mac-Naughton, who was also president of Reed College and the *Oregonian,* and two pre-war state Republican chairpersons, Lamar Tooze Sr. and Chester E. McCarty. Only infirmity prevented Charles Hart, the dean of Portland's bar and Allan Hart's father, from appearing on his behalf. Subcommittee member Garrett Withers, a Kentucky Democrat, was impressed that "some of the finest citizens appeared [for Solomon], bankers, others, men who were not Jews." No representatives of organized interest groups appeared.[41]

The hearing was not the mere formality Morse had predicted. The senators showed keen interest in the nominee's political beliefs and loyalty. They were angry that they could not question him directly but cooled down after learning of Sourwine's instructions. Solomon said: "Langer objected very strenuously to the introduction of any affidavits on my behalf on the grounds that the Committee had no opportunity to interrogate" their makers. "Yet they were willing to accept as evidence the unsupported statements of my attackers." His witnesses had "a rough time." A rehearing was set for Washington, D.C., on June 4. Solomon was told to be present and to furnish a bar association endorsement. Langer also wanted his nephew in Portland, lawyer Cleveland Cory, to submit an evaluation. The Multnomah County

Bar Association duly voted an endorsement, and Cory sent Langer a complimentary letter. Solomon pasted a hodgepodge of current-event clippings into a scrapbook, in seeming anticipation of queries on current events. "Keep cool and calm," Morse's assistant advised.[42]

Solomon did not look "forward with enthusiasm to testifying on his own behalf before a Committee questioning his qualifications," he afterward admitted. That day, Senator Magnuson sat in the committee room, radiating his powerful backing. Gratefully absent was a campaigning Langer. (The FBI had not yet completed a supplementary inquiry into Governor Martin's spy files and could not intervene.) The proceedings were routine at first. "Gus made a routine but short speech," Kell remembered. "The questions were few and supportive and the Chairman announced sentoriously, if there was no further testimony on the confirmation," when Daniel C. Mahoney, attired in an Air Force uniform, rose unexpectedly and asked to testify. Under oath, he charged Solomon with belonging to an unnamed organization intent on overthrowing the government and replacing it with a Union of Soviet America. Solomon had belonged to a law firm that handled Communist Party matters, he charged. "That silenced the committee for a moment," Kell reported. Mahoney flourished reports attributed to Governor Martin's secret operative Lawrence A. Milner in the 1930s. Against Senator Withers's skeptical questioning, he insisted that he was not prejudiced and was appearing on his own behalf, not as a surrogate for his father or Judge McColloch. McCarran and Withers questioned Mahoney's legal points and demanded personal knowledge rather than hearsay. They subpoenaed Milner and continued the hearing. The *Oregon Journal* headlined the story on June 5: "Portland Law Clerk Tags U.S. Judge Commie." The next day, the paper screamed: "Solomon, Commies Linked by Witness."[43]

On June 9, Withers ripped into Milner, sometimes aided by an obviously rankled McCarran. The reluctant, embittered former operative tried to use some of his old reports to insinuate that Solomon was disloyal. He finally confessed to not having knowledge of certain events on which he had reported and to not knowing whether Solomon had been a Communist. He claimed never to have said that he was one. That Milner was a known perjurer in two trials of longshore union president Harry Bridges did not help him.[44]

Character witnesses had been hastily arranged. Former Republican state chair Ralph Cake testified that he did not know Solomon but that Morse's assurances were sufficient for him. The managing partner of Portland's largest law firm, David Lloyd Davies testified favorably. Both Oregon senators, Senator Kefauver, and others testified to Solomon's merits, loyalty, and good reputation. The nominee reviewed two decades of activities and denied Milner's allegations and knowing what prompted them. He avoided Sourwine's pointed questions by balancing his ACLU and ADA backgrounds against a host of politically innocuous affiliations. When asked, he denied Communist Party and Communist-front membership. In a prepared statement, he expressed a belief in the law as the fundamental guarantor of personal liberty and property rights and his uncompromising opposition to any system predicated on suppressing liberty or prompting lawless reigns. A judge's foremost duty, he intoned, was to maintain the integrity of the American system of law and its courts.[45]

Afterward, Solomon generally felt confident of approval. Many "previously lukewarm toward my nomination are now among my most enthusiastic supporters," he said. He walked on side streets "because I am stopped too often on the busy ones." His "position in Oregon has been strengthened considerably as a result of the attack made against me" in the hearing. Presiding over a jury case containing six major legal points "doesn't bother me one bit [after] what I went through in Washington." He had not realized "before how much I really enjoy this business of 'Judging.'"[46]

Unanimous subcommittee approval came on June 21, 1950. Five days later, all but one member of the Judiciary Committee approved his appointment. The next day, while North Korean armored units battered the outskirts of Seoul, the Senate — by voice vote — easily confirmed Solomon. His campaign had successfully contained the controversy to Oregon and profited both from the opposition's failure to coalesce as a single force and from the historic senatorial tradition of concurring in one another's judicial choices. With "no ambitions to go any higher," Solomon gratefully hung Truman's picture in his chambers. Suspicion of him had not been put to rest, however, and he knew it.[47]

Chapter 6

Settling In

Mere talk has to be implemented by action. If you believe in democracy, you must do things in a tangible way.

—Gus J. Solomon, 1950

FRESHMAN JUDGE

From the hurly-burly of politics, Solomon eased into the quiet, marble-trimmed home of Oregon's sole federal district. Chambers and courtrooms, including one set aside for the Ninth Circuit Court of Appeals, filled the sixth floor of the courthouse in downtown Portland. Bankruptcy referees and the U.S. Attorney's Office occupied the fifth floor; the Clerk of Court, staff, and a post office were on the lower floors. Two courtrooms and Senator Wayne L. Morse's office topped the imposing, seven-story building. Only about five percent of the district's cases were heard elsewhere — in Eugene, Pendleton, Medford, and Klamath Falls.

Press coverage of Solomon almost ceased after his appointment to the court. Federal judges seldom were objects of much public attention and were rarely known outside their own districts. Few non-lawyers even knew their names. Nevertheless, in the post-war period, federal judges basked in a warm public trust. They carefully fostered their reputations as alert and strong individuals full of high purpose, above everyday influences, impartial, open-minded, and amply equipped for their great responsibilities. District judges in the early 1950s

led an unruffled existence. Their decisions, except for the occasional criminal case, were scarcely noticed outside legal circles. The federal judge was a pillar of the community. He could expect to serve out his career to the accompaniment of universal esteem; at the occasional banquet in his honor, he would be the object of widespread tributes. And when he retired, he could look forward to encomia in the press extolling his dedicated public service.[1]

Treated as solemn symbols of the law's majesty, district judges evoked and required deference. On the street, men might tip their hats to them, and nobody cursed in their presence. Monroe Sweetland remembered that he and Solomon laughed about the "obsequious and pleasant" manner of attorneys who had recently opposed his appointment. Because of tradition or fear of harming their interests, lawyers behaved in a circumspect, even diffident fashion in a judge's presence. Stylized courtroom arrangements and rituals reinforced institutional solemnity. Everyone rose when jurists entered and left their elevated benches. Only court personnel handed them documents. Judges, court staff, and counsel dressed conservatively and comported themselves civilly. Adding to the dignified aura, Chief Judge Fee and Judges McColloch and Solomon adopted black robes in 1950.[2]

In speeches, federal judges conventionally confined themselves to grand and portentous remarks. Some chose stony faces and reticence in court, as if to appear oracular. But not the gregarious Solomon, who, Bernard Jolles thought, hated "a lot of this pomp." Solomon much preferred plain legal dealing and speaking. Starchy and orotund lawyers and judges — and most particularly the bar's grandees — never appealed to him. Nor did checking his spontaneity. On the bench, Solomon might mention personal experiences or friends, allude to his good appellate record or his former controversial reputation, refer knowingly to a witness's family, call a counsel by first name, label a drug informer a "rat" (then hastily assure the press that informing was legal), tell attorney Bernard Jolles "I love you like a brother but I am going to rule against you," or comment on the Alice-in-Wonderland character of a hearing. The judge "was a true character," John A. Ryan concluded, with "an inner place that could be ignited when he thought something was absurd."[3]

Courthouse life in the 1950s was almost intimate. Because a handful of Portland law firms handled most federal matters, the same few attorneys appeared in court over and over again. As late as 1965, Solomon estimated that about fifty experienced attorneys among about a thousand in the Portland metropolitan area handled the bulk of federal civil litigation. Many considered federal practice impractical or undesirable. Federal remedies had not yet gained much popularity, and little federal law was taught in law schools before the 1960s. In Oregon, "people were fearful of the federal court," Otto R. Skopil Jr. concluded, "including me when I first started practicing." Pat Dooley hated entering the courthouse "because you were just walking into a bunch of abuse." Its jurists "were under the impression that they had been beatified or something."[4]

Federal judges constitute a life-tenured, independent-minded, role-conscious elite group that is protective of their independence and authority. Their tasks "are so elaborately prescribed and delineated by custom, statute, and professional codes that judges are among the most role conscious of American public officials," a legal historian has written. Statutes and tradition confer substantial discretion on district judges; they set the pace, direction, and goals of their courts and made decisions and resolved disputes even after higher courts had laid down controlling doctrines. They could independently affect legal policies and doctrines. Sitting in courts of equal jurisdiction, a district judge was not bound to heed or take note of the decisions of a district judge elsewhere. Within the federal judiciary, issues of great public consequence also reached them first. Higher courts might not address an issue or set of issues for years, if ever, or not offer them sufficient guidance on key points or definitions. And while their demeanor and opinions were reviewable, district judges' rulings were seldom overturned. Over 80 percent of Solomon's first decade of opinions resulted in affirmations of his opinion, including a record seventeen straight affirmations.[5]

"The district courts know what their business is — disposing of cases by trial or settlement with fairness and with the optimum blend of prompt decision and rightness of result," Judge Henry J. Friendly writes. They "also have the responsibility of demonstrating the quality of federal justice to ordinary citizens — parties, witnesses and jurors." District judges labor primarily as fact-finders, and they explain their decisions, if they wish, in the light of the facts that have persuaded them. Unlike their legal interpretations, their basis for interpreting facts is largely immune from review, precedent having established that the facts stood unless "clearly erroneous." In order to be overturned, rulings on motions had to constitute an abuse of discretion. Because courts of appeal reviewed fewer than 15 percent of their opinions and the Supreme Court examined only about 150 circuit decisions in the 1950s, district judges usually had the last word. On appeals, "heed is given to his estimates of credibility, his determination of the facts, his discretion in framing or denying relief upon the facts he found," a member of the overwhelmingly male institution explained. "Justice stops in the district," another judge expanded. The parties "either get it here or they can't get it at all."[6]

A district court's work style prior to the mid-1960s, in one appellate judge's later estimation, was "leisurely, relaxed, clubby, comfortable, perhaps slightly complacent, perhaps slightly amateurish." Unwritten rules and usages and time-encrusted approaches weighed heavily as newcomers such as Solomon learned the ways of judicial craftsmanship, autonomy, and accountability. Mastering and implementing the complex practices and folkways demanded concentration. One thing was clear. Districts tried cases, or "if a trial was not appropriate, the dispute would, in all likelihood, be dismissed — or settled, but without intervention of the courts." Fee believed that settlements were none of a court's affair.[7]

Solomon began as a modest, even self-censoring presence in court affairs. Respectful and eager to learn, he appreciated Judge Fee's advice. Many attorneys believed that neither Fee nor McColloch had wanted him on the bench. Solomon knew of McColloch's enmity but claimed that a "tough" and "very stern" Fee welcomed him. Much of the bar considered the austere, archly conservative chief judge irascible, autocratic, haughty, or tyrannical. McColloch was more popular, except among liberals because of his antagonism to anti-price-fixing laws and for his routine rulings against the Social Security Administration. Solomon meant to get along with both of them.[8]

Solomon had once complained that the federal courts forced the legal profession to waste time, but Fee's "pre-trial conferences are an invaluable aid in the disposition of litigation," he now decided. They narrowed issues, identified the evidence and witnesses to be used at trial, and forged agreements on uncontroverted issues. In contrast, Fee's weekly "calls" appeared to badly waste time and create unnecessary legal expenses. Every Monday, Fee set the master call, motion, and pre-trial conference calendars; demanded case status reports; and, sometimes without prior notice, rendered decisions on cases taken under advisement. Having to be present every Monday while awaiting a decision or planning a case made federal practice largely unaffordable to lawyers who represented poor clients or who were paid only if they won. Competent legal representation, Solomon still believed, ought not to be a luxury.[9]

Fee disapproved of many provisions in the *Federal Rules of Civil Procedure*. Issued in 1938, they were part of the slow reversal of conditions that had largely given contending parties and their counsel control of the legal process. Its instigators intended "to remove technical obstacles and create a flexible, unified civil process." Successive versions of the civil rules addressed the problems of "complexity, waste, and injustice" in the courts. They virtually replaced common-law pleading with notice pleading, and they established pre-trial conferences, evidence "discovery" through depositions, and other mechanisms. To Lawrence M. Friedman, pre-trial proceedings "started to overshadow the trial itself." By the 1960s, a "civil process based on the *Federal Rules of Civil Procedure* has largely replaced trials with motions," according to Stephen Yeazell. To admirers, the civil rules made trials fairer and decisions less subject to trial tactics. Winning by surprise or trickery, the "sporting theory of justice," basically ended. Otto R. Skopil Jr., a future Solomon colleague, believed that the civil rules "eliminated, to a great degree, incompetence in the federal courts." Judge Fee rigidly enforced them in a vain hope that rebellious lawyers would force their rollback by Congress.[10]

To Judge Solomon, the federal rules were "the most significant improvement in the conduct of cases in the last century." Lawyers, he argued, should know what practices and procedures were expected; then they would have no fear of or reluctance about making federal appearances. A lifelong fan of the civil rules, Solomon exacted compliance with their spirit and, with rare exceptions, their intricate details. Silent about the less innovative *Federal Rules of Criminal Procedure* issued in 1946, he gladly implemented them. Among other changes, successively issued criminal rules clarified and expanded defendants' rights, clarified and simplified indictments and pre-trial motions, limited pre-trial discovery, expanded time periods for raising motions for a new trial and for filing an appeal, and liberalized bail provisions. They created more court uniformity.[11]

Fee's influence on Solomon rapidly waned, and whatever small cheeriness he offered dissipated. They stopped discussing cases after Fee wanted him to decide a case contrary to what he intended. After Solomon protested Fee's strictness toward citizenship applicants from Eastern Europe and his grim quest among them for former fascists and Communists, Solomon was kept away from naturalizing citizens, a task he loved. Fee also refused to let him employ a law clerk until 1952 or have his own courtroom until September 1950, when the appellate court offered him its seldom-used courtroom. Fee generally "had his own ideas," Solomon remembered, "and I wasn't about to start getting in any fights with him."[12]

McColloch and Solomon apparently tried to ignore one another, which was difficult when Fee took them to lunch together in private clubs, to Solomon's silent disapproval, that banned Jews from membership. While Oregon's bar generally viewed the Solomon–McColloch break as permanent, a surface peace prevailed in court. "For many years I didn't fraternize with" either judge because they had different views and interests, Solomon blandly remarked. "Judges are like monks without the unifying bonds of a common faith," Judge Patricia M. Wald explains. They "are consigned to one another's company for life" in the federal system. "Lingering resentments and hostilities must be kept under wraps . . . to preserve the image of a court that is impartial and neutral enough to decide other people's disputes."[13]

"I am enjoying my work immensely," Solomon wrote early in 1950. He felt himself thriving, open to new experiences, and busy. The district handled 709 civil and 190 criminal cases his first year, a small number by later standards but a challenge to a neophyte. Like many of his predecessors, Solomon was a virtual stranger to federal practice, and statutory law had changed drastically since his legal studies. He needed, for instance, greater familiarity with the Administrative Procedure Act of 1946, a law first interpreted as greatly narrowing the judicial review of agency rule-making and administration. He needed also to master the Judicial Code of 1948, which awarded courts and circuit organizations new authority. Fee took account of his limitations at first by largely assigning him negligence, longshore, and accident suits.[14]

Solomon had to familiarize himself with the kinds of cases that dominated the docket. Because federal land occupied more than half the state and natural resources were so important in Oregon, issues related to land and the environment featured prominently. So, too, did admiralty law because of Oregon's coast and navigable rivers. But few cases were large or complex. In Solomon's first decade as a judge, the District Court of Oregon was "sort of a specialized court, where people took cases involving the Bonneville Dam, steamship collisions, Indian affairs, federal timber business, and a few diversity of citizenship private law cases [involving citizens or corporations of another state or country] and regulatory cases," future federal judge Alfred T. Goodwin recalled. Subject matter "jurisdiction was rather narrowly limited." Civil cases mainly involved property issues or the Federal Tort Claims Act. In 1957, the criminal cases mostly entailed the interstate transport of stolen cars, forgery, illegal narcotics, stolen securities, income tax violations, and bank theft, robbery, and embezzlement.[15]

Judging proved to be a very different occupation from lawyering. Inevitably, Solomon made mistakes. Early on, he angrily remonstrated with a jury for refusing to convict a person. Jurors were polled about the impact of his remarks before hearing another case, so strong was the implication that they should avoid not-guilty verdicts. Never again, he said, would he remonstrate with juries. Solomon felt self-conscious about his new position. Like his peers, he was keenly conscious of his office and determined that his actions and appearance match the judiciary's image of impartial and fair-minded dispensers of justice. He resolved to put aside personal likes and dislikes, quit being a special pleader, and stop granting any favors outlawed by statutes or rules.[16]

"Solomon liked me and, as a consequence, he gave my office hell" for years, Wendell Gray recalled. Labor lawyer Sidney I. Lezak (subsequently the longtime U.S. Attorney for Oregon) heard that several plaintiff lawyers expected Solomon to be more sympathetic to injury claims than Fee or McColloch were. Instead, his early rulings created "some feeling that he was leaning over backward to assure the Establishment firms that he was not going to be seen as a tool of the plaintiff bar." Bernard Jolles concluded that the new judge went out of his way to avoid any appearance of favoring the International Woodworkers of America, a former client. "The big firms don't get any special treatment from me, and sometimes even my own dear friends don't do as well as they think they should," Solomon commented. Being popular with the bar and not disappointing friends, he liked to say, were bad judicial policies.[17]

Learning how to judge "usually comes by doing," one legal historian writes. Circumstances and an analytical bent threw Solomon on his own abundant resources. Lacking judicial experience, he could not privately seek guidance from former colleagues. And he enjoyed quarrying statute books, casebooks, legal treatises, and legal journals and reporters. "I would rather read the decision" than a pleader's brief on a Supreme Court case, he typically declared. A growing command of the legal literature freed him from relying on interpretations offered in court or in the parties' documents.[18]

On-the-job learning of trial procedures and case management still seemed insufficient to the freshman judge. "Not all the law is in the books," Solomon decided. "The experience of doing is usually the best experience, and the next-best is to share the experience of others." In 1950, he attended the New Judges seminar at his circuit's judicial conference. The yearly conferences and the Ninth Circuit District Judges Association's meetings broadened his perspectives and contacts. He relied, too, on instructions from the chief judge of the Ninth Circuit, and he pondered reports and statistics from the Administrative Office of the U.S. Courts. After 1959, he could take advantage of the studies and standards formulated by federal sentencing institutes and joint councils. Further, he candidly solicited advice from legal experts. Before his first admiralty suit in February 1950, Solomon confessed ignorance of that standard, if arcane, district fare and asked Wendell Gray for a specialized reading list. Three decades later, he still unhesitantly asked litigators for pre-trial reading matter on the main legal issues.[19]

Solomon quickly recognized that no two federal judges did things in the same way. Throughout his tenure, he incorporated whatever seemed useful from others' handling of calendars, trials, witness statements, and other matters. "Every time I hear a good technique, I add it to my repertoire and try to adapt it to my method of handling a calendar or trying a case." Initially, he copied the general civil and criminal jury instructions prepared by Judge William C. Mathes of Los Angeles, and he later used Mathes's improvements. Over time, he copied Judges Hubert L. Will and Edwin A. Robson of Chicago in cutting out much direct testimony by having expert and lay witnesses submit planned testimony as narrative statements. He also duplicated Will's use of a final, pre-trial conference to ready the pre-trial order. He adopted several criminal pre-trial techniques that had been experimentally developed by Judge James Carter of San Diego. Solomon and Judge William T. Beeks of Seattle bolstered one another's adoption of swift trial procedures after extensive pre-trial preparation. Judge John W. Oliver in Kansas City and Chief Judge David L. Bazelon of the U.S. Court of Appeals for the District of Columbia modeled new court approaches to the mental problems suffered by some accused and convicted people. From Judge Sylvester Ryan in New York, Solomon said that he learned to avoid judicial attitudes of omniscience and omnipotence. And from Judge Theodore Levin and other Detroit judges, he learned how to better handle pre-sentence reports from his district's probation office.[20]

Entering an authoritative lifetime office inevitably affected his relationships. In a broad sense, federal judges exist both in and apart from their communities. Some only committed themselves to noncontroversial areas; a few settled into a near-isolation. Solomon never confused distance with judicial detachment or propriety. Nothing in his past made him want to cocoon within the institution; and his activities, contacts, and friendships expanded. Their own relationship, said Monroe Sweetland, took "on much less political shape and more a personal one." "He could be very kind to people off the bench, [to] people who came to him for help and advice," future Oregon appellate judge Herbert Schwab said. Attorney-friends and liberals visited his chambers.[21]

Many people respected Solomon for avoiding the vanities of power. He appeared highly approachable, unceremonious, and obliging. Restaurant employees and theater- and concert-goers "would come up and greet him with great cordiality and affection," Allan Hart remembered, "and Gus always remembered that person's name and asked about that person's family or situation." He "kept track of people, they liked him, he did favors for them." In 1968, a reporter watched "the horse players and hustlers and securities men and bankers" in a cafe respectfully nod to the judge. Despite claiming that judges led lonely lives because they could not fraternize with many individuals, Solomon fraternized widely.[22]

As a new judge, Solomon reached out to the bar. "My door is always open to the young lawyer" for brief chats or legal business, he boasted. In 1950, Gus and Libby Solomon started to invite young attorneys and their wives to their home for parties featuring current-events discussions. "He was extremely kind," Sidney I. Lezak recalled, "particularly [to] new lawyers coming in from eastern or the top California law schools." Solomon appreciated their intelligence, vigor, and resistance to conservative Oregon ways. For decades, he tried to attract capable young lawyers to the state, and he relentlessly tried to place his law clerks — fifty-four of them during his career — in good local law positions. To "see that lawyers who studied out of state had an opportunity to meet each other and rapidly assimilate into the Oregon State Bar," he rotated four or five of them at a time through his monthly lunches in chambers, Douglas G. Houser remembered. "The great 'coup' was to be invited to more than one of Judge Solomon's lunches during the first year of admission." Generally, Solomon tried to promote various attorneys' careers, break down isolation in the bar, and make bar-court relations less formal. Many a lawyer wished his practical kindness extended to his courtroom and chambers.[23]

THE ESTABLISHMENT

Ascension to the bench profoundly affected Solomon's status and authority, elevating his social rank and leadership possibilities and situating him in a well-educated, esteemed, and affluent national subculture. He was thrust into the very Establishment he habitually criticized. Elite legal and corporate circles prized good relations with federal judges, given their impact on the law and their interests. They and Jewish organizations alike now vied for the judge's presence. He was almost automatically invited to sit at or near head tables; to grace educational, charitable, and other prestigious boards and committees; and to attend functions for movers-and-shakers.

More than ever, Solomon became a regular figure on the banquet and award circuits. His service as a Jew in a major federal post in Oregon was unprecedented. The American Jewish Committee asked him to join and, like the Anti-Defamation League, encouraged him to take a prominent role in the organization. In 1959, he began a long period as chair of the ADL's Oregon Regional Advisory Board. From 1962 to 1974, he served on its National Civil Rights Commission. He developed into a consummate insider, sitting on the dais at Jewish conventions and meetings and enjoying easy access to national Jewish leaders. "With all our activities in Jewish and non-Jewish organizations," he later complained, "Libby and I have been forced to eat out as much as five and six times during one week."[24]

Newspapers gradually started writing about Solomon again. He regularly exchanged views or pleasantries with editors, bishops, university presidents, Supreme Court justices, corporate chieftains, White House staff members, and senators. From the outset, the legal profession treated him deferentially. So did a judicial freemasonry disposed to mutual courtesies and to realizing mutual interests. As part of their bountiful exchange of favors and views, district judges recommended one another's children to colleges and law schools and employed them as law clerks. The Solomons regularly entertained visiting and vacationing judges and their spouses and were similarly entertained elsewhere.

Within a few years, Solomon mildly luxuriated in his local celebrity. If a local lawyer failed to recognize him by name or face, he was displeased. At bar association picnics and in a local athletic club, he expected to be a center of attention. But while he liked the attention, he tried to avoid self-importance and other vanities by taking his place on county juries, dialing his own calls, answering the office phone if his secretary was absent, and scorning "stuffed shirts." Do not over-estimate his life, he later cautioned an oral historian. "I have often said that one person can make a difference and that everyone should try." He had "accomplished some things" and participated "in some good fights," he reflected after a quarter-century on the bench, yet "I haven't continuously engaged in worth-while activities."[25]

Solomon's position, recognition, and authority could have made him a self-satisfied insider and consort of local and visiting grandees and eased his absorption into the nation's Establishment — that web of families and large corporations and their banks and law firms, higher federal officials, national media, and renowned research universities and foundations. Despite decades of trying to swim in the political mainstream, he edgily considered himself an outsider, with an outsider's perspective, and sometimes an oppositionist. Belonging to the Establishment did not come easily, given his penchant for skewering "stuffed shirts" and the mistaken views, behavior, and values of a host of lawyers, businesspeople, Jews, fellow activists, and officeholders. As a combative liberal and Jew with a long history of dissent and identification with the downtrodden, Solomon — self-consciously at times — felt himself outside the Establishment. Readying a speech to local realtors, for example — a group that would anoint him Portland First Citizen in 1970 despite his longtime opposition to their racial segregation policies — Solomon wryly anticipated being even less agreeable than the Establishment expected him to be. And, after two decades on the bench, when swearing in the BPA's new administrator, he said: "We have come a long way since those early days, and the Administrators and a few others at Bonneville — like one federal judge that I know — have almost become members of the establishment."[26]

As a Jew, Solomon considered himself an outsider in clubby Establishment settings. Most Jews do not see themselves as insiders in American society. "Instead," Cheryl Greenberg broadly asserts, "they view themselves as outsiders who belong beneath the multicultural umbrellas as an insecure minority with a separate culture and set of beliefs and values." As Arthur A. Goren writes, "Though other groups have been torn between a desire to maintain their ethnic identity and an eagerness for full merger into the American mainstream, the strain within the American Jewish group has been especially intense." Increased personal security and prosperity in post-war America did not diminish Jews' struggles over these issues. As the price of full acceptance, Solomon was not inclined to accept diminution of his or his family's Jewish identities, which he strongly associated with "dignity" — that is, maintaining personal and collective Jewish pride and acknowledging others' pride.[27]

Invitations to events in private clubs tested Solomon's group loyalty and his sense that he should not go where Jews could not belong. At first, the Solomons reluctantly accepted the invitations. Beginning in 1956, they declined them without explanation to avoid embarrassing anyone and disguised the separation between his public and private selves. While not asking for an end to club discrimination, he changed his explanations for refusing. He and Libby could not accommodate themselves to club policies hurtful to Jews and would only enter their premises when the Jewish bans ended, he said. "Because I was a judge, it was difficult for me to write these letters because I wanted to avoid doing anything which would adversely reflect on the position." Between about 1956 and 1959, to avoid embarrassing friends and the appearance of favoring lawyer-friends in court, Solomon largely avoided private gatherings that included attorneys. Few knew why, and the prolonged absence of so prominent and sociable a person confused many at the bar. At the same time, he began pressing Jews to challenge club discrimination.[28]

IDEAS INTO ACTION

As a veteran activist brimming with convictions, Solomon felt his way toward how much or how little he could appropriately do to put his ideas into action. "Mere talk has to be implemented by action," he declared in 1950. "If you believe in democracy, you must do things in a tangible way." But how true could he be to his convictions and aching grievances? How could he avoid becoming an ideologue in court? How ought his new responsibilities affect his passionate interest in liberal and Democratic Party gains? As a legal Realist, he was alert to the political implications of judging and was certain that no judge put aside all prejudices. No judge "can totally escape the implicit and explicit ideas about justice and good social order that he or she acquires over a lifetime." Nevertheless, Solomon and federal appellate judges such as Henry J. Friendly and Jon O. Newman believed that, while their opinions sometimes reflected their own values and policy views, they also must act disinterestedly.[29]

Solomon never entirely escaped his inner dialects, nor — if understood as adherence to certain values and connections — did he wish to escape them. Being Jewish, a liberal, a civil libertarian, and an anti-Communist and being true to larger beliefs and to friends were histories he proclaimed. Amid new responsibilities, he had no wish to abandon the best dreams of his youth. He savored the chance to use judicial review and due process requirements to reveal and rectify errors and abuses in American life. Still, particularly at the outset, he was genuinely concerned about whether, how, and to what extent he might act on his convictions and connections. The political choices had once seemed clear. The judicial choices were not always so.

Early on, Solomon gravitated to an animating concept in America's legal and popular cultures: the autonomous judge. District judges possessed ample opportunities to organize the judicial enterprise and take initiatives, despite such limits as an inability to bring legal actions or treat a problem comprehensively. So, they informally established what kind of cases they were willing to consider. They also had considerable discretion in deciding whether a case presented a single transcendent issue or a tangle of competing ones. And if, under the principle of *stare decisis*, judges had to follow precedent, then they still had a volume of precedents from which to choose. They could sidestep one by distinguishing it or hold over a decision to wait for the right precedent. They might try to ignore Supreme Court decisions, as some southern district judges did in desegregation matters until reversed by the Fifth Circuit. A judgeship, Solomon always believed, offered considerable leeway for him to do right, to do good, and to do it his own way. Citizen-activism had taught him much the same.[30]

Doing good was simplest as a board member, public speaker, and money-raiser for noncontroversial nonprofit groups. Solomon addressed Brotherhood Week dinners for some fifteen years until deciding that the critics had been correct: the events indulged lofty ideals without lessening discriminatory behavior. For years, he chaired the board of Portland's Boys and Girls Aid Society. Until he died, he did everything he could to help Reed College thrive financially and intellectually. For decades, he was prominent in Israeli bond drives and money-raising for Jewish charities. He served as a college, university, and law school trustee or visitor. Only revised judicial rules — and then barely — made him stop soliciting charitable contributions from lawyers and, he said, made him resign his Anti–Defamation League positions because of the organization's lobbying and fund-raising.[31]

Being charitable was very important to Solomon. From Jewish religious tradition, he drew the precepts that giving to the poor was an obligation, not a privilege, and that the poor got their righteous due, not charity. Beginning as an impecunious attorney, he regularly tithed to charities. As a judge, the tithing climbed at the pace of or faster than his combined judicial salary and investment returns. He gave $1,217 in 1954, against net earnings of $15,000, and $14,570 in 1985, when he netted $78,475. One lucrative investment increased his giving. Cousins who owned Cohn Brothers furniture store had persuaded him to invest $5,000 in 1943 to obtain 20 percent interest in a mattress factory they were buying. From 1954 to 1962, the share brought him between $6,600 and $49,300 a year. After the factory obtained half-interest in another manufacturer, Leonneti Enterprises, his income climbed markedly. Leonneti "enabled him to become even more charitable," accountant-friend Henry Blauer observed. At the end of 1965, Solomon shifted its proceeds to a trust for his children and charities. In the next decade, he figured that he probably gave "a greater number of contributions to big Jewish organizations than anyone else in the city." Toward the end of life, he doubled them.[32]

So long as he acted discreetly or added protective remarks, Solomon apparently felt little inhibited by the few rules that applied to federal jurists. An American Bar Association Canon of Judicial Ethics existed, but there was no Code of Judicial Conduct until a nonmandatory 1972 ABA Code furnished them an informed measure of behavior. One Canon rule, he said in 1957, barred his soliciting Jewish lawyers for contributions to Jewish charities. Two years later, however, he did exactly that for the United Jewish Appeal. Smiling, he told an audience of Jewish attorneys that nobody monitored their contributions to this central charity collection and distribution agency and that no amount guaranteed them favorable judicial decisions or new clients. And then he appealed to their values and sense of guilt. In a similar manner, he routinely counseled trusted friends and their adult children on legal and legal-personal matters that would never come before him. In 1949, he gave legal advice to an attorney undergoing a federal loyalty investigation and in 1954 to a liberal fired from a federal job. He interpreted statutes, case law, and legal documents for several individuals, advised them how to handle their counsel, and ascertained from court personnel how their cases were proceeding. At least once he drafted instructions to a lawyer on the facts in a possible case.[33]

Solomon, who quit the litigious ACLU on ascending to the bench, remained a donor (through his wife), a prod, and a critic. Several times, he privately suggested whether or when the ACLU's Oregon branch should litigate an issue or appeal a case. He was involved in the rebirth of the ACLU in Oregon, specifically in delaying it. In November 1951, when eighty-five Oregonians belonged to the ACLU, Libby and Gus Solomon (calling himself a visitor) attended a meeting to consider re-establishing the branch. From fear of its capture by former Progressive Party adherents, the Solomons, Allan Hart, Sidney I. Lezak, and other liberals barely blocked chapter reconstitution. Both sides recruited new members to affect a future vote and control. Assisted by Morris Ernst and other anti-Communists prominent in the national organization, the liberals prevailed. Only in November 1955 did the American Civil Liberties Union of Oregon come into being. Chapter leaders Jonathan U. Newman, Mike Katz, and others subsequently formed a separate Citizens Committee on Racial Imbalance in the Public Schools. Solomon advised on its "background," remembered ACLU leader Charles Davis, which persuaded the Portland School Board to take the first steps toward ending *de facto* school segregation.[34]

For an issue-oriented activist, politics presented another arena for doing good. Judicial robes never obliterated Solomon's basic urge for political connection and accessibility. Away from the bench, he was a partisan whose reputation and actions unerringly attracted young liberals such as Keith Burns and older New Dealers to him. He remained loyal to the Americans for Democratic Action guardians of Cold War liberalism and to promoting the unfinished agenda of Truman's Fair Deal. He contributed rolls of untraceable postage stamps to Monroe Sweetland's losing 1956 race for Oregon secretary of state. He recommended Hubert H. Humphrey to influential Oregonians and discussed state strategy with his supporters during the Minnesotan's 1959–1960 bid for the Democratic presidential nomination. He apparently gave money to presidential hopefuls John F. Kennedy (not an ADA member) in 1960, Humphrey in 1968, and Henry M. "Scoop" Jackson in 1972. While in Florida as a judge, Solomon introduced Jackson, a newly announced opponent of affirmative action and the most enthusiastic Cold Warrior among the Democratic contenders, to a Tampa campaign breakfast in February 1972. To Solomon, a federal judgeship need not interfere, if handled with discretion outside court, with being a liberal Democrat.[35]

LOYALTY

As a liberal with his background, Solomon occupied a thornier seat during the early 1950s than he acknowledged. Everywhere, accusations of disloyalty were blackening reputations and discrediting or silencing advocates of social and political change. "This whole loyalty business is becoming more serious all the time," he wrote in 1950. Disturbingly, individuals who he respected — such as Neuberger, Morse, and former BPA publicist Stephen B. Kahn — were falsely being called Communists. Later, he denied that the McCarthyism of 1950–1955 affected the decisions of his district. "We weren't influenced in any way by McCarthy's attacks on people in public and private life." Nor could he recall any case in the district rooted in a public employee's hysterical firing.[36]

The anti-Communist crusade affected Solomon more than he may have recognized. He hated the paralysis of political courage when Americans feared acting on their true convictions. At the same time, he seemed wary of his loyalty being attacked again. He was not cowed or stifled by the crusade, just careful. Cold War fears ran through his 1952 loyalty hearing deposition for Lillie Sweetland, when Solomon referred to their both having suffered from false charges of disloyalty. He was "heartily in favor of the objectives of the Federal Employees Loyalty Program" and believed that the government should not employ Communists, but "it would be a monstrous distortion of the purposes of the program if it were permitted to be a vehicle for the ambitions or prejudices of unscrupulous persons." During the 1950s, the unabashedly patriotic Solomon appeared to be more vituperatively anti-Communist and more vocally patriotic than at any time afterward. In the 1952 deposition, he defined Communists as not only repellent to democracy but also pathologically motivated. Communism to him never threatened America's existence as much as it did in the 1950s, and the struggle to preserve the nation's way of life never so relentlessly required. The United States of 1953, he declared, simply was the greatest country in the world in its enjoyment of freedom, democracy, and security. He repeatedly expressed a deep belief in the country, the Constitution, the Bill of Rights, and market capitalism. American society suffered many grievous flaws; but, he argued in the 1950s, they were redeemable.[37]

National security-driven deportation cases tested his deepest sentiments. Changes in immigration laws and enforcement, especially against former and current Communist Party members, inspired a plethora of deportation cases. In Communist-related ones, as Donald D. Jackson said of judges in political trials, Solomon had "to confront his own loyalties and weigh them: the ideal of justice, the preservation of peace and order as he sees it, the commandments of law, the values of the society he represents, and, tucked away in a curtained corner of his mind, his own well-being, reputation, and ambition."[38]

Tension between Solomon's views on civil liberty and the admitted authority of Congress and the president to rid the country of foreign-born Communists ran through his opinions and bench remarks. No fear of fraudulent claims by noncitizens, he warned in a 1956 Ninth Circuit deportation review, ought to "eclipse our primary consideration — the importance of according to each of our true citizens their precious rights and privileges to which his citizenship entitles him." In a 1951 case, he had said that as a citizen he disagreed that Communists and gangsters, as statute mandated, ought to be deported if they had entered the country as children. Had he been in Congress or the White House, he would have rejected the "terrible" Walter–McCarran Immigration and Nationality Act of 1952. But then he expressed a common judicial view, one consistent with the subsequent Warren Court's general affirmation of the domestic-security program: Congress alone determined deportation conditions. "I do not believe that the courts should be used to thwart the will of Congress, absent some constitutional basis therefor [sic]." Whatever his sympathies, he had sworn to enforce the laws and "call them down the center" for everybody. He ordered the deportation of the alleged Communist standing before him. Similarly, he permitted the Immigration and Naturalization Service great latitude. After ordering another deportation for Communist Party activities, Solomon remarked: "You know how difficult it is for the Court to find an administrative agency or an official to be guilty of abuse of discretion. It is practically impossible to do that." Congress, he repeated, solely determined deportation requirements.[39]

One liberal counsel for accused Communists wondered what had happened to the doughty civil libertarian. To Sidney I. Lezak's chagrin, Solomon in 1953 ordered Lezak's Philippine-born clients deported under the Walter–McCarran Act. The judge, reversed when the Ninth Circuit in a related case established a separate category for those born in the Philippines, "knew these people" through earlier associations with Levenson and Goodman and the Communists in the Cannery Workers Union. Lezak told others that he had "refrained from taking a look at our arguments because he was still so frightened" by pro-Communist accusations during the nomination fight "that he would not put himself in a position" to make "hackles rise . . . I probably said that Solomon was a phony liberal."[40]

The FBI held darker views. After an old informant raised new charges against Solomon in 1953, it launched a secret seventeen-month inquiry. Agents examined whether in the 1930s and early 1940s Solomon had been a Communist Party member or contributor or if he knowingly had connected to the *Labor Newdealer*, called by one agent "an official newspaper of the Communist-dominated Congress of Industrial Organizations Industrial Union Council." The FBI concluded that Solomon had been no more than a fellow traveler and that the informant was unreliable.[41]

Solomon's several *Bryson v. U.S.* opinions likely afforded momentary pleasure to the FBI. Writing for the Ninth Circuit Court of Appeals, the judge upheld the conviction of a union president for falsely swearing to the National Labor Relations Board that he was not "affiliated" with the Communist Party. Saying that he did not believe Bryson's testimony, Solomon applied *Dennis v. U.S.,* which defined the Communist Party as a conspiracy dedicated to overthrowing the government. Fellow panelist Richard H. Chambers congratulated him for being "the only judge able to make a Communist sentence stick" during 1956. A 1957 opinion prompted another FBI inquiry. Solomon had dismissed the prosecution of *U.S. v. Apex* after the attorney general ordered the U.S. attorney not to provide, as his court directed, statements of prospective witnesses for pre-trial examination. To the FBI, the Warren Court's recent *Jencks v. U.S.* and its extension by lower courts, including Solomon's, opened FBI records to unwarranted judicial scrutiny. Director J. Edgar Hoover immediately ordered a review of Solomon's file, again questioning his political views and affiliations. Hoover's command came amid agency horror over four Warren Court opinions on June 17, 1957 — Red Monday to outraged conservatives. The opinions undermined major loyalty-security methods, blunted the zeal with which the Smith Act could be prosecuted, and reined in forays by the House Un-American Activities Committee.[42]

In *Apex*, Solomon ordered that all relevant FBI reports, not just portions or summaries, be provided to the criminal defendants' counsel before trial. "Although the Government may suffer some hardship as a result of this decision," he judged, "it appears from *Jencks* that the opportunity for the defense to prepare its case is more important to our system of justice" than any prosecutor inconvenience. Only twelve days earlier, *Jencks* had illuminated a perennial criminal law issue: a defendant's ability to secure material that discredited prosecution witness testimony. The Supreme Court had stated that classified information in FBI files pertaining to accused persons had to be given to the defense once it demanded specific relevant and competent documents. The Ninth Circuit affirmed Solomon's dismissal of the *Apex* prosecution. In August, Congress enacted the Jencks Act, which codified much of *Jencks* but made trial judges the arbiters of the evidence that was released to the defense. The statute struck the testimony if prosecutors refused to produce a witness's statement instead of requiring, as had *Jencks*, a dismissal of the indictment.[43]

Because of the ambiguities in the Jencks Act, district courts disagreed over how it should be applied. In *U.S. v. Jacobson*, Solomon expanded its scope to dismiss another prosecution that used secret government information. He ruled that a conscientious objector's lawyers were entitled before trial to see his original FBI reports, not just resumés that excluded witnesses' names. A summary of statements to investigators by unnamed individuals, Solomon wrote, "is a shallow and insubstantial basis for a factual determination. In a court it would be inadmissible. In an administrative hearing, even if admissible, it would be highly suspect." *Jencks* "did not deal with this problem, but the underlying principle there expressed is equally applicable here."[44]

In 1958, Solomon admitted to having "interpreted the Jencks case more broadly than any other District Judge in America." Accused people "came to appreciate their rights of access to information in the files of the investigative and prosecuting authorities," Solomon's law clerk Arden E. Shenker observed. "While the criminal prosecutors may have had the legal discretion to withhold the submittal of that information, in Judge Solomon's court it was wise to supply the information." Outside Oregon, Solomon complained, "I have had to use considerable persuasion to get United States Attorneys to release Jencks Act statements in advance of trial." *Jencks* actually changed no district approach. "We have always required in this court" that in hearings "whenever the Government produced a witness who had made a written statement that statement was available to counsel for the defendant for the purposes of impeachment." After *Jacobson* was added to Solomon's *Apex* ruling, an FBI official ordered that his bulky file be maintained, "as Solomon is still [a] controversial figure." The instruction was repeated a decade later in "view of his controversial character and past rulings against [the] Bureau." The FBI had not stopped worrying about threats posed by the now-veteran judge.[45]

(Above) Solomon's family in about 1911. Standing are his mother Rose, Sam, and Eugene. Seated are his father Jacob, Gus, Delphine, and Claire

(Left) Solomon as a young boy

Solomon and his wife, Libby, in about 1945 (left) and 1959 (below)

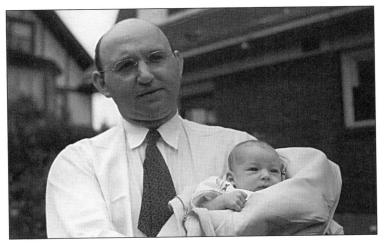

Solomon and his first child, Gerald, in 1942

Solomon (center) with Lillian and Monroe Sweetland

Solomon (second from left) and other members of the Portland Citizens Relocation Committee steering committee on May 22, 1945

A scene from the 1937 longshoremen's strike in Portland

OHS neg. OrHi 78814-8Ar

OHS neg. CN 012201

C. Allan Hart

Sidney I. Lezak

Raymond M. Kell, Solomon, an unidentified man, and Gunther Kraus celebrate Solomon's appointment to the U.S. District Court in 1949

(Left to Right) Otto R. Skopil, Solomon, Robert C. Belloni, William East, and James M. Burns

Solomon at the office

*Attorneys Irvin Goodman and Paul Calicutte, with Tom Mooney (center),
a class war prisoner adopted by the CPUSA, on October 18, 1932*

Solomon, Robert C. Belloni, John F. Kilkenny, and Alfred T. Goodwin

The Gus J. Solomon Federal Courthouse

Judge Solomon

Chapter 7

The Changing Court

*Why don't you give me without all the hocus pocus and all the
rhetoric just the case upon which you rely. I will read them. Just
give me two or three cases. I will study those cases.*

—Gus J. Solomon, 1973

IN CHARGE

During his first years on the bench, Solomon rarely left Portland, so
heavy was Oregon's federal docket. By 1951, he handled most of the
district's cases and seldom could respond to appeals for aid from other
district or appellate courts. He labored six and then seven days a week
because of the mushrooming workload and because Judge McColl-
loch's frequent illnesses kept him in Arizona and Judge Fee was often
absent clearing court backlogs elsewhere. "So, I was home alone, and
I was getting further and further behind," he said. While relishing the
hard work, he fretted about mounting caseloads and backlogs, swelling court expenses, and time- and money-wasting lawyers.[1]

Presiding over what a newspaper called "The Curious Case of the
Hot Bird Ring" sorely tested Solomon. In a steamy San Diego courtroom, the 1953 affair ballooned into the longest trial in his career. The
much-recessed, three-week proceedings crawled over sixteen days.
The defendants, charged with a worldwide conspiracy to illegally im-
port and transport exotic birds, reportedly appeared in "a legal drama
. . . that has all the elements of a movie thriller." A radio station made
the visiting judge, who ran "what the Navy would call a taut ship,"
its Four-Star Citizen-of-the-Day. "Everything that's possible to hap-
pen in a case happened there" to delay and confuse events, Solomon
recounted. One defendant threw fits, was told to stop faking, and was
sent to the hospital with a warning that the trial would continue without him. Two potential witnesses were murdered in Mexico. "There
was jury tampering. One of the lawyers was accused of threatening
witnesses." Jerome Kohlberg Jr. recalled. "Our 'crier' dated one of the

jurors, which nearly resulted in a mistrial, and both the Judge and his law clerk (me) were threatened anonymously." The defendants and defense attorneys were "obstreperous," and "Gus had to sit pretty hard on them, and did. . . . They were trying every trick in the book." Multiple convictions and sentences followed, some reduced on appeal. Later, the chief defense counsel and others were convicted of co-conspiracy and received heavy sentences.[2]

Not long after returning to Portland, the forty-seven-year-old Solomon suffered a coronary attack. Rather than the lengthy recuperation Judge Fee urged, he rested a month at the beach, his first real vacation since 1950, and returned to his grueling pace. The attack alarmed Libby Solomon. "I felt that it was necessary for me to watch what he ate, and go with him whenever he was on assignment," she remembered. During school vacations, they could bring their children. Otherwise, the choice was "whether I stayed home with the boys or took care of Gus, and it was always a heartache to know what to do. But I usually went with him. I was concerned about his health." She watched over the children and his health "like a mother hen," Kohlberg observed.[3]

"They were very close as a couple," Kohlberg and others recognized. Libby Solomon often encouraged him to work less; to attend more of the art, theatrical, and musical events they both enjoyed; and to spend more time with friends and on vacation. The couple cheered one another's participation in liberal, community, and Jewish causes and took pride in each other's accomplishments. "Gus taught me to support the things I really care about," she recalled. The National Council of the American Jewish Congress recruited her, as did the board of a foundation constructing racially integrated housing outside Philadelphia. After attending art school, she served on local arts, zoo, and educational boards. The Solomons quietly commissioned several public artworks, fountains, and musical scores and performances and filled their home with art. Tired of the "stuffiness" and constant self-perpetuation of the Portland Art Association board, they engineered an upset election.[4]

In the district, circumstances changed dramatically when Judge Fee was promoted to the Ninth Circuit Court of Appeals in 1954. The move and McColloch's growing absences lessened the restraints on Solomon's take-charge attitude. For about a year, he conducted most of the court's business. Then, in June 1955, a Republican county judge, William G. East, succeeded Fee. East disapproved of Solomon's courtroom behavior, and he found common cause with McColloch. The Solomon–East relationship ruptured and, according to East, grew "standoffish." But Solomon and others bleakly discovered that East's problems with alcohol were not just rumors. Lawyers complained about his behavior on and off the bench to officials and judges, who struggled to help East regain and maintain sobriety. Western federal judges, Solomon included — fearing for the court's reputation and steeped in a legal culture that idealized autonomous, sovereign judges — tried to shield the district's internal affairs from public view. For a long time, they succeeded.[5]

Through it all, Solomon continued to work hard. In 1960, one newspaper called him a "Human Dynamo," and near the end of his life, a chief appellate judge called Solomon "a veritable judicial work-horse." An early riser, Solomon was usually the first jurist to enter and the last to leave the courthouse. Before any 9 AM hearing or calendar call, he prepared two hours in chambers. There and at home after dinner he worked on speeches, correspondence, and cases. On week-ends, he reviewed his law clerks' work with them. On weekends before trials, he normally reviewed 50 to 125 files to master pleadings, proposed exhibits, and other documents. Every day, he read legal reports, opinions, journals, and articles, legal textbooks, and several newspapers. Every week, he wrote instructions and opinions. As their children grew older, he and Libby attended more plays and concerts, and he began swimming and breakfasting with others at an athletic club. "Used to enjoy playing cards," he said, "but I gave it up when it interfered with my job." Libby Solomon later sighed: "He certainly never left the courthouse even when he wasn't there."[6]

As the 1950s wore on, Solomon developed a plan for his district. McColloch had moved to a nursing home, and East's difficulties encouraged Solomon to take charge months before he became the court's presiding officer. Early in 1958, in line with other districts that were improving their capacities and operations, he started upgrading his district's methods and administration. He pressed it to adopt ways that countered legal uncertainty, unwarranted delays, unneeded costs, and needless hyperbole, disagreements, and spite. Assuming that judges did not bear the sole obligation for good judging, Solomon pressed responsibilities on the bar, law clerks, and court staff. He would not ask them to do what he would not do himself, but neither would he tolerate their doing less than he did. Then, as later, he focused on managing the docket to maintain an orderly and efficient case flow, and manageing cases to better pilot litigation through the courts. "Both of these manifestations of judicial management," Steven H. Wilson writes, "aim broadly to provide the plaintiffs and defendants in federal trials a 'just, speedy, and inexpensive' disposition of their case," as required by the civil rules. Solomon's central role in establishing local rules in 1958, his leadership in their revision, and his legendary implementation of them and the system-wide rules became hallmarks of his career.[7]

Solomon anticipated spirited opposition to new Oregon District rules. He expected lawyers to try to protect their autonomy, prerogatives, and authority and to resist serious alterations in court expectations and routines. Against this tradition, he bluntly asserted that courts had prerogatives and powers to reform themselves. In the interest of efficiency and fairness, the U.S. District for Oregon, he insisted, had an inherent power to control its docket and apply its own rules as to pleadings and practice. Aided by two attorney-friends and after conferring with judges, attorneys, and bar committees, Solomon devised thirty-six local rules to supplement the *Federal Rules of Civil Procedure*. The rules covered a gamut of court and lawyer duties and procedures. Phased in after July 31, 1958, the rules codified various unwritten local practices.[8]

Court reformers such as Solomon argued that in a few years the spiraling caseloads and other forces would overwhelm courts that did not substantially improve themselves. A reform agenda also fit his penchant to move things along as well as his settled view that the bar's ethic extended beyond zealous advocacy. "Like lawyers in every legal system," Robert W. Gordon writes, American attorneys "necessarily also have some duties to third parties, the courts, and the integrity of the substantive and procedural rules of the justice system; but they construe those other duties very narrowly." Not surprisingly, Solomon, with his weighty sense of bar responsibilities, construed its duties broadly. His devotion to local rules, intense pre-trial direction, and other assertive devices placed him in the company of "managerial judges" who were determined to change the legal system. Their advocacy ranged widely, "from highly informal status conferences (sometimes off the record in chambers) to structured regimes relying on formal pretrial conferences or on extensive paper filings," G. Donald Elliott writes. While they disagreed on many issues, managerial judges said "that the system does not work; that *something* must be done to make it work; and that the only possible solution to the problem is *ad hoc* procedural activism by *judges*." Their federal districts tended to codify the successful *ad hoc* procedures.[9]

Solomon soon had the opportunity to be a managerial judge and to stamp his personality and values on the district. In the autumn of 1958, after a year's absence, McColloch retired, leaving an open seat for almost a year. On October 11, 1958, statute awarded the chief judgeship to Solomon, the most senior person. Because East's problems largely kept him off the bench, Solomon essentially filled all court duties until McColloch was replaced. Being called "King Solomon" during the hiatus amused him, and when it ended not a few charged him with still holding fast to the crown. If so, he was a hard-working monarch. He retained almost all of the managerial responsibilities and directed the heaviest caseload to himself. Between Labor Day and the end of December 1959, for example, he conducted nine "jury trials; handled more than 200 pre-trial hearings in which more than half resulted in pre-trial orders; wrote 30 opinions for the District Court as well as the Court of Appeals; handled at least 50 pleas and arraignments in criminal cases; heard 60 motions; and handled the calendar call involving at least 200 items." A year later, he bragged that, largely because of pre-trial efficiencies, he had made quick work of controversies slated for long trials. "Very often I can finish five jury trials a week. On the average, it takes me about 1½ days for a jury trial" in simple cases. A decade later, an obscenity case scheduled by a California district to last five weeks needed fewer than four trial days under Solomon's direction.[10]

In an early action, Chief Judge Solomon terminated the unpopular weekly calls and their unexpected announcements of decisions. Calls were scheduled for the third Monday of each month, which critics said still imposed unwarranted time and financial costs on the parties and lawyers. The local rules retained the district's modified master calendar, but only after setting a final trial date did Solomon assign a trial judge. Until then, he managed routine contract and personal injury suits, small-scale disputes involving the government, and other ordinary cases. On call-days, he set the general calendar, assigned individual pre-trial conference times, and discussed and signed orders. Faced in later years with a growing number of complex securities, patent, anti-trust, and class actions, he usually assigned them and other cases with difficult issues, hefty money claims, or large plaintiff groups to specific judges at the outset.[11]

Solomon ceaselessly defended the local rules as a way to clarify court requirements, speed litigation, and improve the administration of justice. Like calendar control requirements, the rules had a far-reaching effect on judicial decision-making, not just on judicial administration. Beyond giving the Oregon judges more control of the legal process, they shaped how, when, and by whom disputes were resolved and so the final outcomes. Time and again, the bar reacted strongly to the rules, or at least to how he implemented them.[12]

Solomon credited the "tight calendar control, a master calendar system, a current calendar, an educated Bar, and a practical system in which the lawyers do practically all of the work unless the case is actually tried" for the impressive court productivity in Oregon in the 1960s. Under his prompting, the district amended its rules again in 1964 and 1976. Its judges, he said, wished to slow still-rising legal costs and codify their own newer practices, and attorneys wanted to change some rules. New legal developments and system-wide mandates also added provisions, such as a 1964 rule that tightened *habeas corpus* writs and motions and another that banned photography in courtrooms. Pre-trial aspects were spelled out in detail in 1976. The judges "want to streamline the trial in many other ways" without unduly burdening lawyers, he said. In publications and letters, at seminars and conferences, in law schools and law offices, and to his clerks, Solomon preached calendar control and demonstrated techniques to shorten litigation and trials. Probably aware of the criticism of managerial judging, he insisted that his district impaired neither litigant rights nor the quality of advocacy.[13]

On call-days during any three-month period, Solomon estimated that he heard progress reports on about 90 percent or more of the active cases. He prepared by studying four-foot-high stacks of related papers. At a first-time call, he established time schedules for witnesses and discovery of evidence and set a pre-trial conference and trial date. At a later call, Solomon might extend the schedule. If dissatisfied by a case's progress, he unilaterally imposed a schedule, a practice unique to the U.S. District for Oregon. At an advanced stage in the process, he minutely examined proposed pre-trial orders. "During pretrial management," one critic noted in 1982, "judges are restrained only by personal beliefs about the proper role of judge-managers." A year later, amendments to the original 1938 rules clarified judges' pre-trial responsibilities and instructed all districts to issue local rules.[14]

Attorneys uncomfortably felt Solomon's energy focused on them on call-days. It "was the judge's moment," Judy Kobbervig said. "All eyes were on him. He had fun with it." Lawyers jammed the corridors and courtroom, waiting for their tense five-to-ten-minute encounters. Those waiting caught up with gossip, quietly settled suits, and watched the predictable fireworks. "Woe be to those who did not know how many witnesses the lawyer handling the trial planned to call and the issues on which they would be called," M. Christie Helmer remembered. "Woe be to those who responded 'I don't know, Your Honor.'" At calls, Solomon had little patience with uninformed junior counsel sent to handle all of a firm's cases. After a blistering, they had the unenviable task of telling the counsels-of-record to appear immediately. Because of Solomon, Medford attorney James A. Redden grew "more careful about how and who I sued and where," and he and others who were at a distance referred as many cases as possible to Portland lawyers for appearances in the city to avoid costly travel and waiting time. The court, because of its exacting, complicated requirements, "was a place to avoid . . . and the only time [non-Portland lawyers] got in federal court is when they saw some advantage to it or were hauled in by one of the Portland firms."[15]

Solomon assumed that attorneys, not just judges, needed practical guidance. At calls, he used status reports and other matters "to establish the tempo for the cases," which was swift. Monday calls were also meant "to teach lawyers, particularly the younger ones, how to practice in the federal courts" — 75 to 125 at a time. In one exasperated outburst, he ordered one embarrassed attendee to rise. "I want you all to take a good look at Phil Levin. He's always ready for trial anytime I am. He never makes wishy-washy and lame excuses. I want all of you to start doing exactly like Phil Levin does! Stand up and say you're ready for trial whenever I am!" To Otto R. Skopil Jr., Solomon's sometime arbitrary decisions or offensive remarks during calls got in the way of a brilliant educational device.[16]

Redden sympathized with Solomon. The district "didn't have enough judges" for many years, "and unless you keep the cases flowing you really get in trouble." Unless "someone's pushing them," an attorney will "slip that one behind and they'll handle the matter where they're getting pushed by some local state judge." Unless a trial date was set, "lawyers just by nature turn to some other emergency." Often "in litigation one side or one party is in no rush to get it to trial, and if you let them dilly-dally, they will dilly-dally." Thanks to all of Solomon's "you'd better be prepared" speeches, and his and colleagues' requirements, lawyers "don't mess around in federal court" in Oregon.[17]

John F. Kilkenny, who joined the court in 1959, admired the chief judge's trial-shortening techniques, such as his ability in pre-trial conferences to secure concessions that eliminated trial issues and volumes of evidence. The conferences identified the parties' theories and allowed the judge to limit evidence discovery, narrow the scope of trial issues, and rule on issues of law and objections to portions of depositions. What transpired might influence trial tactics or prompt settlements. Everyone knew that between 85 and 90 percent of federal civil disputes are "settled" beforehand and do not reach the trial stage. As a managerial judge, Solomon strongly promoted pre-trial negotiation and settlements. Some suits simply did not belong in court, he declared. Even after trials began, some litigants' agendas were better resolved by negotiations outside court, he thought. A settlement was also superior to a trial if the parties expected a change in circumstances or needed to engage in long-range planning. Future litigation could be prevented if settlements built in flexibility.[18]

When Solomon joined the bench, district judges typically adjudicated legal disputes and stayed above the day-to-day litigation process. Pre-trial conferences were meant to prepare cases for trial; it was merely a welcome side effect if settlements resulted. In the 1960s, a growing number of judges earnestly promoted pre-trial settlements and other active measures. By the 1970s, district judges largely considered themselves problem-solvers and case-managers, not just adjudicators. As Marc Galanter writes,

> There was forthright and ardent embrace of active participation in settlement negotiations. This was based on a warm endorsement of settlement as preferable to adjudication — not on grounds of administrative convenience, but because it produced superior results. . . . Active promotion of settlements is now unmistakably the "established" position in the federal judiciary.

Nationally, 11 percent of civil cases in 1960 proceeded to trial and only 4.4 percent in 1986. What was originally "created as a set of techniques to narrow issues for trial, managerial judging," Elliott wrote in 1986, a year before Solomon's death, "has recently become a set of techniques for inducing settlements."[19]

Solomon denied that the U.S. District for Oregon forced settlements. In fact, he claimed, it applied less pressure to settle than other districts. "I know lawyers resent and I resent when I see how judges in other districts operate [a] pretrial conference in which the judge figuratively takes a bite and hits one fellow over the head and then the other in order to get them to settle the case." Although they might have had other reasons, several lawyers reported settling quickly once Solomon called the other party's offer fair. A resisting litigator from California supposedly yielded to a threat that unless he settled one case Solomon would order him to engage an Oregon co-counsel and thus expensively delay a scheduled major tariff case. Even after a trial started, Redden said, "Gus generally would get on one of the attorneys." He meant "to keep people off balance, and I think always in the back of his mind it was to make it slightly unpleasant so that you'd settle the case. . . ."[20]

Solomon's forceful management during the pre-trial and trial stage could agitate lawyers. His stylized pre-trial order, for example, listed all impending exhibits (which might run up to a thousand in complex suits), witnesses, depositions, and contentions, what portions of the depositions would be introduced, the theories on which counsel depended, and why they ought to win. Other than setting out issues of fact and law, the order might include memoranda of authorities on contested legal issues. After both sides signed, the pre-trial order prevailed. Jack Collins noted that this order included a line "that some lawyers still think is not appropriate" stating "that the pleadings pass out of the case" and the order replaced the original complaint, answer, and reply. "Well, a lot of people didn't understand it and they got caught" omitting something. They questioned any court's authority to discard a complaint and answer. But to Collins the order usefully forced the parties to settle or go to trial and mapped everybody's trial plans. As "Judge Solomon used to say," Collins remembered, "'There are no surprises in this court.'"[21]

Solomon used trials, pre-trial settings, speeches, meetings, swearing-in ceremonies, and oral and published reminders to gain compliance with the local and national rules. At a swearing-in admitting lawyers to federal practice, each attendee expected a short lecture from Solomon and braced for sharp questioning on the rules. "As a realistic matter, no effort to improve the conduct of the legal profession is going to succeed without the help — ideally, the enthusiastic help — of the judges," observers pointed out. Attorneys at their peril ignored the local rules mandated by federal courts during Solomon's tenure. They complied only reluctantly, Solomon publicly said, because they disliked altering the legal system and liked procrastinating. He charged lawyers with being the worst procrastinators among the professions and denied one preliminary injunction because opposing counsel "were procrastinating and instead of getting the remaining issues . . . ready for trial and trying the claims, have engaged in personal attacks against each other and in repetitious and prolix pleadings" and in repeated requests for hearings on already decided matters.[22]

It is no surprise that the bar was reluctant to comfortably accept each and every rule. Everywhere, attorneys and legal scholars disputed the very notion or key aspects of managerial judging. Charging that Oregon's rules impeded cases, raised legal costs, and required unanimous verdicts, attorney John A. Ryan tried to keep his federal caseload to a minimum. "Except for discovery in a limited way, everyone's so-called reform has led to judicial complications and to excessive law work in order to permit it to work."[23]

That Solomon used rule violations as another reason to berate lawyers or force repeated revisions of their submissions won him no friends. Documents submitted to the district court required intricate preparation compared to those submitted to state courts. Counsel had to type them "two inches down from the top of the page and one inch" from the bottom; and, Redden remembered, "you've got to do this, you had to do that . . . and if you didn't do those things, the consequences were pretty grave." Local rules limited attorneys' control over the scope, content, and pace of cases. Their settled ways, reputations, egos, incomes, and clientele were affected. The rules may have increased lawyers' time and costs, but they also saved the court time and let judges handle more trials than before. Overall, they tended to shift costs from the courts to the parties.[24]

Many lawyers told Assistant U.S. Attorney Jack Collins that they automatically doubled their fees because of the costliness of this type of preparation and the chance that Solomon would preside at trial. Attorneys resented "being made to build up legal fees" because of Solomon, Allan Hart said. Drawn-out pre-trial requirements particularly raised the costs of class actions, which might need months of meetings. Firms that charged by the hour and who were able to "justify enormous hourly time [charged] for preparing for Judge Solomon" did not complain, according to U.S. Attorney Lezak. But was "that care commensurate with the ability of clients to pay for their legal services, particularly for clients who didn't have the kinds of funds available that the clients of large firms had?" Lawyers who received contingency fees "had nothing to gain and everything to lose by exercising that kind of care, except that they were required to meet standards that he insisted on." Solomon was unbudging. "We believe that our rules minimize rather than increase the cost of litigation," he said.[25]

Some lawyers and judges believed that Solomon's managerial approach led to *ex parte* behavior, in which speaking to one side when the other was not present constituted judicial failure to insulate the parties from extraneous and impermissible information. "During pretrial supervision, judges make many decisions informally and often meet with parties *ex parte*, and appellate review is virtually unavailable," wrote a judicial management critic. "Sepenuk, come on up here" and talk about an upcoming case, an assistant U.S. attorney heard some mornings. He would hesitate and mention his opponent's absence. "Oh, don't worry about that. I'll call him later," and Solomon generally did. "Nothing particularly evil occurred" in those encounters, but Norman Sepenuk later wished he had cited the Rules of Judicial Conduct and refused. "More than any other judge," Solomon telephoned attorneys on an *ex parte* basis, Lezak recalled. His staff "tried as best possible . . . to remind him of that, of course," and "tried to accommodate ourselves to it in ways that did not" violate the rules. Solomon behaved similarly with private counsel, they knew. He "had an omnivorous desire to get at the evidence," sympathized John A. Ryan, "and he wouldn't have hesitated *ex parte* to call somebody to find out something to determine what the hell was going on, particularly if it was a court case." Nobody raised the *ex parte* issue in appeals.[26]

Solomon's approach to equal opportunity in the court roused no discontent. Shortly after becoming chief judge, Solomon supported hiring the district's first African American employee. Seven years later, he recruited its first African American court reporter, Jerry Harris. "He was really fair minded," Harris recalled. Before a 1965 hearing in Medford, in southwestern Oregon, Solomon said he "would never come back" there again to hold court if Harris encountered discrimination. (There was apparently no problem.) He also tried but failed to hire an African American law clerk. In a 1978 *Oregon Journal* poll of Oregon lawyers, "all six federal judges and magistrates received good-to-excellent marks for sensitivity to women and minorities in day-to-day court work."[27]

In about 1980, Solomon and some businesspeople proposed to Kernan Bagley of the U.S. Marshall's Service that he become the district's first African American U.S. Marshall. Solomon tutored Bagley on winning Republican support and arranged that he meet each prominent African American newly settled in Oregon. Once, Bagley recalled, the judge proudly looked around and said, to the effect: "This is one of the proudest moments in my court. I'm the judge. There's a black U.S. Marshall. There's a black Court Reporter [Harris]. . . . There's a black U.S. Attorney." Judy Kobbervig remembered: "Probably there would have been no other court in the building 15 years ago that would have had that." She also stressed Solomon's even-handedness when she was chief deputy clerk under Chief Judge Belloni and then a prosecutor. "Judge Solomon never made me feel that he was giving me special treatment as a woman or a minority," she said. She, too, feared his temper and appreciated his swift mind and equitable judgments.[28]

UPHEAVAL AND ADAPTATION

An avalanche of cases thundered into the federal courts during Solomon's tenure. By the mid-1950s, the major districts faced big backlogs. From 1940 to 1960, caseloads increased by just under 77 percent; in the next fifteen years, they accelerated to over 106 percent, only to increase again. Conditions other than the case volume worsened matters. Influential segments of the public, mass media, and the bar soon concluded that the federal *and* state courts were in crisis. Critics blamed congestion, delays, and inflated costs in the courts. Some blamed federal judges — meaning the Warren Court majority — substituting themselves for lawmakers and imperially making unwarranted — that is, liberal — public-policy decisions. Federal judges complained that their courts were underfunded and overburdened. "By the 1960s," a student of court reform has written, "it was increasingly apparent that the administrative structure and methods of [the federal] courts were inadequate to the task they faced."[29]

Filings in Solomon's district almost tripled from about 500 cases in 1950 to around 1,300 in 1971, a 240 percent increase while Oregon's population grew by 40 percent. With usually six months between filing and trial dates, Solomon's district required a little over nine months to try a case in 1959; other districts needed from four to 39 months. Oregon's caseload climbed to 1,600 in 1978, with 662 of the cases backlogged, compared to 350 in 1963. Cases inundated all federal courts. Between 1960 and 1987, the litigation rate in all districts increased by more than 350 percent, from 79,200 to 282,274 cases. The increase was some three times more than that recorded in the United States during its previous 175 years. From 1961 to 1981, federal trial court filings climbed by 228 percent, a figure less than half the appellate court escalation. In 1961, Solomon's Ninth Circuit received 434 new case filings; in 1988, 6,334.[30]

The first Attorney General's Conference on Court Congestion and Delays met in 1956. As a step toward gaining control of the docket, district courts imported more and more outside judges. During Solomon's first twenty-one years, he said, "I think I tried more cases in other districts than any other judge in the federal system." By 1971, he had accepted more than fifty assignments in every district of the sprawling Ninth Circuit Court of Appeals and in four other districts. More assignments followed. He ultimately wrote 219 published opinions and countless unpublished ones. For case quality, the Oregonian most liked assignments in Florida, Washington, D.C., and New York City. Manhattan promised stimulating issues, impressive colleagues, cultural pleasures, and time with friends. Comfortable with ethnicity, its judges, a law clerk said, treated Solomon as an enjoyable novelty — a cerebral Jew from faraway Oregon. Prior to becoming a senior judge, Solomon also served once or twice a year as an "extra" judge on Ninth Circuit appeals panels and less often on three other circuits' panels. During his career, he wrote 111 Ninth Circuit opinions and innumerable unpublished ones.[31]

By the early 1960s, there were not only more but also different types of cases and more complex and difficult ones before the U.S. District Court for Oregon. It had no civil rights cases in 1950 but 355 of them forty years later. By then, a third of the criminal cases related to drug charges, property actions had become uncommon, the immigration caseload had appreciably grown, and white slavery cases had disappeared. State courts had taken over its most common criminal charge, auto theft. The federal judges also considered 106 once unheard-of *habeas corpus* convict petitions. Starting in the late 1960s, "'structural reform' litigants challenged federal district judges," Steven H. Wilson writes, "to intervene in and to reform the alleged constitutional deprivations in school discipline, criminal prosecutions, and other domains of public governance traditionally considered to be within the sole purview of state officials."[32]

Major changes in the environment of the federal court system lay behind its perceived problems and responses. Some can be traced to statutes, many of them broadly framed and innovative, which exploded in quantity, scope, and complexity during the 1960s and 1970s. In the civil area, for example, district judges considered once-rare securities law violations, civil rights infractions, private antitrust claims, shareholders' derivative suits, environmental actions, and employment, age, and housing discrimination claims. In the criminal area, they coped with mounds of state and federal convict petitions asking to set aside their sentences, and they massively restructured jails and prison systems in dozens of states (but not Oregon).

Other charges can be traced to the courts, Congress, and groups crafting a "rights revolution," which encompassed fundamental or human rights, a citizen's entitlements, and a government's obligations. "The 'rights revolution,'" Eric Foner writes, "completed the transformation of American freedom from a finite body of entitlements enjoyed mainly by white men into an open-ended claim to equality, recognition, and self-determination." Constitutional doctrines by the early 1970s bore few relationships to those that were in place when Solomon joined the court. He welcomed the Warren Court's expansion of constitutional provisions and statutory reach in such areas as individual expression, electoral reapportionment, civil rights, *habeas corpus*, criminal procedure, and school prayer. A resurrected substantive due process doctrine had made certain rights free from government interference, even though no constitutional clause expressly granted them. The Bill of Rights covered new groups and subject areas. Minimum procedures also had to be followed, and the procedures could not violate individual liberties. Higher standards were mandated for government agencies. The courts acquired more of an oversight role.[33]

Solomon grew less deferential to administrative actions. After the Civil Rights Act of 1964 was passed, he insisted on more acute judicial attentiveness to convicts' procedural due process rights. He also held the Immigration and Naturalization Service to elevated due process terms. When the INS began removing one plaintiff from the country while he had a challenge before his court, Solomon summarily ordered the man's return in 1962. "The INS grumbled that the Court could not intervene in the private preserve of the INS. There was some flexing of muscle, when the U.S. Marshall was directed to take the Director of the INS into custody," law clerk Arden Shenker recalled."[34]

Oregon's three judges in the late 1960s, Judge Goodwin recalled, "had the feeling that the growth of federal jurisprudence was occur-

ring faster than the existing personnel could deal with." Federal remedies had become even more popular, where once the law was silent or
the remedies left to the states. In 1980, Oregon's docket ranged "from
the really routine to the very, very complex, challenging cases in the
areas of constitutional law, environmental law, and patent law, intellectual property law," according to Judge James A. Redden. "Some of
them are almost overwhelming [and] really require a lot of work."[35]

Some changes in the court system's environment can be traced to
transformations in the legal profession. It grew astronomically during
Solomon's tenure, generating more and different sorts of cases. Some
200,000 attorneys were licensed in 1950; a third more were added in
the 1960s, a further 90 percent during the 1970s, and an additional
48 percent from 1980 to 1988. Between 1950 and 1965, Oregon's
federal judges expected to see about 50 lawyers on a recurrent basis. Some 200 to 300 of them put in regular appearances by the late
1980s. Among them were those from new or regenerated public-in-
terest law firms, public defenders, and Legal Aid Societies, and there
were throngs of advocacy lawyers. That so many young attorneys felt
as committed as he had been to law as an instrument of social improvement pleased Solomon.[36]

The growth of law offices in function and size and all-out advocacy likewise effected changes. Corporatization took hold of the
largest firms, while the percentage of sole practitioners declined from
three-fifths to one-third of the legal corps between 1948 and 1980.
Judges, proclaimed legal generalists, presided increasingly over at-
torney-specialists who deployed highly technical resources and arguments. A lawyer need not be a specialist, Solomon sniffed, to conduct
a complicated federal case. He would not countenance a seeming pro-
liferation of wily, intellectually manipulative, merciless, and hyper-ag-
gressive attorneys who treated litigation as warfare and the courtroom
as a battlefield. None should humiliate or unfairly take advantage of
a witness or opponent, he insisted. "If you continue to argue, I am
going to let [the opposing attorney] go ahead and talk, too," he once
cautioned in a water-rights case. "You are not going to get the advantage over him, because I told him he couldn't argue it and now you
are doing the same thing I told him he couldn't do." Elsewhere, he
denied a counsel's request to admit 1,600 pieces of evidence, terming
it "just monstrous."[37]

"Caseload growth has prompted changes in the structure and
behavior of the federal courts designed to cope with [its] growth,"

Judge Richard A. Posner recognized. The courts developed into more complex organizations and grew "busier, more hectic, more 'bureaucratic,' more formal in some respects and informal in others." A new Federal Judicial Center initiated centralized planning, research, and education on efficient docket management and other issues. Congress raised minimum money-claim requirements for courts, provided more judgeships — finally, two new ones for Oregon in 1980 — greatly expanded court workforces, occasionally added districts, and established, as district court adjuncts, bankruptcy judges and U.S. magistrates, later called magistrate judges. Many of these relief measures forced judges into more active managerial roles.[38]

Further, trial and appellate courts encouraged legal conflict resolutions without court intervention; employed special masters, task forces, and expert panels; intensified the use of retired and visiting jurists; delegated routine and preparatory work; created a legion of official and unofficial speed-up strategies; and issued more and more rules. In the new atmosphere of efficiency and speed, federal judges could not engage in "leisured and learned deliberations," Judge Posner has noted. Less time was devoted to each case, and fewer opinions were published. A substantial number of controversies ended in terse dismissals or summary judgments (that is, that no triable issue of material fact existed) and that the judge could decide the case solely on legal issues. Kilkenny, Solomon, and Goodwin picked juries in thirty minutes, Bernard Jolles said. "God help you if you started pettifogging and trying to put on a deal to show the jury anything like that."[39]

Oregon's federal judges frowned on long witness lists, too. In chambers just before a 9:30 AM hearing in Salem, Solomon addressed Ronald B. Lansing. He had fourteen prisoners and a psychiatrist waiting to testify to support an injunction request — until His Honor declared: "Make this short. This won't take much time. Don't give me any long speeches." Only the expert and two prisoners testified. Elsewhere, clumsy attempts by three inexperienced lawyers to drag out a trial, as one confessed later, were quickly waved aside. Economize to clarify matters and save the court time and cost, Solomon preached. "Why don't you give me without all the hocus pocus and all the rhetoric just the cases upon which" the state relied, no more than two or three, he typically suggested.[40]

Solomon's judicial reputation partly rested on his speed and on the dispatch he cultivated in colleagues. He "has helped make the Portland district outstanding among the federal courts in the prompt handling of cases and in the numbers of cases processed by each judge," a 1970 editorial stated. "The Portland district's national reputation is one it did not have when he went on the bench." At their peril, lawyers outside Oregon resisted the tight schedules or ignored the materials sent them before he arrived. Typical of visiting judges, he expected them to do things his way unless rules or directives instructed otherwise. "The word in NY was 'this crazy guy from Ahregone' was cutting the docket mercilessly. You'd better not go in there looking for a postponement," Meyer Eisenberg recalled. In the Manhattan district, Solomon conducted what Eisenberg called a rocket docket: "Tough deadlines on lawyers, summary hearings, no delays, no postponements." Judge John R. Ross pleased Solomon by calling him "The Fastest Gavel in the West." At 9:30 AM he had begun a Nevada car crash case scheduled to last several days. He rapidly picked a jury. Because most facts were admitted, there was little testimony. Solomon barred the introduction of irrelevant evidence, and the jury returned a verdict before noon.[41]

Lateness to court or tardiness after a recess peeved Solomon. In the face of a withering silence or a fine, attorneys learned not to repeat the error. Nor did they necessarily expect written decisions from him. "On the district court, most judges do little writing. They rule from the bench or they may write a short opinion," Solomon observed. Rather than pausing to prepare written opinions on many controverted issues or motions, Solomon often made on-the-spot rulings. Or he might cagily delay ruling on the admissibility of evidence until just before a trial ended, when fewer evidence motions were restated. Having set a blistering pre-trial and trial pace, Solomon rapidly ruled on post-trial curative motions. He seldom ruminated long before issuing final opinions, which were usually short.[42]

District judges rationed themselves to the issues and disputes they truly believed required attention. Facing 182 inmate petitions between 1973 and 1976, Oregon's judges dismissed 143 on their factual pleadings, granted two, and appointed 19 lawyers to argue the remainder. Solomon also said that he generally followed "the rule that administrative remedies must be exhausted before one should be permitted to attack administrative action in court." The critic of delay used delay, too. In 1964, he postponed rendering a decision in the hope that the parties would settle before the Ninth Circuit decided a related case. And he used a little-known legal doctrine to reduce the caseload, saying, "I am a strong believer in the doctrine of abstention."

Federal courts with jurisdiction over a case had statutory discretion under ill-defined conditions to defer to state tribunals considering the same or closely related issues. *Hay v. Bruno* was stayed pending completion of the state courts' review of Oregon's beach law. The Oregon Supreme Court upheld its constitutionality, as then did Solomon's three-judge panel. Another of his panels abstained until an appeal on another unsettled state law ran its course in state courts. Only after informally learning the probable decision did it agree to hear the federal suit without testimony and under a plan to dispose of the claim with a short opinion.[43]

Solomon once heard that a plaintiff in a water case "wasn't asking for a hearing because the depositions and the documents themselves were sufficient. Now, that is my way of trying a lawsuit, anyway." Several colleagues already had adopted his requirements that witnesses replace their live testimony with written statements and that attorneys submit "purged" depositions that contained only disputed information. Both techniques, said George H. Fraser, tended to sharpen the legal issues, permit counsel to convey evidence *they* liked, and either led them to settle before trial or to hurry settlement discussions. Both techniques have "been used regularly, not only in this district, but nationwide and quite generally reduce the time for such trials by fifty percent, or more," Judge Owen M. Panner later concluded. "Neither he, nor those of us who have followed [Solomon] could cope with the increasing volume of litigation without" them. All the district judges in 1980 "were working the kind of hours that he worked for many years."[44]

Solomon was proud of how well-written testimony and its cross-examination and rebuttals had worked in *Weyerhaeuser Co. v. Combustion Equipment Associates*. The suit entailed a host of complex business and technical issues; but he needed fewer than two-and-a-half court days once he had, in writing, a 173-page pre-trial order, 26 depositions, and 71 witness narratives. (Trying fewer of the same controversies, a federal judge in Texas required 32 days of trial, he satisfyingly remarked.) Little cross-examination occurred at trial. Solomon examined 15 post-trial briefs totaling some 2,500 pages before issuing an 84-page opinion, one of the longest in his career. He was pleased by the 24-line Ninth Circuit *per curiam* affirmation of these techniques and of his award to Weyerhaeuser and a similar Ninth Circuit affirmation in a complicated Indian law case, *Carson–Truckee Water Conservancy Dist. v. Watt* (see Chapter 9).[45]

Solomon's reputation for speed — shared by Robert C. Belloni, new to the court in 1967 — elicited frequent invitations to clear backlogs elsewhere. In San Francisco, the two judges handled some two hundred cases dealing with resisitance to the draft in "kind of an assembly line process," Belloni recounted. If an early-morning conference with Solomon won no accommodation, both sides agreed on what was excluded from trial and had the charges scheduled for Belloni to hear later that morning. Almost all the prosecutors and defenders hurriedly made deals. U.S. Attorney Lezak believed their approach was harsh and that Solomon, who had strong views about the draft, was trying to change the Northern California district's well-known leniency toward draft offenders.[46]

In the same vein, Solomon spoke of making "little cases out of big ones." Typical of district judges, he avoided making a decision about constitutionality if neither party had raised the question or if a nonconstitutional opinion serviceably answered an issue. These judges also were reluctant to intervene in state court proceedings unless an individual's rights had been irremediably damaged. In one *habeas corpus* case, Judge Belloni reminded Solomon and another panelist that they had informally agreed with the Oregon Supreme Court "not sua sponte [without prompting or suggestion] to raise the question of by-passing" it. After it ruled, Solomon, for the panel, wrote: "I am not an appeals court. This is the United States District Court. We don't act as an appeal court from the State. The mere fact they make an error doesn't make any difference." As was the convention, the petitioning convict had to show that the error reached constitutional proportions.[47]

NEW COLLEAGUES

Those joining Oregon's federal bench recognized the virtue of moving the docket in a prompt and effective manner. Except for Judge East, Oregon's judges were generally receptive to Solomon's leadership and, surprising themselves, charmed by him. John K. Kilkenny replaced McColloch in August 1959. From the outset, the eastern Oregon Republican and the liberal Portland Democrat liked one another. Kilkenny was receptive to Solomon's lessons and his help in settling in, and they amiably lunched together for years. Kilkenny admitted to only one minor dispute with Solomon in a quarter-century. While he respected his judicial work, however, he never liked what he saw as Solomon's tendency to unnecessarily castigate lawyers. Kilkenny probably said nothing directly. By the 1970s, both men had created "their own little kingdoms and each of them sensed when they were starting to cross into the other's territory and they'd back away," their colleague Judge Otto R. Skopil Jr. remarked.[48]

Kilkenny and Solomon dealt with East's alcohol problem by handling about 95 percent of the caseload. In 1959, East satisfied Ninth Circuit Chief Judge Walter L. Pope that he would remain sober. By 1962, however, complaints about East had reached Senator Maurine Neuberger, who warned of Senate intervention if judicial inaction persisted. Ninth Circuit Chief Judge Richard Chambers decided East had improved, but another relapse brought his disability retirement at the insistence of the Justice Department and the Ninth Circuit. East's actions as a visiting judge in California brought more complaints. In 1966, Senator Morse warned of intervention unless he was kept off all benches. Chief Judge Chambers literally banished him from the Portland courthouse. In the next decade, a restored East, with chambers in Eugene, usefully presided over cases.[49]

Robert C. Belloni, a Democrat, replaced East in 1967. While a county judge, Belloni had accepted the "great legends" about Solomon's ability and heard "scandalous stories" about his bar relations. He meant to have no more than polite, formal dealings with this formidable figure. He later said: "Well, it took him about an hour and a half to completely charm me," and Solomon became "one of the closest friends that I ever had." He "was our teacher, our mentor [and] always there to assist." Belloni came to blame the horror stories about Solomon on unprepared or inexperienced lawyers who were unappreciative of a judge's need for swift action. Skopil, reaching the court in 1972 along with James M. Burns, was also leery of Solomon, having suffered his wrath during court appearances. But he, too, was charmed and decided that Solomon "was one of the most sensitive, concerned people" he had ever known. He "became really a true, true colleague" and personal friend. The chief judge likewise charmed Oregon Supreme Court Justice Alfred T. Goodwin, who replaced Kilkenny when he was raised to the appellate bench. Goodwin had only appeared twice in federal court and, knowing Solomon's reputation, slept poorly beforehand. "Oh, he scared hell of out me when I first appeared before him," he remembered. Now, he was made to feel like a son or nephew. He "was very good about sharing with the younger judges his experiences and methods." Solomon "defended constitutional and statutory rights with wisdom, compassion and dispatch."[50]

Solomon made certain of any newcomers' comfort and law books, loaned his law clerks or his larger courtroom for big cases, and treated them to Americanized Jewish food. He always had time to talk and to act agreeably during their low-key, courteous meetings. At least three times a week the judges discussed trial problems, allocated certain cases, and piloted court affairs. To assure proper trial conduct and avoid miscarriages of justice, Solomon convinced Belloni, Kilkenny, and others to govern — not referee — courtrooms. Neither Kilkenny nor Belloni needed persuasion. They, too, belonged to a historic line of forceful individuals who relished playing a robust judicial hand. They all voiced boundless irritation about imperious, late, or ill-prepared attorneys; obstructive or unfair legal tactics; distasteful statutes they must enforce; and counsel murmuring or rustling papers while an opponent or the judge spoke. As this trio communicated to Norman Sepenuk, "I am a judge. I run the courtroom. You listen to me."[51]

Softer occasions did occur. The tone of naturalization proceedings altered under Solomon. Wanting one of the court's most patriotic ceremonies better publicized, he and the newer judges tried but failed to except them from the ban on cameras and broadcasts in federal courtrooms. He meanwhile pressed local INS officials to stop regarding citizenship applicants "as interlopers who were trying to get things for nothing." The officials appeared to grow more welcoming of applicants, "all of which demonstrates or proves that it is the judge who must take the lead." Local INS officials "really weren't so tough," Solomon said. He loved presiding over naturalization ceremonies; and for years, court employees slipped in to observe an animated, gentler being. "He really put his heart into it," court reporter Jerry Harris recalled. The swearing-in of new citizens stood out from his rapid trials and contrarian, even devilish ways and from the cut-and-dried ceremonies of other judges. Solomon leaned forward on his elbows, inquired if he was easily heard, and grinned throughout the events. One visitor who was not a lawyer called him "the kindest, smilingest judge he had ever seen."[52]

Solomon's basic citizenship talk reminded listeners that he was the son of immigrants and that immigrants had established and strengthened the nation's democratic rights. He extolled patriotism, America as a land of liberty, the Constitution, and a citizen's responsibilities to obey all laws and peacefully improve the nation and its institutions. Hate, prejudice, and bigotry should have no place here, he repeated.

Changing times and reflection on what the dominant culture had done to his own family modified the speech. During the 1950s, he roundly assailed Communist nations. Beginning in the 1960s, Solomon likened unnamed Arab states to Communist ones as subjugators of their peoples. He added that each new citizen could "give full expression to one's own cultural and spiritual heritage." Conformity was not the same as equality, he stressed; diversity was compatible with equality and a common citizenship. Primary loyalty belonged to the United States, but kindly feelings for a former land could properly endure. He rejected the shame that children had felt early in the century when parents spoke a foreign language and the melting-pot idea "that everyone would come out looking and acting and talking like everyone else."[53]

Chief Judge Solomon delighted in his responsibilities, colleagues, and authority. His court's cohesion, the high caliber of its judges (other than East), and their openness to his ideas and administrative direction gladdened him. There was more to their relations than the usual ritual politeness of judicial interaction. Without becoming unduly deferential to one another, the court's judges, he bragged, respected and depended on one another. He claimed that the U.S. District for Oregon was unique in its judges' friendliness to one another and visiting jurists. To Owen M. Panner, sworn in with James A. Redden and Helen J. Frye in 1980, Oregon reputedly had by then the most collegial district court in the nation, largely because of Solomon. Helpfully, the bulk of America's district judges, according to one account, considered themselves "part of a great national fraternity, a brotherhood of individuals who daily encounter the same demands, difficulties, and traumas." Still, multi-judge jurisdictions did not necessarily act collegially, as equals who jointly cooperated to achieve appropriate institutional aims, operations, and functions. When relations among judges grew strained or ruptured, the press and politicians feared that a court was polarizing, undermining judicial independence.[54]

Judicial collegiality, one scholar writes, demands "friendship, civility, intellectual respect, consideration, dialogue and communication, good humor, and shared meals and events." Solomon employed all of them. Discussing cases and sharing problems helped the Oregon judges function like a team or a legal partnership, Judge Goodwin recalled. Solomon figured that sharing meals and opinion drafts helped build collegiality. His jovial lunches in chambers lessened any cloistered atmosphere that might exist, and exchanging opinion drafts avoided ambiguities and errors and minimized inadvertent differences on similar questions among the judges. "He was great on form and substance," Belloni remembered, mainly "the expression of the substance so somebody else could figure out what we were talking about. We used to disagree and sometimes . . . rather noisily [but] always parted friends and remained so."[55]

Solomon was an outsize presence in the courthouse. He treated the district as his domain, although he would have loudly dismissed the idea. A palpable and sometimes towering presence to colleagues, he was for decades a force to be reckoned with. Never "underestimate the fact that Judge Solomon was very active in court" after leaving the chief judgeship. He "always considered it to be his court, and in all reality we acknowledged that it was his court," Judge Skopil declared. Fellow judges "always welcomed any comments he had and followed his advice." After his death, Judge Panner said, "[h]is presence was so strong that I still find myself thinking I need to stop by and visit him."[56]

For most of his judicial tenure, "the dominant figure" in the U.S. District for Oregon was "Gus J. Solomon, whose energy, ability and idiosyncratic judicial autocracy stamped an indelible impression on a generation of lawyers," John C. Beatty asserts. He was "the Pater Nostra [Our Father] of the Courthouse, [who] wanted to keep his hand in everything, wanted to keep control of everything," Sidney I. Lezak commented. In elevators and hallways and by phone and note, Solomon importuned Lezak's office to speed implementation of court decisions, hire his lawyer friends, or take other actions. "What is wrong with Lezak? Call Lezak," he ordered his secretary "and tell him I am concerned" that a deportation order had not been effected. Solomon called his office to discuss its prosecution priorities and "which assistants had done this, that, or the other thing," Lezak complained. Yet, after a jury retired to consider its verdict, Solomon gratified a new prosecutor by mentioning what he had done well or poorly. He "was the federal court even though there were other strong judges, like Kilkenny," Bernard Jolles said. "Whenever you thought of federal court, you thought of Gus Solomon and that's why many lawyers didn't want to go to federal court."[56]

LAW CLERKS

Many intelligent new law graduates across the country competed to be part of Solomon's court. Fifty-four of them became his law clerks.

His hard-working and tough-guy style and his role as teacher-guide largely dictated the tone and content of the clerkships. Solomon wasted little diplomacy on clerks. As in court, he meant to be in charge and, in his own fashion, helpful. Laboring seven days a week himself, he required a clerk to work on almost every holiday and alternately on Saturdays or Sundays. Incoming clerks, he assumed, were bright professionals worthy of conscientious tutoring. In their later careers, they would likely contribute to court collegiality and would be potential community and cause leaders. But foremost he considered clerks to be inexperienced assistants who needed to meet his high expectations and follow directions.

To "loosen the [new] clerks up a bit; hone their sense of humanity; and give them a chance to show" the quality of their logic and writing, Stephen Gillers recalled, Solomon typically assigned them a Social Security Administration disability decision challenge. They checked citations; researched materials for his opinions, findings of fact, memoranda, and jury instructions; analyzed discovery requests and petitions; previewed complicated records; and communicated for him with attorneys. Then they advanced to writing analytical memoranda and opinion drafts. A delighted Arden E. Shenker, for example, prepared a comprehensive review of Indian law and was sent to assist a lawyer arguing before the Supreme Court. Clerks also acted as bailiffs or "criers," so they observed trials. They also washed dishes after lunches in Solomon's chambers.[57]

A new clerk, Michael Pertschuk wrote, "is not commonly possessed of an excess of humility. Among the chosen in law school, secure in the knowledge of his generational superiority, he arrives on the scene as God's gift to the federal judiciary." In 1959, when Pertschuk met Solomon, he encountered an energetic and intellectually quick older man with a keener sense of moral outrage and a talent for inspiring and deflating a clerk. Solomon's clerks had to "be prepared to hear truth, harsh truth, as well as kind encouragement," Pertschuk added. "And watch out if you if you are a fellow who has somehow acquired the notion that you are better than the next man. Don't turn your back on your own tradition and don't look for sentimental indulgence of the moral superiority of the young."[58]

Solomon claimed: "Although I often give them hell, they do learn." In 1972, Mark Silverstein thought that his new employer was the most intimidating person he had ever met. Solomon cut clerks "down to size," played on their insecurities, deflated them by requiring detailed case knowledge, and ripped apart their writing. Those who could withstand the first two weeks of almost nonstop assignments and criticism were allowed a certain playfulness. "The judge would explode," and like a father yell at them. "He would fire us every once in a while. And he would come back and say, 'I guess you are still here.'" Silverstein grew very fond of him. He "cared a lot about us, actually," he said.[60]

Solomon valued relations with law clerks and displayed a warm interest in their welfare. Jewish clerks were encouraged to join a synagogue, and during the High Holy Days he prayed for them. He relentlessly placed former clerks in Portland law firms, and he tapped former clerks' knowledge for his speeches and writings. He referred proudly to about a dozen of them and saw and corresponded with those who still responded to him as a teacher and father figure. Any who associated with the ACLU earned his special regard.[60]

Solomon was not one to treat lawyers diplomatically or suffer fools gladly, his first clerk Jerome Kohlberg Jr. said. He exemplified in a not-so-austere Jewish way the Quakerism that Kohlberg had known as a student at Swarthmore College, where people talked from the heart and "cogitated upon integrity and the things that matter." Stephen Gillers remembered spending "a lot of time" in the courthouse. . . . Mornings, afternoons, evenings, Saturdays, Sundays. More Saturdays. Researching, writing, arguing, researching some more. Arguing some more." After "a while, he did not treat me as a subordinate." Solomon became a "mentor" who explicitly "taught me lessons about legal craft" and "had an enormous influence on my professional life." Gillers's self-styled First Amendment absolutism dwindled when he had to get his arguments and drafts past the exacting judge. They achieved a rare relationship for judge and clerk, Gillers said, as Solomon learned to tolerate his youthful, unduly impetuous, invasive, and presumptuous ways.[61]

John J. Kerr Jr. felt that Solomon "basically adopts you as a son while you are there. If you let him, he would take over your life." As Solomon rarely did elsewhere, he discussed legal issues arising with lawyers and other judges and instructed clerks on such matters. Some were invited home and met friends and relatives. In the courthouse, they were obliged to meet his conservative dress and grooming standards: suits and ties and short hair for the men; no pants suits for the women or any female lawyer making an appearance. Recalcitrant male clerks were ordered into barber chairs. In the 1960s, Solomon reluctantly accepted short, neat beards and trimmed mustaches.[62]

Kohlberg, back in New York, for several years chose successors to clerk for Solomon, mainly from Yale and Columbia law graduates. Competition for a clerkship intensified after law enrollments mushroomed. More than 125 applications arrived in 1973. Liberals gravitated to his court, but he mainly looked for common sense, good judgment, honesty, and integrity, Solomon stated, not a particular social or legal outlook or the best grades.[6e]

Solomon's first female law clerk appeared almost accidentally. Hearing in 1969 that no Portland firm would interview Carol Hewitt, who ranked second in her Willamette University law class, he tried but failed to place her in a local firm. It made him wonder what unexamined biases had stopped him employing a female law clerk. He likened his rationales to non-Jews making excuses to avoid hiring Jewish attorneys. Solomon sent for Hewitt and offered her a clerkship, which she accepted. At the end of her tenure, however, even his warm recommendations failed to find her a place in a local law firm. It was only then, he dubiously claimed, that he became aware of the extensive disadvantages facing women attorneys. He phoned Hewitt's recent Portland interviewers and berated Dennis Lindsay, informing him that the time had come to hire a woman. "We did a lot of business in federal court, and this was a mandate from on high," Lindsay realized. "Perhaps we'd better 'relook' the situation." To its great satisfaction, his firm hired Hewitt. That, Solomon exaggerated, "is how we broke into the bias against women in this area."[64]

Solomon "had a keen sense of a teaching responsibility to his law clerks," recalled Henry Richmond III. To Kohlberg, Solomon was "a teacher both as to the law and what it stood for" and "the righteousness of it" and also "a stickler for writing accuracy, for turning out an opinion that was really professional." Without indicating how he would rule, he taught clerks to draft terse opinions. If the parties did not address important issues, he once instructed, "if it's a widow or orphan, you find the issue." From some more than others, the judge profited from the clerks' ideas and perspectives. Stephen Gillers and John J. Kerr Jr., among others, knowingly disputed him and persuaded him on legal points.[66]

The clerks also appreciated Solomon's instruction in good writing. Lauding Justice Louis Brandeis for laboring over the thirteenth and fourteenth drafts of his opinions, Solomon closely scrutinized the clerks' drafts. To nodding agreement, he shrank ten pages to three or four. Often referring them to the dictionary or writing manuals, he debated word choice, structure, and syntax with them. They might linger half an hour over a single word. Solomon upheld the legal fraternity's schooling in unambiguous expression and the authority of words. He established prizes for good legal writing in colleges and law schools. A wire service publicized his attack from the bench on "legal gobbledygook" when he returned a tax indictment with instructions to rewrite it in plain English. He gleefully opened a "Legalese & Gobbledygook" file to collect new examples. Amid so many doleful events in the 1960s, Solomon sought pleasure where he could find it.[66]

Chapter 8

Judging

To effect justice à la Judge Solomon did not mean seeking near-utopian justice, ultimately, but justice now — pragmatic justice, putting a dispute to rest.

—Ernest Bonyhadi, 1987

JUDICIAL PHILOSOPHY

He had "been too busy to engage in any soul searching about my philosophy of law," Judge Solomon said in 1969, and he had no real interest in doing so. Explaining that he did not mean to sound smug or provincial, the judge admitted that since completing law school "my philosophy of the law has not changed." It was a common judicial stance. "Philosophy of law was never a strong point among American jurists," Cass R. Sunstein writes. "The judicial mind naturally gravitates away from abstractions and toward close encounters with particular cases."[1]

Solomon's legal philosophy was rooted in his earlier legal realism, a strong sense of individual responsibility, and a keen regard for active government. He firmly believed that judges ought to be cautious and self-effacing and restrain their adjudication. He once assured fellow panelists: "I tried to meet the issues which were raised squarely and I did not want to make any new law." Judges, he believed, ought to furnish workable decisions and avoid statements of transcendent principles. They should issue narrow rulings, not decide issues unnecessary for resolving a case and not deliver opinions filled with vaulting declarations. Judges were further obliged to untangle competing principles in a controversy, establish workable priorities for assessing them, and decide the issues on their merits and not on legal technicalities.[2]

While judges must have enough power to pursue their goals, their power had limits, he believed. Courts alone, he specified in 1970, could not stop crime or solve the domestic problems of unrest, civil disturbance, or drugs. Judges, too, should respect the limits Americans imposed on governments. Americans enjoyed a governmental system that demanded morality and self-discipline from citizens, he said. "We want only as much government policing as is necessary to control the few who, through ignorance or defiance, would violate the laws." Further, "Not everything which is wrong can be outlawed, although anything which is outlawed is wrong." Judges must be very cautious about second-guessing the judgments of Congress and the Executive. Because only these branches of government represented the public will, the courts largely should defer to them. "I do not believe that the courts should be used to thwart the will of Congress, absent some constitutional basis therefor [sic]," he remarked in a deportation case. "Although the law is severe and works many hardships, the right to terminate hospitality to aliens and the grounds upon which such determination shall be based are matters solely for the responsibility of Congress and are wholly outside the power of the court to control." During the 1980s, he criticized a two-decade-old tendency in the federal judiciary to find constitutional implications in cases. It was "worse on the appellate courts . . . and maybe the Supreme Court where many of the judges decide cases on issues that were never raised by the litigants."[3]

Solomon did not think "that Congress reaches out to legislate on matters that the government shouldn't legislate on." Because of usually well-drafted statutes, few laws required judicial clarification. He would not invalidate or narrowly interpret one if it expressed a clear, concise purpose. "I decide cases in accordance with the law," he said, "and not with any personal opinions except if the decision is ambiguous and if the law is ambiguous, then I decide the case in accordance with my ideas of what justice is," after taking into consideration the law's social implications. The Administrative Procedure Act also narrowed review of administrative action. Judicial review of Selective Service actions "is designed to prevent isolated instances of arbitrary action."[4]

By and large, Judge Solomon sustained a legal realism, which "assumed that judges were lawmakers and worried about the consequences of unrestrained judicial lawmaking in a democratic society." Proper judging, G. Edward White writes, involved "'judicial restraint,' either as manifested in a cautious exercise of the judiciary's power vis-à-vis other lawmaking branches, or as manifested in judicial efforts to suspend bias and to justify decisions on a 'principled' doctrinal basis, 'principled' denoting the qualities of rationality, impartiality, and intelligibility." Solomon favored judicial restraint even after the 1960s, when few liberals — enamored especially by the Warren Court — still believed in it. If there was a need to right constitutional wrongs, he strongly preferred that district judges did not invalidate the underlying legislative or executive act. Other than that possessed by the Supreme Court, he did not believe in the all-encompassing power of judicial writ.[5]

However much he favored judicial self-restraint, Solomon rejected an unthinking judicial abstinence. "Administrative interpretations are entitled to deference by the courts, but they are not binding," he opined. The government's reach was never boundless. As the Supreme Court of the 1940s and 1950s had ruled, certain clearly defined constitutional rights or the presence of groups unable to protect their own interests in the political process (such as the prison inmates treated in Chapter 11) made judicial deference less possible. No group could use statutes to violate First Amendment freedoms. Regardless of a closed-shop agreement requiring union membership as a condition of employment, he ruled in *Tooley v. Martin–Marietta Corp.* that Seventh Day Adventists, who were unable to join unions because of their religion, could retain their jobs by making charitable contributions in lieu of union membership fees.[6]

Solomon looked for ways to do the sensible thing, even if he had to ignore some issues, temper a principle's application, or risk a reversal. He was inclined to look at a case's specific facts and to fret about the human and institutional effects of his rulings and decisions. "To effect justice à la Judge Solomon did not mean seeking near-utopian justice, ultimately, but *justice now* — pragmatic justice, putting a dispute to rest," Ernest Bonyhadi observed. When facing legal issues rooted in serious social conflict, Solomon imposed as final and as peaceful a solution as possible. "Judge Solomon was anxious to effect a settlement which he thought would produce significant progress in race relations in Portland," Paul R. Meyer recalled. His 1968 "consent decree 'settlement' was as favorable a result as could be obtained without very bloody litigation and extreme exacerbation of race on the waterfront." Meyer's African American B List registrants (employed only if no A List registrant was available) had charged Portland's longshoremen's union and maritime association with discrimination by denying their promotion from probationers to membership with its A-List status. Only four years earlier, the first African Americans had been added to the local union's B List.[7]

"It will be a constant source of irritation for the men on the waterfront" if the lawsuit continued, Solomon warned. "It will be no settlement at all." He refused to order the tight-knit local to admit the plaintiffs or to extend court protection to African Americans who might seek future waterfront employment. Instead, he pressed its leaders to strongly urge their members to vote the plaintiffs into the union. Fearing that publicity would increase the white members' resistance to the settlement and worsen their views of the challengers, he ordered all its provisions kept secret. No plaintiff ought to be "put in a bad light" by union people, he said, and neither "party should be in a position of eating crow. You are going to have to live together and you ought to try to do it with the least amount of difficulty." He locked the consent agreement in his safe for thirteen years, despite a reporter's protest.[8]

Six years later, the union was no longer lily-white. About one hundred B List registrants, mainly white men, had been transferred to the A List, and the remaining two hundred "would be next in line," Solomon noted. He thanked the attorneys and others "for helping to bring about peace on the waterfront in Portland." This consent agreement seemingly built in what Judge Frank N. Coffin later called "workability," that is, "the extent to which a rule protecting a right, enforcing a duty, or setting a standard of conduct — which is consistent with and in the interests of social justice — can be pronounced with reasonable expectation of effective observance without impairing the essential functioning of those to whom the rule applies."[9]

Burton v. Cascade School Dist. Union High School No. 5 similarly displayed Solomon's sense of practical justice, though the plaintiff likely disagreed. The judge awarded the remainder of a year's salary and legal fees to a lesbian teacher who had been wrongfully terminated by a small rural school district during her one-year contract. He had found the "immorality" clause of a state law it used unconstitutionally vague, but he refused reinstatement. "It just wouldn't work out to reinstate this woman in this little area," Solomon said in court. "Let's not kid ourselves. If any district finds out that she is a lesbian, they are not going to hire her, no matter what the law is." Agreeing to expunge her record, he asked: "But, what does that mean? It means she is going to not divulge that fact. As soon as they found out about [her sexual preference], they are going to be unhappy with her." Referring to *Burton*, clerk Mark Silverstein later recalled that Solomon "had a hard time with the notion of lesbianism." In a previous obscenity case he had instructed the jury to treat "homosexuals, flagelists, lesbians, masochists and sadists" as deviant classes and groups; now he lightly referred to the teacher's "peculiar propensity." According to clerk David Walbert, "Gus, [who] wasn't particularly inclined to find sexual conduct to be a fundamental right," struck down the wrongful termination "on good, solid civil libertarian grounds."[10]

Solomon never believed that if a little legal process in some situations was a good thing, then a great deal of legal process in every situation must be much better. He was committed to resolving disputes with as much finality and dispatch as possible. "I thought we ought to decide this case once and for all and not have the case going up and back from the Court of Appeals," he once declared. If he could decide a case on one or two of the issues raised and ignore the others, he did so. He railed against lawyers piling on claims and requests or manipulating established agency and judicial processes to delay legal resolutions or to avoid their clients' responsibilities. "I don't care how much money [the plaintiff millionaire] Stonehill has, I don't think you can request sixteen hundred admissions," he said. This case, he noted, had dragged through the courts for fourteen years and might outlive him. Elsewhere, Solomon expressed frustration about administrative and judicial appeals that stretched over nine years to keep an alleged Communist from deportation.[11]

TRIAL JUDGE

"The trial court is a scene of drama, wit, humor, and humanity, along with the sorrows and the stretches of boredom," Marvin E. Frankel writes. "Even the periods of tedium are charged with the awareness of important stakes. . . . There is power and there is, often more satisfying, the opportunity to forego the exercise of power." Exercising power appealed to Solomon. He amply signaled that he played the leading role in trials (and at calls) and brooked no competitor. His was a popular approach in judicial circles. The "trial judge's primary audience is found in the courtroom itself and consists of the parties (and their families and their counsel), jurors, witnesses, court watchers," Judge Posner wrote. "The appearance of fairness, the maintenance of authority, keeping things moving along — these become ends in themselves for the trial judge, and properly so."[12]

Solomon wanted a courtroom to be a forum where he and any jury could quickly obtain the clear, relevant evidence needed to make fair and workable decisions. It was not a stage for lawyer-actors or lawyer-manipulators. (Any acting was his felt prerogative.) Neither was it a place for counsel to be ill informed or ill prepared. As a practical matter, he urged lawyers before trials to learn beforehand how individual jurists operated. "Each judge has his own methods and peculiarities," he reminded. Out-of-state counsel wisely "called Portland lawyers to find about me." In his court, attorneys would already know what had been proposed and sought as relief and would possess all statements they might cross-examine. These statements were provisionally accepted until the case was under advisement, when Solomon would hear objections, grant requests, and entertain briefs challenging his rulings. Overall, he gave advocates wide latitude to prove their cases, probably to reduce the vulnerability of his verdicts at appeal. One list of his requirements included: "Deal from the top of the deck. Don't try to throw sand in my eyes. . . . And I am not interested in 'string' citations. If you cite a case, read the case first and then give me the facts of the case." Abide by his rulings and, for rehearing purposes, do not restate the same arguments. There must be "no dirty tricks regardless of what a defendant does"; they must be "completely honest & fair." He advised against courtroom oratory and in favor of civility, speed, closely reasoned arguments, well-honed briefs, and the apt but limited citation of precedents.[13]

Justice, not speed, Solomon cautioned fellow judges, "must always be the prime consideration" in trials. "Are they entitled to the Fifth Amendment?" he asked at the outset of a civil trial. He would entitle the defendants to its protection "unless you can get a stipulation from the government and signed by the Attorney General that they are not going to prosecute them." In criminal matters, he advised judges: "Don't rush proceedings involving waivers, arraignments and pleas. Take your time. You can't ask too many questions. And you can't take too many precautions." Once, he closely questioned a check forger ready to plead guilty. Satisfied after fifteen minutes that there had been no coercion, he grilled the defense attorney at length.[14]

At trial, Solomon might assist weak, undiscerning, or inexperienced counsel, although this aid almost entirely escaped the bar's notice. In criminal cases, he declared, a judge's burden increased when a defense lawyer was inexperienced or court-appointed and unpaid. So, newcomer James Heltzel, acting *pro bono*, merely suffered a displeased glance when he violated a local rule by handing a folded document to a court clerk. In one case, Solomon, after repeatedly saying that he did not understand an attorney's questioning of a witness, essentially

took over the task. He steered rookie Douglas G. Houser, acting *pro
bono*, to a volunteer handwriting expert to help him prepare questions.
Do not worry about the law, just learn the facts, he told the nervous
counsel. "I know the law and justice will be done in my courtroom."
The judiciary also bore a heavier responsibility when an outstanding
attorney opposed a mediocre one in complicated trials, Solomon said,
because, unlike run-of-the-mill cases, the difference in preparation,
not presentation, could be conclusive. Wendell Gray saw the judge
quickly decide that his opponents were no match for him and "started
trying their lawsuit for them." Gray remembered: he "didn't want to
see any litigant in his court get short-changed by a lawyer [who] was
not competent." So, "Gus would just kind of take over."[15]

When Solomon died, one former plaintiff recalled his even-
handedness when his side faced huge odds. Dr. Carl Petterson, the
principal plaintiff in several related suits, had challenged the Port of
Portland's 1968 plan to expand the main airport to Columbia River
islands. "Last week's eulogies for Gus Solomon brot [sic] back bit-
tersweet memories," he mused, "bitter, because he ruled against us in
all three of our appearances before him — sweet, because we did win
the case with intended and unintended help from Solomon (he kept
us in court, dismissing the many attempts to get us thrown out, and
by keeping our court costs down)." Solomon knew that a companion
case in New York had lasted seven days in court, "the costs of which
would have finished us off before we had gotten started." Solomon
instructed the government to provide transcripts, saving the plaintiffs
sorely needed funds, and he kept the Portland trials and hearings
brief and affordable while advising them on how to overturn some of
his key rulings.[16]

Like other good judges, Solomon went to great length to keep
one side from being overwhelmed by the other's superior financial
and legal resources. When eight lawyers faced Petterson's one at a
calendar call, he remembered, "Solomon called me by name from the
gallery . . . and then proceeded to chide me to get more help for my
attorney." Solomon subsequently told Marvin Durning, Petterson's
lawyer, that he had made allowances for him handling this case alone:
"I have relieved you of the obligation to have [an Oregon] lawyer
who shall meaningfully participate in the case because I think you
have always complied with our rules." His being overworked would
not be allowed to slow the court's work, he cautioned. Petterson remembered that law clerk Henry Richmond III came "to assure us that

justice was not weighed by the numbers on each side and suggested some sources of volunteer help, all of which we were already exploiting."[17]

The Ninth Circuit Court of Appeals seldom flattered judges by name, but it praised Solomon on several occasions. "The trial court was confronted with a very difficult case. It approached the problem in an orderly and intelligent manner," said one endorsement. "Its printed opinion is an excellent example of good judicial work. . . . The trial judge took up the problems seriatim and 'called them as he saw them.'" In a different instance, the Ninth Circuit commended Solomon's "effort to coordinate federal and state resolution of water rights" and approved of his preventing needlessly costly proceedings for the parties and needless duplication of judicial efforts. In a more complex water case, the court affirmed and adopted all but one of his many holdings, "for the reasons ably stated by Judge Solomon in his two learned opinions." So, too, the Ninth Circuit fully accepted Solomon's standard of review in a complex business case after he largely relied on documentary evidence and written narrative statements from witnesses. And in an unusual Supreme Court tribute, Chief Judge Warren Burger praised a "thorough opinion by Senior Judge Gus J. Solomon."[18]

Solomon's assertive manner also won a Ninth Circuit assent of his criminal courtroom work in 1962. Commenting that a judge "is more than a moderator or umpire," the court rejected challenges to Solomon's jury instructions and to his frequent colloquies with attorneys. Providing that judicial comment "is fair and the jury is clearly instructed that they are to find the facts and may disregard such comments," the Ninth Circuit held, a judge "may assist the jury by commenting upon the evidence and this may include an appraisal of the credibility of witnesses." Some instances, the court continued, in which he "took a personal hand in the proceedings undoubtedly proved helpful to the prosecutor, others unquestionably aided appellants. Perhaps most judges would have taken a less active role in the trial." But Solomon's actions did not "constitute a substantial and unwarranted interference with counsel in the presentation of their cases, nor does it appear that the judge was biased."[19]

APPEALS JUDGE

Solomon's judicial caliber, speed, and dedication earned him welcome as an extra judge on appellate courts. "Sitting with appeals panels . . . is considered a plum assignment that allows district judges to spotlight their legal talents, often by writing the court's opinion," Augustus B. Cochran III writes. More than a quarter of the nation's usual three-person appellate panels employ an active or retired district court or appeals court judge from another circuit. They needed the help. "Cumulatively," one study found, "there has been close to a fifteen-fold increase in the number of cases before the circuit courts since 1925 and almost a tenfold increase" between 1960 and 1988.[20]

Solomon's appellate opinions largely originated in his own circuit. Because of its heavy caseload, the Ninth Circuit used approximately twice the number of extra judges as all other circuits combined. Solomon also tirelessly participated in its conferences and policy-making councils and led seminars for its district judges. He long served on the federal courts' Intercircuit Assignment Committee. Ninth Circuit district judges in 1963 chose him as their representative to the Judicial Conference of the United States, which makes the basic administrative policies of the federal courts. A year later, it unsuccessfully sent him and Chief Judge Chambers to ask the U.S. Judicial Conference to allow it to breach the system-wide ban on photography and broadcasting in nonjudicial ceremonies.[21]

At the appellate level, Solomon savored the intellectual stimulation, collegiality, and enlarged opportunity to shape federal law. Circuit courts had the final say in most matters of law. As a practical matter, they were the courts of last resort, serving as the final arbiters of federal law for all but the small number of cases considered by the Supreme Court. "The appellate judge is deciding cases and writing opinions for the guidance of the bar and the district bench, and for the illumination of other appellate judges, law professors, and law students," Judge Posner wrote. For these audiences "the most important thing is the quality of the decision . . . rather than the judge's courtroom management and deportment."[22]

Appellate courts generally apply settled points of law to a particular conflict. Their panels, Lauren K. Robel summarizes, "decide motions, read briefs, hear arguments, confer about case dispositions, do research, and write opinions." It can be isolating, Solomon concluded. "You lead a very cloistered life. You usually sit with two colleagues," see few lawyers, and know fewer of them. "The argument, if there is an argument, seldom lasts more than a half hour on the side. Most of your work is in chambers, when you are writing things." Free of the hectic pace of the lower court, appellate court judges can be more scholarly and reflective, but they have to closely attend to one another's views. "The central reality of appellate judging is its collective nature," Donald D. Jackson writes. "The excess of ego afforded by the trial bench seem to subside" here. "Personalities soften; appellate judges invariably seem to be gentler men, more congenial, less willful."[23]

"Gus had a *very* congenial relationship with most of the other judges in the [Ninth] circuit, both at the district court level and the court of appeals level," Allan Hart remembered. "He was well respected and well liked in that situation." Solomon was often assigned to write the opinion. In contrast to his usual practice in his own court, he did not try to play the leading role and generally behaved deferentially to fellow panelists. Having drafted one opinion, Solomon informed colleagues that it made little, if any legal contribution: "I have no pride of authorship, and I am willing to make any changes you deem desirable." Solomon later remarked that he was "not sensitive about my decisions nor my work. I enjoy consulting with the judges on opinions, and I am disturbed the protocol apparently prevents one judge from suggesting language and other changes in an opinion." He politely disagreed on points and corrected spelling and grammar in circulated drafts. Once, when he thought a panelist would not be receptive to his suggestions, he diplomatically asked the other judge to make them.[24]

Solomon dissented in full or part in only six of his 111 published Ninth Circuit opinions. An issue had to seem extremely important to trigger a dissent from Solomon. In one case, deference painfully clashed with his Jewishness and anti-fascist past. In 1982, Andrija Artukovic — complicit in Nazi-allied Croatia's murder, imprisonment, and torture of Serbs, Jews, and others — had appealed a judge's revocation of a stay of deportation order. To issue the order, the INS appeals board had relied on a 1978 statutory amendment that barred relief to Nazi collaborators. In the post-argument stage, Solomon's memoranda advocating deportation failed to stop use of "collateral estoppel" principles, that is, the conclusiveness of a judgment in a prior action (relief from deportation in the 1950s) where the subsequent action is on a different cause of action (essentially, applying the amendment retroactively). Solomon drafted several versions of a dissent, restating points in his memoranda, before settling, simply, on "I dissent." For "me to set forth in detail my reasons for the dissent will help no one and may do some harm," he informed panelists. Ultimately, Artukovic was deported.[25]

JUDICIAL TEMPERAMENT

If Solomon had a major failing, his judicial temperament was it. At the district level, it compromised his performance, weakened his relations with the legal profession, and squandered lawyers' respect for him. Even admirers acknowledged this failing. Judge Goodwin felt that others possessed "a higher degree of what I call good judicial temperament than Judge Solomon." He "could be very arbitrary" at times, Judge Skopil concurred. "He was extremely bright," remarked Herbert Schwab of the Oregon Court of Appeals. "But I don't think he had the temperament to be a first-class judge." To Sidney I. Lezak, Solomon's "temperament was so bad it gave the appearance of unfairness that was not justified." A low reversal record was only one reason why Lezak concluded that "his rulings were actually more fair than he was given credit for."[26]

To admirers and critics alike, Solomon's judicial temperament diminished his virtues: sagacity, diligence, a devotion to justice, an imposing depth of legal knowledge, command of the cases, personal compassion, and, usually, generosity. "Despite his storied abrasiveness and indiscretions, Judge Solomon's purely legal abilities are acknowledged even by attorneys who turn ashen at the mention of his name," the *Oregon Journal* found. In 1978, to Solomon's disgust over the poll's propriety and crude methods, the newspaper asked 350 to 400 randomly selected federal bar members about each Oregon federal judge's performance. The 152 respondents, including those who merely had heard about him, gave Solomon (on a one-to-ten scale) an average of 8.4 for legal ability, 5.0 for fairness, 8.2 for diligence, and 3.4 for demeanor. "More than half the lawyers polled saw Solomon as intellectually distinguished . . . despite many scorching comments on demeanor." Eight out of ten respondents felt that he played favorites among attorneys; 70 percent of this group (56 percent of the total) thought favoritism affected his demeanor and 39 percent (27.3 percent of the total) his decisions. Allan Hart ruefully recalled enduring sarcasm and losing key motions and decisions in his good friend's court. Nor did Marvin Durning, the obvious favorite in the airport challenges, escape. Consistently ruling against Durning's clients, Solomon called his arguments "neither organized nor relevant. Plaintiffs have made many allegations of environmental harm and illegal administrative action, but their trial brief has frequently failed to relate their allegations to the legal issues."[27]

Solomon was fairer than the poll revealed. He "had a reputation that was worse than it should have been actually," Judge James A. Redden said. "He wasn't near as bad as the stories." As to impartiality, according to his own records, Solomon, a supporter of Social Security, ruled for the government in fifty-eight Social Security cases from 1964 through 1983 and against it in seventy cases. Lawyers representing businesses did not question the fairness of the former New Dealer, insurance-client advocate, and personal-liability attorney. "I recently tried an antitrust case involving automobile dealers," Solomon said. "In spite of my low regard for automobile dealers, I set aside a verdict only because I was convinced that the award was based solely upon the prejudice of jurors against automobile dealers." Another time, he held a special 7 AM hearing on a Saturday because the suit involved a tied-up vessel. "I knew that the costs of keeping a ship idle are astronomical." He allowed: "Yes, I am a liberal — in politics and economics — but I have never been a liberal with other people's money, that is why business likes to come before me." Solomon even won the grudging respect of insurers and their defenders. Early in his tenure, "the insurance industry, by voluntary agreement, [chose] to follow Judge Solomon's original holding" about what happens when two policies cover an Oregon driver's liability "rather than the rule adopted by the Ninth Circuit" when it reversed him, Randall B. Kester has written. In another trial, Douglas G. Houser recalled, "Judge Solomon made it clear from the beginning of trial that he was exceedingly hostile to the insurance company's position, but he never let his personal feelings interfere with the ultimate outcome of the case." After insurance defense lawyer Edwin J. Peterson tried additional cases before Solomon, he "realized that he was without favoritism, and when all was said and done, he treated both sides about the same."[28]

Nobody charged Solomon with self-absorption or indifference to the quality of the law, the courts, the legal profession — or justice. Although lawyers faced "a considerable amount of grief" from him, Norman Sepenuk concluded, "when the chips were down he would almost invariably reach the right result in a case." Being able to "trust your case to him" was Solomon's cardinal virtue. Strikingly, commentators by and large faulted Solomon's judicial demeanor, not the outcomes in his court.[29]

Solomon now and again confessed to legal errors, mainly after a reversal. Unlike many other judges, he also admitted to changing his mind. In 1977, he frankly reversed his 1975 opinion on a tax-free real-estate exchange method, an action that reverberated through national real-estate circles. The issue in both cases was whether forests could be legally exchanged tax-free for real estate handed over in the future. "I am going to take a good, hard look to see if the cases upon which I relied [in *Starker I*] require I hold that way," he had signaled. Only because of the law's seeming requirements had he allowed what seemed an unfair transaction in 1975, he explained. In *Starker II*, "I now conclude that I was mistaken in my holding [in *Starker I*] as well as in my earlier reading of *Alderson*." He labeled the questioned exchange method a tax-avoidance scheme and reversed himself.[30]

To U.S. Attorney Lezak, "Gus's saving grace . . . after he had a chance to think about something, where he had over-reacted" or acted impulsively, was that he "would back away." In one labor case, for example, Solomon "exploded," threatened night-and-day hearings on a preliminary injunction, and "stomped off the bench," Donald W. McEwen recalled. While "the lawyers were gazing at each other in somewhat stunned amazement, Gus reappeared and shouted" that he would issue a temporary restraint. He was persuaded to do nothing until the parties, as expected, agreed on the arbitration issues the next morning. Even when visibly disturbed, Solomon was strict, not ruthless. One attorney who forgot a calendar-call had his case dismissed. When approached worriedly in chambers, Solomon shouted that the offender should brace for a malpractice suit and stalked away. After a sleepless night, the chastened counsel received an order setting aside the dismissal.[31]

Many lawyers believed that while Solomon was an intelligent, hard-working, and basically fair-minded judge, he subjected them to shortsighted anger and unnecessarily complicated and sometimes unfair demands. Woe be the attorney who violated his high standards or said or did something Solomon considered manipulative, offensive, or an impediment to the court. "Men of conscience trained in the law are not easily tethered when given the sovereignty of judicial power," Justice William O. Douglas wrote. Judge Posner was balder: "Judges can make life hell for the lawyers who appear before them."[32]

In part, Solomon believed that he was rough on lawyers, including his own law clerks, for their own good. He scolded those who used incorrect punctuation, complicated or Latin words rather than simple English, or several sentences or paragraphs when one sufficed. But real hell threatened those who seemed poorly prepared, sloppy, lazy, or greedy; those who appeared to be blusterers, truth-shaders, cheaters, or cynical trial tacticians; or those who equivocally defended positions rather than helped him find out how things really were. "I dislike lawyers who are lazy, who bluff and cheat," he remarked, and "I do something about it." Why had it taken a year and a half for him to hear the defense's theory, he demanded in a case whose elements rambled through criminal and civil courts for decades. "Don't play footsie with me," he told an advocate. "That stuff isn't going to help you either, telling me how correct I am," he informed the opposing lawyer. When the famous California lawyer Melvin Belli listed a witness who, opponents feared, might introduce irrelevant and prejudicial evidence in a case, Solomon rumbled, "Whose idea is this?" Belli confessed uncertainty about calling the witness and then was cautioned from the bench, "Don't try it."[33]

Bar veterans knew what angered particular jurists but still could be amazed by Solomon's aria-like outbursts. Hearing one lawyer say that his client might or might not testify, as was his right, and that the jury ought not draw any inference of guilt or innocence from that decision, Solomon sprang from the bench. Livid, he motioned the stunned attorney to take his place and barked: "Do you want to be the judge? Do you want to tell the jury what the law is?" Another time, Norman Sepenuk heard from court personnel: "Gus feels like you are a son, and you stabbed him in the back" by filing a not-unusual request to withdraw a guilty plea. Two years of cool distance passed before the judge just as unexpectedly restored their friendly relationship. Those at the bar who were not charmed by Solomon before he was a judge seldom were afterward.[34]

Brusque or caustic treatment could befall both beginning and experienced lawyers appearing before Solomon, and few appreciated being caught within his fiery emotional range. Solomon could be impatient, preemptory, condescending, even insulting. The bite of an east European Jewish argumentative style — rich in inflated words and feelings and playfully, often sharply, pointed in phrasings and questions — was felt and easily misunderstood. Countless lawyers thought themselves chided "for 'infractions' that either did not exist or were comparatively minor," Edwin J. Peterson observed. They rankled at being taken to task in front of their peers, their clients, and court personnel rather than in the privacy of chambers or in correspondence. Being "skinned alive in public was hard to take" even when the criticism was justified, said one clerk of court. "Shouting with emotion," Solomon reportedly told Washington representatives: "This is not a case the state of Washington can be proud of." Another advocate heard: "Maybe you don't read very well. . . . If you don't understand English, that is up to you." He reportedly apprised still another: "You've got diarrhea of the mouth."[35]

The judge had a very elastic face and "could make faces" in court, John A. Ryan remembered. An agitated Solomon shook his finger, pounded his fist on the bench, or yelled at offenders, occasionally adding a heart-stopping flight from the bench. One lawyer who had the temerity to remind the judge that he was not enforcing a local rule was left red-faced and stammering when informed, "I'm running this court, and don't need any help from you!" He "was capable of berating you and just tearing up some guy and then moving in his favor," Bernard Jolles commented. Outside Oregon, where he and other visiting judges rarely concerned themselves with building rapport with local bars, he behaved similarly. "He sparked the otherwise dull beginnings of a civil trial yesterday by pouncing verbally on attorneys for talking too much" in Honolulu. In Seattle, more than one lawyer "slipped in to watch his peers at the bar get the business from Solomon." Nonetheless, Solomon's intellectual quickness was widely recognized. Dawdling, long-winded arguments and unneeded declarations, questions, citations, and documentation made him impatient. Lawyers who phoned him were curtly told to call back if they had not stated their idea in fifteen seconds. Solomon's intellectual quickness would have been "a virtue if he had learned to control his temper," Oregon Judge Herbert M. Schwab commented.[36]

Solomon was not one of those courtroom masters who could be routinely tough with attorneys without offending them. To Norman J. Wiener, he was "an outstanding judge" whose autocratic ways set him "almost at war with the federal" bar in Oregon. "There were years when his handling of his courtroom earned the enmity of, maybe hatred, of a great percentage" of it, Solomon's close friend Allan Hart concluded. "He could be savage in his sarcasm, in his humiliation of lawyers standing in front of him." He saw others violating rules or being careless, "but sometimes he was wrong." As "a result of the combination of these qualities, believe me, you didn't come into Judge Solomon's courtroom without thorough preparation and defend what you said . . . without the most careful thoroughness."[37]

Peppery anecdotes stuck to the judge; but storytellers ignored his heartfelt praise of particular attorneys for their contributions to the legal profession, their *pro bono* work, or their dedication to civil rights and civil liberties. Publicly and privately, he singled out individual lawyers for their ability, arguments, diligence, frankness, intelligence, hard work, and social consciousness. In decisions, bench remarks, correspondence, and speeches, he sprinkled compliments on those attorneys who helped worthwhile social movements. Peeved by the Washington attorney general's remark that he was overly friendly to Interior Department lawyer George Dysart, who was known for protecting Indian treaty rights, Solomon unconventionally answered through the press, mentioning his "high regard" for Dysart, who knew "as much or more about Indian law as any person in this area." Sometimes his compliments carried an edge: "Despite the fact [Paul R. Meyer] gets under my skin because he is a very persistent young man, he is an excellent lawyer. I have to give him credit for that. He is one of the best."[38]

The legal profession expected to find blunt and overbearing figures on the bench, and attorneys who believed that every multi-judge federal jurisdiction had its tyrant gave Solomon the title. "A lot of lawyers don't like me," he publicly acknowledged, and many of them called him a "son-of-a-bitch." Popularity was not in a judge's job requirements, he reminded, because fear of offending lawyers hurt good judging and efficient court administration. "The good administrative judges are never liked," Chief Justice Edwin J. Peterson believed. "Gus Solomon was a superb administrator." The "judges who let the lawyers run their courtrooms" won the "popularity contests."[39]

Solomon came to like his tough-guy image and occasionally tended to his legend. Without Libby Solomon, he declared, "I might have been like many other judges — impatient, irascible, and short-tempered; but because of her admonitions to be kind to lawyers, I am the sweet, kind, patient judge that all of you [lawyers] know." He confessed to being tough on counsel, but "I am usually tough on a younger lawyer," he said. New attorneys, he warned, got "preferred treatment, but not for long, and usually not for the things they can learn by reading the rules and by attending" Continuing Legal Education sessions. After his death, his friends remembered Solomon as irascible and temperamental. In 1970, he had preferred to avuncularly assure law students that he was "a teacher at heart, no worse than the professors." Smiling impishly, he confessed to being a "devil's advocate" in courtrooms and, like many judges, an occasional bluffer. Most "of the time, my hot air and bluster are calculated" to make lawyers prepare better and reach the true issues faster; "only rarely do I really lose my temper." In his displays of gruff bravado and other antics, Solomon exposed the lawyer-actor beneath the robe. But attorneys commonly felt that, given the stakes, they must treat his vinegary manner as genuine. He would "either get mad or feign anger at ill-prepared, bumbling lawyers," Judge Goodwin said. One court reporter was amused that lawyers being berated avoided eye contact with Solomon. He would "look down at me," he said, "and he'd wink at me and smile. Sort of an impish little smile he had."[40]

When angry, blood flushed Solomon's face and balding head, and his tenor voice was electric. Outside the courthouse, his friend Morton Goodman "would often temper him down when he became angry with people," and he himself tried to prevent his temper from hazarding legal outcomes. Many arguments in a brief "were calculated to arouse our anger by reflecting upon our competence and even our integrity," Solomon once wrote fellow panelists, "I did not rise to the bait." He said: "If there's ever any doubts in my mind about the state of my emotions when it comes time to pass sentence, I always postpone it until a later date." He suggested that lawyers copy his habit of reviewing critical or angry letters after cooling off in order to remove abrasive language before sending them.[41]

Appellate courts never commented on Solomon's temper, and offended counsel did not raise the issue. His worst eruptions apparently were absent from transcripts before courts reviewed them; and appellate lawyers, if they recognized any alteration, never challenged the record. One court reporter admitted to removing the worst outbursts before Solomon reviewed the transcripts and said that both Solomon and Kilkenny, as the bar suspected, submitted some altered transcripts, though none that changed meaning. Another court reporter complained to Judge Owen M. Panner that he had adamantly refused Solomon the right to change a just-prepared record. On Panner's inquiry, Solomon essentially said not to bother about it. In a different case, Solomon offered to enter corrections but only after the attorneys entered their own to correct possibly flawed spelling.[42]

Lawyers swiftly learned to be well prepared in his court. Trying personal injury cases before Solomon was "a real chore," Bernard Jolles recalled. "Fortunately he did them quickly. So it was painful but quick." A lawyer had to be prepared and "know what your case was about." It was important to have "witnesses lined up so there wasn't a 30 second delay between them." All witnesses had to be present the first trial day because often there was no second one. In "all candor, the best way to avoid his outbursts was to be thoroughly and completely prepared," Edwin J. Peterson decided from courtroom experiences. Part of the lawyers' terror, according to U.S. Attorney Lezak, "was that they knew that the judge was smart, that he was well prepared, and that he might question you about any case . . . or any composition that you cited."[43]

Late in Solomon's career, a Seattle lawyer lodged a complaint of judicial incompetence against him, one rapidly dismissed by the Ninth Circuit's chief judge. The charge focused on the visiting jurist's deteriorating "alertness, stability and ability to attend to the case." Repeated clashes between the complainant and the judge had marked the drawn-out and exasperating trial and post-trial processes in *Domingo v. New England Fish Co.* (see Chapter 9). Solomon disliked the tactics of both parties, "locked horns with the plaintiffs' lead attorney, and initially thought they had a pretty weak case," clerk John J. Kerr Jr. remembered. The attorney "was not afraid of the judge at all. He was from Washington and unlikely to have another case before him." In Solomon's opinion, he called the plaintiffs' lawyers idealistic but inexperienced, stubborn, and poor in judgment; and they made bad-faith, frivolous demands. He "felt that they were too aggressive in pursuing individual claims," clerk Henry J. Kaplan added. "Consequently, he denied most of the individual claims," denying relief to "all but a handful on grounds which I considered to be disingenuous."[44]

The opening day of this five-million-dollar class-action trial in Seattle ignited a Solomon flash point: inflated legal fees. To applause, he complained: "If all the money spent on attorneys were given to the workers, we wouldn't have a case in court." For decades, Solomon assailed excessive fees in class-action suits as well as counsel who did little work or never "gave an inch." He singled out civil rights lawyers "who bleed for the poor and oppressed" and when victorious "ask for exorbitant fees and sometimes get them." His strong views seemingly affected the Seattle case. After the opinion was rendered, he repeatedly refused to order interim payment of $175,000 to the plaintiffs' firm, although he knew that finances constricted its appeal. Borrow more funds from foundations and churches, he advised. To avoid what he considered the firm's potential conflict of interest, he appointed U.S.

magistrates to collect claims and severely limited the firm from helping possible claimants.[45]

In 1984, the Ninth Circuit accepted his basic liability decision in the Seattle case but reversed several of his findings and remanded for new hearings claimants who refiled claims or made new ones. Solomon had overly restricted communications between potential class members and the plaintiffs and their lawyers, it declared: "The trial court seems unnecessarily concerned that counsel would be overzealous in the pursuit of claims." Solomon also erred in refusing relief for discrimination after the date of trial and in making "an unusually low award of $70,000 to cover fees and costs for 6800 hours of service over several years." He justified the low fee by saying that the lawsuit should never have been brought and did not explain how he arrived at the award. Help from U.S. magistrates was no substitute for legal advocates aiding claimants, the Ninth Circuit ruled. Solomon normally took reversals calmly, but this time he asked that another judge handle the remand.[46]

Some lawyers learned to take Solomon's testiness in stride. To Berkeley Lent, it was simply "par for the course: being chewed out by Gus." Another said: "That's not the way I read the decision, your honor." The judge replied: "Maybe you don't read very well. Did it ever occur to you then?" The chance to spar was deftly declined. "Lots of things have occurred to me," the lawyer responded. Once Solomon needled a wary anti-trust counsel. Told that his side was anxious to go to trial, the judge replied: "You are going to trial, don't worry about that." When nothing was heard, Solomon archly continued: "I assume you have something more than hot air on which to base your complaint." The answer: "I hope so." For Pat Dooley, catching "hell" from Solomon "wasn't anything that tore me up." Without notice, he was ordered to represent a former client, a car thief who was on probation. He guessed that the judge merely wished to berate the man. While Solomon peered "like a rat terrier," Dooley pleaded for continued probation, and heard: "If you are criticizing the order of this court, you're talking this man right into McNeill Island" prison. "I thought, 'What the Hell.' So I said, 'Your Honor, I know you're too big a man to punish him for anything I might say.'" His Honor "hit the roof" but only told him to proceed. "Oh, was he mad. He looked at me about three times and just glowered" but continued the probation.[47]

A Honolulu lawyer likened the visiting judge to his former professors in toughly preparing law students for professional rigors. Solomon "very seldom picked on the same person twice in a row," Judge Skopil remarked. And he exercised some caution in the presence of juries. Overzealous counsel must sometimes be rebuked, Solomon typically instructed them, but they were "to draw no inference against the side to which an admonition of the Court may have been addressed during the trial." Lawyers who might assure clients beforehand that each advocate suffered his reproofs preferred not to be the last target and the freshest one in a jury's memory.[48]

Solomon did try to soften criticisms of his behavior. He occasionally sent attorneys and judges brief explanations of his decisions; and in law offices, law schools, and bar meetings, he smilingly assured listeners that he was not so tough. He denied a published account that he had "thundered" in the courtroom about an illegible signature: "Those of you who know me know that I never 'thunder' and that the newspaper reporter must have been mistaken." But he was thin-skinned about the press. In the 1930s, he had cultivated liberal editors and reporters to lessen press attacks on him and his causes. During his judicial nomination fight, he had played the *Oregonian* off against the *Oregon Journal*. His wariness about the press and crude attempts to manage stories continued when he was on the bench. Believing he had a responsibility to the public, he made his opinion file available for the *Journal's* court series. But he also asked to review intended feature stories about him and the court "to correct patent errors of grammar and context only . . . before publication. This is not censorship, only good sense." Editors usually refused these requests. In the end, what the bar or press thought of him did not really perturb Solomon. What was happening to the country did.[49]

Chapter 9

Rights

[The Lloyd] Corporation's rule prohibiting the distribution of handbills within the Mall violates Plaintiffs' First Amendment rights. I do not believe the Corporation may decide what groups may distribute literature within the Mall. Neither do I believe the Corporation may prohibit all distribution of handbills.
—Gus J. Solomon, 1970

TIDAL CHANGES

The "great tides and currents which engulf the rest of men do not turn aside in their course and pass judges by," Justice Benjamin N. Cardozo observed. The tumultuous 1960s and 1970s left Solomon variously — sometimes simultaneously — feeling puzzled, angered, rebuffed, behind the times, wary, or, less often, happy. "We are in a period of great unrest — of a social revolution," he warned in 1963. "Such a period is ordinarily bad for Jews because Jews are the traditional scapegoats for the fascists, the Nazis, the Communists, and all the forces of hatred and malevolence." National unrest between 1967 and 1972 manifested itself in his own hometown in alternative lifestyles; student, anti-war, and draft resistance movements; two small riots in a predominantly African American neighborhood; a bomb exploding outside City Hall; a police clash with anti-war protesters; and the near-disruption of a national American Legion convention. "There was a hell of a lot of foment that may not have had a lot of significance nationally," recalled Portland political activist Joe Uris, "but it was representative of what was going on nationally."[1]

Powerful forces were buffeting the country and the world. The Americas, Europe, and Asia were experiencing turmoil even as the United States' post-war expansion started grinding to a halt around 1965. During the 1970s, economic decline, an oil crisis, stagflation, a sharp increase in income inequality, and other difficulties caused

America's worst economic trauma since the Great Depression. In 1975, the country lost its first war and had its first president driven from office. The scale, thrust, and rapidity of such events worried Solomon. In 1969, he spoke plaintively of how difficult it had become "to keep up. I feel compelled to run faster and faster just to remain in the mainstream of American life." He was not the first long-serving judge to worry that he and his court might be losing touch with the culture and society.[2]

At times, it seemed as if events swept away much that Solomon held dear. His liberal programs and agenda badly suffered through those years — but not initially. "Liberalism entered the 1960s near the height of its power," Alan Brinkley writes, as "Great Society" liberals forced through major legislation and appropriations that affected cities and rural areas, poverty, medical delivery, civil rights, voting, education, arts, and the humanities. But liberalism "departed the decade crippled, defensive, and widely reviled." By 1968, the major pillars of liberalism "had begun to crumble: the commitment to the Cold War, the faith in the possibility of peaceful social change, the belief in the essential health of American culture, even confidence in the American economy." Other "kinds of politics emerged to challenge it."[3]

Protesters' sweeping demands for alterations in American society and its allocation of power made Solomon wary, angry, or both. It violated his liberal notions of merit and fair play to guarantee any group equal results rather than equal opportunities. Often, he feared in 1976, "a member of a minority uses his race or color as a method of attempting to get an advantage to which he is not entitled. In other words, asserting his color rather than recognizing his own actions as a basis for some action." Cascading demands by African Americans, Latinos, students, women, sexual minorities, and the young badly stretched his sympathy for groups that had little power. Black separatists rejected his interracial liberalism and the ideal of a race-blind society. The setting ablaze of campuses and urban ghettos appalled him. The pro-choice movement challenged his orientation as a board member and chair of the Boys and Girls Aid Society of Oregon, which counseled against abortions and refused to perform them. His generation's hard-won accomplishments were being challenged. Calls for individual fulfillment, anti-authoritarianism tied to an "anti-politics," and self-absorbed politics violated his beliefs in the centrality of social needs and of collective, constitutionally rooted politics. He opposed the fractionalization of culture and a radical individualization of interests in society. Demands for teaching Spanish in the public schools challenged his belief in English as the language that was necessary to set all children on the path toward opportunity. Relentless invective by radicals and conservatives stigmatized the term *liberal* when he considered it a badge of honor.[4]

The country's noisy debate over freedom, morality, and citizenship sometimes took directions Solomon opposed. The Cold War consensus was unraveling; and younger, more culturally liberal, socially left, and anti-war elements derided liberals as hopelessly docile and out-of-date. The student-based New Left and overlapping counter culture rejected Solomon's tenets by embracing alternative lifestyles and values, questioning the merits of economic growth, espousing equal outcomes, and opposing anti-Communism and pro-corporate Democratic Party stances. Solomon recoiled from protesters' increasingly confrontational tactics. Often, he misunderstood the protesters, all but failing to recognize his own heritage mirrored in their infectious optimism and idealism and their denouncement of the established order for not living up to the nation's proclaimed ideals. Except among Jews, he did not resonate to the stress on "community" in a wide range of social movements. Imposing dress and grooming standards on his clerks, he repudiated convention-flaunting behaviors, dress, and entertainment. He almost viscerally opposed the new popular attitudes toward formal rules and customs, parental and societal authority, sex, education, and personal appearance.[5]

"I confess that I don't understand the dancing and music of young people," he said, "or their strong belief that they should pick the faculty and select the courses in the schools they attend." Students displeased by his rulings on a draft case picketed his court, "and I have been vilified because of my conservatism. Even some of my law clerks are critical of my views about young people who engage in violent acts and who create situations to get television coverage." He remained as contemptuous of dissidents' theatrical displays and large gestures as he was of those who merely expressed fine sentiments.[6]

Not that Solomon soured with age. In the early 1960s, he admired the many Americans struggling to make their nation freer and more democratic. He welcomed the southern Civil Rights movement, the liberal Warren Court decisions, and resurgent signs of active government. He sympathized with the nation's identity and ethnic revival — at least when it came to Jews — when, as Jonathan D. Sarna writes,

"Americans of all kinds came to focus on roots, race, ethnicity, and gender." Questions of who did or did not belong to a group and what those who belonged deserved lay at the center of the revival — and a lifetime of Solomon's concern. He loved the reawakening ethnicity among Jews and celebrated the decline in anti-Semitism. If in his lifetime he did not "expect to see a world free from anti-Semitism," then his children and grandchildren "may be able to live in such a world."[7]

John F. Kennedy's presidential victory pleased Solomon, and with a Democratic Senate it offered him a chance to advance to the Ninth Circuit Court of Appeals. With no Oregonian on that court since Judge Fee's death in 1959, some Oregonians in 1961–1962 and again in 1963, when another seat became vacant, unofficially claimed a place for a judge from the state. Solomon did not avidly seek either opening, age and public recognition likely having dimmed his ambition; and as a judge, he had to act indirectly when he did seek it. In Washington, his old friend C. Girard Davidson and broadcasting executive and civil libertarian Ancil H. Payne and in Portland, former Republican Representative Walter Norblad and others saw western senators and others on his behalf. Solomon publicly maintained a grave, disinterested stance, telling the press only that he would consider the post if nominated. That year, he spoke to Attorney General Robert F. Kennedy in Portland about district matters and probably about a nomination. Twice that year, the *Oregon Journal* endorsed him. Solomon's doctor issued communiqués saying that his health, which had been questioned — he had suffered a heart attack when he was forty-nine — barred no promotion.[8]

In 1961–1962, a dispute between Senator Maurine Neuberger and Representative Edith Green dissolved his chances. Solomon was not the issue; both officials had recommended him to the Justice Department, and a now-Democratic Senator Wayne L. Morse had concurred. The issue was patronage, which included whether Neuberger's candidate, Allan Hart, or Green's candidate, John C. Beatty, should replace Solomon on the district court. Neuberger refused to sign the senatorial "blue slip," preventing Judiciary Committee review of Solomon. With top Democrats divided and a dispute looming on the district court replacement, the administration settled on a Californian for the court of appeals.[9]

The possible naming of Solomon to the Ninth Circuit in 1963 replayed these scenes, except now Senators Morse and Neuberger feuded. Morse, whose warm relationship with Solomon had not endured, essentially did nothing for him. Neuberger and Green recommended Solomon and held a luncheon in his honor at the U.S. Capitol, but the possibility of a Hart-Beatty district rematch worried the administration because of its possible impact on the approaching 1964 election. Another Californian joined the Ninth Circuit. In the political arena, Oregon is "a very small state" and is overridden by more powerful ones, Hart said of these events. Solomon would have been "a wonderful circuit judge," U.S. Attorney Lezak and others felt. "He was an excellent writer, and his vision and his brilliance would have shone" on the higher court. Whatever "faults that he had were exaggerated because he sat as a trial judge," Lezak continued, and these "would not have existed to anywhere near the extent had he gotten to the Court of Appeals. It's tragic that politics kept him" from it.[10]

While losing a promotion was no wrenching affair for Solomon, the nation's assassinations, riots, and war in Asia were. Unenthusiastic about the conflict in Vietnam, Solomon masked his doubts. Saying privately in 1968 "that Americans generally are sick and tired of the Vietnam war" and that he hoped "something can be done about it," he publicly called President Johnson "right" on the war. Meanwhile, he sadly watched Great Society programs dwindle or die; the welfare state shrink; divisions over the war worsen; bellicose conservatives surge ahead; liberals fissure over issues of class, race, and the Vietnam War; and blue-collar and white ethnic constituencies abandon the Democratic Party. He generally faced such happenings with obstinate confidence in his old principles and the power of intelligence and practical, morally driven acts, and occasionally with self-preserving humor. There were no lamentations for a lost liberalism or lost causes and no reminiscing about faded glories. Solomon had no sense that his basic principles and ideals had run down or failed. He felt pride in having waged seemingly hopeless fights for supposedly radical or dangerous causes that, in the end, won measurable acceptance and legitimacy. Certain about the worth of the nation's values and institutions, he recognized national failings and, fueled by his moral and political dicta, got on with trying to improve matters. Still enamored by the possibilities of using an active government in the name of a more just and equitable society, Solomon did not lose his way, despair, or abandon the old causes, the old ways, the old doctrines.[11]

He self-consciously belonged to a die-hard band of an Americans for Democratic Action-type of New Dealers–Fair Dealers who roundly damned conservatives and radicals alike. An anti-Communist liberal in the tradition of Truman, Humphrey, and Jackson when it came to their defense of New Deal liberalism and color-blind integrationism, Solomon wavered when they called for confronting the Soviet bloc. At the same time, Senator Robert F. Kennedy's new identification with the interests of the dispossessed did not attract him. His liberal New Deal fever burned despite serious charges that events had proven his and his friends' kind of political thinking unworkable or invalid and their sentiments empty rhetoric. Nothing had discredited their convictions, accomplishments, or shrewdness, Solomon insisted. The set of ideological and ethical commitments that had sustained him since youth held, as did his liberal core values regarding social justice, positive government, and social-political inclusiveness.

From the 1960s until his death, Solomon rued the lack of patriotism, the loss of moral authority by institutions, and the growing popular feeling that America was wrong. When social movements and economic and cultural chasms forced an angry debate on American institutions, he defended them. "The government never engages in dirty tricks," he insisted after the Watergate revelations, "but a few misguided government employees do." Governing institutions were no less obliged than during the Great Depression, he argued, to protect and advance individual rights, further equal opportunity, and help generate prosperity. Despite eroding public trust in these principles, government to him remained an essential vehicle of economic and social development and the guarantor of citizens' welfare.[12]

"Gus never lost his interest in developing the economy for people," in whatever "affected the standard of living" and raised "the economic capabilities of the general public," veteran New Dealer Dan Goldy observed. During lunches in his chambers in the mid-1960s, Solomon had Goldy, director of the Oregon Economic Development Office, tutor the judges on active economic policies. To increase outside investment in Oregon, Solomon relayed information on the state's timberland to a Chicago paper-box manufacturer that employed his oldest brother Eugene. And he identified investment opportunities in the state to corporate officials and his former law clerk Jerome Kohlberg Jr., who he introduced to Oregon bankers, lawyers, and politicians.[13]

It was more painful to be called a conservative at the time than Solomon admitted. "What was a liberal in the late 40s and early 50s was not a liberal in the 80s," Judge Skopil dryly said of him. Law clerk Stephen Gillers preferred to locate him "center-right on issues of military preparedness, international affairs [and] communism" and "center-left on social issues." But Solomon knew how liberal he was. If others termed him complicit with the Establishment or said that the solutions offered by his liberal generation constituted the problems of the next one, he affected to be amused. When local realtors, whose residential segregation practices he had long condemned, officially feted him in 1970 as Portland's First Citizen, he remembered: "I realized that I was getting older and more conservative [but I] had no idea that I had made myself so agreeable to the Establishment." Of nationally prominent liberal friends in New York, he commented: "Maybe they are no longer liberal but as reactionary as we are." American Civil Liberties Union and Legal Aid Society people "are critical of me because I don't go along with everything they do, but I didn't believe that I had moved so far right. It worries me." Fidelity to now accepted but once controversial programs and viewpoints made him appear conservative, he implied. Convictions that had nourished him through the perilous 1930s and 1940s sustained him.[14]

THE DRAFT

The Vietnam War swept thousands of alleged draft offenders into federal courts. A democratic social order, Solomon made clear, was harmed by those who he publicly claimed made up 70 percent of the draft and war resisters who appeared before him. In 1969, he caricatured them as bearded, longhaired, drug-using hippies who opposed the Vietnam War; as educational dropouts living with women and taking no responsibility for children they fathered; and as objectors "to the moral code of parents and of [a] society" they damned as materialistic and immoral. Americans must not permit this influential group "to determine whether a law is good or bad, and, if they believe it is bad, permit them to disregard the law." They lacked "the knowledge, experience or expertise to determine" American foreign policy, he said.[15]

David Burner may have exaggerated in stating that American liberalism "was caught and rent to pieces" during the 1960s because liberals advocated "both the free assertion of conviction and careful maintenance of laws, institutions, and a well-ordered polity." Nevertheless, Burner highlighted a major problem in Solomon's centrist liberalism. As a judge, his solicitude for dissidents' rights bumped hard against his yearning for social order and effective *and* humane institutions, especially their control features. The Cold War liberal who valued the draft and disapproved of generational rebellion proved to be sensitive to the rights of alleged draft offenders and not entirely deaf to their idealism. As to the law, some resisters claimed religious exemption from the draft under the First Amendment's free exercise of religion clause; others claimed due process of law protection under the Fifth Amendment. Solomon looked more benignly on conscientious objectors from traditional peace churches and on principled secular dissenters than on the larger run of draft defendants, who he caricatured severely. In any event, he tried to persuade conscientious objectors to accept alternate service, and, over time, he tried to hobble the draft resistance movement.[16]

Like other Vietnam-era judges, Solomon treated the draft as sound policy and its registration provisions as settled law. He refused to determine whether the Selective Service Act was good or bad law. Precedent similarly allowed him to bar arguments about the morality or legality of the Vietnam War, which were central contentions of war resisters. In terms of due process, Solomon applied common tests of administrative agency action in evaluating draft boards' actions. Did the record show they had been arbitrary and capricious, or had their actions been based on a reasonable evaluation of the information the boards possessed? "Court review is designed to prevent isolated instances of arbitrary actions" by them, he stated. One board, he ruled, should have given its reasons for denying a defendant a deferred ministerial classification. "A court should not be forced to speculate on the local board's basis in fact for its decision."[17]

Solomon exhibited similar views while writing for the Ninth Circuit in *U.S. v. Haughton*. The opinion "brought important procedural fairness to the Selective Service process," Stephen Gillers recalled. Enormously powerful draft boards often spoke by fiat; *Haughton* forced them to explain themselves. Otherwise, courts could not know whether a board did not believe the registrant — a nearly unreviewable factual conclusion — or had made a reviewable factual error about his legal entitlement. To Solomon, the decision "established the rule that once a registrant had made a *prima facie* case for classification as a conscientious objector, the Selective Service Board, if it rejects the request, must state the reasons for the rejection." He credited the idea to his law clerk Gillers. "We sold it to my colleagues on the panel, and it was followed in many other circuits," he said. The Supreme Court in 1971 and 1972 generally accepted the rule in *U.S. v. Gillette, U.S. v. Clay*, and *Fein v. Selective Service System Local Board No. 7*.[18]

In New York in the early 1970s, law student Mark Silverstein heard about Solomon's good reputation among "judge-shopping" draft dissidents hoping for light sentences and relatively easy prison berths. Portland attorney G. Bernhard Fedde, considering Solomon "very sensitive on draft cases," was pleased that his client Robert Wollheim would face him. Solomon admired principled, nonviolent opponents of the draft who were willing to accept the consequences of their actions, which is how he characterized Wollheim before imprisoning him. The Ninth Circuit reversed the decision on the grounds that the draft board had punitively reclassified Wollheim after he refused induction. When Wollheim later applied to law schools, Solomon recommended his admission and described him as an "idealistic and courageous young man who was willing to give up his freedom for his convictions." In front of press photographers, he swore Wollheim — subsequently an Oregon appellate judge — into federal practice.[19]

Solomon distinguished "between those people who were against the war in Vietnam and those people who believed in picketing and violence and in the violation of the law." Peaceful marching and handbilling were acceptable protests; throwing rocks was not. Violent resistance threatened to create the chaos he had always feared, just as resisters who were disrespectful in court threatened the orderly court processes he required. "If you think I'm going to permit a circus to be made out of this court, you're mistaken," he told a draft defendant who had the temerity to request assignment of a free lawyer from California rather than one from Oregon. When a convicted draft dissident called his court unjust and likened him to Nazi Adolph Eichman, Solomon listened silently before imposing a thirty-month sentence, reportedly his severest sanction to date. Once the sentence was affirmed by the Ninth Circuit, he halved it to match those he usually gave.[20]

Solomon was more disturbed by religiously motivated conscientious objector cases, he said, "than I am with any other." The historic maltreatment of pacifists disgusted him. "I have all the sympathy in the world for a conscientious objector," he said, "but no sympathy for people who rely on technicalities to avoid their [draft] obligations." After a 1968 sentencing of an Amish defendant, for example, "I did something I seldom do. I took a double martini [at lunch], I was upset as hell. Don't think a judge is God." This man "cannot go home again if he goes into the service." In August 1968, Solomon stumbled on how to keep Jehovah's Witnesses free while making sure they served governmental interests and societal needs. For the Witnesses, who were the subject of the most Selective Service cases in the district by 1967, the "trials were religious experiences, a confirmation of the depth of their beliefs," according to two scholars. Normally, Solomon jailed Witnesses who refused alternate service and fruitlessly offered them a second chance to register, tied to parole. The Oregon judges usually gave Witness-refusers three-to-six-month sentences. Why, Solomon asked a Bible-carrying Witness poised to plead guilty to nonregistration, did he not register and accept alternate service? It violated Biblical passages to cooperate with a military organ, he heard. Temporarily stopping the trial, Solomon called a Unitarian minister to interpret the passages and was told that the defendant believed that civil authorities (judges), not military authorities, were commanding voices of God.[21]

Reconvening, Solomon proclaimed his civilian status as a judge and said that the law and the Bible compelled the accused to register with the draft, obtain conscientious objector status, and accept a hospital assignment, followed by probation. Whenever possible, he tried to keep sincere young men from the disadvantages and lifelong stigmas of imprisonment, he said. The defendant complied, satisfied that the judicial formula removed the moral stigma found in obeying a military command. Nationally, newspapers took note. Solomon seldom used this technique, and then mainly "in cases where I found that the local Draft Board acted not only unwisely but possibly punitively." The Witnesses, he privately wrote, lacked criminal records but were so poorly educated and low in intelligence as to be useless to the military. There was no reason to imprison them "when we can get them to do that which the Selective Service wants them to do." It "is delighted with this solution." He offered to free Witnesses who were persuaded by the new formula. If they served the rest of their sentences in alternate service jobs, then they could leave prison.[22]

Judge Belloni copied his method, and by 1971 the district reportedly led all others in its use. After studying the Scriptures to better question Christian pacifists, Solomon began referring in court to Biblical passages and chiding jurists for not knowing their New Testament. Judges Abraham L. Marovitz in Chicago and John W. Oliver in Kansas City copied the technique, but another judge complained that it made slaves of the Witnesses. Eighteen months later, a *Los Angeles Times* investigation traced a 30 percent national decline in imprisoned Witnesses in part to Solomon's formula. Early in the 1970s, however, with few Witnesses anywhere being sent to prison, the Witnesses decided that such cooperation did indeed violate their beliefs.[23]

When troop involvement in Vietnam and draft cases both escalated between 1966 and 1970, Solomon began expressing uncertainty about the purposes of his draft sentencing and proper draft sanctions. In draft cases, judges enjoyed wide sentencing discretion. They could order imprisonment or supervised probation, suspend jail sentences, or impose fines. They might also reduce imposed sentences, which national statistics masked. In 1965 and 1967, Solomon said that eighteen months was longer than he usually imposed, except when conscientious objectors failed to report to alternate service jobs. During the Tet offensive in early 1968, he feared that deteriorating conditions in Vietnam might invite judicial punitiveness toward draft defendants. He did not consider himself a harsh sentencer in draft cases.[24]

The Oregon Selective Service Panel, a group of about fifty antiwar lawyers, disagreed. The Panel reported that of the twenty-four men Solomon convicted for draft violations between 1966 and June 1969, nine went to prison for an average of 17.5 months; the rest received probation plus civilian work in the national interest. Judges Belloni and Kilkenny awarded an average 17.25-month jail term to the seven men they convicted, and another six received probation requiring civilian work. (According to another study, judges in draft cases imposed an average thirty-four-month sentence in 1969.) The Panel criticized all three Oregon judges, Solomon most of all, for imposing harsher sentences on draft violators than on those they sentenced for fraud, income tax evasion, counterfeiting, forgery, bank robbery, assault, receiving stolen property, and narcotic offenses. The three judges, it concluded, gave little weight to draft offenders' lack of prior criminal convictions and seldom permitted them to plea bargain.

By the 1970s, alarmed by draft resistance, Solomon publicly argued for a two-tier sentencing approach, because, he implied, it would hobble resistance to the war. Draft violators felt neither shame nor regret, he informed federal judges, and they were unstigmatized by detention or conviction. Probation only raised noncompliance. Because "the primary purpose of sentencing Selective Service violators is to deter others, longer sentences should be imposed on those violators who occupy prominent positions in student and anti-draft organizations" — two-and-a-half to three-year terms, and eighteen-month-to-two-year terms for followers. Longer sentences would alienate "the moderates — the middle group," who the judiciary should target as the most easily influenced draft segment — and make them receptive to skilled far left and far right agitators.[25]

Draft prosecutions and convictions appreciably slowed as Americans wearied of the war and as Supreme Court decisions eased draft challenges, more defending lawyers litigated aggressively, troop withdrawals increased, a draft lottery was instituted, and draft calls declined. The percentage of Selective Service convictions fell nationally every year between 1967 and 1975, from about 75 percent to less than 17 percent. The Oregon Selective Service Panel in this period was granted representation of indigent draft offenders and fought charges previously handled by judicial review of the records alone. The district responded to changing opinion by lightening sentences; and, during the early 1970s, its judges, with official cooperation, gradually adopted "a standard sentence, except for the most egregious cases, of six months," according to U.S. Attorney Lezak. The judges tried to arrange imprisonment in relatively safe state and federal prison farm and forest facilities.[26]

THE FIRST AMENDMENT

American Civil Liberties Union General Counsel Marvin Karpatkin in 1971 publicly credited his friend Solomon with courageous civil liberties decisions. The year before, in *Tanner v. Lloyd Corp.* — an important First Amendment case on public access rights to private and governmental properties — the judge had awarded young anti-war dissidents a substantial free speech victory. Security guards, threatening arrest, had cleared three anti-war handbill distributors to sidewalks outside Portland's sprawling Lloyd Center, where the mall's literature ban did not apply. Before he read the briefs, Solomon signaled his notion of the central legal issue and his probable ruling. What he had to decide as a matter of law, contrary to the owner's claim that protesters had no free expression rights on its private property, was "whether a shopping center of the size and magnitude of yours can separate and distinguish between people who want to use those facilities, not for the purpose of the shopping center but for their own purpose, for instance the Salvation Army."[27]

"Yea, yea, yea" came from the plaintiffs' supporters "just loud enough to signify appreciation . . . for remarks or rulings of Judge Solomon during the [bench] trial," their lawyer Carl R. Neil recalled. This "Greek Chorus" would not influence the court, Solomon responded. Many young anti-war people "don't like me. I know that . . . I send them to jail. But that is not the proposition" being considered. Neil thought it "pretty unusual for people of that sort to receive any favorable rulings in a court case in those days." But Solomon cut short the attorney's argument that the leaflets advocated Selective Service violations. *Oregon v. DeJonge,* he reminded, "says that a man is to be held for what is done at that particular time and not who calls the meeting."[28]

As the leading case, the plaintiffs offered *Marsh v. Alabama,* which affirmed First Amendment rights when owners opened a property for use by the public. Lloyd Center countered with *Amalgamated Food Employees v. Logan Valley Plaza,* which likened a shopping center to a company town. At trial, Solomon commented skeptically on *Logan Valley's* relevance, calling it a labor, not a First Amendment case — a minority view among scholars. Finding for the plaintiffs, he wrote that the Supreme Court "held that Marsh's rights occupied a 'preferred position' and weighed heavier than the owner's [property] rights" and that the handbill distribution was identical to Marsh's literature distribution. That it was a shopping center rather than a company town was irrelevant. While *Logan Valley* left open whether an owner could bar picketing unrelated to a property's use, at Lloyd Center the handbilling "was pure speech." The First Amendment went that far even if *Logan Valley* had not. "I do not believe the [Lloyd] Corporation may decide what groups may distribute within the Mall. Neither do I believe the Corporation may prohibit all distribution of handbills," Solomon wrote. Any owner opening "land to the general public for business purposes, to the extent that the land becomes the functional equivalent of a public business district, gives up the right to prohibit" literature distribution or "to decide which literature may be distributed." Otherwise "the public need for uncensored information, on which Marsh was based, could be frustrated."[29]

Affirmed by the Ninth Circuit in a brief *per curiam* ruling, Solomon's attempt to expand on *Marsh* was turned back five-to-four by the Supreme Court in 1972 in what Stephen L. Wasby termed "one of the better-known Supreme Court rulings to have originated in the District for Oregon." It "is of particular interest for its place in the transition from the Warren Court to the Burger Court, because the lower courts drew on pro-civil liberties rulings . . . but were reversed in what many took to be a precursor of a far more conservative position by the newly reconstituted 'Nixon Court.'" Justice Lewis F.

Powell Jr., who wrote for the majority, concluded that allowing on-site distribution of handbills in a shopping center would infringe the owner's property rights "without significantly enhancing the asserted right of free speech." No open-ended invitation to the public to use the mall for any and all purposes had been extended by the owners. The facts of the case, he averred, significantly differed from those in *Marsh* and *Logan Valley*. Where handbilling was unrelated to the Lloyd Center's activity and where respondents had adequate alternative means of communication, Powell found that the lower courts had erred. The more liberal justices on the Court disagreed. When striking the balance between freedom of speech and owners' ability to control property, the balance must weigh more heavily for speech, Thurgood Marshall wrote in dissent.[30]

Similar views informed Solomon's actions on a three-judge district panel that considered a request by the Oregon Socialist Workers Party (SWP) for First Amendment relief from the Oregon Campaign Disclosure Act. He was persuaded by the SWP's contention that disclosing its contributor list would open donors to unconstitutional harassment. He asked its counsel: "Aren't you giving up too much when you say: If the F.B.I. and C.I.A. would stop their harassment, the situation would be different? Isn't that your real point that the [SWP] is a small unpopular party, despised by the great majority?" She replied: "That's accurate." And to the state's attorney: "What should [the SWP] have to prove in order to be entitled to this exemption" to listing contributors? "I assume you concede under *Buckley*, under certain circumstances a political party may obtain an exemption?" He answered: "Certainly." "Go ahead and tell me what they should show."[31]

Buckley v. Valeo recently had established the constitutionality of the Federal Election Campaign Act disclosure requirements and had raised the possibility of First Amendment exceptions to state campaign disclosure acts. In deliberations, Solomon argued that allowable exemptions applied to the SWP because of the government's harassment of the party. Failing to persuade fellow panelists, he issued one of his rare dissents, stressing *Buckley v. Valeo*. "We must preserve the right of splinter parties to participate in the political process. . . . The alternative will force minor parties underground and create a significantly greater risk to our democratic society." Through his law clerk, he tried to have the ACLU adopt the case and persuade the SWP to appeal. There was no appeal; but in a different SWP challenge, the Supreme Court struck down a similar state disclosure requirement in 1982.[32]

NATIVE AMERICAN RIGHTS

Solomon demonstrated a substantial commitment to the rights of Native Americans, although he did not consider that his opinions on those cases significantly contributed to the law. As law clerk Henry J. Kaplan recognized, Solomon had a "sympathetic concern for faithful adherence to the historical promises made to Native Americans." But few outside Indian law circles noticed his benevolent treatment of the claims made by western tribes and poor Native Americans. The cases neither added to nor detracted from his judicial reputation, but they did affect the course of the law on tribal lands and resources that followed in the troubled wake of the post-1953 termination of federal supervision of more than a hundred tribes and bands and after an important 1963 Supreme Court decision on Indian water rights.[33]

Solomon firmly approved of the judiciary's requirement that the federal government and its courts act fairly as guardians of Native American rights and interests. Going further, he resisted efforts to criminalize activities that native people needed to engage in to live partly off the land. Outside the court, he encouraged tribal and governmental initiatives against Indian poverty, joblessness, alcoholism, and delinquency. And he wanted injustices against Native Americans confronted. Once, for instance, he surprised Bend attorney Owen M. Panner with a call suggesting that he investigate the Madras city jail. He had heard that it was unsanitary and that "things were going on there which were very unfair" to members of the tribe that Panner represented.[34]

Early in Solomon's judicial career, federal health, education, and economic development services to terminated tribes all but ended. Terminated tribes floundered. Swaths of Indian Country fell into private and government hands, including in 1961 the million acres of the nation's second largest terminated tribe, the Klamath in southern Oregon. The majority of the 2,133 Klamaths "withdrew" from tribal affiliation and received payment from the sale of their reservation. About 1,000 of their descendants born after the 1954 closing of the tribal roll were left in legal limbo. Public Law 280 meanwhile subjected tribal members in several states, except on Oregon's Warm Springs Reservation, to state civil and criminal laws.[35]

By the early 1960s, termination was largely considered a failure. Tribal legal standing and jurisdiction and various benefits were gradually re-established, and Native American authority was expanded in federal programs. Indians pressed for restored tribal or band status, more assertive tribal governance, and the enforcement of long-ignored treaty rights to water, timber, fish, and wildlife. Federal courts became the customary forums for adjudicating Native American water rights. At the same time, Congress in the McCarran Amendment of 1952 consented to the United States being joined in state courts as a defendant in many Indian water suits.

None of the rights of Native Americans was the source of lengthier litigation than hunting, trapping, and fishing rights. In the 1960s, Washington and Oregon renewed state efforts to curtail or abrogate treaty rights, arresting and fining Indians and seizing their equipment. Indians held "fish-ins" in the Pacific Northwest and Great Lakes regions in defiance of state restrictions on fish limits as well as non-Indian resistance to federal court orders on Indian fishing. Decisions in the 1970s upheld numerous Indian treaty fishing and hunting rights, established some tribes as co-managers of fisheries with state and federal officials, and defined Indian property rights after termination. But in the 1980s, the courts limited tribal civil-regulatory jurisdiction and permitted some state conservation methods to prevail over reservation practices. In 1985, two years before Solomon's death, the Supreme Court, in reversing one of his many attempts to ward off state restrictions of Indians, abrogated the Klamath Tribe's rights to hunt, fish, and trap on land it had ceded, unless it was open to those uses by all Oregon residents.[36]

Solomon, who would have denied any pro-Indian bias, usually indulged tribal claims to fish, game, and water resources. As in *Klamath v. Maison* (*Klamath I*), he normally accorded Indian treaties superiority over any conflicting executive orders or statutes. The Klamath and Modoc 1864 treaty "should be construed literally in favor of the Indians," he ruled elsewhere. Favoring treaty language that enabled Native American to use and control natural resources, Solomon repeatedly reined in the states' authority. Precedents established that they could regulate Indian fisheries, he admitted, but only with actions necessary to conserving fish. Oregon had not met that burden of proof, he ruled in a 1960 Klamath fishing case. In court and to reporters, he also complained about the overly aggressive Indian litigation tactics of Oregon and Washington and their conservation officers' tough treatment of Native Americans. More than once, Solomon threatened to issue injunctions against state officials to enforce his decisions.[37]

Native Americans seemed to lie on his conscience. When he accepted the American Civil Liberties Union of Oregon's highest civil liberties award in 1965, he hinted at the depth of his feelings. Many people "are disturbed over our shabby treatment of the Indians 100 years ago, over Hitler's massacre of 6 millions Jews and the evacuation of Americans of Japanese ancestry during World War II," he declared. His sympathies seem strongest if Indian claimants were poor or living in a traditional manner or if tribes had been badly represented or handled by federal authorities. So, in *Klamath I* tribal members were granted an unrestricted right to take the fish and game on their reservation but not on the nearby national forest, which had been acquired from the tribe at termination. Hunting and fishing "affords a substantial part of the subsistence and livelihood of the Klamath people. Many would be inadequately fed were they deprived of the right to hunt on their reservation as their needs for food require." As with other minorities, though, Solomon rejected their use of threats or force. In *Burgwin v. Mattson*, he summarily upheld FBI agents for acting in good faith and ruled that they had official immunity and probable cause for arresting individuals who agents thought were delivering supplies to Indians at Wounded Knee on the Pine Ridge Reservation in South Dakota.[38]

The origin of Solomon's sympathy for Native Americans is uncertain. Feelings of guilt or obligation, which among liberal non-Indians historically plays a role in setting, enforcing, and interpreting Indian policies, probably moved him. In his court, official promises to Native Americans likely resonated with "a kind of morality profoundly rare in our jurisprudence," as Charles F. Wilkinson said of Indian issues before the Supreme Court. "Somehow, those old negotiations . . . are tremendously evocative. Real promises were made on those plains, and the Senate of the United States approved them, making them real law." Wilkinson's sense "is that most judges cannot shake that. Their training, experience, and finally, their humanity — all of the things that blend into the rule of law — brought them up sharp when it came to signing opinions that would have obliterated those promises." The Umatillas in northeastern Oregon, Solomon ruled, had the right to hunt on all land near their ancestral reservation. A different treaty interpretation would "violate the solemn promise made to the Indians more than a century ago."[39]

Like many of his predecessors, Judge Solomon stressed the federal government's "special obligation to Indians." In a Warm Springs reservation case, for example, he found official failure in distributing a cash judgment. A new distribution plan had to be negotiated and win congressional approval, he ruled. The legislative branch alone could decide any Indian descendants' claim to money, which Solomon had dismissed. The new plan must also be in accord with the Fifth Amendment's due process and equal protection clauses. Indians who had withdrawn from a tribe earned less sympathy than enrolled members, and those who had withdrawn from the terminated Klamath tribe had to win Ninth Circuit reversal of *Kimball I* to achieve standing to sue. On remand, Solomon found that descendants of Klamaths on the final 1957 tribal role had exclusive treaty rights to hunting, fishing, and trapping on ancestral land. In *Kimball II*, the Ninth Circuit Court of Appeals made his remanded opinion "the law of the case" throughout the circuit.[40]

His sympathies did not go unnoticed. Washington's attorney general labeled Solomon prejudiced in 1968 and at an early stage forced him to abandon what became *Sohappy v. Smith*, Judge Belloni's landmark decision on off-reservation Native American fishing rights on the Columbia River. A preemptory challenge was filed to prevent Solomon from sitting on the case, which Solomon blamed on a case in 1959 when he forced Washington to release an unjustly imprisoned African American, Geither Horn (see Chapter 11). He suspected that Oregon legal officials also thought him prejudiced. Appreciative tribal and federal attorneys had already started to collect, circulate, and study Solomon's transcripts and his published and slip opinions on Indians. Their request that he publish his oral opinion in *Klamath I* surprised him. A Nez Perce lawyer later termed his *Confederated Tribes of Umatilla Indian Reservation v. Maison* "legal statesmanship" and wrongly predicted it would become a landmark of Indian law. He had held that Native Americans have the right to hunt on lands near the reservation that are not occupied by non-Indian settlers and that National Forest lands are not "claimed" within the meaning of the plaintiff's treaty.[41]

In Nevada, Solomon twice plunged into a decades-long stream of litigation over Carson and Truckee river water to rule on a dam that affected Pyramid Lake, located on an Indian reservation. In *Carson–Truckee I*, he ordered the secretary of the Interior to sell all of the dam's water, except the amount necessary to fulfill the government's trust obligation to the tribe, and to protect under the Endangered Species Act (ESA) two types of fish in the Lower Truckee River. In *Carson–Truckee II*, he grappled with several core issues in Indian water-rights disputes: how much water was reserved for tribal use; the uses to which the water might be devoted; and who was authorized to represent Indian interests in water rights disputes. Under the ESA, he held that the secretary of Interior's plan rightfully gave the Pyramid Lake Paiute tribal fishery sufficient water to remove two types of lake fish from the government's endangered and threatened list at a later date. This use held priority over storing water for municipal and industrial use. The tribe rightfully intervened in the case to protect its economic interests, he wrote. On Indian rights, the Ninth Circuit upheld him in all respects.[42]

During hearings, Solomon remarked that he had prevented thousands of acres of Nevada land from getting enough water because a mere eight hundred endangered pupfishes existed in Devil's Hole, part of the Death Valley National Monument. He had given Indians priority to obtain the water over fast-growing Reno and Sparks, Nevada. Individuals "had bumper strippers in Nevada saying 'Kill the pupfish' because thousands of people might have been needing that water. But [my opinion] was based upon legislation." He referred to *U.S. v. Cappaert*, which he had written for the Ninth Circuit. It was the first test of the reserved doctrine's application to non-Indian lands. The presidential proclamation that had created the National Monument implicitly reserved the government's right to water against a future water appropriation, Solomon wrote. So, too, the federal government had reserved the water before Nevada or nearby property owners had perfected their water rights. The Supreme Court affirmed this expansion of a federal claim of reserved right to surface water to include underground water, in this instance an amount sufficient to preserve the habitat of the endangered desert pupfish from underground water loss because of nearby pumping. By implication, *Cappaert* could be applied to virtually all types of federal reservations in the arid West. Solomon had, once again, endorsed expanded opportunities for weak or excluded groups.[43]

Chapter 10

Opportunities

*We Jews are committed to the brotherhood of all men and to the
goal of free equality in a free society. Negro and White, Christian
and Jew, must work together in the common effort to make the
promise of equality come true for every citizen.*

—Gus J. Solomon, 1967

EQUAL OPPORTUNITY

Solomon's beliefs about liberal democracy, Judaism's moral impera-
tives, and fundamental Jewish interests made him an apostle of equal
opportunity. Equal opportunity to him meant advancing justice
across racial, ethnic, class, and other divisions to help all Americans
fully participate in society. It meant both obtaining formal civil rights
and developing equality of esteem, which included acknowledging
human dignity.[1]

"Civil rights," as Jonathan D. Sarna has written, "became a central religious issue for American Jews in the postwar era," with Jewish support for civil rights peaking in the early 1960s. After the war,
the American Jewish Congress and the National Association for the
Advancement of Colored People banded together to seek state and
federal anti-discrimination statutes and fair employment practices.
Solomon continually prodded the two groups to pursue their common interests. During the 1950s, broader African American–Jewish
coalitions formed, as Cheryl Greenberg notes, to support "a host of
projects ranging from desegregating hospitals, schools, housing projects, and bowling leagues to barring inquiries by employers or colleges regarding an applicant's race or religion." In the 1970s, Solomon
voiced a common white liberal view: the "barometer of civil rights
in any area is determined by the manner in which Negro people are
treated." He and Libby contributed funds to nonprofit developer Morris Milgram's construction of racially integrated housing in Pennsyl-

vania, and she served on Milgram's board. The Solomons remained most comfortable with moderate civil rights groups. "During those difficult civil rights struggle days of 1963–1964, we always knew we had a supporter and a friend" in the chief judge, the former president of Portland's NAACP recalled.[2]

Solomon repeatedly called for an active urban agenda as a step toward realizing social justice and lessening the country's disruptions. Common among white liberals, he viewed the ghetto disorders of the 1960s as outbursts of frustration rooted in socioeconomic deprivation. "Ghetto areas are the breeding grounds for most of the serious domestic ills of our society," he declared. "The treatment of the Negroes and the riots which from that treatment constitute our No. 1 internal problem." He feared that continuing "violence and rioting may plunge us into a period of racial warfare which may shake the foundations of our great democracy. Law and order must be maintained by black and white alike." Whites must encourage African American leaders who offered "constructive alternatives to violent behavior," he advised; they must improve interracial communication "to prevent further Negro isolation and provide a basis for joint attacks on common problems." Whites had to educate themselves on the urban crisis.[3]

Solomon endorsed massive federal urban employment, education, and housing programs as well as union and governmental aid to unskilled minority workers. "The most serious urban problem is not the inability of a few Negroes to achieve high political office or an important position in a bank or in industry; I think that they can get jobs, particularly if they are qualified," he said. "The place where help must be given is among the unskilled Negroes, Mexican-Americans, and Puerto Ricans who have no skills." He and Hubert H. Humphrey, the 1968 presidential candidate, agreed about the nation's violence: only by promoting economic justice and equality could law and order be obtained. To Solomon, nonviolent change was required "if we are to preserve the best in our society" and avoid the upheavals experienced abroad. He liked the courts being used to this end, as in a 1971 Black Coalition class-action suit against the Portland School District regarding disciplinary regulations and procedures that allegedly violated the due process and equal protection clauses.[4]

That year, the Cheryl James case brought African American rage uncomfortably home. Portland's Black Panther Party and an interracial defense committee had made James's arrest a public issue, stirring "up controversy between the races," Solomon privately complained. He had found her guilty of resisting and forcibly assaulting the FBI agents who had been trying to arrest her brother. Using a noncriminal juvenile statute, he had committed the seventeen-year-old James to the attorney general's custody for no more than eighteen months once she finished high school. Solomon spoke at Portland State University just before James was slated to enter prison. As a question-and-answer period ended, a Black Panther leader, an unidentified African American, and James reportedly walked up and stood silently by his lectern, while people shouted questions at the startled Solomon. The meeting was hastily adjourned. As Solomon and a deputy U.S. marshall strode toward an elevator, James followed, reportedly yelling that the judge did not want to listen to anybody and shouting her version of what happened during the arrests. "In the high-pitched verbal exchange that followed" before the elevator arrived, the campus newspaper reported, Solomon "repeatedly asked James, 'Do you want to go to jail, now?'" Afterward, he reviewed her files and denied all further defense motions. The Ninth Circuit affirmed her punishment. Ten months later, Judge Belloni, calling Solomon's sentence "just," released her from prison.[5]

Falkenstein v. Dept. of Revenue for State of Oregon may have come as a welcome relief amid the racial rancor. It was a case in which Solomon could apply his deepest sentiments free from militant involvement. A decade earlier, he had been instrumental in ending a widespread ban on Jewish membership in Portland-area private clubs. The plaintiffs sought a declaratory judgment and an injunction restraining the state of Oregon from granting tax exemptions to the Elks Club, a fraternal organization that racially discriminated in its membership selection. The court did not allow the Elks Club to intervene. Hoping to dispose of the case with a short *per curiam* opinion, the panel postponed consideration until *Moose Lodge v. Irvis* came down from the Supreme Court, apparently expecting the justices to bar club discrimination. Instead, the Court held that there had been insufficient "state action" to bring the Fourteenth Amendment into play. Further, state issuance of a liquor license did not constitute sufficient state action. Amid worries that the Supreme Court had sounded the death knell to curbing discriminatory club practices, Solomon fervently tackled *Falkenstein*. Intending to find a way around *Moose Lodge*, according to clerk Mark Silverstein, he "decided how he was going to do it, and our job [as clerks] was to figure some way" to persuade the other two judges on the panel. Solomon understood "that the law is extraordinarily flexible and political, and there are ways that things can be done. . . . He was not a guy who was going to be too concerned with being reversed or with precedent. If he thought something was fair, we were going to do it."[6]

Clerk David Walbert added: "We came up with a way of distinguishing ('ignoring' is a little too strong, but not very much)" *Moose Lodge* to reach an opposite result. Writing for the court, Solomon rejected the state's contention that tax exemptions did not encourage or foster racial discrimination. "Unlike the liquor license in *Moose Lodge*, tax exemptions for fraternal organizations benefit both the State and the organizations. Oregon relieves fraternal organizations from the burden of property and corporate excise taxes and, in return, the public benefits from the charitable and benevolent activities of these organizations. This is the kind of 'symbiotic relationship' that was lacking in *Moose Lodge*" but that *Burton* had established earlier. Exemptions gave the Elks a fiscal freedom its lodge did not otherwise enjoy, and so it was obligated to comply with the equal protection clause. The state, as in *Burton*, must ensure that the lodge met its obligation. The state did not appeal the decision.[7]

In *Domingo v. New England Fish Co.* (see Chapter 8), Solomon presided over one of three related class-action suits filed in 1973 under Title VII of the 1964 Civil Rights Act, which banned employment discrimination on the basis of race, color, creed, or sex. The plaintiffs charged that some thousand Alaskan native and Asian American seasonal migrant workers had for decades been denied high-paying jobs and equitable living conditions at some of Alaska's largest salmon canneries. The case involved gathering and analyzing reams of statistical, demographic, and other complex data, nonstop motions, heated courtroom arguments, prolonged complaint collection, and several appeals. Solomon divided the trial issues, determining any liability on a class-wide basis and deciding damages individually. He found a *prima facia* case of discriminatory practices in job allocation and housing but not in feeding the workers. For the first time, a federal court held an American employer liable for discrimination against seasonal migrant workers. Solomon refused to hold the canner liable for practices before 1971. In a subsequent hearing, the judge "recognize[d] that racial hiring goals and quotas are permissible and even desirable when they represent a rational method of eradicating past discrimination, particularly when an employer has a history of deliberate and intentional discrimination." The canner's discrimination, however, "was not of the egregious character that the Courts condemn," and the company was making a good-faith effort to hire qualified non-whites. "I, therefore, doubt that quotas and goals are necessary or even justified." He ultimately granted relief to only eight of the 124 people permitted to lodge claims and awarded them a lump sum of $55,000 for past housing disparities.[8]

While advocating for all minorities, Solomon did not have equal opportunity for women uppermost in his mind. He always opposed guaranteeing women or any other group equal results as distinct from equal opportunity. "I think that the Equal Rights Amendment for Women (SJ61) is a dangerous piece of legislation," he cautioned Senator Morse as early as 1946. "I believe in equal rights, but I don't think the amendment will accomplish anything. I am, of course, in favor of the adoption of Senate Resolution 1187, the women's equal pay bill." Disagreeing among themselves on the nature of equality, congressional liberals divided on SJ61, helping doom it in the Senate.[9]

What Laurie B. Mapes has called "perhaps the most significant sex discrimination case in Oregon" originated in Solomon's court. In *Gunther v. County of Washington,* he — and, finally, the Supreme Court — tried to end the confusion created by two statutes: the 1963 equal-pay-for-equal-work law and Title VII of the 1964 Civil Rights Act. Women jailers had alleged that Washington County paid them substantially less than male jailers for similar work and that they had been fired when they complained. The county claimed that jail closure and inmate transfers to a nearby prison had ended their jobs. But Solomon found that the women's work responsibilities were less than those of the male jailers, and therefore they were not entitled to equal pay. As a matter of law, he held that a sex-based wage discrimination claim could not be brought under Title VII unless it would satisfy the 1963 standard that equal pay was due work that was approximately equal in nature. He also found that the women's complaint did not result in their termination. "No employer, private or governmental, should be prevented from eliminating an unnecessary position merely because all the holders of that position are women — provided there are good, nondiscriminatory reasons why they are all women and why the position should be eliminated" — which, Solomon judged, the county had provided.[10]

The Ninth Circuit affirmed Solomon on five issues, reversed him on one, and remanded the case. The Supreme Court, after a settlement on one issue, heard the appeal. Rejecting any "comparable worth" theory (a pay claim where intrinsic worth or difficulty of jobs were compared), a majority of the Court narrowly decided that a Title VII claim of wage discrimination did not have to meet the equal work requirements of the Equal Pay Act. A woman employee could sue for gender-based pay discrimination even if her employer had no man filling the same job for higher pay. "The Court in *Gunther* only went so far as to permit a litigant to bring an action for intentional sex-based wage discrimination under Title VII without satisfying the [Equal Pay Act's] equal work standard," two legal scholars write. "It left to the lower courts, however, the difficult task of formulating the proof standards to be applied to plaintiffs in such cases." The Court, Laurie B. Mapes adds, established the principle that an employer may violate Title VII "by paying women less than men even if the men and women are not performing similar duties." The case "is noted for expanding the equal pay for equal work doctrine to 'fair pay for productive work.'" Taking exception with Judge Solomon, the Supreme Court "established the precedent that women could bring successful pay discrimination claims even when their duties differed substantially from the duties of men in similar positions."[11]

A JEWISH PLACE

Like members of other self-conscious minorities, Solomon closely monitored his own group's place in society. Twentieth-century American Jewry, as depicted by Arthur Hertzberg, repeatedly gauged "their success in establishing themselves in American society; their continuity as a community; and their legitimacy, that is, their justification to themselves of the value of being Jews." Anti-Semitism figured weightily in the assessment. After the war, Solomon shared the view of major Jewish organizations that anti-Semitism and overt discrimination against Jews were in steep decline; and by the mid-1950s, the organization stopped calling Jews an economically disadvantaged group. They had "come a long way in the past 25 years, when discrimination against Jews was the rule rather than the exception," Solomon declared in 1960. Yet, he knew that companies, law firms, and private clubs still limited Jews' opportunities.[12]

By the mid-1960s, Marc Dollinger writes, American "Jews appeared to resemble the white majority more than they did an ethnic minority." A decade later, Solomon said that Jews held "powerful and important places in American economic, political, and cultural life." Indeed, they occupied some of the highest reaches of American society and were the most economically successful of its white ethnic groups. Changes in American society and culture, as rising intermarriage rates reflected, had made Jews largely acceptable to the white majority. And Oregon, as ever, appeared to Solomon a much better place for Jews than other states.[13]

Being a judge was a great honor, Solomon remarked, but being a Jewish judge imposed a special obligation. "I don't go around parading being a Jew," he said in 1973. "But I just know I feel it is my obligation as a Jew who has achieved some stature, to try to help all people to attain personal dignity." Beginning in the 1960s, he grew more expressively Jewish — more willing, for instance, to criticize non-Jews in public, and not just to fellow Jews; more involved in Jewish organizations; and more prone to storms of worry and conscience about the slackening of American Jewry's historic coalitions.[14]

Solomon still labored over what sort of Jew he was. A person did not "have to be religious in order to be a Jew," he declared, but should identify himself or herself as Jewish. Swimming in the national mainstream did not mean drowning one's ethnic identity. What kept Jews afloat — what basically defined Jewishness for Solomon — was community. Edward S. Shapiro expressed this popular Jewish notion this way: "One was Jewish not because of theological categories but because one chose to identify as a Jew and to affiliate with other Jews." Solomon's Jewish affiliations had multiplied since the late 1930s. To educate their sons, the couple had joined Congregation Beth Israel in about 1946. They attended its Reform services and gave it a Torah Scroll as a Holocaust remembrance. Until 1961, Solomon was a Beth Israel trustee. To please his brother Sam, he also nominally belonged to the Conservative Jewish congregation of their childhood. Religiosity for him remained strongly tied to society and civic duty.[15]

Portland rabbis recognized that Solomon was not particularly religious in practice or interest but that he was, as Rabbi Joshua Stampfer observed, immensely interested "in Jewish culture, Jewish knowledge, and Jewish activism." During his court years, Solomon belonged to small groups that studied traditional Jewish texts. On Sundays, he listened to broadcasts from the Jewish Theological Seminary of America, home of Rabbi Mordecai M. Kaplan. The principles of the Reconstructionist Movement founded by Kaplan appealed to the Solomons for decades. They agreed with Kaplan's core definition of Judaism as an "evolving religious civilization," the sum of what Jews did both culturally and religiously. Reconstructionism, according to Mel Scult, "stressed Judaism's efforts to achieve social justice in addition to individual salvation or fulfillment as the primary values of Jewish life." Reconstructionism pulsated in Solomon's frequent reference to Jewish peoplehood.[16]

Since 1938, Solomon's secular Jewish activities more than any formal religious affiliation or doctrine had filled his central emotional and ideological needs. They also raised his influence in Jewish circles in Oregon and beyond. After 1950, his contributions of time, money, and knowledge to Jewish causes and his prestige as a federal judge made him a *macher*, literally a "doer" in Yiddish, and in some ways a *gonster macher*, a true "big shot." By then, he well understood dizzying Jewish communal politics — that is, in Arthur A. Goren's words, its "organizational diversity, ideological ambiguity, and even [endemic] contentiousness." From 1938 until his death, Solomon labored to bridge Jewish differences, secure Jews equal opportunities, and win Jewish observance of the highest human standards, which usually meant acting with greater courage and for greater ends than in the past. Year after year, he chided Portland Jewry (privately or in Jewish settings) for being unduly cautious and submissive to conservative local ways, for an inadequate sense of social responsibility, for insufficient aid to fellow Jews, for slights by German Jews to Jews of east European background, and for social climbing.[17]

The American Jewish Congress remained Solomon's strongest Jewish affiliation. While heading its Northwest Region and afterward, he strengthened chapters along the West Coast and in Alaska. He addressed its national conventions, presided over its 1960 annual gathering, and served on its Commission on Law and Social Action during much of that decade. In 1974, he and two attorneys re-established a Portland chapter, but it apparently functioned only when Solomon was in town. From 1968 to 1974, he served as an honorary national AJCongress vice president before joining Libby Solomon, formerly on its Women's Division board, on its honorary governing council. He had represented the organization at the 1959 World Jewish Congress in Stockholm, and both Solomons represented it at the 1975 Congress in Jerusalem. In 1967, he addressed its British section. A year later, he was the AJCongress's delegate at an Israeli prime minister's conference of 120 world Jewish leaders.

"At one time," he boasted, "I was the only man in America who was on the National Board" of the Anti-Defamation League, the American Jewish Committee, and the American Jewish Congress, "which had different philosophies and which didn't always agree with the policies of the others." The groups' historic devotion to pluralism, liberalism, and racial integration and their dreams of a social order both "good for the Jews" and others who sought integration into American society deeply appealed to him. Solomon endorsed their policies of combating anti-Semitism while pursuing justice for all citizens and ending discrimination against any sect or group. He supported their extensive litigation, research, educational, and lobbying programs, especially in coalitions with non-Jewish and nonwhite groups.[18]

Several years into his judgeship, Solomon had joined the American Jewish Committee, its Committee on Social Discrimination, and ultimately its national board. To work against bans on Jews in private clubs and to combat Arab propaganda against Israel, he helped reactivate a Portland AJCommittee chapter in 1968. In addition, he headed the Anti-Defamation League's regional board and its Oregon advisory board; he served on its National Civil Rights Commission and, until 1976, on its National Lawyers Committee. When urged by an AJCongress official to resign publicly from ADL in 1960 because of a heated dispute in Florida between the two organizations, he merely repeated the former's viewpoint to the ADL's director. Distant communal controversies did not deflect the experienced activist.[19]

The three organizations and Solomon relied on one another. Their contacts, reports, and letters helped guide and authenticate his anti-discrimination work. When important conflicts developed among Jewish communal leaders and thinkers in the 1950s and early 1960s over the legitimacy of Jewish civil rights commitments, Solomon encouraged their staffs to make the eradication of social discrimination a stronger organizational goal. For years, he exchanged views with their officers and staff on litigation strategies, collaborators, and case possibilities in the West. The AJCongress and the ADL had him evaluate several of their *amici* briefs to the U.S. Supreme Court, and he quietly advised them and the ACLU on handling church-state issues. For unknown reasons, he counseled the ACLU of Oregon and the AJCongress in 1959 to not enter the state courts to challenge the constitutionality of Oregon's textbook law, which allowed publicly funded textbooks in parochial schools. (The Oregon Supreme Court did void the statute at the ACLU's behest.) When the AJCongress in 1965 contemplated a constitutional challenge in state courts to erecting a cross on public land in Eugene, he quietly encouraged the suit. Do not let Eugene's cautious Jewish community veto it, he reportedly advised. As an ADL-ACLU action, it succeeded in the Oregon Supreme

Court but arose later in different guises. "Safe-guarding church-state separation" should be the Oregon ACLU's main task in 1972, he told its gathering. "So far the courts have been almost unanimous but how long can they continue?" But his most sustained battle was against the anti-Semitic discrimination in Portland's legal profession and the area's major private clubs.[20]

LAW FIRM AND CLUB DISCRIMINATION

Beginning as a young judge, Solomon struck at obstacles raised against a significant Jewish presence in executive suites, law offices, housing, private clubs, resorts, and higher education in Oregon and occasionally in California and other states. After years of effort by Solomon and others (who he rarely credited), important Portland law firms hired their first Jewish associates and initiated their promotion based on merit and demonstrated potential. So, too, Portland-area private clubs began to enroll Jews after years of effort by Solomon and his allies. He then helped persuade national Jewish organizations to work actively for the same ends in other locales.

Refusing Jews employment in American law firms was a tradition. In Robert Stevens's understatement, "There was still a hint of anti-Semitism among the larger firms in the 1960s." Solomon proudly confessed to applying "a considerable amount of heat to a number of [Portland] offices to hire Jewish lawyers" over a thirty-year stretch. Unless senior partners received friendly calls and personal introductions to young Jewish lawyers, Solomon believed, their applicants were summarily rejected. Of course, he was now a federal judge, no longer the pre-war operator of an "unofficial, non-paid employment agency." Commitment to equal opportunity and delight at finding jobs for others drove him, but so too did anger about the law firms' refusals to employ him when he was younger and other Jews. In the early 1970s, Solomon still had "lots of grudges" toward "the really established, Waspish Portland law firms," according to clerk Mark Silverstein.[21]

In 1953, "Gus wanted to use me to break the barrier in one or two of the larger law firms," recalled Jerome Kohlberg Jr., who instead decided to return to New York. Three years later, Solomon and Oregon Supreme Court Justice Hall S. Lusk pressed David Lloyd Davies at the city's largest law firm to hire its first Jewish associate. Solomon reminded Davies that he had rejected previous Jewish candidates. "'They had all the amenities and social graces,' he told Davies. 'They wear hats and vests. They are well educated.' Davies said, 'Send me the next fellow.'" Lusk brought his law clerk Leon Gabinet to an interview, and Davies hired him.[22]

Three years later, Solomon recommended Meyer Eisenberg, Oregon Supreme Court Justice William McAllister's law clerk, for a position in top-ranked Portland firms. McAllister, Solomon, and other judges informed them "that the time had come," Eisenberg said, and Solomon "personally introduced me to what seemed to be every managing partner of every large Portland firm, as if I was his long lost son." Eisenberg was sent to interviews with this instruction: "they'll offer you a job — you don't have to take it — but they'll get the message." He remembered: "They did, but I chose to go to Washington. . . . Not long after [the firm] hired their first Jewish associate." In 1967, Edward L. Epstein was promoted "solely on the basis of ability" to a partnership in a major firm. "I have been waiting for this day for the last 10 years," Solomon admitted. Afterward, he pressed for more hiring and merit promotions until all vestiges of discrimination against Jewish attorneys had vanished from local law firms.[23]

Solomon also worked hard against the ban on Jews belonging to exclusive business and social clubs. During the 1930s, he had "realized that there was a correlation between social acceptability and job opportunities or economic opportunities," especially for Jews. "I also learned that many of the real business transactions occur not in offices but in the social clubs." Unless minority lawyers and businesspeople "could meet the people in that industry on social occasions," good jobs and promotions were denied minorities. Jews were further restricted from taking part in the many groups that met in private clubs. Nothing had changed since the Anti-Defamation League depicted a Portland in 1947 where "private and country clubs — University, Arlington, Town, etc. — all excluded Jews." Except for the Aero Club, which "maintained a rigid Jewish quota," clubs did not even bother to enroll a minority member or two to deflect charges of discrimination. During the 1950s and 1960s, Solomon carried on what an allied Allan Hart called a "discreet" campaign against the exclusionary policies. It failed to rouse noticeable local Jewish support.[24]

Solomon had no interest in getting wealthy Jews into prestigious establishments for the snob appeal or in helping anyone for whom belonging would be the last barrier "to passing as Gentiles." Instead, he said, "I was interested in the people who needed a job." Without irony, he pleaded with Jewish audiences on behalf of "millions of Jewish children yet-unborn" who were disqualified by birth from ever becoming heads of corporations. Too many local Jews, he felt, were indifferent or hostile to his appeals because they feared controversy or dreaded challenging the status quo. Some expressed no wish to go where they were unwelcome. Others thought that the local Tualatin Country Club, which Solomon criticized for rejecting non-Jews as members (until the unwritten rule fell in 1967), had equal or superior facilities. Wives of wealthy, prominent Jews particularly "were frightened, unhappy and also worried that their social disabilities were being exposed," he recalled. "That's the scars of persecution showing in their personalities. It's easier to accept second-class citizenship than it is to strike out and stand up against it."[25]

Despite significant post-war advances for Jews, some two-thirds of the nation's business and social clubs banned Jews from membership in the early 1960s. For several years, Solomon quietly lobbied influential non-Jews to overturn restrictive club barriers. The "decent people in these clubs" needed to be made aware of the discrimination. In 1960, he sent publications on discrimination to the Arlington Club board through a sympathetic board member. Nothing changed. Two years earlier, the Multnomah Athletic Club, having revoked its ban, recruited Solomon. Twice weekly, he swam and breakfasted there.[26]

Solomon's fight against law-firm discrimination overlapped with what he exaggerated as his "one-man fight" against club discrimination. Restrictive Portland-area clubs stubbornly resisted pressure from growing numbers of their members and from such nonmembers as Solomon and attorney Moe Tonkon, more than the big Portland law firms did to pressure from lawyers and judges. Few in the clubs feared ever appearing before a federal judge. Also, "many members of the private clubs," Solomon admitted, "are completely unaware that discrimination is practiced against Jews." But after the *Oregonian* in March 1963 reported his criticism of the clubs to a Jewish audience, they began altering their policy in a third of the time that the big law firms had taken.[27]

The news account exposed the quarrel to embarrassing public gaze, and more publicity heaped further unwelcome attention on the clubs. Several Portland luminaries hastened to assure Solomon of their anti-discriminatory pasts, but far more club members felt offended and embattled. They responded in ways that left the judge feeling "vilified and slandered." Keep up the pressure, he advised sympathizers. If they could succeed at the University Club, then other resisters likely would topple. Prominent University Club members — including two bankers and attorneys Samuel Martin, Allan Hart, Hugh Biggs, and John A. Ryan — urged a policy reversal. After talking to Solomon — "Gus didn't mind tussling with people," Ryan admiringly said — they proposed for membership a newcomer to Portland who had been recruited by the American Jewish Committee — corporate head Monford Orloff. Solomon was cautioned not to apply himself.[28]

By October 1964, he claimed, "I am probably the most hated man among the private clubs in Portland because over a period of years, and particularly in the last six months, I have been responsible for the cancellation of a great number of meetings which would have been held there." The press learned that he had warned away musicians Leonard Rose and Issac Stern from gatherings in the offending clubs, and he had repeatedly asked corporate and university officials and some Jews to not sponsor affairs there. The Japanese American Citizens League commended him when a reception was transferred from an offending Waverly Country Club. Threats by an outraged dean that "he would fight me" about moving a law school's event from Waverly was "a very dangerous thing to say," Solomon privately noted. He quietly gathered information to use against the man. As a longtime observer commented, Solomon "hardens when the going gets tough."[29]

After 18 members of the University Club blackballed Orloff, 126 members petitioned the club for a special meeting to transfer membership decisions to its board. Resentment against Solomon heightened. Someone charged that the petitioning lawyers acted only from fear of the chief judge, that Orloff was his front man, and that Solomon actually wanted to belong. Solomon exploded, pledging never to set foot in any Christian-only club again, a pledge he honored. A list of eight of the blackballers leaked, which reportedly "caused the ferment that ended the membership policy." (Solomon had advised circulating the names of two blackballers with significant Jewish clienteles.) A stormy special meeting in which many members did not vote changed the bylaw by a 127-to-54 margin, and the club admitted its first Jew, Moe Tonkon, in 1966.[30]

The fight intensified during a period when the ADL and the AJ-Committee, just as Solomon had been advocating, mounted attacks against barriers to club membership in many places. In 1959, he urged the ADL to adopt a stronger stand on club discrimination. Two years later, he welcomed the AJCommittee's launch of a study of the relation between corporate success and club discrimination. He advised and encouraged Jews engaged in similar struggles in Los Angeles and San Francisco. In Los Angeles, he won new U.S. District Judge Irving Hill's promise to avoid events in discriminatory clubs. The AJ-Committee publicized Solomon's University Club efforts and recommended that its local branches copy them. While its staff said that he had "a tremendous influence on the progress that is now occurring on a national scale in combating social discrimination," Solomon believed that two Jews in the University Club denoted scant success at home. Start pushing public officials to avoid discriminatory venues, he advised. In 1966, the AJCommittee's new National Social Discrimination Committee agreed, as he recommended, to focus initially on downtown social and university clubs rather than the less financially vulnerable country clubs.[31]

Newspapers reported that several Oregon judges and U.S. Attorney Lezak now refused to attend Waverly Country Club receptions. Still, "our non-Jewish friends who want to help us are easily discouraged and . . . unless we keep the pressure on them, they are content to do nothing," Solomon privately wrote. He warned Hubert Humphrey's staff in 1965 that the vice president should not attend a lunch honoring him at the exclusive Waverly. Ignored by Humphrey's staff, Solomon had Jewish organizations and big Jewish party contributors complain in Washington, D.C. The lunch, the press noticed, was abruptly switched to a residence. At breakfast the next morning, an angry Humphrey made an unspecified "damn fool statement" to him. Local clubs now gradually opened to Jews; but, to Solomon, a dozen Jews in the nine-hundred-member University Club after a year seemed a token number. Two years later, when the Arlington Club accepted its first Jew — again, Moe Tonkon — he politely declined its invitation to join. In 1972, the Waverly Country Club accepted its first Jew. Not until 1983, when Solomon was seventy-seven years old, was he satisfied that the "battle basically has been won for Jews" locally, though some club discrimination still existed. But "my job and my age prevent me from doing much now," he said.[32]

JEWISH PARTICULARISM

Solomon worriedly told Jewish audiences as early as 1959 that internal disintegration, not external threats, most threatened them as a group. Having assimilated so thoroughly, he warned, they must vigorously struggle to maintain their separate identity. "Today, we must fight for the rights of equal citizens, born as Jews, to remain Jews." In the past, "we fought for the opportunity to be like everyone else — with equal rights in all areas regardless of race, religion or national origin. Today, we fight for the opportunity to be different — to be proudly and affirmatively Jewish, to give full expression to the cultural and spiritual values of our Jewish tradition and experience."[33]

He welcomed evidence that Jews once enamored of the melting pot were growing more assertively Jewish. With Jews constituting only about three percent of the American population in 1959, he supported attempts by their mainstream organizations to counter group self-destruction (blamed on assimilation, intermarriage, or both) and their programs to stop Jewish upward social mobility from eroding one of the country's distinct subcultures. He encouraged the study of and reflection on Jewish thought and identity, invited proclamations and celebrations of Jewishness, and urged people to connect with their ancestral past and, during the 1970s, to Holocaust-consciousness. Joining heritage tourists, the Solomons traveled to his father's Romanian village. It "was very important for me to know something about my roots," he said.[34]

Spurred by fear that Israel's survival hinged on American support, Israel now acquired a greater significance in Solomon's — and American Jewish — consciousness. Its fate, he insisted, was central to Jewish identity and bound up with the fate of Jews everywhere. The 1967 Six-Day War reactivated largely dormant American Jewish memories of the Holocaust and their attachment to the Jewish state. While the fighting raged, Solomon assured the audience at a receptive, emotional Israeli bond meeting that Jews had discarded a defensiveness toward false charges of dual U.S.-Israeli loyalty. In court, he cited his visit to Israel when telling an apparently Jewish draft resister that he did not understand individuals who would not help their country in time of war. By now, as Edward S. Shapiro writes, no "Jew who did not staunchly support the embattled state could expect to hold a responsible position in a major Jewish organization." That Israel's existence seemed to hang in the balance during the 1973 Arab-Israeli war only strengthened Solomon's views.[35]

For decades, Solomon had been contributing to a Jewish ethnic revival that gained force during the 1960s and especially in the 1970s. But to Stuart Svonkin, the "ethnoreligious particularism" of the revival diminished American Jewry's attachment to "liberal universalism." Other scholars less worriedly termed it a cultural nationalist course or a Jewish "shift in strategic priorities from 'integration' to 'survival.'"

As Arthur A. Goren writes, "Whether Jewish particularism should be maintained — to what degree, in what way and for what reason — or should be abandoned for a higher cosmopolitan fellowship has, of course, been one of the central themes in modern Jewish history." In the 1970s, Jewish particularism seemed weightier for Solomon than before. In 1977, he rejected the ACLU's defense of American Nazis in Skokie, Illinois, and sided with a historic ACLU ally, the AJCongress, in its criticism of the ACLU's defense of the Chicago Nazis' right to march in the heavily Jewish town. Judge Bernard Decker, Solomon argued, had erred in finding that the First Amendment prevented the local authorities from restricting expression. Having so many cases to handle, the ACLU needed to be selective; in Skokie, the Nazis "were using them."[35]

Prominent Jewish leaders such as Solomon expressed growing disillusionment with the United Nations. Jewry's traditional support for internationalism had weakened when the U.N. General Assembly equated Zionism with racism in 1975 and the world body and its agencies adopted other seeming anti-Israeli stands. Israel considered the world organization bankrupt, he said after visiting Jerusalem. The Jewish people, emphasizing the rule of law, had enthusiastically supported the League of Nations, the World Court, and the U.N. in a now largely shattered hope that they "would decide problems on the basis of fairness and justice." He and other worried Jewish leaders increased their efforts to strengthen American opinion favoring Israeli over Arab interests. In Oregon, they heavily backed U.S. Representative Les Au-Coin, a liberal Democrat, and U.S. Senator Robert Packwood, a moderate Republican. They rejected criticisms of Israeli policies by Jews affiliated with the New Left. Solomon, for one, was not inclined to recognize the diverse meanings of Israel among Jews.[37]

More emotionally difficult for Solomon was the troubled relations between Jews and African Americans. The conditions that had created similar interests now appeared to create diverging or conflicting ones. It sounded increasingly false to believe statements that the two groups were one people. By the 1960s, Jewish leaders felt a growing pressure to adopt an ethnic nationalist approach to racial liberalism. Signs of disquiet over race actually had appeared in the 1950s, when alliances were largely in place, according to Michael E. Staub. While "all Jewish liberals articulated their commitment to black civil rights, many were actually not convinced that anti-racist activism was itself a great idea." The "growing movement within the civil rights community to-

ward mass action strategies appeared to threaten the system of civil
stability Jews relied on," Cheryl Greenberg explains. Disagreements
between the two groups visibly worsened in the 1960s because of
urban riots, anti-Semitic statements by some African American militants, the Black Power movement's denouncement of Israel after the
Six-Day War, and conflicts in New York City and elsewhere in 1968.
"The first half of the 1960s," writes Staub, "was a time of tremendous
uncertainty, ambivalence, and internal divisiveness for American Jewish liberalism."[38]

At many Jewish meetings by 1963, Solomon glumly heard protests
against Jews who "devot[ed] so much of their time to the protection
of Negro rights." Nobody, he heard, had guaranteed Jews anything,
and the quota systems preferred by African Americans had historically diminished Jewish opportunities. By then, as Marc Dollinger
notes, "Every major national Jewish organization made opposition
to hiring quotas a priority." They had come to reject the once-shared
principle of collective security and collaboration with non-Jews and
nonwhites. During the early 1970s, "many Jewish groups lobbied
the federal government *against* zealous enforcement of affirmative
actions for anyone," John D. Skrentny adds. They "filed more than
thirty complaints of reverse discrimination" with the federal government. In the midst of the nation's intensifying racial backlash, Solomon first tried a difficult balancing act. As he counseled: "Negro and
White, Christian and Jew, must work together in the common effort
to make the promise of equality come true for every citizen." Still,
he sternly added that both races must place "law and order" high on
their agendas. His attitudes had hardened before the Cheryl James
case in 1971 made him feel unfairly targeted by African American
and white militants.[39]

Solomon rued and resisted the unraveling of Jewish–African
American ties, but he sided decisively with most Jewish groups over
the Supreme Court's *De Funis v. Odegaard* in 1972. What Greenberg
terms "the first open break between Black and Jewish civil rights
agencies" centered on an African American's preferential law school
admission. It "was actually the logical culmination of years of slow
divergence of interest, visions, and priority." To mainstream Jewish
organizations, preferential admission of nonwhites violated standards
of individual merit and smacked of the quota system once deployed
against Jews in higher education and elsewhere. It flew in the face
of the race-blind society of which Jews such as Solomon dreamed.

In *De Funis*, he asked Portland's ADL chapter to endorse the national
ADL's *amicus* brief to the Supreme Court. The brief had argued that
the lower court had distorted "the remedy of 'affirmative action,'"
which threatened to destroy its utility. Rejecting a qualified applicant
"in favor of a less qualified candidate is morally wrong," the brief
concluded, "and in the aggregate, practically disastrous." To redress
minority grievances, the ADL and other Jewish groups suggested different options to the Court.[40]

While the justices in 1974 dismissed *De Funis* because any decision there would have no effect on De Funis's rights — he was about
to graduate — the issues that exposed the break between the two
groups reached them again four years later in *Regents of University of
California v. Bakke*, a white applicant's challenge to reserved minority
places in a medical school. Nearly all major Jewish organizations supported the plaintiff. Before the decision, the Solomons had declined
a Portland NAACP official's appeal to help finance her organization's
defense of the university policy; they firmly endorsed the AJCongress's
pro-Bakke position instead. In *Bakke*, the Supreme Court rejected racial quotas and reserved slots for "minorities," but it ruled that universities could use race as a "plus-factor" in admissions so long as other
factors were considered in a process that analyzed each applicant individually. Finding that Allan Bakke had been denied entry in violation of the equal protection clause, it ordered his admission. Solomon
considered the opinion a victory for equal opportunity.[41]

Chapter 11

Crime and Punishment

To require that an indigent defendant in a felony case be represented by a lawyer if he wants one, in my view, is elementary justice.

—Gus J. Solomon, 1965

SENTENCING

Solomon felt recurring unease about the purposes, rightness, and effectiveness of his sentencing decisions. Publicly reviewing his first nine years as a judge, he estimated having made serious sentencing errors at least half the time. He accepted full responsibility for those mistakes. Thanks to statutes prior to the Sentencing Reform Act, district judges possessed substantial sentencing discretion so mitigating and aggravating factors could be weighed. Probation in its many forms was only one among many ways judges had to individualize sentences, and incarceration was far from automatic. Almost half of those convicted in federal courts were not imprisoned between the 1950s and 1987, when the act became effective.[1]

Solomon wanted his sentences to deter people from contemplating the same crime. Yet, he did not think that jail effectively deterred drug offenders or that lengthy sentences solved the drug problem. During his first decade on the bench, he wanted prisons to rehabilitate convicts; but absent viable alternatives, he felt obliged to protect society by jailing some people without knowing whether it helped them. Invariably, he imprisoned "sociopaths. . . . Maybe it is going to help, and maybe it won't." Some "criminals have personalities so bent toward crime that their rehabilitation seems beyond our current knowledge and means," he said. "But the great majority of those imprisoned are capable of profiting from a good institutional program of therapy." He shared in what one scholar calls a national consensus in the 1950s "favoring rehabilitation of offenders by means of a scientifically based penology."[2]

What trial judges primarily wished to accomplish — restraint, deterrence, rehabilitation, or retribution — guided sentencing, and Solomon had some definite ideas. "We take some of our most restless elements," he said, "cage them up in small cells, behind high walls, and subject them to harsh and rigid treatment and then expect them to come out prepared for useful citizenship." Not surprisingly, the recidivism rate was high. Punishment was "the means, not the end, of criminal justice" to him; "sentences should have two general objectives — deterrence and rehabilitation." Solely because of its effectiveness, Solomon called himself a great believer in probation, except for a few categories, such as crimes that shocked the community. As a critic of punitive sentencing, he was disturbed to hear from Clerk of Court Donal Sullivan in the 1960s that he was regarded as a "hard sentencer" and "an unfair judge." The 1969 Oregon Draft Panel, for one, had created an impression that all Oregon judges punitively sentenced draft offenders. Solomon denied imposing unduly long draft sentences, and Sullivan supplied reassuring statistics that ranked him as "one of the lighter" sentencers nationwide.[3]

One of the most difficult and unpleasant responsibilities of the judicial office, Judge Robert E. Keeton writes, is "making sentencing decisions in criminal cases." One type of case — involving the death penalty — Solomon simply avoided. At least twice he pleaded nonexistent calendar conflicts to escape reviewing death penalties in the Ninth Circuit. He once told a rabbi that he avoided criminal cases involving Jewish defendants because he would "throw the book at them." As a senior judge, he refused criminal cases in his district but could not easily do so in appellate courts. It was "not pleasant to send people to the penitentiary," Solomon remarked. "There are a lot of other things most judges would prefer doing." Sentencing was "the thing he agonized most with," clerk John J. Kerr Jr. saw. "He really labored over it." In chambers beforehand, having evaluated the record and possible punishment with colleagues, he still fidgeted as if he had "a problem he was working through."[4]

Solomon took to heart warnings from Judge Sylvester Ryan in New York to avoid attitudes of omniscience and omnipotence. Ryan suggested that jurists stab themselves with a pin after the second or third sentencing to know that they too bled. Among the contemporary art and awards and tributes in Solomon's chambers were two somber paintings — *The Brook*, by Gandy Brody and a painting of a candelabra depicting death. They were reminders of his own humanity, and he could gaze at them just before incarcerating somebody. And he looked for help on determining punishment, as in the studies and formulations of goals, standards, and policies issued after 1958 by Sentencing Institutes, where participating judges discussed and became more self-conscious about their sentencing decisions. He relied, too, on pre-sentence reports from his district's probation office. Early on as chief judge, he installed a popular weekly procedure, an early version of a sentencing council. All the judges discussed the pre-sentence reports, questioned their authors, and sought a nonbinding consensus. It "offends ours sense of justice and fair play," they informed the press, to have a similar offense involving like circumstances and by offenders with similar backgrounds to be sentenced differently.[5]

Not surprising for someone who was sensitive to minority stigmatization and ill treatment and to income and class issues, Solomon closely examined and encouraged his fellow judges' interest in the possible psychological, social, and economic influences on those they judged. What motivated these individuals? Were they able to assist in their own defense? How well could a jurist gauge this ability? "I believe that true [juvenile] delinquency is the result of bad inter-personal relationships," he typically said. He sometimes delayed a trial if the defendant accepted his offer of a voluntary psychiatric evaluation. For a long time he turned to psychiatrists for aid, including treatment of potential probationers, if free or low-cost mental facilities could be located. Judges also had too much difficulty obtaining definite psychiatric evaluations regarding the accused's ability to assist in the defense, he said. Interested in nonstatutory changes in the classic insanity defense, Solomon exchanged letters, articles, opinions, and reports during the 1960s on psychiatric-legal matters with Judge John W. Oliver, whose jurisdiction included the federal prison in Missouri, and Chief Judge David L. Bazelon of the U.S. Court of Appeals for the District for Columbia. Bazelon's *Durham* rule in 1954, that the "accused is not criminally responsible if his unlawful act was the product of mental disease or mental defect," had earned both praise and criticism. The rule "was nothing short of a judicial vote of confidence in the sophistication of psychiatrists," Lucas A. Powe Jr. writes. Among other results, it prompted Sydney I. Lezak to initiate U.S. Attorney's Probation, which diverted the mentally ill for counseling, not trial. Chief Judge Solomon's sympathetic support proved essential to its initiation in Oregon, while Lezak awaited Justice Department approval of this type of probation.[6]

In 1969, Solomon organized a daylong seminar on psychiatry and the courts. Judge Oliver and Kansas City psychiatrists addressed judges and psychiatrists from the Pacific Northwest at a time when the District for Columbia's appeals court was backtracking on *Durham*. Solomon endorsed the rough guidelines for court psychiatric evaluations that emerged from the seminar. In Israel, he lectured the country's Supreme Court justices and others on these practices. He also met inconclusively with Oregon psychiatrists on issues discussed at the seminar. Soon, the District for Columbia discarded Bazelon's rule as unworkable and adopted a new test.[7]

Before any sentencing, Solomon looked closely at an individual's social circumstances. Liberal jurists during his tenure, Lucas A. Powe has written, "believed that until the root causes of crime were seriously attacked, some Americans necessarily would be forced into criminal activity." As Solomon had argued in 1952, "Slum conditions, unemployment, hunger, discrimination, the lack of mechanical skills, as well as the lack of motivation and a sense of dignity, all contribute to crime." Far more pressure existed on "the poorer, less-educated elements of the community" to "do wrong" than on community leaders. The "temptation to get a quick dollar by improper means is stronger among persons who are rejected, frustrated, unhappy or disturbed and who feel that society has treated them unfairly," as among people of color, he declared. In sentencing, he assessed a person's social or community position and economic status before making decisions.[8]

All judges, he claimed, pondered the temptations of and unconscionable demands on defendants from impoverished backgrounds. He referred sympathetically to them but not to well-paid or high-status defendants. "The Government has been very good to professional people," Solomon said at one sentencing. "They are the privileged classes of America, and in my view" must maintain "a very high standard and meet the responsibilities imposed by their privileged status." For tax cheats, "I believe that jail terms should be imposed in most cases, and the more prominent the individual the more compelling the reason for jail time." In his court, failure to pay income taxes almost automatically spelled imprisonment and maybe an added fine. Any alternative to imprisonment weakened the incentive of professional people to pay taxes, he argued. Solomon apparently thought that the certainty of jail time was more important than its length. According to Lezak, the judge expected parole boards to quickly release tax cheats. Because of the personal shame involved for professional people and community leaders, Solomon likely figured that an actual sixty-to-ninety-day incarceration had the same general deterrent effect as a longer term.[9]

CRIMINALS

On the issue of guilt, neither criminal defendants nor convicts received much sympathy from Solomon unless their constitutional rights had been violated. The felt need to convict the guilty and keep them in prison sometimes overcame his attentiveness to their rights. Solomon viewed defendants' claims suspiciously and appeared not to have presumed the innocence of most formally charged persons. He did insist that everyone must enjoy due process of law. As in other legal and juridical areas, serious tension existed between Solomon the civil libertarian and Solomon the enemy of crime and social disruptions and the proponent of effective, well-ordered, humane penal institutions.[10]

"Frankly, Judge Solomon's instincts were quite pro-government," one federal prosecutor-turned-criminal defender concluded, although he "certainly tried to conduct a fair trial." If used in a constitutional manner, Solomon said, wiretaps, informers, and undercover agents were necessary "to protect our nation from internal as well as external enemies" and from those who sold drugs. While generally approving of the Warren Court's expansion of the rights of the accused and prisoners, "Solomon, the liberal judge, refused to suppress evidence as a version of a Supreme Court decision that would elevate the rights of criminals to an extremely high degree," U.S. Attorney Lezak approvingly said. More broadly, Solomon was "a liberal judge giving relatively conservative rulings, trying to make the Warren Court system work." He "wanted to interpret the rulings in a way which did not unnecessarily allow people who were guilty to escape by virtue of technicalities." Lezak called him a criminal prosecutor's judge. He "was particularly good" on white-collar and fraud cases and "also very good on tax and customs cases," but he distinguished between tax and anti-trust cases and never jailed anti-trust violators.[11]

In Solomon's "heart he believed that if people came into court after indictment, they were most likely guilty," law clerk Stephen Gillers said. The judge had warned Gillers that "most defendants . . . are guilty. The great majority of them would like to avoid the consequences of their acts. They don't want a fair trial; they want to be freed." Expect them to reveal only selected information, he warned, and to ask their counsel to falsify records and engage in other underhanded tactics. Criminals would do or say almost anything to avoid punishment, he believed. Solomon shared a common bar attitude that repetitive and transparent dishonesty characterized criminal defendants and that they were usually guilty, although not necessarily of every charge.[11]

To clerk Henry J. Kaplan, Solomon's Ninth Circuit opinion in *U.S. v. Brooklier* typified this bias. A seven-week trial had convicted five men for extorting or conspiring to extort money from pornographers and bookmakers. When considering their appeal, Solomon labeled them members of La Cosa Nostra, "a secret national organization engaged in a wide range of racketeering activities, including murder, extortion, gambling, and loan sharking." Cooly rejecting all twelve appellant contentions, the judge "carefully skirted every meritorious argument offered by defense counsel, in order to reach the 'correct' result," Kaplan remembered; "some of the evidentiary rulings set appalling precedents."[13]

"The Government had to turn square corners" in criminal prosecutions in his court, clerk Mark Silverstein countered. "What kind of a fair trial do you think that a defendant in a small community can get if his confession is published in a newspaper or read over a telecast, even if his confession is excluded at the trial because it was illegally obtained?" Solomon once asked. Prosecutors had been known, he added, to provide the press all matter of excludable pre-trial information. He diligently protected a defendant's right before trial to secure material that had the potential to discredit prosecution witness testimony. Citing the Supreme Court's *Brady v. Maryland* and appellate decisions, Solomon held in *Simms v. Cupp* that even when the defense did not request it — because it did not know that a completely different description of the perpetrator was missing from the requested police file — the state had a duty to disclose potentially exculpatory evidence on the issue of guilt.[14]

Solomon also was alert to the possibility of forced confessions and to the denial of competent counsel to the accused, problems that had disturbed him since the 1930s. He welcomed the Warren Court's landmark *Mallory*, *Jackson*, *Draper*, and *Gideon* decisions, which strengthened the rights of individuals charged with crimes. "To require that an indigent defendant in a felony case be represented by a lawyer if he wants one, in my view, is elementary justice," as *Gideon* expressed. In *Horn v. Rhay*, Solomon released a convict after nearly

twenty-four years of a life sentence. In 1935, Ghether Horn, "an il-
literate transient worker without friends or funds," had confessed to
murder. The judge found that Horn's confession was not free and voluntary but obtained through police trickery and coercion. Applying
the then-current "fair trial" rule for state criminal trials, Solomon also
found against the state of Washington for its failure to arraign Horn or
give him an attorney for approximately sixty days after his arrest.[15]

Solomon set aside the waivers of counsel and indictment, the second-degree murder plea, the conviction, and the life sentence of another alleged murderer — McWilliams, who had only an eighth-grade
education. He lambasted the prosecutor and the trial judge. Neither
had explained to McWilliams the differences among manslaughter,
first-degree, and second-degree murder pleas. "The racial overtones
of the homicide (McWilliams was a Caucasian, his wife was Indian,
and Robinson, her paramour, was a Negro) and the circumstances
of the [deadly] fight would have been relevant to any attorney who
might have defended McWilliams," Solomon concluded. Nor had a
confession given while McWilliams was "still under the influence of
alcohol" been challenged. "Due process requires a judge to find out
whether there is a factual basis for the alleged crime before he accepts
a guilty plea requiring a life sentence from a defendant who is not
represented by counsel," Solomon said.[16]

Solomon was no absolutist about due process of law or any other
constitutional principle. He held that the facts in *McCoy v. Cupp*, involving the search of a suspected rapist's vehicle, did not meet the
stringent test under *Mapp v. Ohio*, the landmark 1961 application
of the Bill of Rights search-and-seizure restrictions to the states. He
unblushingly followed the Supreme Court's lead between 1965 and
1969 as it tightened and then eliminated the retroactive application of
its new criminal procedure rules unless a rule's purpose was to protect
the innocent. He refused in *Shannon v. Cupp* to retroactively apply the
Escobedo and *Miranda* enhancements of the rights of the accused to
counsel. In *Klamert v. Cupp*, he refused to free a felon who had been
inadequately warned of his *Miranda* right to remain silent and who,
while being transported, volunteered his guilt and later claimed he
had been too drunk to know what he had been saying.[17]

Three of Solomon's criminal determinations won Supreme Court
approval — and accolades from prosecutors. In *Naughten v. Cupp*,
the Court upheld his finding on a state judge's instruction to jurors
that there was a "presumption of truthfulness" about the testimony of

witnesses, while only prosecution witnesses had appeared. Solomon found the instruction proper under Oregon law and held that it did not deprive the accused of due process of law. The man's evidence of guilt, he determined, "was so overwhelming that the instruction, even if erroneous, was harmless under *Harrington v. California.* . . ." The appellate court reversed him. In overturning the Ninth Circuit, Chief Justice Rehnquist wrote: "Certainly the instruction by its language neither shifts the burden of proof nor negates the presumption of innocence." Any instruction had to be not only "undesirable, erroneous, or even 'universally condemned,'" but also violate a Fourteenth Amendment right, he wrote for the Court. To the dissenting Justices Brennan, Douglas, and Marshall, however, the "practical effect of the court's instructions was to convert the state's burden of proving guilt beyond a reasonable doubt to proving guilt by a preponderance of the evidence."[18]

In a brief opinion related to search and seizure, *Cupp v. Murphy,* the Supreme Court — which was beginning to limit Fourth Amendment protections — upheld Solomon's denial of *habeas corpus* to an Oregon inmate who had permitted police without a warrant to take scrapings from under his fingernails. Solomon found that the fingernail evidence could easily have been destroyed if the police had not immediately gathered it and that the accused had a full and fair hearing on all issues. Again reversed, he was nevertheless upheld by a Supreme Court that agreed that the police had probable cause to arrest him at the time of detention and fingernail scraping. Citing *Chimel v. California* on searches incident to a valid arrest, the Court held that the very limited intrusion undertaken to preserve easily destroyed evidence did not violate the Fourth and Fourteenth amendments.[19]

In *Nelson v. O'Neil,* the Supreme Court held, as had Solomon in a Ninth Circuit dissent, that the defendant had not been denied rights protected by the confrontation clause of the Sixth and Fourteenth Amendments. Justice Potter Stewart "adopted much of my reasoning," Solomon said, "but did not mention that there was a dissent." The Ninth Circuit majority had affirmed the lower court ruling that a robber-kidnapper's conviction was improper under the confession requirements of *Bruton* and affirmed a grant of *habeas corpus.* Solomon had countered, "We may be nearing the day when a co-defendant's confession in a joint trial will be barred, but I do not believe *Bruton v. United States* . . . or any other case cited by the majority goes that far."[20]

PRISONERS

Appeals by felons in state and federal facilities similarly evidenced the serious tension between Solomon's civil libertarianism and his respect for proper and humane governmental and institutional authority. "I think the recent trend has been to grant prisoners greater rights, and I favor this trend," he said in 1973. "Nevertheless, I recognized some of the problems and attempted to deal with them in the opinions which I am enclosing" — including *Capitan v. Cupp,* on whether a prisoner received a fair hearing before transfer to another prison.[20]

Solomon insisted that convicts have equitable access to the courts to seek release by *habeas corpus,* challenge confinement conditions, and prepare appeals. In 1959, he termed Oregon's new statute providing legal assistance to indigent inmates "humane and admirable legislation." He liked *Fay v. Noia,* in which the Supreme Court, by applying the Civil Rights Act to the states, provided for court redress of deprivation of civil rights by people acting under state law. Solomon's *Balleaux v. Holmes,* which anticipated *Fay* by some four years, had tried to establish the right of Oregon inmates to easily prepare *habeas* petitions by invalidating several prison regulations, but he excluded from the ruling those prisoners being held in isolation cells. "The Court appreciates the fact that prison authorities must maintain effective discipline, and must prevent unscrupulous prisoners from preying on the weak and ignorant," he concluded. While those excluded "may not initiate court action, communicate with counsel, or have access to legal materials," which he granted all other prisoners, he cautioned that this "administrative control, even if reasonable and moderate, must yield to the basic right to have access to the courts." Oregon's ACLU, which Solomon had quietly urged to file an *amicus* brief in this action, told him that other ACLU chapters had used his decision to win improvements in their prison systems. The Ninth Circuit in 1961, however, sharply rejected Solomon's invalidations of the regulations, denied any right to court-appointed counsel for indigent state prisoners in federal *habeas* actions (which he had hinted should occur), and restated as a circuit court rule that no judge could control or supervise state prison regulations and practices.[21]

Under Chief Judge Solomon — and in the spirit of his old Legal Aid Society commitment — the district labored to upgrade legal assistance to all prisoners and improve the state of Oregon's answers to inmate petitions. It supported initiatives in 1969–1970 by Professors Ross R. Runkel of Willamette University and Frederic R. Merrill of the

University of Oregon whereby their law students helped state prisoners prepare writ applications. In the 1970s, Solomon called on Governor Robert Straub to seek federal funds for the Oregon State Bar's legal assistance program. The bar organization was put on notice that the district's judges "believe that *Johnson v. Avery* requires" that convicts in state facilities must enjoy competent legal advice.[23]

Solomon sided with indigent inmates who sued Oregon for not providing them lawyers and paralegals and for denying them reasonable access to prison law libraries. "I believe that the state has both a duty not to interfere with prisoner access to the courts," he wrote in *Washington v. Penwell,* "and an affirmative duty to assure them effective access to the courts." A state may choose among reasonable alternatives to effect access, he added. He told the parties to propose a consent decree that went further than federal courts had been requiring and was assured that it happened.[24]

Solomon was alert to prisoners being demeaned or degraded — to a point. *Shannon v. Gladden* presented the question of whether the Oregon State Penitentiary's confinement of unruly, sometimes naked inmates in cold, pitch-dark, tiny isolation cells constituted cruel and unusual punishment. Calling the conditions "deplorable" and expressing "deep concern," Solomon in 1967 nonetheless accepted that "most of the offensive practices had already been abandoned and that the warden intended to issue new regulations. He accepted the legality of isolation cells under the new directive, implying a considerable institutional discretion to maintain control over unruly prisoners, and dismissed the complaint. "The task of administering a modern penal institution is a difficult one," he wrote in *Capitan v. Cupp.* "I do not pretend to assume the role of warden." Further, "I believe that the courts should not attempt to run prisons." Courts, however, had recently required that serious changes in confinement conditions "must comport with at least the most basic elements of procedural due process." In this light, he found in 1972 that Capitan, because he had no hearing or chance to refute charges against him before or shortly after the move, had been wrongfully transferred two thousand miles from the penitentiary to the U.S. Penitentiary in Leavenworth, Kansas. Solomon next found that the prisoner, Capitan, was returned for a hearing that was a sham. Neither the prison nor Oregon's Attorney General Office could be trusted to provide a fair hearing, he declared. In a rehearing, U.S. Magistrate George Juba approved the Leavenworth transfer. Satisfied on due process grounds (and later affirmed),

Solomon unsuccessfully attempted to arrange Capitan's incarceration closer to his family in Oregon.[25]

The politically liberal Solomon struggled to reconcile his convictions about due process of law, equal access to the law, and other constitutional liberties with his tough-minded attitudes toward punishment and sane, effective prison administration and, ultimately, with his deep sense that institutions must be strengthened and humanized. He ended up looking "for a maximum of reform with a minimum of institutional change," as Godfrey Hodgson writes of liberal reformists during the 1960s and 1970s. In the same vein, he looked for a maximum of effect in his official retirement with a minimum of change in the court and his duties.[26]

Chapter 12

Final Years

If he really retired, he would die.

—Libby Solomon, 1997

SENIOR JUDGE

For nearly six years, Solomon mulled over taking senior status at age sixty-five. A form of semi-retirement, it would permit him to work part-time at full pay, with his position filled by a newly selected district judge. His health was an unacknowledged factor. For twenty years, he had ignored advice to slow down because of health problems. His gall bladder had been removed when he was forty-nine, a year after his heart attack. Two years later, he complained that long evening meetings exhausted him. At fifty-six, a mild coronary condition was diagnosed. His angry outbursts worried physicians. When he "got into one of his tirades, he raised his blood pressure. It's amazing he didn't have a stroke," Dr. Arnold Rustin recalled. In 1965, Dr. Morton Goodman warned that a impending three-week trial would send Solomon to the hospital or the grave. Take time off, he ordered, and prescribed reducing his blood pressure and weight and taking medicine for his gouty arthritis. Still driving himself mercilessly, Solomon suffered a second coronary attack in 1966. Mild recurrences followed. Newspapers remarked on the chief judge's punishing schedule and less than robust health. Quietly, Solomon again tried but failed to make Allan Hart his replacement.[1]

In 1968, the Solomons made the first of several visits to a California weight-reduction spa. (When "I work hard I eat too much," he said.) The judge returned to his seven-day work schedule, but at sixty-four, experienced internal bleeding. Tests indicated that he was all right, "but it might have been different." He was now ingesting nitroglycerin pills, antacids, sleeping pills, and "relaxers." Reluctantly, he decided to take senior status in September 1971, obstinately denying that health was a consideration. Retirement came "primarily because I believe that

we need another judge," he claimed. It was not good for either them
or the court, he said, that all the judges were required to work seven
days a week. If replaced, Solomon rightly figured that the beleaguered
district would need him even after it added a new position from an
expected expansion of the judiciary. Taking life easier would satisfy
his wife, and Belloni would become chief judge. Colleagues did not
push him to retire, he said, but he guessed that they were glad when
it happened.[2]

Led successively by Chief Judges Belloni, Skopil, and Burns, the
district made piecemeal changes over the next dozen years under
Solomon's watchful eye. They nourished its good working relations
and, for a time, the court policies identified with his regime. Belloni
"sort of followed in Gus' footsteps because Gus was just down the hall
so he couldn't very well do anything without Gus knowing about it,"
Judge Skopil remarked. "As time went on we changed some things,
but we did it over a long period of time because it was a transition
for Judge Solomon." No policies were discussed outside his presence.
Under Skopil, U.S. Magistrate Edward Leavy, deemed the least fearful
of their number, was sent to test Solomon's views of proposals. Gradually, the judges delegated day-to-day management to committees, informed law firms of their desire to lighten the court atmosphere and
improve bench-bar relations, and, after Congress revised the statute,
adopted a rotating chief judgeship. Solomon was persuaded to phase
out his chamber's lunches for fear that some speaker might reappear
as a party in a case.[3]

"If he really retired, he would die," Libby Solomon remembered
feeling. Working at least fifty-hour-weeks and keeping to his busy
speech, board, and convention schedules, the judge barely slowed
down. He wrote more than sixty district and appellate opinions in
1970 and a burst of eighty-four during the 1971 retirement year. The
next year, he wrote sixty-seven opinions. That September, he reported
intermittent heart pains — it tired him, he laughed, to think about
how many assignments were ahead in and out of Oregon. Fifty opinions marked 1973. Endurance remained a source of pride. "In spite
of my 'retirement' and occasional chest pains and labyrinthitis [dizzi-
ness]," he chortled in 1974, "I am still carrying a full load in Oregon. I
recently worked on the Court of Appeals in the D.C. and Seventh Circuits, and I will soon work on the Appeals Courts in the Second and
Ninth Circuits." By 1975, he exalted that Oregon "dispos[ed] of more
cases per judge than in practically any other court in the country." In

1976, he wrote fifty-three opinions; in 1977, fifty-seven. A troubled spouse struggled to have him take retirement seriously.[4]

In his seventies, the senior judge zestfully clung to a full court schedule. When in Portland, he conducted the Monday calls. Their preparation jeopardized his health, Libby Solomon warned Judge Skopil. After angina pains forced Solomon to leave a concert in 1975, he ignored medical advice to stay in bed. Illnesses "never seemed to slow him down a bit. He really didn't acknowledge that he had that trouble," Dr. Rustin commented. "Talking to him either as a physician or a friend, one would not know he was a cardiac patient." His report on work he completed in Florida "is simply further evidence that Judge Gus Solomon is one of the most productive Judges in America," a chief judge there remarked. He wrote Solomon that he was "amazed at your accomplishments in our Court, most especially when I realized that you were in the hospital for almost a week and must have felt poorly at other times." Solomon had only consented to hospitalization for a suspected heart attack after a replacement judge was located. Upon release, he resumed trial responsibility.[5]

Starting in the mid-1970s, casual allusions to his mortality began slipping into Solomon's letters and bench remarks. "What a wonderful way to die," he said of the ACLU's Osmond K. Fraenkel, who died on his way to work in 1983. But his main hope or ambition was continuing "as a judge for at least thirty more years." Take any judgeship offered, he advised attorneys. "It's a damn good job." Feeling his battling days against anti-Semitism behind him, he nevertheless searched for an instrument through which, he said, Jewish lawyers could act at their "Brothers' Keeper." At seventy-eight, Solomon helped found the International Association of Jewish Lawyers.[6]

During Skopil's regime, Libby Solomon finally convinced her husband's colleagues to do something about the judge's Monday calls. Eliminating the calls, Judge Skopil remembered, constituted "the first outward expression of a change of reign in the district court." Under Chief Judge Burns, the judges in a close vote installed an independent calendar system in which a filed case automatically received a judge who controlled his or her own calendar. Oregon was one of the last federal districts to make this change. While silent about being removed from the calls and skeptical about altering procedures in which he still believed, Solomon apparently accepted that times had changed. His colleagues' collegiality, respect, and sensitivity to his ego considerably eased matters. They let him fulfill his wishes to sit only on civil cases, especially large, complicated ones, and to swear in attorneys and new citizens. Solomon contentedly believed that age had barely dented his capacity for hard work and had taken no real toll on his mental clarity or grip on the law — and that his capable peers recognized it.[7]

TO THE END

Not that Solomon was always content. Entering his mid-seventies, the intermittently ill jurist fretted about whether "the techniques which I use and which I have tried to get other Judges to use to cut down trial time" — which he termed his greatest judicial contribution — had much affected the federal judiciary. Comments in 1982 by members of a national commission on his proposed amendments to the civil rules discouraged him. Judges "write long articles and they make speeches about the need for cutting down trial time and speeding up the calendar, but they don't do very much about it, and I have found that they are critical of my techniques even when" they are effective.[8]

Solomon still saw the great merits of his calendar and trial techniques, yet no more than a handful of district judges outside Oregon reported adopting them. Those elsewhere who had received his speeches, writings, and press interviews on these matters responded noncommittally, if at all. Among his many correspondents in the bar, courts, and law schools, only Milton Handler of Columbia University, known since their student days there, openly disagreed with him. Handler, a national expert on complex litigation, told him that his "techniques would have to be substantially modified in dealing with the big, complex litigations which I handle." There was "no Open Sesame, no sure-fire technique that will work in all type of cases," he warned.[9]

Solomon's colleagues did adopt one or more of his techniques. For Judge Owen M. Panner, "those of us who tried cases in front of [Solomon] as lawyers and then became judges learned the importance of understanding the issues in the case and insisting that lawyers try the issues that are involved and not extraneous matters." The mandate that direct testimony be submitted beforehand in writing, subject to cross-examination in court, "has been used regularly, not only in this district, but nationwide and quite generally reduces the time for such trials by fifty percent or more." The consequent reduction in trial time in the U.S. District for Oregon, Judge Skopil estimated, ranged from 50 to 90 percent.[10]

Declining health might have contributed to Solomon's pessimistic appraisal of his influence. In his mid-seventies, he experienced worsening difficulties, including a disconcerting heart rhythm disturbance. Heart pain demanded frequent rest in chambers, and some hearings continued there while he lay on his back. A litigator once watched him swallow nitroglycerin pills and, "unstinting in his devotion to a case," persevere. Then prostrate cancer was diagnosed, painfully affecting his leg and foot. During 1986, Solomon underwent harrowing radiation treatment. Apprehensive but uncomplaining, he doggedly finished cases under advisement.[11]

The fading campaigner appreciated that friends once again tried to secure him the prestigious Devitt Distinguished Service to Justice Award. He suggested possible endorsers and arguments. As his major judicial contribution, he instructed, emphasize the "cutting down trial time and speeding up the calendar." Cancer spreading into his bones overtook their effort, however. In considerable pain, he retired to bed. Awaiting his end, he ceased taking his heart medicine and suffered another heart attack. He died on February 15, 1987, at age eighty.[12]

Nearly eight hundred mourners attended his funeral, where he was eulogized "as a man of courage, compassion and wisdom" and as an individual and judge who pursued justice. Speakers also remembered his irascible and temperamental nature — "as Solomon, the man of integrity, would have liked," a newspaper said — and his zestful wonder at being a judge. For months, publications printed obituaries and memorials, dwelling on a few opinions — mainly those affecting civil liberties — on his earlier political and legal activism, and on his positive human qualities and love of justice. Colorful stories of his demanding treatment of lawyers ran through lawyers' commentary. Solomon passed into legal folklore as a just, smart, capable, and unusually tough judge — and his district court, mainly because of him, as a distinguished one.[13]

In 1988, the American Inns of Court, which promotes collegiality, education, and ethics among member lawyers, judges, and legal educators, charted the Gus J. Solomon American Inn of Court in Portland. The same year, the Japanese American Citizens League conferred a posthumous award for his aid to Japanese Americans, as "one of the earliest, active, and unwavering proponents against the suspension of civil and human rights." In 1989, Solomon's legal, judicial, and Democratic Party admirers had Portland's federal courthouse named in his honor. In 1997, the Jewish Federation of Portland established Solomon's Legacy, named for the judge and the biblical Solomon, to conduct a topical forum for Jewish lawyers and obtain volunteers for its agencies. Solomon would have enjoyed these honors and used their ceremonies to urge listeners to help him fulfill the best dreams of his youth.[14]

Notes

ABBREVIATIONS

ACLU	American Civil Liberties Union
ADA	Americans for Democratic Action
BPA interview	interview with Gus J. Solomon, for Bonneville Power Administration, in possession of Gene Tollefson
FBI/HQ	Federal Bureau of Investigation, Reports on Gus J. Solomon, in possession of the author.
FRC/location	Federal Records Center (by location)
FRD	*Federal Rules Decisions*
GS	Gus J. Solomon
GS Judiciary file	Gus J. Solomon's file in Senate Judiciary Committee, Record Group 46, NARA/Washington
GSOHS	Gus Solomon oral history, OHS Research Library
GSOJM	Gus Solomon oral history, Oregon Jewish Museum
NARA/location	National Archives and Records Administration (by location)
OCF	Oregon Commonwealth Federation
OHSRL	Oregon Historical Society Research Library
OJM	Oregon Jewish Museum
OSC	Oregon Supreme Court Case, Oregon State Archives
PFJ	Personal: Federal Judgeship folder in Gus J. Solomon Papers
Salt Lake Hearing	"Hearings on Nomination of Gus J. Solomon, May 4, 1950, Salt Lake City, Utah" before Subcommittee of the Senate Judiciary Committee, vol. 1 in Gus J. Solomon Papers, OHSRL
UO	University of Oregon
Washington Hearing	"Hearingson Nomination of Gus J. Solomon, June 5, 1950, Washington, D.C." before Subcommittee of the Senate Judiciary Committee, vol. 2 in Gus J. Solomon Papers, OHSRL

Unless otherwise noted, all materials are from the Gus J. Solomon Papers, MS 2886, at the Oregon Historical Society Research Library, Portland. MS 2886 is an unprocessed collection; folder names, rather than numbers, are indicated in citations. Unless otherwise stated, all legal materials are in named case files in the Solomon Papers.

CHAPTER 1

1. Personal and family information are from GSOHS, tape 1, side 1; GSOJM, tape 1, side 1; biographical questionnaire, Judicial Conference of the United States, mailed June 18, 1976, in "Solomon Biographical Material"; American Jewish Archives biographical questionnaire, n.d.; newspaper obituary of Jacob Solomon, n.d.; GS to cousin (Jakow Peisik), Feb. 13, 1959, "Personal Correspondence, 1959," MS 2886; *(Portland) Scribe*, July 24, 1936; Gary Miranda, *Following a River: Portland's Congregation Neveh Shalom, 1869-1989* (Portland, Ore.: Congregation Neveh Shalom, 1989), 53, 82.

2. Joseph Kissman, "The Immigration of Rumanian Jews up to 1914," in *YIVO Annual of Jewish Social Science* (New York: Yiddish Scientific Institute-YIVO, 1947/1948), 2:160; Keith Hitchens, *Rumania, 1866-1947* (New York: Oxford University Press, 1994), 166; Michael R. Marrus, *The Unwanted: European Refugees in the Twentieth Century* (New York: Oxford University Press, 1985), 34.

3. Gerald Sorin, *Tradition Transformed: The Jewish Experience in America* (Baltimore: John Hopkins University Press, 1997), 93.

4. Arthur A. Goren, "Jews," in *Harvard Encyclopedia of American Ethnic Groups*, ed. Stephen Thernstrom (Cambridge: Harvard University Press, 1980), 579; Simon Kuznets, "Immigration of Russian Jews to the United States: Background and Structure," *Perspectives in American History* 9 (1975): 35-124; Gerald Sorin, *A Time for Building: The Third Migration, 1860-1920* (Baltimore: Johns Hopkins University Press, 1992), 14, 35.

5. Paul G. Merriam, "The 'Other Portland': A Statistical Note on Foreign-Born, 1860-1910," *Oregon Historical Quarterly* 80 (Fall 1979): 258-68; Sorin, *Tradition Transformed*, 97; Carl Abbott, *Portland: Planning, Politics, and Growth in a Twentieth-Century City* (Lincoln: University of Nebraska Press, 1983), 121; William Toll, *The Making of an Ethnic Middle Class: Portland Jewry over Four Generations* (Albany: SUNY Press, 1982).

6. Sorin, *Tradition Transformed*, 93; William Toll, "Voluntarism and Modernization in Portland Jewry: The B'Nai B'rith in the 1920s," *Western Historical Quarterly* 10 (January 1979), 22; idem, "Ethnicity and Stability: The Italians and Jews of South Portland, 1900-1940," *Pacific Historical Review* 54 (May 1985): 175.

7. E. Kimbark MacColl, with Harry H. Stein, *Merchants, Money and Power: The Portland Establishment, 1843-1913* (Portland, Ore.: Georgian Press, 1988), 357-461.

8. Robert D. Johnston, *The Radical Middle Class: Populist Democracy and the Question of Capitalism in Progressive Era Portland* (Princeton: Princeton University Press, 2003), 99; 1910 Manuscript Census of Portland, District 162, Sheet 7A; GS, untitled speech, April 16, 1965, in "Speeches," MS 2886; GS birth certificate, in possession of the author.

9. Eric L. Goldstein, "Fitting In and Standing Out: The Paradoxes of Jewish Identity in the American World of 'Difference,'" in *"Jewishness" and the World of "Difference" in the United States*, ed. Marc L. Raphael (Williamsburg, Va.: Department of Religion, College of William and Mary, 2001), 4; E. Kimbark MacColl, *The Growth of a City: Power and Politics in Portland, Oregon, 1915 to 1950* (Portland, Ore.: Georgian Press, 1979), 395.

10. GSOJM, tape 1, sides 1 and 2; GSOHS, tape 1, side 1; Libby Solomon interview; American Jewish Archives biographical questionnaire, n.d.

11. GSOHS, tape 1, side 1; David Biale, "The Melting Pot and Beyond: Jews and the Politics of American Identity," in *Insider/Outsider: American Jews and Multiculturalism*, ed. David Biale et al. (Berkeley: University of California Press, 1998), 18.

12. GSOHS, tape 1, side 1, and tape 10, side 1.

13. GSOHS, tape 1, side 2; Toll, *Making of an Ethnic Middle Class*, 118.

14. William Toll, "Ethnicity and Stability: The Italians and Jews of South Portland, 1900-1940," *Pacific Historical Review* 54 (May 1985), 175; GSOHS, tape 1, sides 1 and 2; GSOJM, tape 1, side 2.

15. Steve M. Cohen and Arnold M. Gisen, *The Jew Within: Self, Family and Community in America* (Bloomington: Indiana University Press, 2000), 203; Steven Lowenstein, *The Jews of Oregon, 1850-1950* (Portland: Jewish Historical Society of Oregon, 1987), 92-156; Deborah Dash Moore, *At Home in America: Second Generation New York Jews* (New York: Columbia University Press, 1981), 16.

16. Henry L. Feingold, *A Midrash on American Jewish History* (Albany: State University of New York Press, 1982), 128-40; Mordecai Waxman, "The Ideology of the Conservative Movement," in *Understanding American Judaism: Toward the Description of a Modern Religion*, ed. Jacob Neusner (New York: Ktav Publishing, 1975), 2:250-4; GS, B'nai B'rith contribution, in "Speeches No. 34 Thru 59," MS 2886; Lowenstein, *Jews of Oregon*, 152.

17. GSOHS, tape 1, side 1, tape 14, side 1; Victoria Saker Woeste, "Insecure Equality: Louis Marshall, Henry Ford, and the Problem of Defamatory Antisemitism, 1920-1929," *Journal of American History* 91 (Dec. 2004): 878.

18. GS, The Jewish Role in the American Civil Rights Movement, Sept. 28, 1967, in "Trip to England-Sept. and Oct. 1967," MS 2886; GSOJM, tape 1, side 1; GS, "My

Encounters with Discrimination and What I Did about Them," Jan. 3, 1973, in "Speeches No. 110," MS 2886.

19. GSOJM, tape 1, side 1; GS, untitled speech, Jan. 22, 1974, in "Naturalization Speeches," and B'nai B'rith contribution, "Speeches No. 34 Thru 59," MS 2886.

20. GSOJM, tape 1, side 1; Ellen Eisenberg, "Transplanted to the Rose City: The Creation of East European Jewish Community in Portland, Oregon," *Journal of American Ethnic History* 19 (Spring 2000), 88.

21. GSOJM, tape 1, side 1.

22. GSOHS, tape 1, side 1; GSOJM, tape 1, side 1.

23. GSOJM, tape 1, side 1; Morton Goodman interview; Ted Swett oral history, 18.

24. Charles E. Wright oral history, 54; James E.B. Breslin, *Mark Rothko: A Biography* (Chicago: University of Chicago Press, 1993), 34-36; *Oregonian* (Magazine), May 11, 1980; Gilbert Sussman oral history, tape 1, side 1; Mollie Bluementhal oral history, 8.

25. GS, Introduction to Hy Samuels, Dec. 9, 1970, "Speeches No. 60 Through No. 109," MS 2886; (Lincoln) *Cardinal*, January 1923 class issue.

26. A "second-generation" Jew is either the native-born child of immigrants or a Jewish adult living between the 1920s and 1945.

27. GSOHS, tape 1, side 2; GSOJM, tape 1, side 2.

28. GSOHS, tape 1, side 2; GSOJM, tape 1, side 2; Report of Aug. 4, 1939, Solomon Report, FBI/HQ 77-10137; Burton R. Clark, *The Distinctive College* (New Brunswick: Transaction, 1992 [1970]), 109-17; "The First Quarter Century: Retrospect and Appraisal 1911-1936," *Reed College Bulletin* 15 (Nov. 1936): 49; Jane J. Feldstein, ed. *Rabbi Jacob Weinstein: Advocate of the People* (New York: Ktav Publishing, 1980), 14, 20; Allan N. Wald, "The Menorah Group Moves Left," *Jewish Social Studies* 38 (Summer-Fall 1976): 289-320; Solomon quoted in Louis I. Neiman to GS, Jan. 18, 1956, in "Personal Correspondence 1953 through 1958," MS 2886.

29. GSOHS, tapes 1 and 2, side 2; GSOJM, tape 1, side 2; GS to William L. Josslin, July 9, 1949, in "GS/PFJ,"; GS to Florence W. Lehman, April 7, 1972, in "Reed College Correspondence 1955 to 1979," MS 2886.

30. GSOHS, tape 1, side 2, and tape 2, sides 1 and 2; GSOJM, tape 1, side 2; GS to Max Gordon, Oct. 15, Nov. 3, 1971, in "Max Gordon"; GS, "My Encounters with Discrimination," MS 2886.

31. MacColl, *Growth of a City*, 162-72; Johnston, *Radical Middle Class*, 221-2, 243, 253; GSOHS, tape 1, side 2.

32. Reports of Aug. 4, July 31, 1939, Solomon FBI Report, FBI/HQ 77-10137; GSOJM, tape 1, side 2, tape 2, side 1, tape 5, side 2.

33. Peter Novick, *That Noble Dream: The "Objectivity Question" and the American Historical Profession* (Cambridge: Cambridge University Press, 1988), 172; GSOJM, tape 2, side 1; GSOHS, tape 1, side 1, tape 2, sides 1 and 2.

34. GS, Remarks at Orientation Program for First Year Class, College of Law, Willamette University, Aug. 28, 1970, in "Speeches No. 60 Through No. 109," MS 2886.

35. GSOHS, tape 2, side 1; GSOJM, tape 1, side 2; GS, untitled speech, April 16, 1965, MS 2886; Max Gordon, *Live at the Village Vanguard* (New York: St. Martin's Press, 1980), 8; GS to Gordon, Nov. 3, 1971, in "Max Gordon," MS 2886; Reports of July 31, Aug. 15, 1939, Solomon FBI Report FBI/HQ 77-10137.

36. GSOHS, tape 2, side 2; Julius Goebel Jr., *History of the School of Law Columbia University* (New York: Columbia University Press, 1955), 289-303, 490n73; GS, Remarks at Orientation Program, MS 2886; William O. Douglas, *Go East, Young Man* (New York, 1974), 150; Peter Irons, *The New Deal Lawyers* (Princeton: Princeton University Press, 1982), 6-7; Robert Stevens, *Law School: Legal Education in America From the 1850s to the 1980s* (Chapel Hill: University of North Carolina Press, 1983), 137-9.

37. Laura Kalman, *Abe Fortas: A Biography* (New Haven: Yale University Press, 1990), 16, 29; Jerold S. Auerbach, *Unequal Justice: Lawyers and Social Change in Modern America* (New York: Oxford University Press, 1976), 150; GSOHS, tape 2, side 1; GS, Speech to Young Lawyers, c. 1951, in "Speeches No. 1 Thru 34"; GS, Speech to ACLU, Nov. 16, 1985, in "E.B. MacNaughton Award–1985," MS 2886.

38. GSOJM, tape 1, side 2; GS to Jerry Pratt, Oct. 26, 1966, in "Jerry Pratt Oregonian Article and TV Show," MS 2886; *Oregonian*, Aug. 25, 1968. As a judge, he rejected an invitation to join a Columbia legal fraternity.

39. GSOHS, tape 2, side 1, tape 4, side 2; GS, Speech to ACLU, MS 2886; GSOJM, tape 3, side 2; Michael Alexander, *Jazz Age Jews* (Princeton: Princeton University Press, 2001), 75. Historically, free speech was for Jews an important indicator of a tolerant government.

40. GSOHS, tape 2, side 1.

41. GSOHS, tape 2, side 1; "Judge Solomon, Activist and Workaholic, Prizes Common Sense, Judgment in Lawyers," *Multnomah Lawyer* 84 (January 1984).

42. Between 1927 and 1929, Oregon experienced the highest business failure rate in the nation. GSOHS, tape 2, side 1; Robert E. Burton, "The New Deal in Oregon," in *The New Deal: The State and Local Levels*, eds. John Braeman, Robert H. Bremner and David Brody (Columbus: Ohio State University Press, 1975) 2:356; Stevens, *Law School*, 197; GSOJM, tape 1, side 2.

43. GSOJM, tape 1, side 2; GS to Lowell Turrentine, Sept. 5, 1973, in "Stanford Law School," MS 2886; GSOHS, tape 2, side 2.

44. GSOHS, tape 2, side 2; Arnold Rustin interview.

CHAPTER 2

1. GSOHS, tape 2, side 2; MacColl, *Growth of a City*, 137-411.

2. Lawrence M. Friedman, *American Law in the 20th Century* (New Haven: Yale University Press, 2002), 461.

3. GSOHS, tape 2, side 2, tape 3, side 1.

4. E. Kimbark MacColl, with Harry H. Stein, *Merchants, Money and Power: The Portland Establishment, 1843-1913* (Portland, Ore.: Georgian Press, 1988), 335-461; Johnston, *Radical Middle Class*, 56, 60.

5. Appellant's Abstract of Record in *Solomon v. Glickman*, 140 Or. 364 (1932), Oregon Supreme Court Case File 7319, in Oregon State Archives [hereafter OSC and case file number]; GSOHS, tape 2, side 2.

6. GS, Speech to Young Lawyers, MS 2886.

7. GS, Speech to Young Lawyers, MS 2886; Robert W. Gordon, "The Legal Profession," in *Looking Back at Law's Century*, eds. Austin Sarat et al., (Ithaca, NY: Cornell University Press, 2002), 291.

8. Charles E. Silberman, *A Certain People: American Jews and their Lives Today* (New York: Summit Books, 1985), 23; GS, Joint Defense Appeal Human Relations Award Dinner—Portland, Ore., Nov. 13, 1960, in "Joint Defense Appeal—Award 11/13/60,"; "My Encounters with Discrimination and What I Did About Them", Jan. 3, 1973, in "Speeches No. 110"; Speech to Lawyers for United Jewish Appeal, March 31, 1959, in "United Jewish Appeal"; Speech to a New York City Synagogue Group of Lawyers [1957], in "Speeches No. 1 Thru 34," MS 2886; GSOJM, tape 2, sides 1 and 2.

9. GS, "My Encounters with Discrimination" and Speech to Young Lawyers, MS 2886.

10. Ibid.

11. Auerbach, *Unequal Justice*, 159, 186; Leo Levenson oral history, tape 3, side 1; *Oregon Journal*, Jan. 10, 1971.

12. GS to Walter, July 11, 1973 in "Stephen Gillers, MS 2886"; GSOHS, tape 2,

side 2 and tape 3, side 1; GSOJM, tape 2, side 1; Report of Aug. 4, 1939, Solomon FBI Report FBI/HQ 77-10137.

13. Richard Abel, *American Lawyers* (New York: Oxford University Press, 1989), 178-81; Levenson oral history, tape 3, side 2; Esther L. Brown, *Lawyers and the Promotion of Justice* (New York: Russell Sage Foundation, 1938), 172-5; William Weinfeld, "Income of Lawyers, 1929-48," *Survey of Current Business* 29 (Aug. 1949), 18-24; Auerbach, *Unequal Justice*, 158-9; David L. Davies in Washington Hearing 3:284; Allan Hart interview; Sol M. Linowitz with Martin Mayer, *The Betrayed Profession: Lawyering at the End of the Twentieth Century* (New York: Scribner's 1994), 91.

14. Charles E. Wright oral history, 39; GSOHS, tape 4, side 1.

15. GSOHS, tape 4, side 1; Robert A. Leedy oral history, 27; Raymond M. Kell, "History of Kell, Alterman & Runstein," 2-3; Wright oral history, 46.

16. GSOHS, tape 3, side 1; Leonard J. Arrington, "The New Deal and the West: A Preliminary Statistical Inquiry," *Pacific Historical Review* 38 (Aug. 1969): Table 2; Burton, "The New Deal in Oregon," 356; Richard Lowitt, *The New Deal and the West* (Bloomington: Indiana University Press, 1984), 144; William H. Mullins, *The Depression and the Urban West Coast: Los Angeles, San Francisco, Seattle and Portland* (Bloomington: Indiana University Press, 1991), 8-18; David Peterson del Mar, *Oregon's Promise: An Interpretive History* (Corvallis: Oregon State University Press, 2003), 185-7.

17. Auerbach, *Unequal Justice*, 158-9; Brown, *Lawyers*, 185-90.

18. Levenson oral history, tape 3, sides 1 and 2; GSOHS, tape 2, side 2 and tape 3, side 1; *Oregonian* (Magazine), May 11, 1980; GSOJM, tape 2, side 1.

19. Erling J. Hangerud in Salt Lake Hearing 1:48-51; Kell, "History," 33; GSOJM, tape 2, side 1; *McLean v. Sanders*, 139 Or. 144 (1932), OSC Case File 7206; *Walling v. Lebb*, 140 Or. 691 (1932), OSC Case File 7381; *Solomon v. Glickman*, 140 Or. 364 (1932), OSC Case File 7319; *Glickman v. Solomon*, 140 Or. 358 (1932), OSC Case File 7318; GS in Washington Hearing, 3:341; Linowitz with Mayer, *Betrayed Profession*, 97.

20. Unidentified newspaper clipping, Oct. 19, 1932, Levenson Papers; GSOHS, tape 3, side 1 and tape 4, sides 1 and 2; Zechariah Chafee, Jr., *Free Speech Speech in the United States* (Cambridge: Harvard University Press, 1941), 478-80. Solomon usually retained the pre-war term "civil rights" for "civil liberties," and I have usually changed it in brackets to the latter.

21. GS in Washington Hearing, 3:304, 341; Irving Korn to GS, June 1, 1950 in "Hearing re Confirmation," MS 2886; *Oregon Journal*, July 1, 1958; GSOHS, tape 3, side 1; *Oregonian* (Magazine), May 11, 1980; Levenson oral history, tape 3, side 2.

22. GS, "My Encounters with Discrimination," MS 2886; *Oregonian*, May 3, 1934; GSOHS, tape 4, side 1; briefs in *Oregon v. Jordan*, 146 Or. 504 (1934) in OSC Case File 7909; *Oregon v. Jordan*, 146 Or. 504 (1934); *Powell v. Alabama*, 287 U.S. 45 (1932), *Brown v. Mississippi*, 297 U.S. 278 (1936).

23. GSOHS, tapes 4 and 5, side 1; GSOJM, tape 2, side 1; *Oregon Journal*, July 1, 1958; *Oregonian*, Feb. 17, 1987.

24. Levenson oral history, tape 3, side 1; GS, Statement to Julius A. Bernard of FBI, Sept. 3, 1953, in "Personal Correspondence 1953 throughout 1958," MS 2886.

25. This and the next paragraph derive from GS, Stanford Law School Class of 1929 Reunion Dinner in "Speeches No. 60 Through No. 109," MS 2886; James Caputo Sr. interview; *Maneff v. Lamer*, 148 Or. 455 (1934) in OSC Case File 7947; *Stone v. Shaw Supply Co.*, 148 Or. 416 (1934) in OSC Case File 7951; *Richey Loan Co. v. Cheldelin*, 148 Or. 170 (1934) in OSC Case File 7909"; Berg Gets $7500 Damages," unidentified Portland clipping, Levenson Papers; *Harlow v. Chenoweth*, 158 Or. 343 (1938) in OSC Case File 8588; *Vale v. State Industrial Accident Commission*, 160 Or. 569 (1939) in OSC Case File 8734; Krause in Salt Lake Hearing 1:58; and *Northwestern Mut. Life Ins. Co. v. Cohn Bros.*, 102 F.2d. 74 (1939).

26. GSOHS, tape 4, side 2; GSBPA interview; Robert E. Burton, *Democrats of Oregon:*

The Pattern of Minority Politics, 1900-1956 (Eugene: University of Oregon Books, 1960), 71, 76, 87; Burton, "The New Deal in Oregon," 362.

27. Richard L. Neuberger, *Our Promised Land* (New York: Macmillan, 1938), 151; and see Wesley A. Dick, "Visions of Abundance: The Public Power Crusade in the Pacific Northwest in the Era of J.D. Ross and the New Deal" (Ph.D. diss., University of Washington, 1973), and Jay L. Brigham, *Empowering the West: Electrical Politics Before FDR* (Lawrence: University Press of Kansas, 1998).

28. Kell, "History," 2; Morton Tompkins to Charles Brannan, July 5, 1949, and Tompkins to Tom Clark, July 5, 1949, in "GSJ/PFJ," MS 2886; GSOHS, tape 4, side 2 and tape 5, side 1; C. Allan Hart oral history, tape 10, side 1; GS, Speech to Young Lawyers, MS 2886; Marquis Childs, *The Farmer Takes a Hand: The Electric Power Revolution in Rural America* (Garden City: Doubleday, 1952), 207-9.

29. As used by Austin Sarat and Stuart Scheingold, eds., *Cause Lawyering: Political Commitments and Professional Responsibilities* (New York: Oxford University Press, 1998). Cause lawyer is a term that came to include public interest, civil rights, civil liberties, feminist, and poverty lawyers. Carl D. Thompson to Sweetland, Nov. 14, 1940, in "Peoples Utility Districts (2)," OCF Papers; Public Ownership League of Washington materials in unlabeled scrapbook; Gene Tollefson, *BPA and the Struggle for Power at Cost* (Portland: Bonneville Power Administration, [1985]), 185, 199-200.

30. Levenson oral history, tape 3, side 1; GSOHS, tape 5, side 2; GSOJM, tape 3, side 1; *Harris v. Backman*, 160 Or. 520 at 529 (1939) in OSC Case File 8729; Frank E. Gordon to Cordon, May 22, 1950, in "Miscellaneous," MS 2886; GS to James Loeb Jr., June 6, 1941, reel 13, ADA Papers.

31. GS to Jerome M. Britchey, June 10, 1939, reel 177, ACLU: Roger Baldwin Years; *Congress of Industrial Organizations v. Bain* and *American Federation of Labor v. Bain*, 165 Or. 183 (1940) in OSC Case File 8969; GS affidavit, Jan. 27, 1939, in *Harris v. Backman* in OSC Case File 8729. Almost since its inception, the ACLU had linked freedom of expression and association with the struggle for workers' rights.

32. GS to ACLU, Nov. 20, 1940, reel 8, ACLU/Selected Papers; GS to Elizabeth Willer, [Feb. 6, 1939] in "Miscellaneous," MS 2886; briefs and oral argument in *Congress of Industrial Organizations v. Bain* and *American Federation of Labor v. Bain* in OSC Case File 8969.

33. Irvin Goodman to Roger N. Baldwin, Dec. 21, 1933; Emily Nunn to Forrest Bailey, Feb. 15, 1932; Elizabeth Gurley Flynn to Lucille Milner, July 29, 1934; Baldwin to Goodman, Jan. 4, 1933, and Aug. 23, 1934, and GS to Milner, Nov. 22, 1934, reel 7, ACLU/Selected Papers; GS to Mr. and Mrs. Fred W. Friendly, March 10, 1983 in "Civil Rights," MS 2886.

34. Eldridge F. Dowell, *A History of Criminal Syndicalism Legislation in the United States* (Baltimore: Johns Hopkins University Press, 1939), 118-22; Oregon Code of 1930, section 14-3113, as amended by chapter 459 of the Oregon Laws of 1933; National Lawyers Guild, Oregon Chapter, *Report of the Civil Liberties Committee* ([Portland:]: Author, May 24, 1938); Jerry Lembcke and William M. Tattam, *One Union in Wood* (Madeira Park, BC, and New York: Harbour Publishing and International Publishers, 1984), 58-59; MacColl, *Growth of a City*, 484-5.

35. Cass R. Sunstein, *One Case at a Time: Judicial Minimalism on the Supreme Court* (Cambridge, Mass.: Harvard University Press, 1999), x-xi.

36. GS, ACLU-E.B. MacNaughton Civil Liberties Award Speech, Dec. 8, 1965 in "Speeches No. 60 Thru No. 109," MS 2886; Jerold S. Auerbach, "The Depression Decade" in *The Pulse of Freedom: American Liberties: 1920-1970s*, ed. Alan Reitman (New York: Norton, 1975), 67, 78. Also see Mullins, *Depression*, 27, 58, 83; Alan L. Gallagher, "The American Civil Liberties Union in Oregon from 1920 to 1955," [unpublished manuscript] 15 in "History-Oregon," ACLU of Oregon; *New York Times*, Jan. 10, 1937, and Millie R. Trumbull to Baldwin, Feb. 20, 1938, reel 166, ACLU: Roger Baldwin Years.

37. Levenson oral history, tape 3, side 2; GS to Milner, Dec. 15, 1934, and June 6, 1935, Baldwin to GS, Dec. 21, 1934 , GS to Baldwin, May 15, 1935, GS to Wirin, Sept. 1, 1934, Flynn to Milner, July 29, 1934, Milner to Members of Portland Committee of the American Civil Liberties Union, Sept. 21, 1934, Milner to Flynn, Sept. 24, 1934, GS to Samuel P. Puner, Aug. 20, 1935, and Milner to GS, Sept. 24, 1935, reel 7, ACLU/ Selected Papers; Samuel Walker, *In Defense of American Liberties: A History of the ACLU* (New York: Oxford University Press, 1990), 118.

38. GS to Milner, June 6, 1935, reel 7, ACLU/Selected Papers; petition, June 8, 1935, in *Oregon v. Pugh*, 151 Or. 561 (1935) in OSC Case File 8167.

39. GS to Puner, June 19, 1935 and Aug. 20, 1935, reel 7, ACLU/Selected Papers; brief in OSC Case File 8167.

40. GS in Proposed Rule Changes, Sept. 13, 1975, p. 34, in "Rules (Old Drafts of Changes)."

41. I partly rely on Richard C. Cortner, *The Supreme Court and Second Bill of Rights: The Fourteenth Amendment and the Nationalization of Civil Liberties* (Madison: University of Wisconsin Press, 1981), 87-97, and William E. Leuchtenburg, *The Supreme Court Reborn: The Constitutional Revolution in the Age of Roosevelt* (New York: Oxford University Press, 1995), 237-58.

42. GS to Milner, Nov. 22, 1934, reel 7, ACLU/Selected Papers; GSOHS, tape 4, side 2.

43. GS to Milner, Nov. 22, 1934, and Baldwin to GS, Dec. 21, 1934, reel 7, ACLU/ Selected Papers; *Oregon v. DeJonge*, 152 Or. 315 (1935); Charles E. Rice, *Freedom of Association* (New York: New York University Press, 1962), 132.

44. GSOHS, tape 4, side 2; Portland Committee Minutes, Sept. 6, 1935, and GS to ACLU, Oct. 22, 1936, reel 7, ACLU/Selected Papers; Cortner, *The Supreme Court*, 93-94; Dan T. Carter, *Scottsboro: A Tragedy of the American South* (New York: Oxford University Press, 1971 [1969]), 334; *Herndon v. Georgia*, 295 U.S. 441 (1935).

45. GSOHS, tape 4, side 2; Hart oral history, tape 4, side 2; GS, ACLU-E. B. MacNaughton Civil Liberties Award Speech, Dec. 8, 1965, in "Speeches No. 60 Thru No. 109," MS 2886; ACLU *amici curiae* rehearing brief in *Oregon v. DeJonge*, 152 Or. 315 (1935) in OSC Case File 8168; GS, ACLU-MacNaughton; Cortner, *The Supreme Court*, 92-93; GS to ACLU, Jan. 25, 1936, reel 7, ACLU/Selected Papers.

46. GSOHS, tape 4, side 2; GS to ACLU, Jan.14 and 25, 1936, reel 7, ACLU/ Selected Papers.

47. Osmond K. Fraenkel to GS, March 10, 1936, reel 7 and GS to ACLU, Dec. 6, 1935, and Oct. 22, 1936, reel 8, ACLU/Selected Papers; Harry A. Poth Jr. to GS, Oct. 27, 1936, reel 139, ACLU: Roger Baldwin Years; GSOHS, tape 4, side 2.

48. GSOHS, tape 4, side 2; GS to Milner, Dec. 15, 1934, and GS to ACLU, April 21, 1936, reel 7 and GS to ACLU, Oct. 22, 1936, reel 8, ACLU/Selected Papers; Tarshis in Salt Lake Hearing 1:40-42.

49. Fraenkel in Ann Fagan Ginger, *Carol Weiss King: Human Rights Lawyer, 1895-1952* (Niwot: University Press of Colorado, 1993), 217-8; Transcript of Record, *DeJonge v. Oregon*, 299 U.S. 353 (1937).

50. GS in Washington Hearing, 3:345; scrapbook of clippings, Levenson Papers; Appendix to "Excerpts from the Diary of Osmond K. Fraenkel Relating to the American Civil Liberties Union," unp., Princeton University. For part of the State's exact argument before the high court, see Chafee, *Free Speech in the United States*, 386.

51. *DeJonge v. Oregon*, 299 U.S. 353 (1937).

52. GS to ACLU, Jan. 6, 1937, reel 8, ACLU/Selected Papers; DeJonge in David R. Hardy, "The 1934 Portland Longshoremen's Strike" (B.A. thesis Reed College, 1971), 73.

53. *Gitlow v. New York*, 268 U.S. 652 (1925); *Stromberg v. California*, 283 U.S. 359 (1931); *Near v. Minnesota*, 283 U.S. 697 (1931); *Grossjean v. American Press Co.*, 297

U.S. 233 (1936); Martin Shapiro, *"DeJonge v. Oregon,"* in *Encyclopedia of the American Constitution,* eds. Leonard Levy and Kenneth L. Karst (New York: Macmillan Reference USA, 2000), 2:760.

53. Mark Silverstein interview; *Oregonian,* Nov. 2, 1937; GS, ACLU-E.B. MacNaughton Civil Liberties Award Speech, Dec. 8, 1965, in "Speeches No. 60 Thru No. 109," MS 2886; Oregon Laws of 1933 chapter 459 as amended by Oregon Laws of 1937 chapter 362. For modern interest in Solomon's role in DeJonge, see Fred W. Friendly and Martha J. H. Elliott, *The Constitution: That Delicate Balance* (New York: Random House, 1984), 75-80, and Cortner, *The Supreme Court,* 87-97.

54. GS, ACLU-E.B. MacNaughton; GSOHS, tape 4, side 1; Weinfeld, "Income of Lawyers," 18.

CHAPTER 3

1. GS, Speech to Young Lawyers; Blanche W. Cook, *Eleanor Roosevelt* (New York: Penguin Books, 1992), 1:4; Wendell Gray oral history, 154, 160.

2. Gordon, "The Legal Profession," 221.

3. GS in Washington Hearing, 3: 334.

4. "The politics of [twentieth-century] liberalism was ineluctably a politics of place." Thomas J. Sugrue, "All Politics is Local: The Persistence of Localism in Twentieth-Century America," in *The Democratic Experiment: New Directions in American Political History,* eds. Meg Jacobs et al. (Princeton: Princeton University Press, 2003), 302.

5. GSOHS, tape 3, side 2 and tape 4, side 1.

6. GSOJM, tape 2, side 2.

7. Green, Trashis, Sussman, and Peoples in Salt Lake Hearing 1:34, 42-46, 111; E.F. Bennett to editor, *Oregonian,* c. June 1950, clipping in 1933 Scrapbook; Gordon to Cordon, May 22, 1950, in "Nomination Letters," GS, [Deposition,] March 1952, in "Personal Correspondence 1953 through 1958;" Sweetland to Peyton Ford, Aug. 5, 1949, in "GSJ/PFJ," MS 2886.

8. David Plotke, *Building a Democratic Political Order: Reshaping American Liberalism in the 1930s and 1940s* (Cambridge: Cambridge University Press, 1996), 81, places the highpoint of national popular mobilization—a concept I borrow—in approximately 1935-1937.

9. GS to Guy Cordon, Jan. 26, 1950, in Senate Judiciary file; Warren F. Kuehl and Lynne K. Dunn, *The Covenant: American Internationalists and the League of Nations, 1920-1939* (Kent, Ohio: Kent State University Press, 1997), 44-47; Robert C. Accinelli, "Militant Internationalists: The League of Nations Association, The Peace Movement, and U.S. Foreign Policy, 1934-38," *Diplomatic History* 4 (Winter 1980), 36; *Oregonian,* Sept. 11 and 12, 1929, Feb. 28, 1932, and June 25, 1933; *Oregon Journal,* Sept. 10, 1929; GSJHSO, tape 2, side 1. The association had renamed itself since Solomon's student days.

10. GS to A. L. Wirin, Aug. 31, Sept. 1 and 17, 1934, Goodman to Baldwin, Dec. 21, 1933, and Lucille B. Milner to Members of Portland Committee of the American Civil Liberties Union, Sept. 21, 1934, reel 7, ACLU/Selected Papers; GSOHS, tape 4, side 2; William Bigelow and Normal Diamond, "Agitate, Educate, Organize: Portland, 1934," *Oregon Historical Quarterly* 89 (Spring 1988), 5-29.

11. Gallagher, "American Civil Liberties Union," 12-13; Albert F. Gunns, *Civil Liberties in Crisis: The Pacific Northwest* (New York: Garland, 1983), 214-7; GS, ACLU-E.B. MacNaughton; GS to Baldwin, May 15, 1935, Baldwin to David Epps, Apr. 27, 1936, GS to ACLU, April 21, May 4, and 9, and June 11, 1936, and the Mannisto, Reinis, and Baer deportation files, reel 7, ACLU/Selected Papers.

12. [L.A. Milner, Daily Report,] Jan. 17 and 28, 1936, in Oregon Military Department Records: Communist Activity Intelligence Reports, 1932-1939, Oregon State Archives, Salem; *Oregonian,* Dec. 2, 1937; *Oregon Journal,* Feb. 16, 1938; GS to ACLU, Jan. 14,

1936, GS to Baldwin, Jan. 21, 1936, reel 7, ACLU/Selected Papers.

13. Appendix to Appellants Brief, Tables 1 and 2, in *American Federation of Labor v. Bain*, 165 Or. 183 (1940) in OSC Case File 8969.

14. Appendix to Appellants Brief, Tables 1 and 2 in *American Federation of Labor v. Bain*, 165 Or. 183 (1940) in OSC Case File 8969; Stuart Jamieson, *Labor Unionism in American Agriculture* (New York: Arno Press, 1976 [1946]), 204-205; MacColl, *Growth of a City*, 468; Bigelow and Diamond, "Agitate, Educate," 5-29; Robert C. Donnelly, "Organizing Portland: Organized Crime, Municipal Corruption, and the Teamsters Union," *Oregon Historical Quarterly* 104 (Fall 2003): 337.

15. Jerry Lembcke and William M. Tattam, *One Union in Wood* (Madeira Park, BC, and New York: Harbour Publishing and International Publishers, 1984); Gary Murrell, *Iron Pants: Oregon's Anti-New Deal Governor, Charles Henry Martin* (Pullman: Washington State University Press, 2000), 173-4; Ronald L. Filippelli, "Northwest Lumber Strike of 1935," in *Labor Conflict in the United States*, ed. Ronald L. Filippelli (New York: Garland, 1990), 329; Robert A. Christie, *Empire in Wood: A History of the Carpenters' Union* (Ithaca: Cornell University, 1956), 299; GS in Washington Hearing 3: 357-8; GS to ACLU, Nov. 10, 1938, reel 8, ACLU/Selected Papers.

16. GS to ACLU, March 11, April 11, Nov. 10, 1938, reel 8, ACLU/Selected Papers; *Oregonian*, Feb. 16, 1938; Portland *Labor Newdealer*, Feb. 4, 1938.

17. *Oregonian*, Feb. 17, 1987; L.A. Milner, Daily Report, March 21, 1937, in Oregon Military Department Records: Communist Activity Intelligence Reports, 1932-1939, Oregon State Archives, Salem; cf. Bureau of Police, "Weekly Report of Communist Activities," April 9, 1937, Police Historical Records: Red Squad, City of Portland Stanley Parr Archives and Records Center [City of Portland Archives].

18. GS to Arnold Forster, Dec. 8, 1960, in "AJCongress-ADL Correspondence With Reference to Mindlin-Jewish Floridian," MS 2886; GS to ACLU, April 11, 1938, reel 8, ACLU/Selected Papers.

19. GSOJM, tape 2, side 1; Kermit L. Hall, *The Magic Mirror: Law in American History* (New York: Oxford University Press, 1989), 289.

20. "Interview: Gus J. Solomon on the Beginnings of Legal Aid in Oregon," *Oregon Historical Quarterly* 88 (Spring 1987): 52-60; Earl Johnson Jr., *Justice and Reform: The Formative Years of the American Legal Services Program* (New Brunswick, NJ: Transaction Books, 1978), 9; GS, No Man is Above the Law and No Man is Below It, May 2, 1967, in "Speeches No. 60 Through No. 109," MS 2886; GSOJM, tape 2, side 1.

21. GS Legal Aid interview, 54-55; GS, No Man is Above the Law; GSOJM, tape 2, side 1; Minutes of the Regular Meeting of Multnomah Bar Association, Sept. 25, 1935 and Feb. 25, 1936, in "MBA Minutes 1921-37," Multnomah County Bar Association. The Legal Aid Committee, chaired successively by Robinson and Crawford, and including Solomon and Judge George M. Woodley, oversaw it.

22. "Report of the Committee on Legal Aid," *Oregon State Bar Bulletin* I (Dec. 1935), unp., II (1936), 11-13, III (1937-1938), 11-13 and IV (1938-1939), 67-69; Leíonie N. Brooke, "Legal Aid as Part of the Social-Welfare Program of Multnomah County," *Commonwealth Review* 22 (Nov. 1940), 172-3.

23. GS Legal Aid interview; Brooke, "Legal Aid," 175-6; GS, Uphold the Law—A Citizen's First Duty, April 30, 1965 in "Speeches No. 60 Through No. 109," MS 2886; *Oregonian*, Oct. 11, 1961.

24. GSOJM, tape 2, side 1; Lawyers Hit County's Jury Selection Plan," unidentified Portland clipping, ca. 1937, Levenson Papers; GS to Milner, Feb. 17, 1937, reel 8, ACLU/Selected Papers; GS, ATLA Convention, Portland, Oregon, August 4, 1971, in "Speeches No. 60 Through No. 109," MS 2886; Chester E. McCarty in Salt Lake Hearing 1:94. The club apparently disbanded after two years.

25. Hart oral history, tape 5, sides 1 and 2 and tape 6, side 2; Hart interview; GS, ATLA Convention; Auerbach, *Unequal Justice*, 193-209; Ann Fagan Ginger and Eugene

M. Tobin, eds., *The National Lawyers Guild: From Roosevelt Through Reagan* (Philadelphia: Temple University Press, 1988); Percival R. Bailey, "Progressive Lawyers: A History of the National Lawyers Guild, 1936-1958" (Ph.D. diss., Rutgers University, 1979); GS to Milner, Feb. 17, 1937, reel 8, ACLU/Selected Papers; Minutes of Regular Meeting of Multnomah Bar Association, Feb. 16, 1937, in "MBA Minutes 1921-37," Multnomah County Bar Association.

26. Auerbach, *Unequal Justice*, 198; Hart oral history, tape 5, side 2; Sussman in Salt Lake City Hearing 1:33-34.

27. Brown, *Lawyers*, 147-53; Hart interview; Hart oral history, tape 6, side 1; National Lawyers Guild, Oregon Chapter, *Report of the Civil Liberties Committee* ([Portland,]: Author, May 24, 1938); Sussman in Salt Lake Hearing 1:33-34; GS in Washington Hearing 2:332-3.

28. GSOHS, tape 4, side 2 and tape 3, side 2; GS to Baldwin, Feb. 4, 1936, reel 7, ACLU/Selected Papers; Transcript of Proceedings, Nov. 28, l976, in *Oregon Socialist Workers 1974 Campaign Committee v. Meyers*, unpub. opinion (Dist. Or. 1972), NARA/Seattle; GSBPA interview; GS, "My Encounters with Discrimination" in "Speeches No. 110 Through...," MS 2886.

29. GSBPA interview; GSOHS, tape 4, sides 1 and 2; Raymond M. Kell, "History of Kell, Alterman & Runstein," in possession of Lee Davis Kell.

30. San Diego *Evening Journal*, Oct. 9, 1953; GS, Speech to Young Lawyers, MS 2886. PUDs developed the technique of employing electric recipients in line building before Solomon proposed it.

31. GSOHS, tape 4, side 2; GSBPA interview.

32. Morton Tompkins to Charles Brannan, July 5, 1949, and Sussman to Brannan, June 30, 1949, in "GSJ/PFJ," MS 2886; GSOHS, tape 4, side 2; GSBPA interview, unp; unlabeled scrapbook; GS to Sweetland, Dec. 2, 1941, in "Oregon Commonwealth Federation," Sweetland Papers.

33. This and subsequent paragraphs are based on Kell, "Memoirs;" Hart oral history, tape 10, side 1; "PUD Bill Draws Warm Debate During Hearing," unidentified newspaper clipping, Feb. 1 [1940]; GS, Speech to Young Lawyers, MS 2886; Tompkins to Brannan, July 5, 1949, Tomkins to Tom Clark, July 5, 1949, and Sussman to Brannan, June 30, 1949, in "GSJ/PFJ," MS 2886; Salem *Capital Journal*, Oct. 8, 1937; *Oregon Journal*, Feb. 27, 1938, and Oct. 15, 1949; GSBPA interview; GSOHS, tape 3, side 2; Tollefson, *BPA*; GSOJM, tapes 2 and 3, side 1; GS to Loeb, June 6, 1941, reel 13; ADA Papers and GS to Sweetland, Oct. 30, 1941, and Dec. 2, 1941, in "Oregon Commonwealth Federation," Sweetland Papers.

34. Kell, "History," 7.

35. GSOJM, tape 2, side 2.

36. GSOHS, tape 5, side 2.

37. GS, [Deposition,] March 1952, in "Personal Correspondence 1953 throughout 1958," MS 2886; Executive Committee Minutes, July 30, 1938, in "Board and Executive Minutes," OCF Papers; Floyd J. McKay, *Editor for Oregon: Charles A. Sprague and the Politics of Change* (Corvallis: Oregon State University Press, 1998), 86.

38. Plotke, *Building a Democratic Political Order*, 141; Burton, *Democrats of Oregon*, 39-40, 64-66, 76, 81-83.

39. This and subsequent paragraphs are based on Jill H. Herzig, "The Oregon Commonwealth Federation: The Rise and Decline of a Reform Organization," (M.A. Thesis, University of Oregon, 1963); Burton, *Democrats of Oregon*, 84, 88; Hugh T. Lovin, "Toward a Farmer-Labor Party in Oregon, 1933-38," *Oregon Historical Quarterly* 76 (June 1975), 135-51; Sweetland interview; GSOHS, tape 5, side 1 and tape 3, side 2; GSOJM, tape 2, side 1; and GS in Washington Hearing 3:334.

40. GS to ACLU, Nov. 10, 1938, reel 8, ACLU/Selected Papers.

41. Sweetland interview; Sweetland, Oregon Commonwealth Federation Report,

June 30, 1937, in "Board and Executive Minutes," OCF Papers; Stuart McElderry, "Building a West Coast Ghetto: African-American Housing in Portland, 1910-1960," *Pacific Northwest Quarterly* 92 (Summer 2001), 138-9; Burton, *Democrats of Oregon*, 88; Murrell, *Iron Pants*, 155-6, 171.

42. Annual Report of Monroe Sweetland, Dec. 14, 1940, OCF Papers; Herzig, "Oregon Commonwealth Federation," 80, 87. Sweetland also reported, "Oregon is fortunate in that this problem [communist influence in AFL and CIO unions] has assumed no such proportions here as in other West coast states."

43. Sweetland interview.

44. Hart interview; Sweetland interview; Minutes of Board of Directors of OCF, Jan. 2, 1940, and June 9, 1940, in "Board and Executive Minutes" and Harlow Lenon and Gus Solomon to Dear Friend, Jan. 31, 1940, OCF Papers.

45. GS to Robert S. Allen, Sept. 21, 1938, in "Miscellaneous Personal Correspondence;" Hangerud Deposition, [April 1950] in "Senate Confirmation"; Sussman in Salt Lake Hearing 1:32; GS, Deposition, March 1952 in "Personal Correspondence 1953 throughout 1958," MS 2886; Dr. Morton Goodman interview.

46. GS, [Deposition,] March 1952, in "Personal Correspondence 1953 throughout 1958," MS 2886; Sweetland interview; Minutes of Board of Directors, Oct. 15, 1939, in "Board and Executive Committee Minutes," OCF Papers; Sweetland to Ford, Aug. 5, 1949, in "GSJ/PFJ."

47. *Oregonian*, Aug. 28 and Dec. 11, 1939; Minutes of Board of Directors, Oct. 15, 1939, in "Board and Executive Committee Minutes" and Res 57, [Dec. 1939], OCF Papers; Sweetland to Baldwin, Jan. 7, 1941, reel 8, ACLU/Selected Papers.

48. William Barry Furlong, "The Midwest's Nice Monopolists: John and Mike Cowles," *Harper's* 226 (June 1963): 66-67; GSOJM, tape 4, side 1.

49. GSOHS, tape 5, side 2 and transcript; Libby Solomon interview; GS, Joint Defense Appeal Human Relations Award Dinner; GSOJM, tape 4, side 1; Stuart Svonkin, *Jews Against Prejudice: American Jews and the Fight for Civil Liberties* (New York: Columbia University Press, 1997), 7.

50. Toll, *Making*, 180-3; Lowenstein, *Jews of Oregon*, 199-200.

51. Leonard Dinnerstein, *Antisemitism in America* (New York: Oxford University Press, 1994), 105-48; Donald S. Strong, *Organized Anti-Semitism in America: The Rise of Group Prejudice During the Decade 1930-1940* (Westport: Greenwood Press, 1979 [1941]), 36, 51, 145-6, 151, 174; Marc Dollinger, *Quest for Inclusion: Jews and Liberalism in Modern America* (Princetown: Princetown University Press, 2000), 61-75; Harry A. Whitten, "Subversive Activities: Their Extent and Meaning in Portland" (Senior thesis Reed College, June 1939), 55-109; Karen E. Hoppes, "An Investigation of the Nazi-Fascist Spectrum in the Pacific Northwest: 1924-1941" (M.A. thesis Western Oregon State College, 1983), 29, 31, 58, 63-64, 68; Leland V. Bell, "The Failure of Nazism in America: The German American Bund, 1936-1941," *Political Science Quarterly* 85 (December 1970): 585-99.

52. Sarna, *American Judaism*, 261; Alan Brinkley, "Coughlin, Charles Edward," http://www.anb.org/articles/15/15-00869.html American National Biography Online Feb. 2000 (accessed January 2, 2005); Dollinger, *Quest for Inclusion*, 73

53. *Oregonian*, April 6, 1938; Portland *News-Telegram*, Jan. 27, 1939; Report of Meeting of the Silver Shirt Region, Turn Verein Hall, Portland, Oregon, June 16, 1938, and C.L. Mannheimer to [David Robinson?,] Sept. 25, 1939, in "Silver Legion of America Oregon Ephemera," Rennar Papers; Sweetland to Baldwin, March 17, 1942, reel 197, ACLU: Roger Baldwin Years; Richard W. Steele, *Free Speech in the Good War* (New York: St. Martin's, 1999), 273fn10; Robinson to Max Delman, Feb. 27, 1946 in "Bernie Cantor."

54. GS, Speech to Business Girls, YWCA, March 19, 1953, in "Speeches No. 60 Through No. 109;" Minutes of OCF Executive Committee, Jan. 2, 1939 and Minutes

of the Board of Directors, June 9, 1940, in "Board and Executive Committee Minutes," OCF Papers; [David Robinson?,] "How Can the Activities of the German-American Bund in Oregon be Counteracted and Minimized?," [c. 1938] in "Friends of New Germany–Portland, Or.," Rennar Papers; GS to ACLU, April 11, 1938, reel 8, ACLU/ Selected Papers; GSOHS, tape 5, side 2.

55. GSOHS, tape 5, side 2; *Oregonian*, April 6, 1938; [GS,] judicial conference biographical questionnaire, [June 18, 1976], in "Solomon Biographical Material," GS, Outline of Speech – Feb. 3, 1958 – A.J.C. in "Jewish Organizations (Current)," MS 2886; Svonkin, *Jews Against Prejudice*, 23.

56. Morris Frommer, "The American Jewish Congress: A History, 1914-1950," Ph.D., Ohio State University, 1978; Jerome A. Chanes, "Who Does What? Jewish Advocacy and Jewish 'Interest'" in *Jews in American Politics*, ed. L. Sandy Maisel (New York: Rowman and Littlefield, 2001), 105; Charles R. Epp, *The Rights Revolution: Lawyers, Activists, and Supreme Courts in Comparative Perspective* (Chicago: University of Chicago Press, 1998), 54.

57. GSOJM, tape 2, side 1; *Oregonian*, Oct. 6, 1939; Sweetland interview.

CHAPTER 4

1. Levenson oral history, tape 3, sides 1 and 2; Sussman in Salt Lake Hearing 1:34-35; *Oregonian* (Magazine), May 11, 1980.

2. Minutes of the Board of Directors, OCF, June 9, 1940, OCF Papers; GS to Loeb, June 6, 1941, reel 13, ADA Papers; *Oregonian*, June 11 and Aug. 16, 1940, March 20, Aug. 6, Sept. 4 and 26, 1941; *Oregon Journal*, Sept. 24, 1941; Lise Namikas, "The Committee to Defend America and the Debate between Internationalists and Interventionists, 1939-1941," *Historian* 61 (Summer 1999): 843-63.

3. Norman [Littell?] to Sweetland, Feb. 3, 1940, in "Personal 1936-42," Sweetland Papers; Kell, "History," 2; Solomon FBI Report FBI/HQ 77-10137; GS in Washington Hearing 3:355; GS, untitled speech, April 16, 1965; Hangerud Deposition, [April 1950], in "Senate Confirmation." In 1940, a new BPA lawyer, Raymond M. Kell, learned that Solomon had been thought too liberal to employ.

4. GSOHS, tapes 2 and 5, side 2; Libby Solomon interview and conversations; GSOJM, tape 4, side 1.

5. Ibid.

6. Libby Solomon interview; Goodman interview.

7. GS to Sweetland, Dec. 2, 1941, in "Oregon Commonwealth Federation," Sweetland Papers; Hangerud Deposition, [April 1950], in "Senate Confirmation," MS 2886; Tollefson, *BPA*, 185.

8. Libby Solomon to editor, *Oregonian*, March 13, 1946.

9. Alan Brinkley, *The End of Reform: New Deal Liberalism in Recession and War* (New York: Alfred A. Knopf, 1995), 154; GSOHS, tape 4, side 2; "interviews with Allan Hart: Recollections of the Development of Bonneville Power Marketing Policies during Paul J. Raver's Term as BPA Administrator, September 1, 1939-December 31, 1953," p. 75, Hart Papers; unidentified clipping, c. Dec. 14 or 15, 1941, in untitled scrapbook; Minutes of Extraordinary Executive Board Meeting, July 26, 1942, in "Board and Executive Committee Minutes," OCF Papers; Nathalie Panek to GS, Oct. 1949, in "Federal Judgeship (Congratulations)," MS 2886; *Astorian-Budget*, Feb. 2, 1942; *Oregon Journal*, May 14, 1942.

10. Robert N. MacGregor to Baldwin, March 8, 1941, Neuberger to Baldwin, March 15, 1941, and Sweetland to Baldwin, March 17, 1941, reel 197 and Hays to Portland City Council, Sept. 12, 1941, reel 201, ACLU: Roger Badwin Years; Lenon to Baldwin, May 6, 1940 and Baldwin to Frances Bowman, Apr. 14, 1942, reel 8, ACLU/Selected Papers; GS, Joint Defense Appeal; GS, Speech to ACLU, Nov. 16, 1985, in "E. B. MacNaughton Award–1985," MS 2886.

11. Baldwin to Pearl Buck, Aug. 5, 1943, and Baldwin to Nathan Greene, Aug. 6, 1943, reel 219, ACLU: Roger Baldwin Years; Jehovah's Witnesses file, reel 8, ACLU/Selected Papers; Shawn F. Peters, *Judging Jehovah's Witnesses: Religious Persecution and the Dawn of the Rights Revolution* (Lawrence: University Press of Kansas, 2000), 8-16; *Oregonian*, Dec. 4, 1944; GS to Baldwin, May 22, 1944, and Aug. 8, 1944, reel 3, ACLU/Japanese; John Morton Blum, *V Was For Victory: Politics and American Culture During World War II* (New York: Harcourt Brace Jovanovich, 1976), 172.

12. Blanche H. Pickering to Sweetland, Dec. 12, 1942, Reuben G. Lenske to Sweetland, July 18, 1943, and Sweetland to Lenske, Aug. 17, 1943, in "Politics 1942-43-44" and Sweetland to David C. Epps, May 7, 1942, in "Dave Epps," Sweetland Papers; Leland N. Fryer to Loeb, Nov. 19, 1943 and March 14, 1945, reel 13, ADA Papers; GS to Baldwin, April 10, 1945, reel 8, ACLU/Selected Papers.

13. Steve Kahn to Sweetland, July 15, 1943, in "Public Power I," Sweetland Papers; Steele, *Free Speech*; Geoffrey R. Stone, *Perilous Times: Free Speech in Wartime* (New York: Norton, 2004), 235-311.

14. MacColl, *Growth of a City*, 555-84.

15. GS to Baldwin, July 12, 1944, reel 3, ACLU/Japanese; McElderry, "Building a West Coast Ghetto."

16. GSOHS, tape 1, side 1, tape 5, side 2 and tape 11, side 2 and its transcript; Archie Silberman to James M. Burns, Nov. 28, 1983, in "Solomon Longevity Ceremony," MS 2886; GS to Morse, Dec. 20, 1944, and July 1, 1946, in "Gus Solomon," Morse Papers; Kell, "History," 9, 24; Kahn to Sweetland, June 28, 1943, in "Public Power I," Sweetland Papers; Thomas B. Stoel interview.

17. Minutes of Extraordinary Executive Board Meeting, July 26, 1942, in "Board and Executive Committee Minutes," OCF Papers; GSOHS, tape 1, side 1.

18. Frank A. Warren, *Noble Abstractions: American Liberal Intellectuals and World War II* (Columbus: Ohio State University Press, 1999), 108-29; Steven M. Gillon, *Politics and Vision: The ADA and American Liberalism* (New York: Oxford University Press, 1987), 10; Sweetland interview; Report of Aug. 30, 1949, Solomon FBI Report FBI/HQ 77-10137; [GS,] "Confidential Please," [1950] in "Senate Confirmation," MS 2886.

19. GS to Loeb, June 6, 1941, reel 13, Loeb to GS, July 24, 1946, and Panek to Loeb, July 29, 1946, reel 76 and generally Loeb, Fryer and Howard Y. Williams correspondence for 1941-1946, reels 13 and 76, ADA Papers; Minutes of Extraordinary Executive Board Meeting, July 26, 1942, and Smith to Loeb, Jan. 7, 1942, in "Union for Democratic Action," OCF Papers; Warren, *Noble Abstractions*, 113-4; Gillon, *Politics*, 11.

20. Transcript of GSOHS, tape 4, side 1; GS to ACLU, Nov. 20, 1940, reel 8, ACLU Selected Papers; Minutes of the Board of Directors of OCF, Jan. 2, 1940, OCF Papers; file "Gus J. Solomon–Federal Judgeship in Oregon," MS 2886; Lucille Furman to Libby Solomon, Oct. 21, 1940, and Dorothy McAllister to Libby Solomon, Oct. 23, 1940, in "Libby Solomon," MS 2886; Sussman to Brannan, June 30, 1949, and Sweetland to Ford, Aug. 5, 1949, in "GJS/PFJ"; *Oregon Journal*, April 24, 1940; Willis M. Mahoney to William Boyle Jr., Aug. 5, 1949, in "Correspondence re federal judgeship, 1949," Donald Sterling Papers; Libby Solomon interview.

21. [GS,] "Confidential Please" in "Senate Confirmation," MS 2886; GS to Baldwin, May 22, 1944, reel 3, ACLU/Japanese; Mason Drukman, *Wayne Morse: A Political Biography* (Portland: Oregon Historical Society Press, 1997), 122-4, 134-7; Morse to Frank W. Kuehl, Feb. 17, 1948, and GS to Morse, Dec. 20, 1944, in "Gus Solomon," Morse Papers.

22. GSOHS, tape 5, side 2; GSJMO, tape 3, side 1; Terry J. Yamada to Libby Solomon, Nov. 30, 1988, in "Americans With Japanese Ancestry"; Minoru Yasui to GS, Oct. 27, 1949, in "Federal Judgeship (Congratulations)," MS 2886; *Pacific Citizen*, Feb. 27, 1987.

23. GSOHS, tape 5, side 2; GSJMO, tape 3, side 1; GS, untitled speech, [c. 1946-1949] in "Miscellaneous," MS 2886.

24. GSOJM transcript tape 3, side 1.

25. John J. Kilkenny oral history, tape 8, side 2.

26. Eric Foner, *The Story of American Freedom* (New York: Norton, 1998), 241; Walker, *In Defense*, 135-46; Warren, *Noble Abstractions*, 113; Edward E. Henry, Report of Alien Evacuation Conditions in the Portland Area of the State of Washington [sic], April 1, 1942, reel 1, ACLU/Japanese; Ellen Eisenberg, "'As Truly American As Your Son:' Voicing Opposition to Internment in Three West Coast Cities," *Oregon Historical Quarterly* 104 (Winter 2003), 542-65; McKay, *Editor for Oregon*, 125.

27. Ellen Eisenberg, "Looking the Other Way: Portland Jewry's Non-response to Japanese Internment" and "To Be the First to Cry Down Injustice? Western Jews and the Problem of Japanese Internment," unpublished papers in possession of the author.

28. GSOJM, tape 3, side 1; Arthur Garfield Hays to Earl Bernard, April 7, 1942, and Baldwin to Ernest Besig, Feb. 8, 1943, reel 2, ACLU/Japanese; GSOHS, tape 5, side 2; GS to Peter H. Irons, June 9, 1982 in "Americans With Japanese Ancestry"; GS to Edward J. Ennis, June 6, 1986, in "Article on Min Yasui," MS 2886; Peter H. Irons, *Justice at War* (New York, 1983), 81, 116, 171-3; Walker, *In Defense*, 139; Judy Kutulas, "In Quest of Autonomy: The Northern California Affiliate of the American Civil Liberties Union and World War II," *Pacific Historical Review* 67 (May 1998), 201-3; Charles Davis, "Land of the Free?," *Oregon State Bar Bulletin* 59 (July 1999), 24; Randall B. Kester oral history, tape 4, side 1.

29. GSOHS, tape 5, side 2; GS to Irons, June 9, 1982, in "Americans With Japanese Ancestry"; Randall B. Kester, "A Time of Change, 1927-1950," in *The First Duty: A History of the U.S. District Court for Oregon*, ed. Carolyn M. Buan (Portland: U.S. District Court of Oregon Historical Society, 1993), 187-9; *U.S. v. Yasui*, 48 F. Supp. 40 (1942); *Yasui v. U.S.*, 320 U.S. 115 (1943); *U.S. v. Yasui*, 51 F.Supp. 234 (1943); Yasui to GS, Oct. 27, 1949, in "Federal Judgeship (Congratulations)," MS 2886.

30. GSOHS, tape 5, side 2 and tape 6, side 1 and transcript; GSOJM, tape 3, side 1 and tape 2, side 2; GS to Baldwin, Aug. 8, 1944 and Wirin to Clifford Forester, Aug. 21, 1944, reel 3, ACLU/Japanese; *Ex Parte Mitsuye Endo*, 323 U.S. 283 (1944).

31. GSOJM, tape 3, side 1; GS, untitled speech [1946-1949], MS 2886; *Oregonian*, Dec. 18, 1944; GSOHS, tape 9, side 1.

32. Linda Tamura, *The Hood River Issei: An oral history of Japanese Settlers in Oregon's Hood River Valley* (Urbana: University of Illinois Press, 1992), 215-23; GS to Baldwin, April 10, 1945, reel 8, ACLU/Selected Papers; Forester to GS, April 25, 1945, reel 233, ACLU: Roger Baldwin Years; Verne Dusenberry, *et. al*, "Multnomah County Bar Association Report: The Japanese Problem in Oregon," *Oregon Law Review* 24 (April 1945), 208-19.

33. GSOHS, tape 6, side 1; GSOJM, tape 3, side 1; GS, untitled speech [1946-1949]; McKay, *Editor for Oregon*, 187.

34. Judicial Conference Biographical Questionnaire in "Solomon Biographical Material," MS 2886; Marvin G. Pursinger, "Oregon's Japanese in World War II: A History of Compulsory Relocation" (Ph.D. diss. University of Southern California, 1961); GSOHS, tape 6, sides 1 and 2 and transcript; GSOJM, tape 3, side 2; Tamura, *Hood River Issei*, 228; Goodman interview; "Nisei Praise WRA Activity," unidentified Portland clipping, [1946] and Joseph K. Tagawa to GS, March 16, 1946, in "Miscellaneous," MS 2886; generally U.S. War Relocation Authority, Oregon Records, 1942-1946, Record Group 210 NARA/Washington D.C.; GS to Irons, June 9, 1982, in "Americans With Japanese Ancestry," MS 2886.

35. GSOHS, tape 6, sides 1 and 2 and transcript; GSOJM, tape 2, side 2; Tagawa to GS, March 16, 1946, in "Miscellaneous," MS 2886; Goodman interview; GS to ACLU, May 9, 1947, reel 248, ACLU: Roger Baldwin Years; Hart oral history, tape 17, sides 1

and 2; *Oyama v. California*, 332 U.S. 633 (1948).

36. *Oregonian*, March 6, 1945, and March 10, 1945, *Time* 45 (March 19, 1945), 19; Blair Stewart to Tom Clark, Oct. 25, 1945, WRA Press Release, April 27, 1945; E.B. Mac Naughton, Jim Landye, Gus Solomon and Vern Dusenberry to Morse, March 23, 1945; WRA to All Relocatees, Jan. 31, 1946, and WRA, *Northwest Area Final Report of Reporting Officer* (1946), in U.S. War Relocation Authority, Oregon Records; GSOHS, tape 6, side 1; GSOJM, tape 3, side 2; and Pursinger, "Oregon's Japanese."

37. WRA, *Final Report of Activities of the Portland, Oregon District Office*, 7, in U.S. War Relocation Authority, Oregon Records; "Nisei Praise WRA Activity," unidentified Portland clipping, [1946] in "Newspaper Clippings," MS 2886; Roger Daniels, *Concentration Camps USA: Japanese Americans and World War II* (New York: Hot, Rinehart & Winston, 1971), 162.

38. Kell, "History," 10; GS to Baldwin, July 12, 1944, reel 3, ACLU/Japanese; Weinfeld, "Income of Lawyers," 18-19.

39. GS in Washington Hearing 3:324; McCarty in Salt Lake Hearing 1:93.

40. *In the Matter of the Petition of the Board of Directors of the Tillamook People's Utility District*, 160 Or. 530 (1939) in OSC Case File 8728; Betty L. Brown, "People's Utility Districts in Oregon," *Oregon Law Review* 22 (Dec. 1940), 1-73.

41. *Ravlin v. Hood River People's Utility District*, 165 Or. 490 (1940) and 165 Or. 569, in OSC Case File 8966; *Ollilo v. Clatskanie People's Utility District*, 170 Or. 173 (1942), in OSC Case File 9242; *In the Matter of the Petition of the Board of Directors of the Northern Wasco County People's Utility District v. Kelly*, 171 Or. 691 (1943), in OSC Case File 9291.

42. Kell, "History," 9; George H. Fraser oral history, tape 7; Weinfeld, "Income of Lawyers," 19; Green in Salt Lake Hearing 1:114.

43. *Seufert and Northern Wasco County People's Utility District v. Stadelman*, 178 Or. 646 (1946), in OSC Case File 9636; *Gurdane v. Northern Wasco County People's Utility District*, 183 Or. 565 (1948), in OSC Case File 9918; *Stringham v. Union County People's Utility District, Herman v. Same*, and *Conley v. Same*, 182 Or. 565 (1947) in OSC Case File 9838; *Fullerton v. Central Lincoln People's Utility District*, 185 Or. 28 (1948), in OSC Case File 9977.

44. GS to Sweetland, Jan. 17, 1949, in "GSJ/PFJ"; GS to Joel D. Wolfson, June 28, 1949, "Present Clients of Gus J. Solomon," [c. July 1949], GS to Sweetland, Jan. 17, 1949, Kenin to James C. Petrillo, June 29, 1949 and GS to Sweetland, Jan. 17, 1949 in "GSJ/PFJ"; GS, incomplete list of legal areas and clients, [1949], GS to Morse, March 3, 1945, July 1, 1946, May 23, 1947, June 25, 1948, Jan. 5, 1949 and April 22, 1949, Morse to Herman D. Kenin, May 28, 1947, and Morse to Kuehl, Feb. 17, 1948, in "Gus Solomon," Morse Papers; Sam H.Wilderman to Cordon, Jan. 30, 1960, in "Miscellaneous," MS 2886; *Weinstein v. Watson*, 184 Or. 508 (1948), in OSC Case File 9954; Krause and Green in Salt Lake Hearing 1:58-59, 109, 112; GS to Davidson, Feb. 1, 1949, and Sept. 28, 1948, Cecil C. Moore to Sweetland, Oct. 5, 1949, Davidson to GS, Sept. 27, 1948, and GS to Davidson, Feb. 1, 1949, in "Gus Solomon," Davidson Papers; GSOHS, tape 6, side 2; GSBPA interview; Kell, "History," 22-24; Drukman, *Wayne Morse*, 138; GS, judicial conference biographical questionnaire in "Solomon Biographical Material"; Weinfeld, "Income of Lawyers," 18-24; Kell, "History," 36.

45. Kell, "History," 20; "The Making of the Modern Democratic Party in Oregon: An interview with Howard Morgan," *Oregon Historical Quarterly* 95 (Fall 1994), 373; Floyd J. McKay, "With Liberty for Some: Oregon Editors and the Challenge of Civil Liberties, 1942-55" (Ph.D. diss. University of Washington, 1995), 64.

46. Burton, *Democrats of Oregon*, 103-7; Sweetland to Ford, Aug. 5, 1949, in "GSJ/PFJ."

47. *Oregonian*, Sept. 9, 1946; GS to Loeb, Dec. 20, 1946, Panek to Sweetland, May 14, 1946, and Panek to Stanley Earl, May 15, 1946, reel 76, ADA Papers.

48. GS to Loeb, May 18, 1948, reel 76, ADA Papers; Curtis D. MacDougall, *Gideon's army* (New York: Marzani and Munsell, 1965), 3:7632; Sweetland to Ford, Aug. 5, 1949, in "GSJ/PFJ"; Nancy H. Robinson to Donald Dawson, Oct. 6, 1949, in "Senate Nomination," MS 2886.

49. *Oregonian*, Sept. 9, 1946, Sweetland to Ford, Aug. 5, 1949, in "GSJ/PFJ"; Panek to Earl, May 15, 1946, Panek to Loeb, July 19, 1946, Hart to Panek, July 29, 1946, Loeb to Sweetland, Nov. 21, 1946, Loeb to GS, Dec. 11, 1946 and Dec. 27, 1946, GS to Loeb, Dec. 20, 1946, Sweetland to Loeb, March 24, 1947 and Feb. 14, 1948, Panek to GS, May 7, 1947 and Nellie L. McKinley to Panek, June 7 and 25, 1947, and Minutes of Board of Portland ADA Chapter or of its Executive Committee, July 1947, Aug. 27, Sept. 29, and Dec. 8, 1947, and Jan. 13, 1948, reel 76, ADA Papers; GS to Panek, Nov. 8, 1949, in "Federal Judgeship (Congratulations)," MS 2886.

50. Panek to GS, May 7, 1947, McKinley to Panek, June 7, 1947, and June 25, 1947, McKinley to Sal B. Hoffman, Nov. 10, 1947, Minutes of the Board of Portland ADA Chapter, Jan. 2, 1948, GS to Panek, April 10, 1947, and Ancel H. Payne to Evelyn Dubrow, Sept. 20, 1948, reel 76, ADA Papers; Richard L. Neuberger, "The Cities of America: Portland, Oregon," *Saturday Evening Post* 219 (March 1, 1947), 108; Eleanor Bradley to Sweetland, Aug. 16, 1948, and Bradley to Loeb, Nov. 2, 1948, in "ADA corr. 1948-49" and Sweetland to Nicholas Granet, Feb. 15, 1950, in "DNC corr. 1948-1952," Sweetland Papers; Burton, *Democrats of Oregon*, 107.

51. Gillon, *Politics*, ix, 23, 41, 59ff.; Brinkley, *End of Reform*, 6-8, 154, 167, 170-4, 226.

52. *New York Times*, March 31, 1947.

53. GSOHS, tape 9, side 1; Tollefson, *BPA*, 293; Minutes of Portland Chapter, Oct. 8, 1947, and GS to Loeb, June 11, 1948, reel 76, ADA Papers.

54. Burton, *Democrats of Oregon*, 103; Portland Board and Executive Committee Minutes, 1947-1948, and Payne to Loeb, Sept. 13, 1948, reel 76, ADA Papers.

55. Waldo Schumacher, "The 1948 Elections in Oregon," *Western Political Quarterly* 2 (March 1949), 122.

56. Sweetland to Ford, Aug. 5, 1949, in "GSJ/PFJ"; Robinson to Dawson, Oct. 6, 1949, with attachment in "Senate Nomination," MS 2886; Pat Dooley oral history, tape 4, side 1.

57. Schumacher, "1948 Elections," 121, 123; Sussman to Brannan, June 30, 1949, in "GSJ/PFJ"; Burton, *Democrats of Oregon*, 109; Karl M. Schmidt, *Henry A. Wallace: Quixotic Crusade 1948* (Syracuse: Syracuse University Press, 1960), Table 7; MacDougall, *Gideon's army*, 3:762; Gillon, *Politics*, 56; *Portland ADA Annals* 5 (March 1949), reel 76, ADA Papers.

CHAPTER 5

1. Howard Morgan oral history, 193-4.

2. Kell, "History," 16-22; GSOHS, tape 6, side 2.

3. Kell, "History," 16-22; Eugene *Register-Guard*, June 30, 1949. As Sheldon Goldman has written, Truman "primarily treated judgeships as patronage, in service" of his partisan and personal agenda. Sheldon Goldman, *Picking Federal Judges: Lower Court Selection from Roosevelt Through Reagan*, (New Haven: Yale University Press, 1997), 76.

4. *Oregonian*, July 6, 1949, and see "Gus Solomon" file, Morse Papers. Lee Epstein and Jeffrey A. Segal, *Advice and Consent: The Politics of Judicial Appointment* (New York: Oxford University Press, 2005), 26.

5. Kell, "History," 25; GS to Sweetland, Jan. 17, 1949, GS to Joel D. Wolfson, June 20, 1949, and GS to Gene Solomon, July 6, 1949, in "GSJ/PFJ"; GSOHS, tape 6, side 2; GS in Washington Hearing 3:328.

6. GSOJM, tape 1, side 1.

7. James Redden oral history, tape 21, side 1; GS in Washington Hearing 3:364;

Woodford J. Howard Jr., *Courts of Appeals in the Federal Judicial System: A Study of the Second, Fifth, and District for Columbia Circuits* (Princeton: Princeton University Press, 1981), 17.

8. Kell, "History," 22-25; GSOHS, tape 6, side 2; GS to Davidson, Oct.18, 1949, in "Federal Judgeship (Congratulations)," MS 2886.

9. Kell, "History," 24; GS to Sweetland, Jan. 17, 1949, in "GSJ/PFJ"; Joel B. Grossman, *Lawyers and Judges: The ABA and the Politics of Judicial Selection* (New York: John Wiley, 1965), 42; GSOHS, tape 6, side 2; William D. Hassett to E.B. MacNaughton, July 11, 1949, White House Central Files: Official File; MacNaughton to Cordon, Jan. 6, 1950, and GS to Ivar Peterson, June 21, 1950, in "Gus Solomon," Morse Papers; GS to Davidson, July 11, 1949, in "Gus Solomon," Davidson Papers; Davidson to Sweetland, July 12, 1949, in "Davidson correspondence 1948-51," Sweetland Papers; GS to Davidson, Oct.18, 1949, in "Federal Judgeship (Congratulations)," MS 2886.

10. Sweetland oral history, tape 11, side 2; Sweetland interview; Kell, "History," 16, 24, 26; Michael J. Ybarra, *Washington Goes Crazy: Senator Pat McCarran and the Great American Communist Hunt* (Hanover, NH: Steerforth Press, 2004), 464.

11. Lisle A. Rose, *The Cold War Comes to Main Street* (Lawrence: University Press of Kansas, 1999), 3-5.

12. Richard M. Fried, *Nightmare in Red: The McCarthy Era in Perspective* (New York: Oxford University Press, 1990), 70, 83-87; Floyd J. McKay, "With Liberty for Some: Oregon Editors and the Challenge of Civil Liberties, 1942-55" (Ph.D. diss. University of Washington, 1995), 201; *U.S. v. Brooklier* 674 F.2d 4126 (9th Cir. 1982) .

13. Sweetland to J. Howard McGrath, June 29, 1949, in "DNC," Sweetland Papers; *Oregonian*, July 7, 1949 and Aug. 17, 1949; GS to Morse, July 9, 1949 in "GSJ/PFJ."

14. Kell, "History," 25-26; Micheal J. Gerhardt, *The Federal Appointments Process: A Constitutional and Historical Analysis* (Durham, N.C.: Duke Univeristy Press, 2000), 110; Nancy H. Robinson to Chapman, June 6, 1949, in "GSJ/PFJ."

15. Sweetland to William M. Boyle Jr., June 29, 1949, and Sweetland to Harry S. Truman, June 30, 1949, in "GSJ/PFJ"; Ben Buisman to Truman, July 29, 1949, Sweetland to Donald Dawson, Oct. 6, 1949, and Robinson to Dawson, Oct. 6, 1949, White House Central Files: Official File; GSOJM, tape 3, side 2, transcript.

16. GS to Davidson, May 16, 1949, and Davidson to GS, Oct. 8, 1949, in "Gus Solomon," Davidson Papers; Phyllis Kormarek de Luna, *Public Versus Private Power During the Truman Administration: A Study of Fair Deal Liberalism* (New York: Peter Lang, 1997), 23, 31; Gary A. Donaldson, *Truman Defeats Dewey* (Lexington: University Press of Kentucky, 1999), 20-24, 27-28, 191.

17. Morse to GS, Feb. 4, 1949, in "Gus Solomon," Morse Papers; Sweetland interview; Morse to GS, Sept. 21, 1949, and Kell to Harold M. Stephens, Sept. 29, 1949, in "GSJ/PFJ."

18. Neuberger to McGrath, Aug. 4, 1949, in "Additional Judiciary," McGrath Papers; Baldwin to GS, Sept. 19, 1949, Wolfson to GS, June 17, 1949, and Tompkins to Brannan, July 5, 1949, in "GJS/PFJ"; William J. Seufert to Cordon, January 21, 1950, in "Nomination Letters," MS 2886; "Copies of letters urging the appointment from the people listed below were sent to Wayne Morse on February 1, 1950," E. E. Benedict to Boyle, [1949], Russell M. Colwell to Truman, July 30, 1949, and Seufert to Truman, July 30, 1949, in "Gus Solomon," Morse Papers; Elton Watkins to McCarran, Jan. 5, 1950, in Solomon Judiciary file.

19. Baldwin to GS, Sept. 19, 1949, in "GJS/PFJ"; Mitchell to Boyle, Aug. 30, 1949, in "Democratic National Committee," Mitchell Papers; Palmer Hoyt to Clark, Aug. 5, 1949, in "Gus Solomon," Morse Papers; GS to Davidson, Feb. 8, 1961, Davidson Papers (UO); GSOHS, tape 8, side 2; GS to Estes Kefauver, Dec. 30, 1949, and Jan. 20, 1950, and GS to Hubert H. Humphrey, Jan. 20, 1950, in "Nomination Letters."

20. Unfortunately for Latourette, McGrath had recently replaced his supporter

Attorney General Clark. Sussman to Brannan, June 30, 1949, Tompkins to Brannan, July 5, 1949, Robinson to Chapman, Sept. 1, 1949 and GS to Wolfson, June 20, 1949, in "GJS/PFJ"; Willis Mahoney to Louis Johnson, Aug. 5, 1949, White House Central Files: Official File; Mahoney to Donald J. Sterling, July 28, 1949, in "Corr. re Federal Judgeship, 1949," Sterling Papers; GS to Kefauver, Dec. 30, 1949, in "Nomination Letters," MS 2886; Donald R. McCoy, *The Presidency of Harry S. Truman* (Lawrence: University Press of Kentucky, 1984), 188, 212, 214-5, 224, 235-6; Robert J. Donovan, *Tumultuous Years: The Presidency of Harry S. Truman* (New York: Norton, 1982), 62, 65; L. B. Nichols to Mr. Tolson, Oct. 5, 1949, Solomon FBI Report FBI/HQ 77-10137.

21. GS to Sweetland, Aug. 1, 1949, in "GJS/PFJ."

22. GS to Gene Solomon, July 6, 1949, in "GSJ/PFJ"; GS to Louis Goodman, Dec. 5, 1949, in "Federal Judgeship (Congratulations)," MS 2886; GS to Herbert S. Marks, June 14, 1950, and GS to Davidson, May 5, 1950, in "Nomination Letters," MS 2886; Davidson to GS, Oct. 8, 1949, in "Gus Solomon," Davidson Papers; GS to Morse, Mar. 18, 1950 and Morse to GS, Mar. 23, 1950, in "Gus Solomon," Morse Papers; GS to Wolfson, June 20, 1949 in "GJS/PFJ."

23. GS to William L. Josselin, July 9, 1949, and GS to Morse, July 9, 1949, in "GJS/PFJ"; Davidson to GS, Oct. 8, 1949, and GS to Davidson, Oct. 10, 1949, in "Gus Solomon," Davidson Papers; GSOHS, tape 7, side 1; McKay, *Editor for Oregon*, 189; Salem *Oregon Statesman*, July 7, 1949; *Oregonian*, July 7, 1949; Thomas R. Mahoney to Howard F. Burns, May 4, 1950, in "Nomination Letters," MS 2886.

24. Kell, "History," 26; *Oregonian*, June 6, 1949.

25. Ibid.; GS, "My Encounters with Discrimination," MS 2886; Mitchell to Charles R. Cater, Aug. 30, 1949, in "Judges," Hugh B. Mitchell Papers; GSOHS, tape 7, side 1.

26. Edward S. Shapiro, *A Time for Healing: American Jewry Since World II* (Baltimore: Johns Hopkins University Press, 1992), 28-59; Dinnerstein, *Antisemitism*, 170; Anti-Defamation League of B'Nai B'rith, *Anti-Semitism in the United States in 1947* (New York: Author, 1947), 73-75.

27. Wegner, *New York Jews and the Great Depression*, 201.

28. Wolfson to GS, June 17, 1949, and GS to Wolfson, June 20, 1949, in "GJS/PFJ"; GS to John S. Sinai, March 18, 1950, in "Nomination Letters," MS 2886; McCarran to Sinai, May 15, 1950, and Watkins to McCarran, Jan. 27, [1950], Solomon Judiciary file.

29. Kell, "History," 28; GSOHS, tape 6, side 2; *Oregonian*, Oct. 18, 1949; Sweetland to George W. Norris, June 11, [1937], in "Federal Judgeship," OCF Papers.

30. GSOHS, tape 4, side 2; GS to Baldwin, Sept. 16, 1949, in "GJS/PFJ"; Louis E. Starr to Pat McCarran, Jan. 30, 1950, Solomon Judiciary file; Chester E. McCarty oral history, tape 5, side 2; McCarty in Salt Lake Hearing I:97-99; generally "Corr re Federal judgeship, 1949," Sterling Papers; *Oregon Journal*, July 8, Aug. 3, and 26, Oct. 18, and Dec. 2, 1949.

31. *Oregon Journal*, Feb. 1, 1978, and Aug. 24, 1949; GS to Davidson, July 6, 1949, in "Gus Solomon," Davidson Papers; Sweetland oral history, tape 11, side 2; Sweetland interview; Kell, "History," 26; "Oregon Lawyers 4 1/2-to-1 Republican," 1949 clipping in 1933 Scrapbook.

32. George Rossman to Cordon, Jan. 6, 1950, Charles H. Leavy to John R. Steelman, Jan. 23, 1950, Leavy to Magnuson, Jan. 23, 1950, and Leavy to Kefauver, Jan. 23, 1950, in "Nomination Letters," MS 2886; Cordon to Alfred P. Murrah, Nov. 21, 1949, and Leavy to GS, Nov. 15, 1949, in "Nomination Letters," MS 2886; Arthur D. Hay to Cordon, Jan. 6, 1950, and James R. Bain affidavit, May 1, 1950, Solomon Judiciary file.

33. William O. Douglas, *The Court Years, 1939-1975: The Autobiography of William O. Douglas* (New York: Random House, 1980), 194; Goldman, *Picking Federal Judges*, 86; Charles H. Sheldon and Linda S. Maule, *Choosing Justice: The Recruitment of State and Federal Judges* (Pullman: Washington State University Press, 1997), 149-53; McCarran

in Grossman, *Lawyers and Judges*, 64-66; GS to Morse, Jan. 5, 1950, Morse to Burns, Dec. 28, 1949, Burns to McCarran, Dec. 15, 1949, and Morse to McCarran, Dec. 28, 1949, in "Gus Solomon," Morse Papers; GS to Davidson, Jan. 21, 1950, in "Nomination Letters," MS 2886.

34. From Office of Director, Federal Bureau of Investigation to Official Indicated Below by Check Mark, [Oct. 1949] and A. Rosen to Mr. Ladd, Oct. 5, 1949, Solomon FBI Report FBI/HQ 77-10137; GS to Baldwin, Sept. 16, 1949, in "GJS/PFJ."

35. Harold W. Chase, *Federal Judges: The Appointing Process* (Minneapolis: University of Minnesota Press, 1972), 73; McGrath to Truman, Oct. 13, 1949, White House Central Files: Official File; Sweetland oral history, tape 11, side 2; Sweetland interview; *Oregonian*, Oct. 15, 1949; Kell, "History," 28; Robert A. Carp and C.K. Rowland, *Policymaking and Politics in the Federal District Courts* (Knoxville: University of Tennessee Press, 1983), 54-55; Samuel Lubell, *The Future of American Politics* (New York: Harper and Row, 1965), 86-87, 198.

36. Unidentified Oct. 18, 1949, clipping in 1933 Scrapbook; GS to Kefauver, Dec. 30, 1949, in "Nomination Letters," MS 2886; Sweetland oral history, tape 11, side 2; Cordon to McCarran, Jan. 18, 1950, Solomon Judiciary file.

37. Morse to GS, March 23, 1950, in "Gus Solomon," Morse Papers.

38. Sidney Teiser to Cordon, Jan. 6, 1950, Teiser to Clark, July 7, 1949, Edward E. Sox to Morse, Jan. 6, [1950], Dennis Lindsay to McCarran, Jan. 19, 1950, Harold J. Gallagher to Maurice D. Sussman, Jan. 23, 1950, Morse to H. Peterson, Jan. 21, 1950, Burns to McCarran, Jan. 27, 1950, Morse to Burns, Dec. 28, 1949, Morse to McCarran, Dec. 28, 1949, and GS to Morse, Feb. 1, 1950, in "Gus Solomon," Morse Papers; GS to Baldwin, Jan. 9, 1950, in "Nomination Letters," MS 2886; *Oregonian*, Jan. 20, 1950; *Oregon Journal*, Dec. 21, 1949, Jan. 18 and 19, 1950.

39. James H. Polhemus to GS, Nov. 23, 1949, and Waldemar Seaton to GS, Oct. 17, 1949, in "Federal Judgeship (Congratulations)," MS 2886; GS to Morse, Jan. 4, 1950, in "Gus Solomon," Morse Papers; GSOHS, tape 7, side 1; GSOHS, tape 7, side 1; Daniel C. Mahoney to McCarran, Jan. 9, 1950, Solomon Judiciary file; [GS,] "Confidential Please," [1950], in "Senate Confirmation," MS 2886.

40. Gerhardt, *Federal Appointments Process*, 69; Kell, "History," 29, 32; GS to Herbert S. Marks, June 14, 1950, in "Nomination Letters."

41. GS to Morse, May 11, 1950, in "Gus Solomon," Morse Papers; Sweetland interview; Withers in Washington Hearing 3:240.

42. GS to Davidson, May 5, 1950, in "Nomination Letters," MS 2886; Morse to GS, April 22, 1950, GS to Morse, May 11, 1950, and Nicholas Jaureguy to Morse, May 27, 1950, in "Gus Solomon," Morse Papers; unsigned Solomon deposition, May 11, 1950, in "Hearings re Confirmation," MS 2886; Gunther F. Krause to McCarran, May 10, 1950, and Cleveland Cory to William Langer, [1950] and May 29, 1950, William Langer Papers; Washington Hearing 2:135-37; Pete to GS, June 17, 1950, in "Misc.," MS 2886.

43. GS to McCarran, July 12, 1950, Solomon Judiciary file; Reports of March 24 and June 14, 1950, Special Agent in Charge, Portland to FBI Director, May 12 and June 5, 1950, Mr. Rosen to Mr. Ladd, June 6, 1950, and FBI Director to Ford, June 8, 1950, Solomon FBI Report FBI/HQ 77-10137; Washington Hearing 2:142-78; Kell, "History," 29-30; GSOHS, tape 7, side 1. Solomon remembered a "Solomon-Communist?" headline in the *Oregon Journal*, which I could not find in the microfilm edition, though it could have appeared in an uncopied edition. The Library Association of Portland Newspaper Index does list "Solomon-ex-red?" on June 5, 1950.

44. Washington Hearing 3:177ff.

45. Washington Hearing 3:328-54; David L. Davies to Clark, July 1, 1949, in "GSJ/PFJ"; cf. Davies to Cordon, Feb. 1, 1950, Solomon Judiciary file; Kell, "History," 33. Earlier, Davies had confidently termed Solomon not the ablest or most qualified of the

candidates but the one most likely to be seriously considered, so his big firm probably wanted to be in the victor's graces now.

46. GS to Peterson, June 13 and 30, 1950, in "Gus Solomon," Morse Papers; GS to Irving Hoff, June 13, 1950, and GS to Marks, June 14, 1950, in "Nomination Letters," MS 2886.

47. Solomon Judiciary file; GS to Marks, July 3, 1950, in "Nomination Letters," MS 2886.

CHAPTER 6

1. Bernard Schwartz, *Swann's Way: The School Busing Case and the Supreme Court* (New York: Oxford University Press, 1986), 5.

2. Sweetland interview.

3. Bernard Jolles oral history, tape 5, side 2; San Diego *Evening Tribune*, Oct. 9, 1953; *Oregon Journal*, Oct. 14, 1959, and April 22, 1971; Transcript of Proceedings in re Hearing on Order to Show Cause, Aug. 5, 1958, p. 36, NARA/Seattle in *MacKay v. McAlexander*, unpub. opinion (D.Or. 1958); *Honolulu Star-Bulletin*, Feb. 4, 1960; Donald W. McEwen to Don S. Willner, May 14, 1987, in "Don McEwen Autobiographical Materials," U.S. District Court of Oregon Historical Society Papers; John A. Ryan oral history, 18.

4. GS, The Charge to the Jury, June 29, 1965, in "Speeches No. 60 Through No. 109," MS 2886; Alfred T. Goodwin oral history, 450; Otto J. Skopil Jr. oral history, tape 10, side 2; Dooley oral history, tape 3, side 2.

5. Howard, *Courts of Appeals*, xxiii; Honolulu *Advertiser*, Feb. 4 and 5, 1960.

6. Henry J. Friendly, "The 'Law of the Circuit' and All That," *St. John's Law Review* 46 (March 1972): 406-7; Robert A. Carp and C.K. Rowland, *Politics and Judgment in the Federal District Courts*, (Lawrence: University Press of Kansas, 2000), 5, 41; GS, "Techniques for Shortening Trials," F.R.D. 65 (1976), 488; Charles E. Wyzanski Jr., "The Importance of the Trial Judge" in *Courts, Judges and Politics: An Introduction to the Judicial Process*, Walter F. Murphey and C. Herman Pritchett, eds. (New York: Random House, 1961), 325; Robert Carp and Russell Wheeler, "Sink or Swim: The Socialization of a Federal District Judge," *Journal of Public Law* 21 (1972), 359.

7. Richard A. Posner, *The Federal Courts: Challenge and Reform* (Cambridge: Harvard University Press, 1996), 185-6; Randall B. Kester, "That Was Then and This is Now— Changes in Federal Practice," *Oregon Benchmarks* 10 (May 1995), 2; GS, Multnomah County Bar Luncheon—New Rules, Sept. 10, 1964 in "Speeches No. 34 Thru 59," MS 2886; Wolf Heyderbrand and Carroll Seron, *Rationalizing Justice: The Political Economy of Federal District Courts* (New York: State University of New York Press, 1990), 1, 138.

8. GS, Endorsement of Fee, March 3, 1954, in "Miscellaneous Personal Correspondence," MS 2886; GSOHS, tape 7, side 1; Dooley oral history, tape 3, side 2; Leedy oral history, 40; Kester, "Time of Change," 174, 180; Ryan oral history, 28; *Oregon Journal*, Jan. 31, 1978.

9. GS to Baldwin, July 12, 1944, reel 3, ACLU/Japanese; GS to Murrah, Dec. 13, 1949, in "Federal Judgeship (Congratulations)," MS 2886; GSOHS, tape 7, side 1; GS, New Rules of Court, Aug. 13, 1958, in "Speeches No. 1 Thru 34," MS 2886.

10. Friedman, *American Law*, 254-5; Stephen Yeazell, "The Misunderstood Consequences of Modern Civil Process," *Wisconsin Law Review* (1994), 631-3; Skopil oral history, tape 10, side 2; Kester, "Time of Change," 180-1. The "essence of Notice Pleading is that about all you have to do is tell somebody that you're suing them about something that occurred at a particular time and place and that you'd like to have some damages or some other relief." The "parties don't know what the lawsuit's all about when they start the case but they find it out as they go along." Jack Collins oral history, 3.

11. GS, Speech to Oregon Institute of Real Estate Appraisers, March 27, 1957; GS,

New Rules of Court in "Speeches No. 1 Thru 34," MS 2886.

12. GSOHS, tapes 7 and 11, side 1.

13. John F. Kilkenny oral history, tape 8, side 2 and tape 9, side 1; GSOHS, tape 14, side 1; Patricia M. Wald, "Some Real-Life Observations About Judging," *Indiana Law Review* 26 (1992), 179.

14. GS to Vincett Mitchell, Feb. 4, 1950, in "Nomination Letters"; Laurie Bennett Mapes, "A Period of Complexity, 1950-1991," in *The First Duty: A History of the U.S. District Court for Oregon*, ed. Carolyn M. Buan (Portland: U.S. District Court of Oregon Historical Society, 1993), 224-5.

15. GSOHS, tape 10, side 2; Goodwin oral history, 449-50; *Oregon Journal*, Aug. 18, 1971; Mapes, "Period of Complexity," 224-5; GS to John G. Day, Aug. 7, 1968, in "Automobile Accident Cases—Office of Secy of Transportation,"; GS, Crime, Punishment and Juvenile Delinquency, Nov. 6, 1957 in "Speeches No. 1 Thru 34," MS 2886. For a review of Solomon's earliest indemnity, insurance, admiralty, and transportation cases, see Kester, "Time of Change," 201-9.

16. GSOHS, tape 13, side 1, transcript only; *Oregon Journal*, Jan. 31, 1978.

17. Gray oral history, 156, 158; Sidney I. Lezak interview; Jolles oral history, tape 5, side 2; GS to George C. Levin, May 8, 1962, in "Personal Correspondence 1962."

18. Howard, *Courts of Appeals*, 225; Transcript of Proceedings, Nov. 13, 1969, p. 97, in *Tanner v. Lloyd Corporation*, 308 F.Supp. 128 (D.Or. 1970).

19. Beverly Blair Cook, "The Socialization of New Federal Judges: Impact on District Court Business," *Washington University Law Quarterly* (Spring 1971), 255-6, 259; GS, The Charge to the Jury, June 29, 1965, in same-titled folder; GS, Speech—Portland Psychological Society, Oct. 14, 1959, in "Speeches No. 1 Thru 34," MS 2886; Gray oral history, 154; Transcript of Proceedings II, Aug. 10, 1981, p. 196, FRC/San Bruno in *Carson-Truckee Water Conservancy Dist. v. Watt and Pyramid Lake Paiute Tribe of Indians*, 537 F.Supp. 106 (D.Nev. 1982) and *Carson-Truckee Water Conservancy Dist. v. Watt and Pyramid Lake Paiute Tribe of Indians*, 549 F.Supp. 704 (D.Nev. 1982).

20. GS, "Techniques for Shortening Trials," 486, 496; Murrah to GS, Aug. 20, 1974, in "Techniques for Shortening Trial (Narrative Statements)"; GS, The Charge to the Jury, June 29, 1965 in same-titled folder, MS 2886; GSOHS, tape 7, side 1, tapes 8 and 12, side 2; GS to William C. Mathes, April 26, 1956, in "Personal Correspondence 1953 throughout 1958," MS 2886; *Oregonian*, Nov. 8, 1964.

21. Wright oral history, 55; Sweetland interview; Keith Burns interview; Herbert Schwab interview.

22. Hart oral history, tape 24, side 2; *Oregonian* (Magazine), Aug. 25, 1968; GSOHS, tape 13, side 1.

23. San Diego *Evening Tribune*, Oct. 9, 1953; Hart oral history, tape 25, side 1; Jonathan Newman to Devitt Distinguished Service to Justice Award, Dec. 23, 1986, in "Nomination for the Devitt Award"; Lezak interview; Douglas G. Houser to Thomas B. Stoel, Dec. 21, 2000, in author's possession.

24. GS to Norman H. Stone, May 8, 1962, in "Personal Correspondence 1962," MS 2886.

25. GSOJM, tape 4, side 1.

26. GS to Panek, Dec. 14, 1970, in "First Citizen Award—Congratulatory Messages"; GS, Swearing in of Don Hodel, Bonneville Power Administrator, Dec. 1, 1971, in "Speeches No. 60 Through No. 109," MS 2886.

27. Cheryl Greenberg, "Pluralism and its Discontents: The Case of Blacks and Jews," in *Insider/Outsider: American Jews and Multiculturalism*, David Biale, Michael Galchinsky, and Susannah Heschel, eds. (Berkeley: The University of California Press, 1998), 60; Arthur A. Goren, *The Politics and Public Culture of American Jews* (Bloomington: Indiana University Press, 1999), 13.

28. Lowenstein, *Jews of Oregon*, 173; GSOJM, tape 2, side 2; GSOHS, tape 11, side

2; GS to Charles A. Hart, Oct. 3, 1957, in "Social Clubs"; Libby Solomon interview.

29. GS, Brotherhood Week Speech, Feb. 22, 1950, in "Speeches No. 1 Thru 34," MS 2886; Bradley C. Canon and Charles A. Johnson, *Judicial Policies: Implementation and Impact* (Washington: GC Press, 1999), 46; Henry J. Friendly, "Reactions of a Lawyer-Newly Become Judge," *Yale Law Journal* 71 (July 1961), 218-38; Jon O. Newman, "Between Legal Realism and Neutral Principles: The Legitimacy of Institutional Values," *California Law Review* 72 (January 1984), 204. The bulk of cases pose little or no significant conflict between a district judge's legal views and personal values.

30. Heyderbrand and Seron, *Rationalizing Justice*, 43; Jack Bass, *Unlikely Heroes: The Dramatic Story of the Southern Judges of the Fifth Circuit who Translated the Supreme Court's Brown Decision into a Revolution for Equality* (New York: Simon and Schuster, 1981).

31. "Solomon Biographical Material" file; *Oregonian*, Feb. 23, 1950; GSOHS, tape 14, side 1.

32. Gus J. Solomon tax returns in possession of Richard B. Solomon; Blauer interview; *Oregonian*, Dec. 9, 1971; GS to Norman Wapnick, Oct. 12, 1976, in "Personal Corr. 1976," MS 2886.

33. Erwin C. Surrency, *History of the Federal Courts* (New York: Oceana Publications, 1987), 293; GS to Dr. Sanford Wollin, May 6, 1957, in "Personal Correspondence 1953 through 1958"; GS, Speech to Lawyers for United Jewish Appeal, March 31, 1959, in same-titled folder; Louis Kaufman with Annette Kaufman, *A Fiddler's Tale: How Hollywood and Vivaldi Discovered Me* (Madison: University of Wisconsin Press, 2003), 158; GS to Tom S. Wilson, Nov. 9, 1949, in "Federal Judgeship (Congratulations)"; GS to Dr. Hyman Miller, Dec. 14, 1954 and Miller to GS, Dec. 21, 1954, in "Miscellaneous Personal Correspondence"; files for Nan Honeyman Robinson, Louis and Annette Kaufman, Dr. Louis Goodman, and Jerome Kohlberg Jr, all MS 2886.

34. Hart to George E. Rundquist, Nov. 30, 1951 and March 8, 1952, Incomplete list of persons present at 11/20 mtg., Charles Davis to [Stevie] Remington, Oct, 1970 and Notes on Oregon Affiliate History, October 1970, in "History-Oregon," American Civil Liberties Union of Oregon; Gray oral history, 154; Charles Davis interview.

35. Sweetland interview; Noreen Kelly McGraw oral history, tape 3, side 2; Burns interview; Loeb to GS, Aug. 6, 1959 and Hubert H. Humphrey to GS, Aug. 20, 1959, in "Personal Correspondence 1959"; GS to Arnold Forster, Dec. 8, 1960, in "AJCongress-ADL Correspondence With Reference to Mindlin-Jewish Floridian"; Henry M. Richmond, III interview.

36. GS to Ivar Peterson, Jan. 18, 1950, in "Gus Solomon," Morse Papers; GSOHS, tape 9, side 1, transcript only.

37. GS, Deposition, March 1952, in "Personal Correspondence 1953 throughout 1958"; GS, Brotherhood Week Speech, Speech to Congregation Neveh Zedek Talmud Torah, Remarks on the Anniversary of the Constitution, c. 1951 and Speech to Business Girls, March 19, 1953, in "Speeches No. 1 Through 34," MS 2886.

38. Jackson, *Judges*, 223.

39. *Yip Mie Jork v. Dulles*, 237 F.2d 393 (9th Cir. 1956); Transcript of Proceedings in Transcript of Record, U.S. Court of Appeals for the Ninth Circuit, p. 60, bail application oral opinion and oral opinion, March 7, 1956, in *Niukannen v. Boyd*, 148 F.Supp. 106 (D.Or. 1956) aff'd 241 F.2d 938 (9th Cir. 1959).

40. Lezak oral history, tape 2 side 1; Lezak interview; *U.S. v. Absolar*, unpub. opinion (D. Or. 1953) rev'd *Mangaong v. Boyd*, 205 F.2d. 553 (9th Cir. 1953).

41. Report of Nov. 24, 1953, in Solomon FBI Report FBI/HQ 100-372256.

42. Richard H. Chambers Memorandum, Oct. 21, 1957, in *Bryson v. U.S.*, 238 F.2d 657 (9th Cir. 1956); *U.S. v. Apex*, unpub. opinion (W.D.Wa. 1957) aff'd 270 F.2d 747 (9th Cir. 1958); Solomon FBI Reports FBI/HQ 62-104029-570 and Mr. Rosen to C.A. Evans, July 10, 1957, and J. Edgar Hoover to Attorney General, July 12, 1957 FBI/HQ

77-10137; *Jencks v. U.S.*, 353 U.S. 657 (1957); Arthur J. Sabin, *In Calmer Times: The Supreme Court and Red Monday* (Philadelphia: University of Pennsylvania Press, 1999).

43. *U.S. v. Apex*, unpub. opinion (W.D.Wa. 1957) aff'd 270 F.2d 747 (9th Cir. 1958).

44. *U.S. v. Jacobson*, 154 F.Supp. 103 (W.D.Wa. 1957).

45. Transcript of District Court Proceedings, pp. 50-51, in Transcript of Ninth Court Record, April 10, 1958, NA/Seattle in *Niukkanen v. Boyd*, 148 F.Supp. 106 (D.Or. 1956); Arden E. Shenker Clerks' Survey, 1996; GS, The Conduct of the Criminal Trial, July 1, 1965, in "Speeches No. 60 Through No. 109," MS 2886; handwritten notes for Mr. Nease, Dec. 23, 1958 and for Mr. Tavel, Feb. 5, 1968, Solomon FBI Report FBI/HQ 77-10137; *Oregonian*, March 23, 1962.

CHAPTER 7

1. GSOHS, tape 7, side 1.

2. *Oregonian*, Oct. 16, 1953; "In Recognition: Gus J. Solomon 'Four-Star Citizen-of-the-Day'" and GS to Leon R. Yankwich, Nov. 4, 1953, in *U.S. v. Steiner*, unpub. opinion (S.D. Ca. 1953) aff'd in part, rev'd in part *Steiner v. U.S.*, 229 F.2d 749 (9th Cir. 1956); GSOHS, tape 9, sides 1 and 2, and tape 14, side 1; Kohlberg to Author, April 9, 1996; Kohlberg oral history, tape 1, side 2.

3. Libby Solomon interview; Kohlberg oral history, tape 2, side 1.

4. Kohlberg oral history, tape 2, side 1; GS, Speech: Ceremony for Judge Solomon in "Solomon Longevity Ceremony, December 2, 1983," MS 2886; GSOHS, tape 14, side 1; GS to Kallen, Dec. 21, 1959, Kallen Papers; *Oregonian*, Nov. 12, 1959, and Aug. 15, 1973; GS to Judge and Mrs. Alexander Bicks, Dec. 7, 1959, in "Personal Correspondence 1959," MS 2886; Libby Solomon in *Portland State University Magazine* 11 (Spring 1996): 18; GS to Stone, May 8, 1962, in "Personal Correspondence 1962," MS 2886.

5. East oral history, tape 3, side 2 and tape 4, side 1; Neva Elliott oral history, tape 3, side 2; Kilkenny oral history, tape 9, side 1; Smith oral history, tape 8, side 2; Norman J. Wiener oral history, 51-52.

6. Honolulu *Advertiser*, Feb. 4, 1960; David L. Bazelon to GS, Dec. 2, 1983, in "Solomon Longevity Ceremony, December 2, 1983"; GS, interview, March 21, 1967, in "Speeches No. 60 Through No. 109"; Richmond interview; Kohlberg OHSRL interview; Paul J. Rank, The Honorable Gus. J. Solomon, Dec. 14, 1973, in "Oregon State Bar, County Bar Associations CLE Sessions and American Bar Association"; Libby Solomon interview.

7. Steven H. Wilson, *The Rise of Judicial Management in the U.S. District Court, Southern District for Texas, 1955-2000* (Athens: University of Georgia Press, 2002), 6.

8. GS, "New Rules of Court," MS 2886.

9. Gordon, "The Legal Profession," 290; Donald E. Elliott, "Managerial Judging and the Evolution of Procedure," *University of Chicago Law Review* 53 (Spring 1986), 309.

10. Meyer Eisenberg to Author, Jan. 10, 2001; GS to Judge and Mrs. Alexander Bicks, Dec. 7, 1959, in "Personal Correspondence 1959," MS 2886; Honolulu *Advertiser*, Feb. 4, 1960; GS to Simon H. Rifkind, Dec. 15, 1967, in *U.S. v. Baranov*, 293 F.Supp. 610 (S.D.Ca. 1968).

11. GS to Murrah, June 4, 1968, in "Copies of Letters to Judge Alfred P. Murrah," MS 2886; GS, New Rules of Court; GS, Federal District Court Rules—1976 in "Rules—CLE Session, April 24, 1976," MS 2886; GS, Proposed Rule Changes, Sept. 13, 1975, in "Rules (Old Drafts of Changes)."

12. GSOHS, tape 10, side 1.

13. *Rules United States District Court for the District for Oregon* (St. Paul, 1958, 1964, 1976); GS to Murrah, June 4, 1968, in "Copies of Letter to Judge Alfred P. Murrah, June 4, 1968," MS 2886; GS, Proposed Rule Changes; GS, Federal District Court Rules—1976. Individual case management approaches received broad national application in

the amended Federal Rules of Civil Procedure in 1983 and in the Manual of Complex Litigation.

14. GS, Remarks to Davies Biggs Office, Sept. 16, 1975, in same-named folder, MS 2886; Donal D. Sullivan interview; Judith Resnik, "Managerial Judges," *Harvard Law Review* 96 (Dec. 1982), 413; Owen M. Panner, "Surviving in Federal Court," *Oregon Benchmarks* 8 (Summer 1992) unp.

15. Judy Kobbervig interview; Skopil oral history, tape 9, side 1 and tape 10, side 2; Panner, "Surviving in Federal Court;" M. Christie Helmer, "Pants Suits on Women Don't Cut It in Judge Solomon's Court," in *The First Duty: A History of the U.S. District Court for Oregon*, ed. Carolyn M. Buan (Portland: U.S. District Court of Oregon Historical Society, 1993), 312; Sullivan interview; Redden oral history, tape 5, side 1.

16. GS to Murrah, June 4, 1968, in "Copies of Letter to Judge Alfred P. Murrah, June 4, 1968," MS 2886; Panner, "Surviving in Federal Court"; Skopil oral history, tape 9, side 1 and tape 10, side 2.

17. Redden oral history, tapes 20 and 5, side 2; Wendell Gray appreciated Solomon's speedy ways and fairness and expressed a distinctively minority view that all bar members liked them. Gray oral history, 159.

18. Kilkenny oral history, tape 9, side 1; *Oregonian*, Jan. 26, 1975; GS to Roy W. Harper, Oct. 25, 1974, in "oral history"; GS, "Alternate Methods of Dispute Resolution," *Preventive Law Reporter* 2 (June 1984), 2; GSOHS, tape 8, sides 1 and 2; GS, Proposed Rule Changes; Donald W. McEwen to Don S. Willner, May 14, 1987, in "Don McEwen Autobiographical Materials," U. S. District Court of Oregon Historical Society Papers; GS to Belloni, July 1, 1974, in untitled folder, MS 2886; Gray oral history, 157; Redden oral history, tape 5, side 2.

19. Herbert M. Kritzer, "The judge's role in pretrial case processing: assessing the need for change," *Judicature* 66 (June-July 1982), 30; Marc Galanter, "'...A Settlement Judge, Not a Trial Judge:' Judicial Mediation in the United States," *Journal of Law & Society* 12 (Spring 1985), 1-18, "The emergence of the judge as a mediator in civil cases," *Judicature* 69 (February-March 1986), 261 and "Beyond the Litigation Panic," in *New Directions in Liability Law*, ed. Walter Olson (New York: Academy of Political Science, 1988), 25; Elliott, "Managerial Judging," 308.

20. GS, "Alternate Methods of Dispute Resolution," 2; GSOHS, tape 8, sides 1 and 2; GS, Proposed Rule Changes; McEwen to Willner, May 14, 1987, in "Don McEwen Autobiographical Materials," U.S. District Court of Oregon Historical Society Papers; GS to Belloni, July 1, 1974, in untitled folder, MS 2886; Gray oral history, 157; Redden oral history, tape 5, side 2.

21. Collins oral history, 3, 6-8, 11-12.

22. "Urgent Notice," *Oregon State Bar Bulletin* 38 (Oct. 1977), 40; Edwin A. Robson to GS, Oct., 1965, in "New Rules—1964," MS 2886; Linowitz with Mayer, *Betrayed Profession*, 167-8; GS, Speech to Anchorage Bar, July 28, 1958, in "Speeches No. 1 Thru 34," MS 2886; GS, Opinion 1468, July 19, 1979, in *Domingo v. New England Fish Co.*, 445 F. Supp. 421 (W.D. Wa. 1977).

23. Ryan oral history, 20.

24. Redden oral history, tape 5, side 1.

25. Collins oral history, 13; *Seattle Post-Intelligencer*, n.d. clipping in "Personal Corr. 1976," MS 2886; Hart oral history, tape 25, side 1; Carl Petterson to E. Kimbark MacColl, Sr., Feb. 20, 1987, in author's possession; Lezak interview; GS to Bruce R. Thompson, May 28, 1976, in "Rules—CLE Session, April 24, 1976," MS 2886. A contingency fee is paid only out of any damages awarded to the winning lawyer's client.

26. Resnik, "Managerial Judges," 413; anonymous source; Sepenuk oral history, tape 3, side 1; Lezak interview; Ryan oral history, 19.

27. GS, "My Encounters with Discrimination," MS 2886; Jerry Harris interview; Gillers interview; *Oregon Journal*, Feb. 2, 1978.

28. Kernan Bagley oral history, tape 4, side 1 and tape 5, side 1; Kobbervig interview.

29. Robert H. Bork, "Dealing with the Overload in Article III Courts," 70 F.R.D. 232 (1976); "Lagging Justice," *Annals of the American Academy of Political and Social Science* 328 (March 1960), entire issue; Henry P. Chandler, "The Direction of Administration of Trial Courts," 21 F.R.D. 65 (1957); John A. Sutro, "Can the Courts Find Improvement Through Science?" 45 F.R.D. 77 (1968); "Addresses During the National Conference on the Causes of Popular Dissatisfaction with the Administration of Justice," 70 F.R.D. 79 (1976); Mark W. Cannon, "Innovation in the Administration of Justice, 1969-1981: An Overview" in *The Politics of Judicial Reform*, ed. Phillip L. Dubois (Lexington, MA: Lexington Books, 1982), 35.

30. *Oregon Journal*, Aug. 18, 1971; *Oregonian*, Jan. 26, 1975; Milton D. Green, "The Situation in 1959," *Annals of the American Academy of Political and Social Science* 328 (March 1960), 7, 11; GS, Federal District Court Rules—1976; Posner, *Federal Courts*, 59; Stephen L. Wasby, " 'Extra' Judgesin a Federal Appellate Court: The Ninth Circuit," *Law and Society Review* 15 (1980-1981), 369-84; Arthur D. Hellman, "The Crisis in the Circuits and the Innovations of the Browning Years" in *Restructuring Justice: The Innovations of the Ninth Circuit and the Future of the Federal Courts*, ed. Arthur D. Hellman (Ithaca, NY: Cornell University Press, 1990), 5.

31. GSOHS, tape 7, side 1 and tape 9, side 2; GS to Roy W. Harper, March 7, 1972, in "Intercircuit Assignment Committee"; GS to Lil and Monroe Sweetland, Dec. 4, 1970, and GS to Max Gordon, Dec. 7, 1970, in "First Citizen Award—Congratulatory Messages," MS 2886; Kohlberg oral history, tape 2, side 1; GS to Helen Bradley, [1961], in "Personal Correspondence 1961," MS 2886.

32. Mapes, "Period of Complexity," 224-5; Collins oral history, 14; Sullivan interview; Wilson, *Rise of Judicial Management*, 140.

33. Foner, *The Story*, 303; *Goldberg v. Kelly*, 397 U.S. 254 (1970); *Oregonian*, Jan. 26, 1975; Mapes, "Period of Complexity," 225.

34. Shenker to Author, [1996]. For two Solomon restrictions on administrative regulations which ultimately were overturned, see *National Center for Immigrants' Rights v. INS*, 791 F.2d 1351 (9th Cir. 1986) granted and vacated, 481 U.S. 1009 (1987) on appeal after remand 913 F.2d 1350 (9th Cir. 1990) rev'd 502 U.S. 183 (1991) and *Eaton v. Ford Motor Credit Co.*, unpub. opinion (D.Or. 1977) aff'd in part and rev'd in part *Milhollin v. Ford Motor Credit Co.*, 585 F.2d 753 (9th Cir. 1978) rev'd 444 U.S. 555 (1980).

35. Goodwin oral history, 449; James Redden oral history, tape 21, side 1.

36. Lawrence M. Friedman, *Total Justice* (New York: Russell Sage Foundation, 1985), 8; Richard H. Sander and E. Douglass Williams, "Why Are There So Many Lawyers?: Perspectives on a Turbulent Market," *Law and Social Inquiry* 14 (Summer 1989): 432; Richard Abel, *American Lawyers* (New York: Oxford University Press, 1989), 178-81; GS, Charge to the Jury; Goodwin oral history, 450-1.

37. GS, Federal District Court Rules—1976; Transcript of Proceedings I, Aug. 10, 1981, p. 38, FRC/San Bruno in *Carson-Truckee Water Conservancy Dist. v. Watt and Pyramid Lake Pauite Tribe of Indians*, 549 F.Supp. 704 (D.Nev. 1982); Transcript of Proceedings, Aug. 6, 1973, p. 6, U.S. District Court for Oregon in *U.S. v. Stonehill*, 420 F.Supp. 46 (C.D.Ca. 1976).

38. Posner, *Federal Courts*, 124, 185, 339*fn*5; Heydebrand and Seron, *Rationalizing Justice*, 1, 39. The still hard-pressed Oregon judges granted Magistrate Judges near-equal authority.

39. Posner, *Federal Courts*, 185; Jolles oral history, tape 4, side 2; *Oregonian*, July 27, 1967.

40. Lansing interview; *Shannon v. Gladden*, unpub. order (D.Or. 1967); Neil Goldschmidt, "Proceedings on Renaming of the United States Courthouse to the Gus

J. Solomon United States Courthouse," 749 Fed. Supp. 79; Transcript of Proceedings, Jan. 23, 1970, p. 18, FRC/Seattle in *Kimball v. Callahan*, unpub. opinion (W.D. Wa 1973).

41. *Oregon Journal*, Dec. 4, 1970; Skopil to Devitt Distinguished Service to Justice Award, Jan. 5, 1987, in "Nomination for the Devitt Award"; Eisenberg to Author, Jan. 10, 2001; GSOHS, tape 9, side 2 cf. Edward C. Reed Jr. to GS, Aug. 27, 1986, in blue binder.

42. Posner, *Federal Courts*, 185; Goldschmidt, "Proceedings on Renaming of the United States Courthouse"; Transcript of Proceedings, Jan. 23, 1970, p. 18, FRC/Seattle in *Kimball v. Callahan*, unpub. opinion (W.D. Wa 1973); Jolles oral history, tape 4, side 2; GSOHS, tape 11, side 2; GS, untitled interview in "Speeches No. 60 Through No. 109," MS 2886. "The Federal rules of evidence were an incoherent mess until 1975, when Congress codified them," Lawrence M. Friedman did note. Friedman, *American Law*, 268.

43. "Prisoner Petitions and Civil Complaints for the years 1973, 1974, 1975," in *Washington v. Penwell*, unpub. opinion (D.Or. 1975); *U.S. v. Harris*, 302 F.Supp. 1194 (D.Or. 1968); GS to C. Delos Putz Jr. Jan. 8, 1964, in "Personal Correspondence 1964"; GS to Judges Carter and Kilkenny, Oct. 4, 1968, in *Hay v. Bruno*, 344 F.Supp. 286 (D.Or. 1972); *Thornton v. Hay*, 254 Or. 584 (1969); Memorandum on Doctrine of Abstention from Defendants, Sept. 7, 1972, and GS to Goodwin and Burns, Aug. 16, Sept. 11, and 14, 1972, in *Delorme v. Pierce Freightlines Co.*, 353 F.Supp. 258 (D.Or. 1973).

44. Transcript of Pretrial Conference, July 10, 1981, p. 3, FRC/San Bruno in *Carson-Truckee Water Conservancy Dist. v. Watt and Pyramid Lake Paiute Tribe of Indians*, 537 F.Supp. 106 (D.Nev. 1982); George H. Fraser oral history, 2; Owen M. Panner to Author, Dec. 31, 2001.

45. GSOHS, tape 7, side 1 and tape 8, side 2; *Weyerhaeuser Co. v. Combustion Equipment Associates, Inc.*, unpub. opinion (D.Or. 1979) aff'd 654 F.2d 569 (9th Cir. 1981); *Carson-Truckee Water Conservancy Dist. v. Watt and Pyramid Lake Paiute Tribe of Indians*, 537 F.Supp. 106 (D.Nev. 1982); GS to Alice L. O'Donnell, Oct. 25, 1984, in "oral history," MS 2886.

46. Belloni oral history, 210-1; Lezak interview.

47. GS to Day, Aug. 7, 1968, in "Automobile Accident Cases"; Judge Belloni to Judges Solomon, Skopil, Burns and Juba, June 20, 1972, in "Willamette-U. of Ore. Project to Man Desk at Oregon State Penitentiary," MS 2886; Transcript of Proceedings, April 10, 1970, pp. 25-27, in *Colson v. Cupp*, 318 F.Supp. 1381 (D.Or. 1970).

48. Kilkenny oral history, tape 9, side 1; Skopil oral history, tape 10, side 2.

49. GS to Murrah, June 4, 1968, in "Copies of Letters to Judge Alfred P. Murrah"; GS to Day, Aug. 7, 1968, in "Automobile Accident Cases"; Wiener oral history, 51-52; Walter L. Pope to Emanuel Celler, June 9, 1959, GS to Chambers, May 12, 1962, and Dec. 15, 1965, Chambers to GS, March 19, 1962, Warren Olney to Chambers, April 10, 1962, Morse to GS, Jan. 4, 1966, Chambers to East, Aug. 2, 1967, and GS to Kilkenny, March 18, 1968, in "Chief Judge—Correspondence with reference to JUDGE EAST," MS 2886.

50. Belloni oral history, 159-60; Skopil oral history, tape 9, side 1, tape 10, side 2; Goodwin oral history, 397, 404, 411, 422-44 , 450; Alfred T. Goodwin, "The First Duty: A Review Essay," *Western Legal History* 7 (Winter/Spring 1994), 146.

51. Belloni oral history, 160-1, 163-4, 172, 212; Norman Sepenuk oral history, tape 3, side 1.

52. GS, Associated Press Meeting—Oct. 25, 1963, in "Taking of Pictures in Courtroom—Correspondence concerning"; GSOHS, tape 11, side 2; Kathi Wright interview; Jerry Harris interview; Jean Meeker to GS, Aug. 24, [1980s], in "Naturalization," MS 2886.

53. GS, Speech at Swearing in Ceremony for New Citizens, June 4, 1953, in

"Speeches No. 1 Thru 34"; GS, Remarks to Citizenship Swearing In, Jan. 14, 1960 with addendum, c. 1984, in "Solomon-Biographical Materials," MS 2886.

54. *Oregon Journal*, Oct. 24, 1958; GS, Speech on District Court for Oregon history, c. 1980s, in untitled folder; Gus J. Solomon—First Citizen Award—Dec. 1970, in "Speeches 106...," MS 2886; "The Honorable Gus J. Solomon," 1; Robert A. Carp and C.K. Rowland, *Policymaking and Politics in the Federal District Courts* (Knoxville: University of Tennessee Press, 1983), 128.

55. James L. Oakes, "Judicial Collegiality" in *Encyclopedia of the American Constitution*, eds. Leonard Levy and Kenneth L. Karst (New York: Macmillan Reference USA, 2000), 3:1451; Goodwin oral history, 403-4, 411; GS to Judges Skopil, Belloni, Burns, Juba, Leavy and Hogan and Mr. Christ, Sept. 23, 1979, in *Tooley v. Martin-Marietta Corp.*, 476 F.Supp. 1027 (D.Or. 1979); GSOHS, tape 13, side 2; Skopil oral history, tape 10, side 2; Belloni oral history, 161-2, 165.

56. Skopil oral history, tape 9, side 1; Panner, "The Honorable Gus J. Solomon," 1, John C. Beatty, Book Review, *Oregon Historical Quarterly* 97 (Winter 1996-97), 298; Lezak interview; Lezak oral history, tape 5, side 1; GS to Helen Bradley, Jan. 13, [1969], in "Personal Corr. 1969"; McEwen to GS, June 16, 1986, in "Nomination for the Devitt Award," MS 2886; Jolles oral history, tape 5, side 2.

57. Stephen Gillers, "Gus J. Solomon: 'On the Side of God,'" *National Law Journal*, April 27, 1987; GSOHS, tape 12, side 2; Shenker, in Clerks' Survey, 1996; Kerr interview.

58. Michael Pertschuk, Portland's First Citizen: The Law Clerk's Impression, in "Gus J. Solomon—First Citizen Award—Dec. 1970," MS 2886.

59. GS to Vincent E. Mitchell, Nov. 5, 1970, in "Personal Corr. 1970"; Silverstein interview.

60. GSOHS, tapes 7 and 11, side 1; Eisenberg to Author, Aug. 14, 2000; GS to Dick Adelman *et. al.*, Sept. 28, 1971, in "Sentences in Selective Service and Income Tax Cases and in Narcotics Cases—May 8, 1970 (Phoenix Seminar)"; "National Indian Timber Symposium (April 24, 1984, N. Mexico)," MS 2886.

61. Kohlberg oral history, tape 2, side 1; Gillers in *Congressional Record*, June 13, 1989, S 6569; Gillers interview.

62. Kerr interview; Silverstein interview; Richmond interview.

63. GS to Stanley Heisler, July 5, 1968, in "Social Clubs"; GS to Lawrence S. Wilson, Sept. 12, 1974, in "Personal Corr. 1974," MS 2886.

64. GSOHS, tape 4, side 1 and its transcript; section omitted from GS, Realtors of Portland First Citizen Award, Jan. 22, 1971, in "Gus J. Solomon—First Citizen Award—Dec. 1970," MS 2886; *Oregonian* (Magazine), Sept. 10, 1989.

65. Richmond interview; Kohlberg OHS interview; Walbert to Author, May 22, 1996; GS to C. Delos Putz Jr., Jan. 8, 1964, in "Personal Correspondence 1964"; Kerr interview; Gillers interview. See *U.S. v. Van Leeuwen*, 414 F.2d 759 (9th Cir. 1969) rev'd 397 U.S. 249 (1970) for Gillers's views being accepted by Solomon but ultimately reversed.

66. Gillers, "Gus J. Solomon;" Hart oral history, tape 25, side 1, *Washington Post*, Aug. 30, 1967; GS to Ep [Palmer Hoyt,] Nov. 6, 1967, in "Legalese & Gobbledygook," MS 2886.

CHAPTER 8

1. GS, Stanford Law School Class of 1929 Reunion Dinner, April 12, 1969, in "Speeches No. 60 Through No. 109," MS 2886; Friedman, *American Law*, 489; Sunstein, *One Case At a Time*, xi.

2. GS to Chambers, Nov. 26, 1956, in *Bryson v. U.S.*, 238 F.2d 657 (9th Cir. 1956).

3. *Oregonian*, Dec. 5, 1973; GS, Sentences in Selective Service and Income Tax

Cases, May 8, 1970, in "Sentences in Selective Service and Income Tax Cases and in Narcotics Cases—May 8, 1970 (Phoenix Seminar)"; GS, Draft. Ethics...*Lorillard Case* in "Speech—Univ. of Ore. School of Business Administration," MS 2886; oral opinion, March 7, 1956, in *Niukannen v. Boyd*, 148 F.Supp. 106 (D.Or. 1956); GSOHS, tape 13, sides 1 and 2 and transcript for side 2.

4. GSOHS, tape 13, side 1; *Gold v. Confederated Tribes of Warm Springs Indian Reservation*, 478 F.Supp. 190 (D.Or. 1979); *Carson-Truckee Water Conservancy Dist. v. Watt*, 549 F.Supp. 704 (D.Nev. 1982); *U.S. v Dillon*, 249 F.Supp. 38 (D.Or. 1968).

5. G. Edward White, *Earl Warren: A Public Life* (New York: Oxford University Press, 1982), 218-9.

6. I rely on Powe, *Warren Court*. *Henderson v. State of Oregon*, 405 F.Supp. 1271 (D.Or. 1975); Opinion, May 27, 1977, in *Gold v. Confederated Tribes of Warm Springs Indian Reservation*, 478 F.Supp. 190 (D.Or. 1979); *Tooley v. Martin-Marietta Corp.*, 476 F.Supp 1027 (D.Or. 1979) aff'd 648 F.2d 1239 (9th Cir. 1981).

7. Proposed Rule Changes, 29, in "Rules (Old Drafts of Changes")," MS 2886; Ernie Bonyhadi, "Judge Gus J. Solomon, 1906-1987," *Multnomah Lawyer* 87 (April 1987): 2; Paul R. Meyer to Ted De Bra, Feb. 26, 1992, in possession of Meyer.

8. Transcript of Proceedings, Dec. 6, 1968, pp. 3-8, 15, William Sanderson to GS, Jan. 22, 1970 and GS to Frank Pozzi and Paul R. Meyer, Jan. 31, 1974, in *Hill v Local 8, International Longshoremen's and Warehousemen's Union*, unpub. opinion (D.Or. 1968).

9. GS to Pozzi and Meyer, Jan. 31, 1974, in *Hill v Local 8, International Longshoremen's and Warehousemen's Union*, unpub. opinion (D.Or. 1968); Frank M. Coffin, *On Appeal: Courts, Lawyering, and Judging* (New York: Norton, 1994), 284.

10. Transcript of Proceedings, Feb. 1, 1973, pp. 3-5, 7, FRC/Seattle in *Burton v. Cascade School Dist. Union High School No. 5*, 353 F.Supp. 258 (D.Or. 1973) aff'd 512 F.2d 850 (9th Cir. 1975) cert den 423 U.S. 839; Silverstein to Author, [May] 1996; "Instructions to Jury," in *U.S. v. Baranov*, 293 F.Supp. 610 (S.D. Ca. 1968); David F. Walbert to Author, May 22, 1996.

11. Transcript of Proceedings, Nov. 9, 1971, pp.26-27, FRC/Seattle in *Petterson v. Resor*, 331 F.Supp. 1302 (D.Or. 1971); Transcript of Proceedings, Aug. 6, 1973, p. 6, U. S. District Court for Oregon in *U.S. v. Stonehill*, 420 F.Supp. 46 (C.D. Ca. 1976); Transcript of Proceedings, June 30, 1958, p. 5, NARA/Seattle in *MacKay v. McAlexander*, unpub. opinion (D.Or. 1958); *McKay v. Turner*, unpub. opinion (D.Or. 1960).

12. Marvin E. Frankel, "The Search for Truth: An Unimperial View," *University of Pennsylvania Law Review* 123 (May 1975), 1032; Jolles oral history, tape 4, side 1; Posner, *Federal Courts*, 35-36.

13. GS, Remarks to Davies Biggs Office, Sept. 16, 1975, in same-named folder, MS 2886; Transcript of Proceedings, Aug. 6, 1973, p. 5 with attachment, U.S. District Court for Oregon in *U.S. v. Stonehill*, 420 F.Supp. 46 (C.D.Ca. 1976); GS, Multnomah Bar Association, June 27, 1967, in "Multnomah Bar Assn. Panel Discussion with Fed. Judges,"MS 2886.

14. Honolulu *Advertiser*, Feb. 5, 1960; Transcript of Proceedings, Aug. 6, 1973, p. 5, U.S. District Court for Oregon in *U.S. v. Stonehill*, 420 F.Supp. 46 (C.D. Ca. 1976); GS, The Conduct of the Criminal Trial, July 1, 1965, in "Speeches No. 60 Through No. 109," MS 2886; *Oregon Journal*, Oct. 14, 1959

15. GS, The Conduct of the Criminal Trial, July 1, 1965, in "Speeches No. 60 Through No. 109," MS 2886; James Heltzel conversation; Transcript of Proceedings, Jan. 23, 1970, p. 20, FRC/Seattle in *Ryan v. Cupp*, unpub. opinion (D.Or. 1970); Douglas G. Houser to Thomas B. Stoel, Dec. 21, 2000, in author's possession.

16. Dr. Carl Petterson to E. Kimbark MacColl, Feb. 20, 1987, in author's possession.

17. Petterson to MacColl, Feb. 20, 1987; Transcript of Proceedings, Nov. 9, 1971, pp. 2, 13-15, FRC/Seattle in *Petterson v. Resor*, 331 F.Supp. 1302 (D.Or. 1971).

18. *U.S. v. Hanna Nickel Smelting Co.*, 400 F.2d 944 (9th Cir. 1968); *U.S. v. Adair*, 723 F.2d 1394 (9th Cir. 1983); *Carson-Truckee Water Conservancy District. v. Clark and Pyramid Lake Paiute Tribe of Indians*, 741 F.2d 257 (9th Cir. 1984); *Carson-Truckee Water Conservancy Dist. v. Watt*, 741 F.2d 257 (9th Cir. 1982); *Weyerhaeuser Company v. Combustion Equipment Associates, Inc.*, 654 F.2d 569 (9th Cir. 1981); *Cappaert v. U.S.*, 426 U.S. 128 (1976); and also see *U.S. v. Heider*, 347 F.2d 695 (9th Cir. 1965).

19. *Smith and Corey v. U.S.*, 305 F.2d 197 (9th Cir. 1962).

20. Augustus B. Cochran III, *Sexual Harassment and the Law* (Lawrence: University Press of Kansas, 2004), 79; Donald R. Songer, Reginald S. Sheehan, and Susan B. Haire, *Continuity and Change on the United States Courts of Appeals* (Ann Arbor: University of Michigan Press, 2000), 15.

21. Songer, et al., *Continuity and Change Change*, 8, 14; Wasby, "'Extra' Judges," 370; *Oregonian*, Sept. 12, 1963; GS, "Associated Press Meeting—Oct. 25, 1963" and GS to J.E. Simpson, April 30, 1964, in "Taking of Pictures in Courtroom—Correspondence concerning," MS 2886.

22. GS to Murrah, June 19, 1974, in "Techniques for Shortening Trial (Narrative Statements)," MS 2886; Posner, *Federal Courts*, 36, 350.

23. Lauren K. Robel, "Caseload and Judging: Judicial Adaptations to Caseload," *Brigham Young University Law Review* (1990): 37; GSOHS, tape 11, side 2; Jackson, *Judges*, 304.

24. Hart interview; GS memorandum, April 9, 1957, in *Bryson v. United States of America*, 238 F.2d 657 (9th Cir. 1956); GS to Chambers, Oct. 22, 1965, in *Yip Mie Jork v. Dulles*, 237 F.2d 383 (9th Cir. 1956); GS to Goodwin, Sept. 24, 1972, in "Court of Appeals 1971, 1972, 1973, 1974 and 1975," MS 2886.

25. GS to Panel, Nov. 22 and May 12, 1982 and Goodwin to Panel, Feb. 16, 1982, in *Artukovic v. Immigration and Naturalization Service*, 693 F.2d 694 (9th Cir. 1982) in possession of the author. Published cases have precedential effect; unpublished ones lack binding effect on future judges.

26. Goodwin oral history, 444; Skopil oral history, tape 10, side 2; Schwab interview; Lezak interview.

27. *Oregon Journal*, Jan. 31, Feb. 2 and 7, 1978; Hart oral history, tape 25, side 1; Transcript of Proceedings, Nov. 9, 1971, pp. 13, 18, 26, FRC/Seattle in *Peterson v. Resor*, 331 F.Supp. 1302 (D.Or. 1971); *Petterson v. Froehlke*, 354 F.Supp. 45 (D.Or. 1972).

28. Redden oral history, tape 5, side 2; GS to Michael Pertshuk, May 2, 1968, in "Personal Corr. 1968"; *Oregonian* (Magazine), Aug. 25, 1968; *Oregon Journal*, Oct. 27, 1979; Kester, "Time of Change," 201-2; Houser to Stoel, Dec. 21, 2000, in Author's possession; Edwin J. Peterson to Author, Nov. 21, 2003.

29. Sepenuk oral history, tape 3, side 1; Jolles oral history, tape 5, side 2.

30. *Starker v. U.S.*, unpub. opinion (D.Or. 1975); Transcript of Proceedings, March 23, 1977, p. 23 and June 3, 1977, p. 7 and Opinion 1349, p. 848, FRC/Seattle in *Starker v. U.S.*, 432 F.Supp. 864 (D.Or. 1977) aff'd in part and rev'd in part 602 F.2d 134 (9th Cir. 1979); *Wall Street Journal* clipping [spring 1979] and "Real Estate Changing and the Starker Decisions" (Executive Seminars, Inc.) in *Starker v. U.S.*, 432 F.Supp. 864 (D.Or. 1977). The Ninth Circuit's landmark Starker III partly overrode Solomon.

31. Lezak interview; McEwen to Willner, May 14, 1987, in "Don McEwen Autobiographical Materials," U.S. District Court of Oregon Historical Society Papers; Jolles oral history, tape 4, side 1.

32. William O. Douglas, *The Court Years, 1939-1975: The Autobiography of William O. Douglas* (New York: Random House, 1980), 195; Posner, *Federal Courts*, 340.

33. "Legalese & Gobbledygook" folder, MS 2886; *Washington Post*, Aug. 30, 1967; Baker, Or. *Democrat-Herald*, Dec. 21, 1970; Transcript of Proceedings, Aug. 6, 1973, pp. 79, Dec. 3, 1973, p. 22 and May 27, 28, 29 and 30, 1975, p. 284, U.S. District Court for Oregon in *U.S. v. Stonehill*, 420 F.Supp. 46 (C.D.Ca. 1976); Cosgrave oral history, 14.

34. *Oregon Journal*, Jan. 21, 1978; Sepenuk oral history, tape 3, side 1.

35. *Herald*, June 18, 1959; Peterson to Author, Nov. 21, 2003; Sullivan interview; Transcript of Proceedings, Dec. 16, 1982, pp. 99, 100, FRC/San Bruno in *Carson-Truckee Water Conservancy Dist. v. Watt*, 549 F.Supp. 704 (D.Nev. 1982); "The Honorable Gus J. Solomon Portland, 1906-1987," *Oregon State Bar Bulletin* 47 (May 1987), 17.

36. Ryan oral history, 17; Jolles oral history, tape 5 side 2; *Honolulu Star-Bulletin*, Feb. 4, 1960; *Seattle Post-Intelligencer*, Nov. 10, 1976; "Proceedings to Renaming the United States Courthouse to the Gus J. Solomon Courthouse," 749 F.Supp. 87 (1991).

37. Wiener oral history, 51; Hart oral history, tape 25, side 1. Edwin J. Peterson, however, believed that "as time passed, grudging respect replaced" lawyers' "fear" of Solomon and his wrath, and "as the years went on, ultimately" they felt "a sort of affection for him." Peterson to Author, Nov. 21, 2003.

38. *Oregon Journal*, Aug. 18, 1971; *Burgwin v. Mattson*, unpub. opinion (D.Or. 1973); *Shannon v. Gladden*, unpub. order (D.Or. 1967); footnote 6 of *U.S. v. Adair*, 723 F.2d. 1394 (9th Cir. 1983); Transcript of Proceedings, June 7, 1983, p. 67 and Transcript of Proceedings II, Aug. 10, 1981, p. 262, FRC/San Bruno in *Carson-Truckee Water Conservancy Dist. v. Watt and Pyramid Lake Paiute Tribe of Indians*, 537 F.Supp. 106 (D.Nev. 1982) and *Carson-Truckee Water Conservancy Dist. v. Watt and Pyramid Lake Paiute Tribe of Indians*, 549 F.Supp. 704 (D.Nev. 1982); *Bailleaux v. Holmes*, 177 F. Supp. 361 (D.Or. 1959); GS, No Man is Above the Law in untitled folder, MS 2886; GSOHS, tape 4, side 2 transcript only; *Oregon Journal*, Aug. 1, 1968; Transcript of Proceedings, March 12, 1973, p. 12, FRC/Seattle in *Kimball v. Callahan*, unpub. opinion (D.Or. 1973); Transcript of Proceedings, Dec. 6, 1968, p. 14 in *Hill v Local 8, International Longshoremen's and Warehousemen's Union*, unpub. opinion (D.Or. 1968).

39. GS, Speech to University of Oregon Law School, Jan. 27, 1967, in "Speeches No. 60 Through No. 109," MS 2886; *Oregon Journal*, Oct. 27, 1979; GS to Donald J. Sterling Jr., Jan. 3, 1978, in "Judges Poll"; Edwin J. Peterson interview; Peterson to Author, Nov. 24, 2003.

40. GS, Remarks to Stanford Law Society of Oregon, Nov. 17, 1971, in "Stanford University"; GS, Federal District Court Rules—1976, MS 2886; *Oregonian*, Feb. 19, 1987; GS, Introductory Remarks University of Oregon Law School, Jan. 9, 1970, in "Speeches No. 60 Through No. 109," MS 2886; Silverstein interview; Gillers interview; Kohlberg oral history, tape 2, side 1; *Honolulu Star-Bulletin*, Feb. 4, 1960; Jolles oral history, tape 4, side 1; Goodwin oral history, 442; Reminiscences of Dale A. Ray, 28. His law clerks reminisce about learning to take his criticisms in stride—or at least developing thicker skins—and so become better lawyers and human beings.

41. Goodman interview; Memorandum, April 9, 1957, in *Bryson v U.S.*, 265 F.2d 9 (9th Cir. 1956); *Oregon Journal*, Oct. 27, 1979.

42. Jerry Harris interview; Reminiscences of Dale A. Ray, 26-28; Owen M. Panner interview; Transcript of Proceedings, May 21, 1982, pp. 197-8, FRC/San Bruno in *Carson-Truckee Water Conservancy Dist. v. Watt and Pyramid Lake Paiute Tribe of Indians*, 537 F.Supp. 106 (D Nev. 1982).

43. Jolles oral history, tape 4, side 2; Peterson to Author, Nov. 21, 2003; Lezak interview.

44. Abraham A. Arditi to James R. Browning, Oct. 12, 1981; GS to Browning, Nov. 19, 1981; Browning, "In Re Charge of Judicial Misconduct," n.d.; and GS to Bruce Rifkin, Aug. 21, 1984, in *Domingo v. New England Fish Co.*, 445 F.Supp. 421 (W.D. Wa. 1977); John J. Kerr Jr. interview; Kaplan to Author, May 31, 1996.

45. *Seattle Post-Intelligencer*, Nov. 10, 1976; GS to Chambers, April 1972, in *Simms v. Cupp*, 354 F.Supp. 698 (D.Or. 1972); GSOHS, tape 4, side 2 transcript and tape 12, side 1; GS, ATLA Convention, Portland, Oregon, Aug. 4, 1971, in "Speeches No. 60 Through No. 109," MS 2886; Robert Windrem, "Fee Delays May Destroy Public Interest Firm" *American Lawyer* 1 (Sept. 1979), 9.

46. GS to Bruce Rifkin, Aug. 21, 1984, in *Domingo v. New England Fish Co.*, 445 F.Supp. 421 (W.D. Wa. 1977) aff'd in part and rev'd in part 727 F.2d 1427 (9th Cir. 1984).

47. Berkeley Lent oral history, tape 12, side 2; Transcript of Proceedings, Dec. 16, 1982, p. 99, FRC/San Bruno in *Carson-Truckee Water Conservancy Dist. v. Watt and Pyramid Lake Paiute Tribe of Indians*, 537 F.Supp. 106 (D.Nev. 1982); Excerpts of Proceedings in *Mitchell v. OECO*, unpub. opinion (D.Or. 1974); Dooley oral history, tape 3, side 2.

48. *Honolulu Star Bulletin*, Feb. 4, 1960; Skopil oral history, tape 9, side 1; Instructions in *U.S. v. Baranov*, 293 F.Supp.610 (S.D. Cal 1968); Peterson interview.

49. GS, "New Rules of Court"; GS to Robert M. Christ, Dec. 20, 1977, in "Judges Poll," MS 2886; GS to James W. Southwell, Nov. 14, 1973, in *Burgwin v. Mattson*, unpub. opinion (D.Or. 1973); GS to Lillian and Joe Paradise, Sept. 4, 1968, GS to Jerry Pratt, March 2, 1969, and GS to Dick McLaughlin, June 2, 1969, in "Jerry Pratt Oregonian Article and TV Show," MS 2886; GS to Donald J. Sterling Jr., Jan. 3, 1978, and GS to Jamie Duncan, Jan. 27, 1978, in "Judges Poll," MS 2886

CHAPTER 9

1. Benjamin N. Cardozo, *The Nature of the Judicial Process* (New Haven: Yale University Press, 1921), 168; GS, American Jewish Committee—Las Vegas. Dec. 8, 1963, in "Speeches No. 34 Thru 59," MS 2886; *Oregonian*, Dec. 28, 1999.

2. GS, Stanford Law School Class of 1929 Reunion Dinner, April 12, 1969, in "Speeches No. 60 Through No. 109,"MS 2886.

3. Alan Brinkley, "1968 and the Unraveling of Liberal America" in *1968: The World Transformed*, eds. Carole Fink, Philipp Gassert and Detlef Junker (Cambridge, Eng.: Cambridge University Press, 1998), 220, 228.

4. Portion of oral opinion in *Armstrachan v. Continental Airlines*, unpub. opinion (D.Or. 1976) in "U.S. District Court—Correspondence with Lawyers on Pending Matters"; GSOHS, tape 14, side 1. "Anti-politics" did not mean taking power but getting away from power and letting power transform itself.

5. Foner, *The Story*, 293.

6. GS, Stanford Law School Class of 1929 Reunion, April 12, 1969, in "Speeches No. 60 Through No. 109," MS 2886.

7. Sarna, *American Judaism*, 317; GS, American Jewish Committee—Las Vegas.

8. GSOHS, tape 11, side 2 and tape 14, side 1; *Oregon Journal*, June 10, 1961, and Mar. 16, 1961; *Oregonian*, Sept. 19, 1963; Robert F. Kennedy to GS, Oct. 24, 1961, Walter Norblad to Genevieve W. Stark, Aug. 18, 1961, Norblad to Audrey Henry, Aug. 18, 1961 and Norblad to Ruth Duncan, n.d., in "Personal Correspondence 1961," MS 2886; "Gus Solomon" folder, Davidson Papers (OHSRL).

9. *Oregonian*, June 2, 1961, and June 11, 1961; n.d. 1962 clippings from *Oregonian, Oregon Journal* and *Christian Science Monitor*, Lezak Scrapbook.

10. *Oregonian*, Sept. 12, 1963, Sept. 18, 1963, Sept. 19, 1963, Nov. 12, 1963, and Nov. 12, 1963; Hart oral history, tape 26, side 1; Lezak interview.

11. GSOHS, tape 10, side 1; GS to Jack R. Cluck, March 13, 1968, in "Personal Corr. 1968," MS 2886; *Oregonian* (Magazine), Aug. 25, 1968.

12. GS, Speech to Internal Revenue Service Staff, June 19, 1976, in "Speeches No. 110 Through...," MS 2886; GSOHS, tape 14, side 1.

13. Dan Goldy interview; Stone to GS, Oct. 30, 1959, in "Personal Correspondence 1959"; GS to Kohlberg, March 16, 1960, in "Personal Correspondence 1960," MS 2886; Kohlberg oral history, tape 2, side 2; Sara Bartlett, *The Money Machine: How KKR Manufactured Money and Profits* (New York: Warner Books, 1991), 103-4.

14. Skopil oral history, tape 10, side 2; Gillers interview; GS to Lil and Monroe Sweetland, Dec. 4, 1970, GS to Panek, Dec. 14, 1970, GS to Sylvia and Jesse Epstein,

Dec. 4, 1970, and GS to Madeline and Arthur Gage, Dec. 4, 1970, in "First Citizen Award—Congratulatory Messages," MS 2886; GSOHS, tape 13, side 2.

15. *Oregon Journal*, Nov. 20, 1969.

16. David Burner, *Making Peace With the 60s* (Princeton: Princeton University Press, 1996), 8.

17. GSOHS, tape 10, side 1; Lawrence M. Baskir and William A. Strauss, *Chance and Circumstance: The Draft, the War, and the Vietnam Generation* (New York: Knopf, 1978), 67-97; Stephen M. Kohn, *Jailed For Peace: The History of American Draft Law Violators, 1658-1985* (Westport, CT: Greenwood Press, 1986), 89; GS, Sentences in Selective Service and Income Tax Cases, May 8, 1970, in "Sentences in Selective Service and Income Tax Cases and in Narcotics Cases—May 8, 1970 (Phoenix Seminar)," MS 2886; *New York Times*, April 9, 1969; *U.S. v. Lonseth*, 300 F.Supp. 857 (D.Or. 1969).

18. *U.S. v. Haughton*, 413 F.2d 736 (9th Cir. 1969); Gillers to Author, Oct. 17, 1997; GS to Charles J. Meyers, Nov. 9, 1977, in "Stanford University," MS 2886; *Gillette v. U.S.*, 401 U.S. 437 (1971); *Clay v. U.S.*, 403 U.S. 698 (1971); *Fein v. Selective Service System Local Board No. 7*, 405 U.S. 365 (1972). On *Haughton*, see R. Charles Johnson, *Draft, Registration and The Law* (Occidental, CA: Nolo Press, 1985), 201.

19. Silverstein interview; G. Bernhard Fedde interview; Portland State University *Vanguard*, May 18, 1971; Robert Wollheim interview; *Oregonian*, June 12, 1968, and Dec. 19, 1984; GS, To Whom It May Concern, May 4, 1979, in *U.S. v. Wollheim*, unpub. opinion (D.Or. 1969).

20. GSOHS, tape 10, side 1; *Oregonian*, Feb. 12, and (Magazine), March 23, 1969.

21. *Oregonian*, Sept. 16, 1965, June 1, 1967, and (Magazine) Aug. 25, 1968; GS to Judges Kilkenny and Belloni, Sept. 5, 1967, in unnamed folder, MS 2886; Baskir and Strauss, *Chance and Circumstance*, 96; George Q. Flynn, *The Draft, 1940-1973* (Lawrence: University Press of Kansas, 1993), 250; *Oregon Journal*, Sept. 16, 1965; GSOHS, tape 10, side 1; *Los Angeles Times*, Dec. 29, 1968. Only a registrant was eligible for conscientious objector classification and an alternative public-service job.

22. GSOHS, tape 10, side 1; Transcript of Proceedings Sentencing in *U.S. v. Stephens*, unpub. opinion (D.Or. 1967); Transcript of Proceedings—Sentencing in *U.S. v. Risene*, unpub. opinion (D.Or. 1967); GS to William F. Howland, Feb. 9, 1968 and GS to Judges Kilkenny and Belloni, Sept. 5, 1967, in unnamed folder, MS 2886; Fedde interview.

23. *Oregon Journal*, April 22, 1971; *Oregonian*, Sept. 28, 1967, and (Magazine) Aug. 25, 1968; Belloni oral history, 210; *Los Angeles Times*, Dec. 29, 1968; GSOHS, tape 10, side 1; Abraham L. Marovitz to GS, Jan. 15, 1969, in "Personal Corr. 1969"; John J. Oliver to GS, Jan. 19, 1968, in unnamed folder; Oliver to Sidney Willens, May 7, 1987, enclosed in Willens to Libby Solomon, May 12, 1987, in "Judges condolences," MS 2886; Fedde interview; Baskir and Strauss, *Chance and Circumstance*, 97.

24. This and the next paragraph are based on *Oregon Journal*, Sept. 16, 1965, and Aug. 7, 1969, *Oregonian*, June 1, 1967, Aug. 4, 1967, Aug. 7 and 9, and (Magazine) March 23, 1969 and GS to Oliver, Feb. 19, 1968, in unnamed folder, MS 2886. Docketed draft cases in Oregon by a lenient U.S. Attorney's Office went from 15 to 25 percent of criminal cases between 1966 and June 1969.

25. GS, Sentences in Selective Service and Income Tax Cases and "Sentencing in Selective Service and Income Tax Cases," 485-6.

26. Beverly B. Cook, "Sentencing Behavior of Federal Judges: Draft Cases—1972," *University of Cincinnati Law Review* 42 (1973): 598-600; Baskir and Strauss, *Chance and Circumstance*, 67-97; Kohn, *Jailed For Peace*, 89; Lezak oral history, tape 5, side 1; Lezak interview; Gerald Robinson interview; GS, Sentences in Selective Service and Income Tax Cases; Wollheim interview.

27. *Oregon Journal*, Jan. 21, 1971; Transcript of Proceedings, 72, 111 in *Tanner v. Lloyd Corp.*, 308 F.Supp. 128 (D.Or. 1970).

28. Carl R. Neil interview; Transcript of Proceedings, 61, 72, in *Tanner v. Lloyd*

Corp., 308 F.Supp. 128 (D.Or. 1970).

29. Transcript of Proceedings, 43, 45, in *Tanner v. Lloyd Corp.*, 308 F.Supp. 128 (D.Or. 1970); Howard Ball, *Courts and Politics: The Federal Judicial System* (Englewood Cliffs: Prentice-Hall, 1987), 46; Margaret A. Blanchard, *Revolutionary Sparks: Freedom of Expression in Modern America* (New York: Oxford University Press, 1992), 392-3 and Lizabeth Cohen, "From Town Center to Shopping Center: The Reconfiguration of Community Marketplaces in Postwar America," *American Historical Review* 101 (Oct. 1996): 1068-71; cf. Lucas A. Powe Jr., *The Warren Court and American Politics* (Cambridge: Harvard University Press, 2000), 458.

30. *Lloyd Corp. v. Tanner*, 407 U.S. 551 (1972); Wasby, "The District for Oregon in the U.S. Supreme Court," 952-3.

31. Transcript of Proceedings, Nov. 18, 1976, p. 31, FRC/Seattle in *Oregon Socialist Workers Party 1974 Campaign Committee v. Meyers*, unpub. opinion (D.Or. 1977).

32. *Buckley v. Valeo*, 424 U.S. 1 (1976); Kilkenny to GS, Feb. 25 and April 28, 1977, in *Oregon Socialist Workers Party v. Meyers*, unpub. opinion (D.Or. 1977); GS to Gillers, June 2, 1977, and Gillers to Joel Gora, June 6, 1977, in "Stephen Gillers," MS 2886; *Brown v. Socialist Workers '74 Campaign Committee*, 459 U.S. 87 (1982).

33. Kaplan to Author, May 31, 1996; *California v. Arizona*, 373 U.S. 546 (1963); Mary Pearson, "Hunting Rights: Retention of Treaty Rights After Termination—*Kimball v. Callahan*," *American Indian Law Review* 4 (1976), 127.

34. GS, Address at Confederated Tribes Tribal Judges Conference—November 1, 1962, in same-named folder, MS 2886; Panner interview.

35. I partly rely on Joseph P. Mazurek, Julie Wrend and Clay Smith, *American Indian Law Deskbook* (Niwot, CO.: University Press of Colorado, 1998); William C. Canby Jr., *American Indian Law* (St. Paul: West Publishing Co., 1988) and Emily Rader, "The Unfulfilled Promise of the *Winters* Doctrine" in *Law in the Western United States*, ed. Gordon M. Bakken (Norman: University of Oklahoma Press, 2000).

36. *Klamath Indian Tribe v. Oregon Department of Fish and Wildlife*, unpub. opinion (D.Or. 1983) aff'd 729 F.2d 609 (9th Cir. 1984) rev'd *Oregon Department of Fish and Wildlife v. Klamath Indian Tribe*, 473 U.S. 753 (1985).

37. *Klamath & Modoc Tribes and Yahooskin Band of Snake Indians of Klamath Reservation v. Maison*, 139 F.Supp. 634 (D.Or. 1956); *U.S. v. Adair and The State of Oregon*, 478 F.Supp. 336 (D.Or. 1979) as modified aff'd *U.S. & Klamath Indian Tribe v. Adair & The State of Oregon*, 723 F.2d 1394 (9th Cir. 1983); *Confederated Tribes of Umatilla Indian Reservation v. Maison*, 186 F.Supp. 519 (D.Or. 1960); *Oregon Journal*, Aug. 1, 1968; Transcript of Proceedings, March 12, 1973, p. 12 in *Kimball v. Callahan*, unpub. memorandum (D.Or. 1973).

38. GS, "ACLU-E. B. MacNaughton Civil Liberties Award Speech, Dec. 8, 1965," in same-named folder, MS 2886; *Klamath & Modoc Tribes and Yahooskin Band of Snake Indians of Klamath Reservation v. Maison*, 139 F.Supp. 634 (D.Or. 1956) consolidated with *Confederated Tribes of the Umatilla Indian Reservation v. Maison*, 186 F.Supp. 519 (D. Or., 1960) aff'd in part and rev'd in part 338 F.2d 620 (9th Cir., 1964); *Burgwin v. Mattson*, unpub. opinion (D.Or. 1973).

39. Charles F. Wilkinson, *American Indians, Time and the Law* (New Haven: Yale University Press, 1987), 121-2; *Confederated Tribes of Umatilla Indian Reservation v. Maison*, 262 F.Supp. 871 (D.Or. 1966).

40. *Gold v. Confederated Tribes of Warm Springs Indian Reservation*, 478 F.Supp. 190 (D.Or. 1979); *Kimball v. Callahan*, unpub. memorandum (D.Or. 1973) rev'd 493 F.2d 564 (9th Cir. 1974); *Kimball v. Callahan*, unpub. opinion (D.Or. 1976) aff'd in part and remn'd 590 F.2d 768 (9th Cir. 1979).

41. *Oregon Journal*, Aug. 1, 1968; Transcript of Proceedings, March 12, 1973, p. 12 in *Kimball v. Callahan*, unpub. memorandum (D.Or. 1973); *Sohappy v. Smith*, 302 F.Supp. 899 (D.Or. 1969); Mapes, "Period of Complexity," 247-50; GS to Wayne Davies,

May 16, 1956, in *Klamath & Modoc Tribes and Yahooskin Band of Snake Indians of Klamath Reservation v. Maison*, 139 F.Supp. 634 (D.Or. 1956); Theodore H. Little to GS, Aug. 16, 1966, in *Confederated Tribes of Umatilla Indian Reservation v. Maison*, 262 F.Supp. 871 (D.Or. 1966) aff'd *Holcomb v. Confederated Tribes*, 382 F.2d 1013 (9th Cir. 1967). A slip opinion is either not published or not yet published in a reporter. Slip opinions generally are available from the court or, since Solomon's death, on it's web site.

42. *Carson-Truckee Water Conservancy Dist. v. Watt and Pyramid Lake Pauite Tribe of Indians*, 549 F.Supp. 704 (D.Nev. 1982) aff'd in part, vac in part *Carson-Truckee Water Conservancy District v. Clark and Pyramid Lake Paiute Tribe of Indians*, 741 F.2d 257 (9th Cir. 1984); Lloyd Burton, *American Indian Water Rights and the Limits of Law* (Lawrence: University Press of Kansas, 1991), 35.

43. Transcript of Proceedings I, Aug. 10, 1981, p. 49 and Transcript of Proceedings II, May 21, 1982, p. 140, FRC/San Bruno in *Carson-Truckee Water Conservancy Dist. v. Watt and Pyramid Lake Pauite Tribe of Indians*, 549 F.Supp. 704 (D.Nev. 1982); *U.S. v. Cappaert and State of Nevada*, 508 F.2d 313 (9th Cir. 1974) aff'd *Cappaert v. U.S.*, 426 U.S. 128 (1976); Mazurek, et. al, *American Indian Law*, 192.

CHAPTER 10

1. GSOHS, tape 11, side 2.

2. Sarna, *American Judaism*, 309, 310; GS to Stanley Heisler, July 5, 1968, in "Social Clubs," MS 2886; Cheryl Greenberg, "Pluralism," 65; GS, Speech to B'nai B'rith Lodge in Portland, Jan. 9, 1952 and Brotherhood Speech, Feb. 27, 1963, in "Speeches No. 34 Thru 59"; GS, Uphold the Law—A Citizen's First Duty, April 30, 1965, in "Speeches No. 60 Through No. 109"; GS, Jewish Role; Mayfield K. Webb to the Family of Judge Solomon, [Feb. 24, 1987], in "Condolences"; Morris Milgram to GS, March 6, 1971, in "Gus J. Solomon-First Citizens Award-Dec. 1970"; Milgram to Gus and Libby Solomon, March 5, 1971, in "Elisabeth Solomon-Morris Milgram," MS 2886; Libby Solomon interview; Mayfield K. Webb to the Family of Judge Solomon, [Feb. 24, 1987], in "Condolences," MS 2886.

3. Omitted from GS, "Realtors of Portland First Citizen Award," Jan. 22, 1971, in "Gus J. Solomon-First Citizen Award-Dec. 1970," MS 2886; GS, Jewish Role.

4. GS, Speech—Multnomah County Bar Association, MS 2886; *The Black Coalition v. Portland School District No. 1*, unpub. opinion (D.Or. 1971) aff'd 484 F.2d 1040 (9th. Cir. 1973).

5. Lezak to Josiah Nunn, June 1, 1971, "Cherly James Defense Committee Racial Matter—Black Panther Party," FBI Report, June 10, 1971; GS to Lezak, July 19, 1971, and Order, June 11, 1971, in *U.S. v. James*, unpub. opinion (D.Or. 1971) aff'd 464 F.2d 1228 (9th Cir. 1972); GSOHS, tape 9, side 1; Portland State University *Vanguard*, May 18, 1971; GSOHS, tape 9, side 1; *Oregon Journal*, March 14, 1973.

6. GS to Judges Hamley and Taylor, April 25 and May 9, 1972, Judge Taylor to Judges Hamley and Solomon, April 26, 1972, and Lee Johnson and G.F. Bartz to GS, March 28, 1972, in *Falkenstein v. Department of Revenue for State of Or.*, 350 F.Supp. 887 (D.Or. 1972) stay denied 409 U.S. 1032 (1973); *Moose Lodge No. 107 v. Irvis*, 407 U.S. 1963 (1972); Silverstein interview.

7. David F. Walbert to Author, May 22, 1996; *Burton v. Wilmington Parking Authority*, 365 U.S. 715 (1961).

8. Opinion 1468, July 19, 1979, in *Domingo v. New England Fish Co.*, 445 F.Supp. 421 (W.D. Wa. 1977) aff'd in part and rev. in part 727 F.2d 1427 (9th Cir. 1984).

9. GS to Morse, July 1, 1946, in "Gus Solomon," Morse Papers; William H. Chafe, *The American Woman: Her Changing Social, Economic, and Political Roles, 1920-1970* (New York: Oxford University Press, 1972), 187-8.

10. Mapes, "Period of Complexity," 233; *Gunther v. County of Washington*, unpub. opinion (D.Or. 1976) aff'd in part and rev'd in part 602 F.2d 892 (9th Cir. 1979) aff'd

452 U.S. 1961 (1981); Joel W. Friedman and George M. Strickler, *The Law of Employment Discrimination*, (Westbury, CT: Foundation Press, 1997), 950-69.

11. Friedman and Strickler, *Law of Employment*, 963; Mapes, "Period of Complexity," 233-4.

12. Arthur Hertzberg in *The New York Review of Books*, Nov. 21, 1985; John D. Skrentny, *The Minority Rights Revolution* (Cambridge: Harvard University Press, 2002), 191-2; GS, Joint Defense Appeal Human Relations Award Dinner.

13. Marc Dollinger, "The Other War: American Jews, Lyndon Johnson, and The Great Society," *American Jewish History* 89 (Dec. 2001), 457; GS, Jewish Role; GSOJM, tape 2, side 2.

14. *Portland Jewish Review*, Sept. 1973.

15. GS to Kallen, Oct. 12, 1961, Kallen Papers; Shapiro, *Time for Healing*, 200; GS, Speech to a Lawyer Group in a New York City Synagogue, early 1970s, in "Speeches No. 1 Thru 34," MS 2886; Rabbi Joshua Stampfer interview; Libby Solomon interview; GS to Wapnick, Oct. 12, 1976, in "Personal Corr. 1976," MS 2886.

16. Stampfer interview; Libby Solomon interview; Charles S. Liebman, "Reconstructionism in American Jewish Life," in *American Jewish Yearbook 1970*, eds. Morris Fine and Milton Himmelfarb (New York: American Jewish Committee and Philadelphia: Jewish Publication Society of America, 1970), 6; Mel Scult, "Kaplan, Mordecai Menahem," American National Biography Online, http://ww.anb.org/articles/08/08-01739.htm (accessed Oct. 10, 2004).

17. Goren, *Politics and Public Culture*, 29.

18. GSOHS, tape 14, side 1; Greenberg, "Pluralism," 65; Svonkin, *Jews Against Prejudice*, 4-8.

19. American Jewish Committee Portland Unit Organizing Committee Minutes, March 12, 1969, in "AJ Committee Meeting Dec. 3, 1968"; Richard Cohen to GS, Dec. 1, 1960, GS to Foster, Dec. 8, 1960 and Maslow to GS, Jan. 10, 1961, in "AJCongress-ADL Correspondence With Reference to Mindlin-Jewish Floridian," MS 2886.

20. GS to Foster, Dec. 8, 1960, in "AJCongress-ADL Correspondence With Reference to Mindlin-Jewish Floridian"; *Commission on Law and Social Action Report* (Sept.-Oct. 1959), in Box 32 and Cohen to Maslow, March 15, 1965, in "Church and State—1965," American Jewish Congress Papers; *Dickman v. School Dist. No. 62C*, 232 Or. 238 (1961); *Lowe v. City of Eugene*, 254 Or. 518 (1969); *ACLU Newsletter* 10 (Fall 1972).

21. Stevens, *Law School*, 246; GSOJM, tape 2, side 1; Silverstein interview; GS, Speech to Lawyers for United Jewish Appeal. U.S. Attorney Lezak, among others, considered it completely improper for Solomon to put employment "pressure on people who had cases before him." Lezak interview.

22. Kohlberg oral history, tape 1, side 2; GSOHS, tape 4, side 1; Leon Gabinet to Author, Jan. 26, 2005.

23. Eisenberg to Author, Aug. 14, 2000, and Jan. 10, 2001; GS to Edward L. Epstein, Sept. 5, 1967, and GS to Simon H. Rifkind, Dec. 15, 1967, in "Personal Corr. 1967"; GSOHS, tape 4, side 1 and tape 11, side 2.

24. GSOHS, tape 11, side 2; Anti-Defamation League of B'nai B'rith, *Anti-Semitism in the United States in 1947* (New York and Chicago: Author, [1948]), 75; Hart oral history, tape 23, side 2. Protests by White Stag-owner Max Hirsch against attending meetings in discriminatory clubs prompted their being moved.

25. GSOHS, tape 11, side 2; GS, Joint Defense Appeal Human Relations Award Dinner; GS, "My Encounters with Discrimination"; GS, Brotherhood Speech, Feb. 27, 1963, in "Speeches No. 34 Thru 59," MS 2886; *Portland Jewish Review*, Sept. 1973.

26. Dinnerstein, *Antisemitism*, 156; GS to Colwell, Nov. 4, 1960, in "Social Clubs"; [GS,] "Notes on luncheon with Mike Frey—4/17/63," in "Social Clubs"; Verne Perry to GS, May 28, 1958, in "Personal Correspondence 1953 through 1958," MS 2886.

27. GS, Jewish Role; Lowenstein, *Jews of Oregon*, 173.

28. GS, Brotherhood Speech; *Oregonian*, March 1, 1963; GS to Tom L. McCall, March 5, 1963, in "B'nai B'rith Brotherhood Award, 2/9/66," in same-titled folder, MS 2886; [GS,] "Notes on Luncheon"; GS, Jewish Role; Hart oral history, tape 23, side 2; Ryan oral history, 37-38.

29. GS to Lawrence Bloomgarden, Oct. 9, 1964, Walter N. Fuchigama to GS, Oct. 24, 1966, and GS to Seymour H. Kaplan, Oct. 19, 1966, in "Social Clubs," MS 2886; GSOHS, tape 11, side 2; *Oregonian* (Magazine), Aug. 25, 1968.

30. GS to Bloomgarden, Oct. 9, 1964, and Oct. 22, 1964, in "Social Clubs"; GSOHS, tape 11, side 2; *Oregonian* (Magazine), Aug. 25, 1968, and March 25, 1979.

31. Howard S. Smith to GS, Oct. 23, 1963, Bloomgarden to GS, Nov. 10, 1964, March 12 and Aug. 2, 1965, Irving Hill to GS, Dec. 2, 1965, GS to Theodore Weisman, Dec. 15, 1965, GS to Smith, Jan. 16, 1966, "Anti-Semitism's Last Hurrah in American Business," *Careers Today* (Jan. 1969) [American Jewish Committee reprint], and Report of the First Meeting, National Social Discrimination Committee, June 20, 1966, in "Social Clubs," MS 2886.

32. GS to Kaplan, Oct. 19, 1966, and GS to R.H. Willis, Nov. 30, 1969, in "Social Clubs," MS 2886; GS, Jewish Role; GSOHS, tape 11, side 2; *Oregon Journal*, June 12, 1965; *New York Times*, June 12, 1965; *Oregonian*, Sept. 26, 1967 and March 25, 1979; GS, Responsa Club Speech, December 14, 1983, in "Speeches No. 110 Through...," MS 2886

33. GS, B'nai B'rith Contribution.

34. GSOJM, tape 4, side 1; GSOHS, tape 14, side 1.

35. GS, Presentation of Israel Prime Minister Medal and Introduction of Milton Margulis as 1967 Man of the Year-State of Israel Bonds, June 6, 1967, in "Speeches No. 60 Through 109," MS 2886; Baker (Or.) *Catholic Sentinel*, June 9, 1967; Robinson interview; Shapiro, *Time for Healing*, 201; Joshua M. Zeitz, "'If I am not for myself...': The American Jewish Establishment in the Aftermath of the Six Day War," *American Jewish History* 88 (June 2000), 253-86.

36. Svonkin, *Jews Against Prejudice*, 178; Peter Novick, *The Holocaust in American Life* (Boston: Houghton Mifflin 1999), 184; Goren, *Politics and Public Culture*, 13; GSOHS, tape 14, side 1.

37. *Oregonian*, Jan. 23, 1969; GS, Introduction of Senator Robert Packwood, Nov. 11, 1971, in "B'nai B'rith and ADL"; Packwood to GS, April 30, 1981, in unnamed folder; GS to Les AuCoin, May 27, 1983, in "Solomon Longevity Ceremony," MS 2886.

38. Michael E. Staub, *Torn at the Roots: The Crisis of Jewish Liberalism* (New York: Columbia University Press, 2002), 10, 51, 52, 66, 77; Cheryl Greenberg, "The Wrong Means to the Right Ends? Jewish Ambivalence Toward Black Civil Rights Actions," paper in author's possession.

39. Dollinger, "The Other War," 460; Skrentny, *Minority Rights Revolution*, 284; GS, Brotherhood Speech; GS, Jewish Role; Svonkin, *Jews Against Prejudice*, 178.

40. Cheryl Greenberg, "Negotiating Coalition: Black and Jewish Civil Rights Agencies in the Twentieth Century" in *Struggles in the Promised Land: Toward a History of Black-Jewish Relations in the United States*, eds. Jack Salzman and Cornel West (New York: Oxford University Press, 1997), 167; Minutes of Oregon Regional Advisory Board Meeting, June 20, 1972, in "B'nai B'rith and ADL"; Brief of Anti-Defamation League of B'nai B'rith as *Amicus Curiae* in Support of Jurisdictional Statement or in the Alternative Petition for Certiorari, *De Funis v. Odegaard* in the Supreme Court of the United States, October Term, 1973, No. 73-235, in author's possession.

41. *De Funis v. Odegaard*, 416 U.S. 312 (1974); *Regents of the University of California v. Bakke*, 438 U.S. 265 (1978); Libby Solomon to Lorna, Dec. 30, 1977, in "Elisabeth Solomon—Miscellaneous," MS 2886.

CHAPTER 11

1. U.S. Department of Justice, Bureau of Justice Statistics, *1994 Sourcebook of Criminal Justice Statistics* (Washington: Government Printing Office, 1995), Table 5.27.

2. GS, Crime, Punishment and Juvenile Delinquency, Nov. 6, 1957, in "Speeches No. 1 Thru 34," MS 2886; GS, Sentences in Selective Service and Income Tax Cases (Phoenix Seminar); Jonathan Simon, "Visions of Self-Control: Fashioning a Liberal Approach to Crime and Punishment in the Twentieth Century," in *Looking Back at Law's Century*, eds. Austin Sarat, et al. (Ithaca, NY: Cornell University Press, 2002), 109.

3. GS, Crime, Punishment and Juvenile Delinquency; GSOHS, tape 12, side 2; GS to Pratt, Oct. 26, 1966, in "Personal Corr. 1966," MS 2886; Donal Sullivan interview; *Oregonian* (Magazine), Aug. 25, 1968; Portland State University *Vanguard*, May 18, 1971.

4. Robert E. Keeton, *Keeton on Judging in the American Legal System* (Charlottesville: Lexis Law Publishing, 1999), 167; Kaplan interview; conversation with Rabbi Jonah Geller; GSOHS, tape 10, side 2; Kerr interview.

5. *Portland Jewish Review*, Sept. 1973; GSOHS, tape 13, side 1 and tape 12, side 2; GS, Speech—Portland Psychological Society, Oct. 14, 1959; Kilkenny oral history, tape 9, side 1; Skopil oral history, tape 10, side 2; *Oregon Journal*, Feb. 4, 1978.

6. GS, Crime, Punishment and Juvenile Delinquency; *Oregon Journal*, April 22, 1971; *U.S. v. Brawner*, 471 F.2d 969 (D.C.C.A. 1972).

7. GS to Judges Lindberg, Powell, Boldt, Beeks and Goodwin, Oct. 4, 1968, GS to Oliver, Jan. 31, 1969, Daniel V. Voiss to GS, Feb. 19, 1969 and GS to Judges Kilkenny and Belloni, March 10, 1969, in "Psychiatrists-Psychologists," MS 2886; Powe, *Warren Court*, 443.

8. Powe, *Warren Court*, 446; GS, Uphold the Law; GS, Speech to B'nai Brith Lodge in Portland, Jan. 9, 1952, in "Speeches No. 1 Thru 34," MS 2886.

9. GS, Speech to B'nai B'rith Lodge; Statement at Time of Sentencing Dr. Parlova, Feb. 14, 1962, in "Criminal Cases, Miscellaneous," MS 2886; GS, "Sentencing in Selective Service and Income Tax Cases," 485; Alfred Bonotto Sentencing, June 2, 1971, in *U.S. v. Bonotto*, unpub. opinion (D.Or. 1971); Lezak interview; Goodwin oral history, 437.

10. During most of his tenure, the courts interpreted the phrase (due process of the law) to mean that minimum procedures had to be followed in every case and that the law the procedures enforced must not violate a person's liberties.

11. Sepenuk oral history, tape 3, side 1; GS, Speech to Internal Revenue Service Staff; Leazk interview; Lezak oral history, tape 2, side 1.

12. Gillers interview; GS to Gillers at end of GS to Walter, July 11, 1973, in "Stephen Gillers." "The statistical fact remains that the preponderant majority of those brought to trial did substantially what they are charged with." Marvin E. Frankel, "The Search for Truth: An Unimperial View," *University of Pennsylvania Law Review* 123 (May 1975), 1037.

13. *U.S. v. Brooklier*, 674 F.2d 4126 (9th Cir. 1982); Kaplan to Author, May 31, 1996.

14. GS, Associated Press Meeting—Oct. 25, 1963, in "Taking of Pictures in Courtroom—Correspondence Concerning," Gillers interview; *U.S. v. Crozier*, 274 F.2d 1293 (9th Cir. 1982) rev'd 468 U.S. 1206 (1984); Silverstein interview; *Simms v. Cupp*, 354 F.Supp. 698 (D.Or. 1972) aff'd (9th Cir. 1972); *Brady v. Maryland*, 373 U. S. 83 (1962).

15. GS, Uphold the Law; *Horn v. Rhay*, unpub. opinion (E.D. Wa. 1959).

16. *McWilliams v. Randall*, 275 F.Supp. 700 (D.Or. 1967).

17. Powe, *Warren Court*, 425; *Shannon v. Cupp*, 294 F.Supp. 1113 (D.Or. 1969); Transcript of Proceedings, July 23, 1970, p. 13, NARA/Seattle in *Klamert v. Cupp*, unpub.

opinion (D.Or. 1970); *McCoy v. Cupp*, 298 F.Supp. 329 (D.Or. 1969); *Mapp v. Ohio*, 367 U.S. 643 (1961).

18. *Naughten v. Cupp*, unpub. opinion (D.Or. 1971) rev'd 476 F.2d 845 (9th Cir. 1972) rev'd *Cupp v. Naughten*, 414 U.S. 141 (1973). *Harrington* upheld the introduction of a nontestifying codefendant's confession at a joint trial as harmless error under *Chapman*. *Harrington v. California* 395 U.S. 250 (1969).

19. *Murphy v. Cupp*, unpub. opinion (D.Or. 1977) rev'd 461 F.2d 1006 (9th Cir. 1972), rev'd *Cupp v. Murphy*, 412 U.S. 291 (1973); *Chimel v. California*, 395 U.S. 752 (1969).

20. *O'Neil v. Nelson* 422 F.2d 319 (9th Cir. 1970) rev'd *Nelson v. O'Neil*, 402 U.S. 622 (1971). *Bruton v. United States*, 391 U.S. 123 (1968).

21. GS to Gillers at end of GS to Walter, July 11, 1973, in "Stephen Gillers," MS 2886; *Capitan v. Cupp*, 356 F.Supp. 302 (D.Or. 1972).

22. *Balleaux v. Holmes*, 177 F.Supp. 361 (D.Or. 1959); rev'd *Hatfield v. Ballleaux*, 290 F.2d 632 (D.Or. 1961) cert. denied 36 U.S. 862 (1962); *Fay v. Noia*, 372 U.S. 391 (1963); Rowland Watts to GS with attachment, June 7, 1959, in *Balleaux v. Holmes*, 177 F.Supp. 361 (D.Or. 1959); Remington to Joe Floren, [1970], in "History-Oregon," American Civil Liberties Union of Oregon.

23. GS, Appointment of Counsel Under Criminal Justice Act and in Habeas Corpus Cases, March 21, 1968, in same-named file; GS to Frederic R. Merrill, Nov. 26, 1973, in "Willamette-U. of Ore. Project to Man Desk at Oregon State Penitentiary"; Ross R. Runkle to GS, Aug. 22, 1969 and GS to Runkle, Sept. 22 and 30, 1969, in "Willamette Law School"; Keith Burns to GS, Sept. 7, 1976, in "Personal Corr. 1976," MS 2886; Oregon State Bar, "Detention and Correction Report" in *1976 Committee Reports* and *1977 Committee Reports*; *Oregon State Bar Bulletin* 38 (Oct. 1977), 40-41.

24. William J. Knudsen Jr. to GS, April 10, 1978, and consent decree in *Washington v. Penwell*, unpub. opinion (D.Or. 1975) aff'd 700 F.2d 570 (9th Cir. 1983).

25. *Shannon. v. Gladden*, unpub. order (D.Or. 1967); unpublished opinions and orders and Norman A. Carlson to GS, May 4, 1973, in *Capitan v. Culp*, 356 F.Supp. 302 (D.Or. 1972) aff'd unpub. opinion (9th Cir. 1974).

26. Godfrey Hodgson, *America in our Time* (Garden City, NY: Doubleday, 1976), 475.

CHAPTER 12

1. GSOHS, tape 9, side 1 and tape 10, side 2; GS to Kallen, April 13, 1961, Kallen Papers; Dr. Arnold Rustin interview; GS to Chambers, June 8, 1965, in "Chief Judge—Correspondence with reference to JUDGE EAST"; Goodman interview, tape 1, side 1; *Oregon Journal*, Aug. 19, 1966; Hart oral history, tape 25, side 2, tape 26, side 1, tape 27, side 2 and tape 28, side 2; Hart to Fortas, March 22, 1966, Hart to Maurine B. Neuberger, March 22, 1966, Hart to GS, April 10, [1966] and GS to Hart, April 22, 1966, in "Personal Corr. 1966," MS 2886; Fortas to Hart, March 25, 1966, Hart Papers; *Pendleton East Oregonian*, April 5, 1966.

2. GS to Maslow, Nov. 18, 1968, in "AJCongress-Trip to Israel, Greece and Turkey, December 1968, January 1969"; GS to Maslow, July 3, 1970, in "Trip to Israel-January 1971"; GS to Watford Reed, Aug. 8, 1971, in "Retirement of Judges"; GS to Lil and Monroe Sweetland, Dec. 4, 1970, in "First Citizen Award—Congratulatory Messages"; GS to Ed [Edward Weinfeld,] Oct. 5, 1971, in "Sentences in Selective Service and Income Tax Cases and in Narcotics Cases—May 8, 1970 (Phoenix Seminar)," MS 2886.

3. Skopil oral history, tape 10, side 1 and tape 10, side 2; Lezak oral history, tape 5, side 1; Wiener oral history, 52; Panner oral history, tape 15, side 1; Libby Solomon interview.

4. Libby Solomon interview; Paul J. Rank, The Honorable Gus J. Solomon, Dec. 14, 1973, in "Oregon State Bar, County Bar Associations CLE Sessions and American Bar

Association"; GS to Abraham L. and Barbara Kaminstein, Sept. 21, 1972, in "Abraham L. Kaminstein"; GS to Robert M. Christ, Dec. 20, 1977, in untitled folder; GS to Murrah, June 19, 1974, in "Techniques for Shortening Trial (Narrative Statements)"; *Oregonian*, Jan. 26, 1975; Libby Solomon to Lorna, Dec. 30, 1977, in "Elizabeth Solomon—Miscellaneous," MS 2886.

5. Libby Solomon interview; GS to Martin Gang, April 23, 1975, in "Personal Corr. 1975," MS 2886; Rustin interview; Charles B. Fulton to GS, Feb. 28, 1977, in untitled folder; Samuel M. Rosenstein to James M. Burns, Dec. 30, 1983, in "Solomon Longevity Ceremony, December 2, 1983," MS 2886.

6. Reporter's Transcript, Oct. 10, 1979, p. 75 in *U.S. v. Stonehill*, 420 F.Supp. 46 (C.D. Ca 1976) in U.S. District Court for Oregon; GS to Gillers, May 24, 1983, in "Stephen Gillers"; "Judges' Profile," [mid-1980s], in "Solomon Biographical Material"; *Oregonian*, Jan. 12, 1984; GS, Responsa Club Speech, December 14, 1983, in "Speeches No. 110 Through...;" Gus Solomon, et. al., "Dear ," [May 1984], in "International Association of Jewish Lawyers and Jurists," MS 2886.

7. *Oregonian*, Sept. 7, 1973; Skopil oral history, tape 10, side 2; Redden oral history, tape 20, side 2; Collins oral history, 18; GSOHS, tape 8, side 2, tape 9, side 1; GS to Gillers, Dec. 30, 1982, in "Stephen Gillers," MS 2886.

8. GS to Gillers, Dec. 30, 1982, in "Stephen Gillers," MS 2886; GSOHS, tape 8, side 2.

9. Philip Neville to George D. Leonard, Oct. 9, 1968, in "Personal Corr. 1968"; Milton Handler to GS, April 16, 1975, and other correspondence in "Techniques for Shortening Trial (Narrative Statements)."

10. Panner to Author, Dec. 13, 2001; Skopil to Devitt Distinguished Service to Justice Award, Jan. 5, 1987, in "Nomination for the Devitt Award," MS 2886.

11. Sepenuk oral history, tape 3, side 1; Florence Lehman to Paul Bragdon and Larry Large & Co., Feb. 12, 1987, in Gus J. Solomon Alumni File; Milton Pollock to Libby Solomon, Feb. 16, 1987, in "Judges' condolences"; Cleve and Jean Cory to Libby Solomon, [1987], in "Condolences," MS 2886.

12. GS to Annette and Louis Kaufman, April 25 and 30, 1985, and Aug. 25, 1986, in same-titled folder; GS to Sidney M. Aronovitz to Devitt Distinguished Service to Justice Award, Nov. 21, 1986, and Skopil to Devitt Distinguished Service to Justice Award, Jan. 5, 1987, in "Nomination for the Devitt Award"; Lehman to Bragdon and Large & Co., Feb. 12, 1987, in Gus J. Solomon Alumni File; Milton Pollock to Libby Solomon, Feb. 16, 1987, in "Judges' condolences"; Burns interview; Peter Voorhies to Libby Solomon, Feb. 198, 1987, in "Condolences," MS 2886; *Oregonian*, Feb. 16, 1987; conversation with Richard B. Solomon.

13. *Oregonian*, Feb. 16, 17, 18, and 19, 1987; Stephen Gillers, "On the Side of God," *National Law Journal*, April 27, 1987; *New York Times*, Feb. 17, 1987; (Columbia Law School) *Observer*, May 1987; The 1987 Ninth Circuit Judicial Conference, "A Tribute to the Memory of Circuit Judge Ben C. Duniway [and] District Judge Gus J. Solomon"; *Pacific Citizen*, Feb. 27, 1987.

14. Panner to Libby Solomon, Aug. 26, 1988, and charter in "Inns of Court"; Terry J. Yamada to Libby Solomon, Nov. 30, 1988, in "Americans with Japanese Ancestry"; Proceedings to Renaming the United States Courthouse to the Gus J. Solomon Courthouse in 749 F.Supp. 87 (1991); (Portland) *Jewish Review*, Feb. 1, 1997.

Selected Bibliography

MANUSCRIPT COLLECTIONS AND UNPUBLISHED MATERIAL

American Civil Liberties Union Papers, Mudd Manuscript Library, Princeton University. (microfilmed as American Civil Liberties Union: The Roger Baldwin Years, 1917-1950).

American Civil Liberties Union in the Pacific Northwest, Allen Library, University of Washington (selected from the Princeton collection).

American Civil Liberties Union National Office: Japanese American Evacuation Cases, 1942-1945, Allen Library, University of Washington (selected from the Princeton collection).

American Civil Liberties Union of Oregon Papers, American Civil Liberties Union of Oregon.

American Jewish Congress Papers, American Jewish Historical Society.

Americans for Democratic Action Papers, Wisconsin State Historical Society.

Anti-Defamation League of B'nai B'rith, Pacific Northwest Regional Office, Allen Library, University of Washington.

C. Girard Davidson Papers, acc # 24835, Oregon Historical Society.

C. Girard Davidson Papers, Knight Library, University of Oregon.

Osmond K. Fraenkel, Excerpts from the Diary of Osmond K. Fraenkel Relating to the American Civil Liberties Union, Mudd Manuscript Library, Princeton University.

C. Allan Hart Papers, Mss 2931, Oregon Historical Society.

Houghton Cluck Caughlin and Shubat Papers, Allen Library, University of Washington.

Horace M. Kallen Papers, American Jewish Archives.

Raymond M. Kell, "History of Kell, Alterman & Runstein," in possession of Lee Davis Kell

Raymond M. Kell, "Memoirs," in possession of Lee Davis Kell.

William Langer Papers, Fritz Library, University of North Dakota.

Leo Levenson Papers, in possession of Charles L. Kobin.

Phil Levin Papers, in possession of Dr. Gerald Levin.

Sidney I. Lezak Scrapbook, in possession of Sidney I. Lezak.

J. Howard McGrath Papers, Harry S. Truman Library.

Warren G. Magnuson Papers, Allen Library, University of Washington.

Materials Relating to Dr. Carl Petterson's Suits Against the Portland Airport, in possession of the author.

Multnomah County Bar Association Minutes, 1921-37, Multnomah County Bar Association.

Hugh B. Mitchell Papers, Allen Library, University of Washington.

Wayne L. Morse Papers, Knight Library, University of Oregon.

Oregon Commonwealth Federation Papers, Knight Library, University of Oregon.

George Rennar Papers, Oregon Historical Society.

Hon. Gus J. Solomon Alumnus Record, Reed College Archives.

Hon. Gus J. Solomon Papers, Mss 2886, Oregon Historical Society.

Lillian S. Spear Papers, Allen Library, University of Washington.

Donald J. Sterling Papers, Mss 2619-1, Oregon Historical Society.

Monroe Sweetland Papers, Mss 1747, Oregon Historical Society.

Harry S. Truman Papers: President's Personal File, Harry S. Truman Library.

United States District Court Historical Society Papers, Mss 2925, Oregon Historical Society.

United States War Relocation Authority Oregon Records, 1942-1946, Microfilm 10 copy from NARA at Oregon Historical Society

White House Central Files: Official File, Harry S. Truman Library.

GOVERNMENT RECORDS

Court Records, Federal Records Center–Pacific Alaska Region, Seattle.

Court Records, Federal Records Center–Pacific Region, San Bruno.

Court Records, United States District Court for Oregon, Portland.

Federal Bureau of Investigation, Reports on Gus J. Solomon, in possession of the author.

Oregon Military Department Records: Communist Activity Intelligence Reports, 1932-1939, Oregon State Archives, Salem.

Oregon Supreme Court Case Records, Oregon State Archives, Salem.

Police Historical Records: Red Squad, City of Portland Stanley Parr Archives and Records Center.

Record Group 21, National Archives and Records Administration–Pacific Alaska Region, Seattle.

Record Group 46, National Archives and Records Administration–National Archives Building, Washington.

Record Group 276, National Archives and Records Administration–Pacific Region, San Bruno.

PUBLISHED MATERIAL

Abbott, Carl. *Portland: Planning, Politics, and Growth in a Twentieth-Century City* (Lincoln: University of Nebraska Press, 1983).

Abel, Richard. *American Lawyers* (New York: Oxford University Press, 1989).

Auerbach, Jerold S. *Unequal Justice: Lawyers and Social Change in Modern America* (New York: Oxford University Press, 1976).

Auerbach, Jerold S. "The Depression Decade" in *The Pulse of Freedom: American Liberties: 1920-1970s,* ed. Alan Reitman (New York: Norton, 1975).

Baskir, Lawrence M. and William A. Strauss, *Chance and Circumstance: The Draft, the War, and the Vietnam Generation* (New York: Knopf, 1978).

Bigelow, William and Norman Diamond, "Agitate, Educate, Organize: Portland, 1934," *Oregon Historical Quarterly* 89 (Spring 1988).

Brinkley, Alan. *The End of Reform: New Deal Liberalism in Recession and War* (New York: Alfred A. Knopf, 1995).

Brooke, Leionie N. "Legal Aid as Part of the Social-Welfare Program of Multnomah County," *Commonwealth Review* 22 (Nov. 1940).

Brown, Esther L. *Lawyers and the Promotion of Justice* (New York: Russell Sage Foundation, 1938).

Burton, Robert E. "The New Deal in Oregon" in *The New Deal: The State and Local Levels*, eds. John Braeman, Robert H. Bremner and David Brody (Columbus: Ohio State University Press, 1975).

Burton, Robert E. *Democrats of Oregon: The Pattern of Minority Politics, 1900-1956* (Eugene: University of Oregon Books, 1960).

Carp, Robert A. and C.K.Rowland. *Policymaking and Politics in the Federal District Courts* (Knoxville: University of Tennessee Press, 1983).

Carter, Dan T. *Scottsboro: A Tragedy of the American South* (New York: Oxford University Press, 1971).

Chafee, Zechariah Jr., *Free Speech in the United States* (Cambridge: Harvard University Press, 1941).

Christie, Robert A. *Empire in Wood: A History of the Carpenters' Union* (Ithaca: Cornell University, 1956).

Clark, Burton R. *The Distinctive College* (New Brunswick: Transaction, 1992).

Cook, Blanche W. *Eleanor Roosevelt* (New York: Penguin Books, 1992).

Cortner, Richard C. *The Supreme Court and Second Bill of Rights: The Fourteenth Amendment and the Nationalization of Civil Liberties* (Madison: University of Wisconsin Press, 1981).

Daniels, Roger. *Concentration Camps USA: Japanese Americans and World War II* (New York: Hot, Rinehart & Winston, 1971).

Dinnerstein, Leonard. *Anti-semitism in America* (New York: Oxford University Press, 1994).

Dollinger, Marc. *Quest for Inclusion: Jews and Liberalism in Modern America* (Princeton: Princeton University Press, 2000).

Dollinger, Marc. "The Other War: American Jews, Lyndon Johnson, and The Great Society," *American Jewish History* 89 (Dec. 2001).

Donnelly, Robert C. "Organizing Portland: Organized Crime, Municipal Corruption, and the Teamsters Union," *Oregon Historical Quarterly* 104 (Fall 2003).

Douglas, William O. *The Court Years, 1939-1975: The Autobiography of William O. Douglas* (New York: Random House, 1980).

Drukman, Mason. *Wayne Morse: A Political Biography* (Portland: Oregon Historical Society Press, 1997).

Eisenberg, Ellen. "Transplanted to the Rose City: The Creation of East European Jewish Community in Portland, Oregon," *Journal of American Ethnic History* 19 (Spring 2000).

Elliott, E. Donald. "Managerial Judging and the Evolution of Procedure," *University of Chicago Law Review* 53 (Spring 1986).

Feingold, Henry L. *A Midrash on American Jewish History* (Albany: State University of New York Press, 1982).

Foner, Eric. *The Story of American Freedom* (New York: Norton, 1998).

Frankel, Marvin E. "The Search for Truth: An Umpireal View," *University of Pennsylvania Law Review* 123 (May 1975).

Friedman, Joel W. and George M. Strickler, Jr., *The Law of Employment Discrimination* (Westbury, CT: Foundation Press, 1997).

Friedman, Lawrence M. *American Law in the 20th Century* (New Haven: Yale University Press, 2002).

Gerhardt, Michael J. *The Federal Appointments Process: A Constitutional and Historical Analysis* (Durham: Duke University Press, 2000).

Gillon, Steven M. *Politics and Vision: The ADA and American Liberalism* (New York: Oxford University Press, 1987).

Goldman, Sheldon. *Picking Federal Judges: Lower Court Selection from Roosevelt Through Reagan* (New Haven: Yale University Press, 1997).

Gordon, Robert W. "The Legal Profession" in *Looking Back at Law's Century*, eds. Austin Sarat et al. (Ithaca, NY: Cornell University Press, 2002).

Goren, Arthur A. "Jews" in *Harvard Encyclopedia of American Ethnic Groups*, ed. Stephen Thernstrom (Cambridge: Harvard University Press, 1980).

Goren, Arthur A. *The Politics and Public Culture of American Jews* (Bloomington: Indiana University Press, 1999).

Greenberg, Cheryl. "Pluralism and its Discontents: The Case of Blacks and Jews," in *Insider/Outsider: American Jews and Multiculturalism*, David Biale, Michael Galchinsky, and Susannah Heschel, eds. (Berkeley: The University of California Press, 1998).

Grossman, Joel B. *Lawyers and Judges: The ABA and the Politics of Judicial Selection* (New York: John Wiley, 1965).

Hall, Kermit L. *The Magic Mirror: Law in American History* (New York: Oxford University Press, 1989).

Harmon, Rick. "Interview: Gus J. Solomon on the Beginnings of Legal Aid in Oregon," *Oregon Historical Quarterly* 88 (Spring 1987).

Herzig, Jill H. "The Oregon Commonwealth Federation: The Rise and Decline of a Reform Organization," M.A. thesis, University of Oregon, 1963.

Heyderbrand, Wolf and Carroll Seron, *Rationalizing Justice: The Political Economy of Federal District Courts* (New York: State University of New York Press, 1990).

Howard, J. Woodford, Jr., *Courts of Appeals in the Federal Judicial System: A Study of the Second, Fifth, and District for Columbia Circuits* (Princeton: Princeton University Press, 1981).

Johnson, Earl Jr., *Justice and Reform: The Formative Years of the American Legal Services Program* (New Brunswick, NJ: Transaction Books, 1978).

Johnston, Robert D. *The Radical Middle Class: Populist Democracy and the Question of Capitalism in Progressive Era Portland* (Princeton: Princeton University Press, 2003).

Kester, Randall B. "A Time of Change 1927-1950" in *The First Duty: A History of the U.S. District Court for Oregon*, ed. Carolyn M. Buan (Portland: U.S. District Court of Oregon Historical Society, 1993).

Kohn, Stephen M. *Jailed For Peace: The History of American Draft Law Violators, 1658-1985* (Westport, CT: Greenwood Press, 1986).

Lahav, Pnina. *Judgment in Jerusalem: Chief Justice Simon Agranat and the Zionist Century* (Berkeley: University of California Press, 1997).

Lembcke, Jerry and William M. Tattam, *One Union in Wood* (Madeira Park, BC, and New York: Harbour Publishing and International Publishers, 1984).

Linowitz, Sol M. with Martin Mayer, *The Betrayed Profession: Lawyering at the End of the Twentieth Century* (New York: Scribner's, 1994).

Lowenstein, Steven. *The Jews of Oregon, 1850-1950* (Portland: Jewish Historical Society of Oregon, 1987).

MacColl, E. Kimbark. *The Growth of a City: Power and Politics in Portland, Oregon 1915 to 1950* (Portland: Georgian Press, 1979).

MacColl, E. Kimbark with Harry H. Stein, *Merchants, Money and Power: The
Portland Establishment 1843-1913* (Portland: Georgian Press, 1988).

Mapes, Laurie Bennett. "A Period of Complexity 1950-1991," in *The First
Duty: A History of the U.S. District Court for Oregon*, ed. Carolyn M. Buan
(Portland: U.S. District Court of Oregon Historical Society, 1993).

Mazurek, Joseph P. et al., *American Indian Law Deskbook* (Niwot: University
Press of Colorado, 1998).

McElderry, Stuart. "Building a West Coast Ghetto: African-American Housing in Portland, 1910-1960," *Pacific Northwest Quarterly* 92 (Summer
2001).

McKay, Floyd J. *Editor for Oregon: Charles A. Sprague and the Politics of Change*
(Corvallis: Oregon State University Press, 1998).

McKay, Floyd J. "With Liberty for Some: Oregon Editors and the Challenge of
Civil Liberties, 1942-55" (Ph.D. diss. University of Washington, 1995).

Mullins, William H. *The Depression and the Urban West Coast: Los Angeles, San
Francisco, Seattle and Portland* (Bloomington: Indiana University Press,
1991).

Murrell, Gary. *Iron Pants: Oregon's Anti-New Deal Governor, Charles Henry Martin* (Pullman: Washington State University Press, 2000).

National Lawyers Guild, Oregon Chapter, *Report of the Civil Liberties Committee* (Portland, May 24, 1938).

Neuberger, Richard L. *Our Promised Land* (New York: Macmillan, 1938).

Panner, Owen M. "Surviving in Federal Court," *Oregon Benchmarks* 8 (Summer 1992).

Panner, Owen M. "The Honorable Gus J. Solomon: A Tribute," *Bulletin of the
U.S. District Court for Oregon Historical Society* 3 (Spring 1987).

Plotke, David. *Building a Democratic Political Order: Reshaping American Liberalism in the 1930s and 1940s* (Cambridge: Cambridge University Press,
1996).

Posner, Richard A. *The Federal Courts: Challenge and Reform* (Cambridge: Harvard University Press, 1996).

Powe, Lucas A., Jr., *The Warren Court and American Politics* (Cambridge: Harvard University Press, 2000).

Resnik, Judith. "Managerial Judges," *Harvard Law Review* 96 (Dec. 1982).

Schumacher, Waldo. "The 1948 Elections in Oregon," *Western Political Quarterly* 2 (March 1949).

Shapiro, Martin. "*DeJonge v. Oregon*," in *Encyclopedia of the American Constitution*, eds. Leonard Levy and Kenneth L. Karst (New York: Macmillan
Reference USA, 2000).

Shapiro, Edward S. *A Time for Healing: American Jewry Since World II* (Baltimore: Johns Hopkins University Press, 1992).

Songer, Donald R., Reginald S. Sheehan, and Susan B. Haire, *Continuity and
Change on the United States Courts of Appeals* (Ann Arbor: University of
Michigan Press, 2000).

Sorin, Gerald. *Tradition Transformed: The Jewish Experience in America* (Baltimore: John Hopkins University Press, 1997).

Sorin, Gerald. *A Time for Building: The Third Migration, 1860-1920* (Baltimore: Johns Hopkins University Press, 1992).

Steele, Richard W. *Free Speech in the Good War* (New York: St. Martin's, 1999).

Stevens, Robert. *Law School: Legal Education in America From the 1850s to the 1980s* (Chapel Hill: University of North Carolina Press, 1983).

Sunstein, Cass R. *One Case At a Time: Judicial Minimalism on the Supreme Court* (Cambridge, Mass.: Harvard University Press, 1999).

Svonkin, Stuart. *Jews Against Prejudice: American Jews and the Fight for Civil Liberties* (New York: Columbia University Press, 1997).

Toll, William. *The Making of an Ethnic Middle Class: Portland Jewry Over Four Generations* (Albany: State University of New York Press, 1982).

Toll, William. "Voluntarism and Modernization in Portland Jewry: The B'Nai B'rith in the 1920s," *Western Historical Quarterly* 10 (January 1979).

Toll, William. "Ethnicity and Stability: The Italians and Jews of South Portland, 1900-1940," *Pacific Historical Review* 54 (May 1985).

Tollefson, Gene. *BPA and the Struggle for Power at Cost* (Portland: Bonneville Power Administration, [1985]).

Walker, Samuel. *In Defense of American Liberties: A History of the ACLU* (New York: Oxford University Press, 1990).

Wasby, Stephen L. "'Extra' Judges in a Federal Appellate Court: The Ninth Circuit," *Law and Society Review* 15 (1980-1981).

Warren, Frank A. *Noble Abstractions: American Liberal Intellectuals and World War II* (Columbus: Ohio State University Press, 1999).

Weinfeld, William. "Income of Lawyers, 1929-48," *Survey of Current Business* 29 (Aug. 1949).

Wilson, Steven H. *The Rise of Judicial Management in the U.S. District Court, Southern District for Texas, 1955-2000* (Athens: University of Georgia Press, 2002).

INTERVIEWS

C. Allan Hart, Recollections of the Development of Bonneville Power Marketing Policies during Paul J. Raver's Term as BPA Administrator, September 1, 1939-December 31, 1953, in C. Allan Hart Papers, Oregon Historical Society

Jerome Kohlberg, Jr., 1991, Oregon Historical Society

Hon. Gus J. Solomon, in possession of Gene Tollefson

Author's Interviews

Henry Blauer

Helen Bradley

Richard BrownsteinKeith Burns

James Caputo, Sr.

Charles Davis

G. Bernhard Fedde

Ken Fitzgerald

George H. Fraser

Maurice O. Georges

Stephen Gillers

Ivan Gold

Dan Goldy
Dr. Morton Goodman
Fred Granta
Jerry Harris
C. Allan Hart
Hilde Jacob
Henry J. Kaplan
Mike Katz
John J. Kerr, Jr.
Judy Kobbervig
Ronald B. Lansing
Reuben Lenske
Sidney I. Lezak
Charles Luce
Paul R. Meyer
Carl R. Neil

Hon. Owen M. Panner
Hon. Edwin J. Peterson
Henry M. Richmond III
Gerald Robinson
Dr. Arnold Rustin
Hon. Herbert M. Schwab
Arden E. Shenker
Mark Silverstein
Elisabeth Solomon
Richard B. Solomon
Rabbi Joshua Stampfer
Thomas B. Stoel
Donal D. Sullivan
Monroe E. Sweetland
Hon. Robert Wollheim
Kathi Wright

ORAL HISTORIES
Oregon Historical Society
(United States District Court Oral History Project)

Kernan Bagley
Hon. Robert C. Belloni
Hugh L. Biggs
Hon. Wallace P. Carson, Jr.
Jack G. Collins
Walter Cosgrave
C. Girard Davidson
Hon. Pat Dooley
Hon. William G. East
Neva Elliott
Ken Fitzgerald
Hon. Alfred T. Goodwin
Wendell Gray
C. Allan Hart
Bernard Jolles
Randall B. Kester

Hon. John F. Kilkenny
Jerome Kohlberg, Jr.
Robert A. Leedy
Berkeley Lent
Sidney I. Lezak
C. E. Luckey
Chester E. McCarty
Howard Morgan
Maurine Neuberger
Hon. Owen M. Panner
Dale A. Ray
John Ryan
Norman Sepenuk
Hon. Otto R. Skopil, Jr.
Leo Smith
Hon. Gus J. Solomon

Other Oral Histories

Blumenthal, Mollie, Oregon Jewish Museum, interviewed by Shirley Tanzer, Feb. 17, 1976.

Davidson, C. Girard Davidson, Harry S. Truman Library, interviewed by Jerry N. Hess, July 17,1972, July 18, 1972.

Fraser, George H. Fraser, in possession of George H. Fraser, interviewed by Thomas B. Stoel, April 27, 1993.

McGraw, Noreen Kelly (Saltveit) McGraw, Marylhurst University, interviewed by Lillian Pereyra, Oct. 6, 2001.

Levenson, Leo, Oregon Jewish Museum, interviewed by Michelle Glazer, July 13, 1976.

Morgan, Howard, Oregon Historical Society, interviewed by Clark Hansen, Aug. 24, 1992.

Maurine B. Neuberger, Oregon Historical Society, interviewed by Clark Hansen, Sept. 3, 1991.

Redden, Hon. James A., in possession of Hon. James A. Redden, interviewed by Michael O'Rourke, Jan. 26, 1995.

Simon, Max, Oregon Jewish Museum, interviewed by Molly Mae Pierrii, March 7, 1975.

Solomon, Hon. Gus J., Oregon Jewish Museum, interviewed by Janet Zell, Feb. 16, 1976 and by Marianne Feldman, June 23, 1976.

Sussman, Gilbert, Oregon Jewish Museum, interviewed by Lois Shenker, Jan. 1, 1976.

Swett, Ted, Oregon Jewish Museum, interviewed by Shirley Tanzer, Feb. 15, 1982.

Sweetland, Monroe, Oregon Historical Society, interviewed by Rick Harmon, Nov. 25, 1986.

Index